DYLAN JONES is the editor of *GQ* magazine and a regular columnist for the *Independent* and the *Mail on Sunday*. A former editor at the *Observer* and the *Sunday Times*, he has won seven British Society of Magazine Editors awards.

CAMERON ON CAMERON

Conversations with
DYLAN JONES

FOURTH ESTATE · London

Fourth Estate
An imprint of HarperCollins*Publishers*
77–85 Fulham Palace Road
Hammersmith
London W6 8JB

Visit our authors' blog at www.fifthestate.co.uk
Love this book? www.bookarmy.com

This Fourth Estate paperback edition published 2010

1

First published in Great Britain by Fourth Estate in 2008

A catalogue record for this book is
available from the British Library

ISBN 978-0-00-728537-2

Typeset in Minion by G&M Designs Limited,
Raunds, Northamptonshire

Printed and bound in Great Britain by Clays Ltd, St Ives plc

For Edie & Georgia

CONTENTS

PREFACE   *The Book of Dave*   XV

PROLOGUE   *'There is no looking back, no quarter. This is the*
                 moment. The time is now'   xvii

ONE   *'You either carry on the same approach, or you*
               make changes'   1
               David Cameron's Prius – the *Spectator* – Eton – 'Trojan horse' –
               hugging the hoodie – *From Russia with Love* –
               that parliamentary CV

TWO   *'Reading them [Alastair Campbell's diaries] is like*
               gulping a triple espresso'   25
               By-elections – YouTube – Glasnost – the *Guardian* racing pages –
               Brasenose – Alastair Campbell – the White House tennis rota

THREE   *'Why am I going to Rwanda? Because I think it's a*
               good idea'   55
               Robert Harris – Gordon Brown's coronation – Michael Green –
               a PR disaster – William Hague – cannabis, casinos – IDS

FOUR   *'It is amazing what a new Prime Minister can get away with'*   89

Elton John – the 'big clunking fist' – a turnaround in the polls – the Prime Minister lying on television

FIVE   *'I love you, David Cameron!'*   115

'Hollywood black tie' – Mr Bean – the election that never was – twenty-four-hour drinking – social responsibility – stop and search

SIX   *'I don't think the fact that there are lots of people going to different churches makes for a divided country'*   157

Single mothers – homosexuality – the Royal Family – multiculturalism – Sharia law – terrorism – the grammar school problem – God's own BlackBerry

SEVEN   *'Yes, I do bounce policy ideas off Samantha and because she doesn't think like another politician it's very refreshing'*   191

The NHS – the problems of living with a profoundly disabled child – Cameron's kitchen cabinet – Samantha's rules

EIGHT   *'Every day there is another murder, another assault, another rape, another front-page horror story'*   215

Penal reform – Jack Straw's sleeping habits – social responsibility – bureaucratic bravery – the strange case of the Notting Hill mutterer

NINE   *'Gordon Brown better watch out today, as I'm wearing my Blue Peter badge'*   241

PMQs – the EU treaty – Boris Johnson's Che Guevara watch – acting out *The Godfather* – the implosion of a Prime Minister – Jeremy Clarkson

TEN   'Social responsibility is the essence of liberal
       conservatism. This is the Britain we want to build'   275
       Carla Bruni – another YouGov poll – SNAFU – income tax –
       Northern Rock – non-doms – corruption – Nick Clegg –
       it's the economy, stupid

ELEVEN   'I'm going to be as radical a social reformer as Mrs
          Thatcher was an economic reformer'   299
          Boris Johnson – Mayor Bloomberg – Gordon Brown's
          leadership challenge – the *Spectator* – the Olympics – success
          in Crewe – the coming election

TWELVE   'The age of irresponsibility is giving way to the age
          of austerity … Unless we deal with this debt crisis,
          we risk becoming once again the sick man of Europe'   323
          The collapse of Lehman Brothers – 'Yachtgate' – Davos –
          Gordon Brown's YouTube moment – the worsening economy –
          success in the polls – the death of Ivan

THIRTEEN   'I don't talk about Broken Britain but I do talk
            about the Broken Society and the parts of our
            society that are broken. I don't believe I overstate
            my case at all'   359
            The expenses scandal – 'no drama Obama' – public sector
            cuts – *The Wire* – the conference speech – the election
            campaign – being stuck in a lift with Carla Bruni

Index of Question-and-Answer topics   403

ACKNOWLEDGEMENTS

Firstly I'd like to thank my employers at Condé Nast, Nicholas Coleridge and Jonathan Newhouse, for their continued support and encouragement. I'd also like to thank my brilliant agent, Ed Victor, for … well, pretty much everything, actually. Thanks also to Matthew d'Ancona, David Bailey, Iain Mills, Fergus Greer, Steve Hilton, Andy Coulson, Gabby Bertin, Liz Sugg, Mariella Kroll, Richard Campbell-Breeden and Jonathan Heaf. John Elliott commissioned and edited the book, and I'd like to thank him enormously. Many journalists and columnists have inadvertently helped with the construction of this book, including the many uncredited writers responsible for the hundreds of newspaper and broadcast news items which have helped inform it. I have tried to credit everyone, and apologize to those I haven't (I have read almost every newspaper piece written about David Cameron since 2005, all of which have been helpful in some way). Francis Elliott and James Hanning's *Cameron: The Rise of the New Conservative* was obviously extremely instructive, and it contains possibly the most comprehensive detail of Cameron's life and career to date. YouGov have been largely responsible for the narrative arc of the book, although Gordon Brown has also contributed a little. Finally, I'd like to thank both David Cameron for allowing me to spend a year with him, and my wife Sarah for not complaining while I did.

'We need a culture that ensures we all know two things. First, the fact that we are all in this together, that we are more than solitary individuals, pursuing our private ambitions without a thought for the society we form part of, and that there is such a thing as society. Second, the fact that the government is not the only collective institution in our lives, and that society is not the same thing as the state.

'I believe that these two facts urgently need greater emphasis because too many people believe the opposite. They believe we are isolated individuals – free to do what we like, when we like, how we like. They believe that "society" means "the state" – that only the police, the law, and the government have any power or any legitimacy.

'You see these attitudes everywhere. They are symptoms of the "what's it got to do with you?" culture. Everyone who has ever tried to uphold social responsibility, to make clear the expectations we have of each other, has heard that phrase. Someone drops litter in the street. You object – and you get an earful because they think it is the government's responsibility to keep the streets clean and pick up litter.

'They seem genuinely outraged that their behaviour could be questioned by a mere member of the public – as if one slave had just told another what to do. "What's it got to do with you?", they say – usually with the F-word thrown in for good measure. And they might add, "it's a free country". It is free, but it is also a country. We inhabit the same space. We share the culture. We are all neighbours.

'Citizenship is not about structures. It is not about understanding the workings of Parliament, or knowing the law. It is about relationships. The quality of relationships is what defines a country, what makes it happy or unhappy'

– David Cameron

PREFACE

The Book of Dave

David Cameron is the first Tory leader in a generation to have a real chance of becoming Prime Minister. After over a decade in the wilderness, suddenly the Tories have a sharp-suited firebrand with a media-friendly face, a big bag of energy and the chance of winning an election for them. Cameron is young, committed, and in a relatively short space of time has managed to galvanize his party and the British public alike. In three short years he has moved the Conservatives closer to the centre ground, made the party electable and proved that he can be a more than formidable adversary.

Can he go all the way? Can David Cameron stay the distance until Gordon Brown decides, finally, to hold the election he promised us in 2007?

While the British public like the way he looks, what people still aren't quite so sure of is the exact nature of some of Cameron's policies; and having watched him make his party electable (in much the same way as Tony Blair did with the Labour Party in the mid-nineties), and having watched him fight the phoney war against Blair, they now want him to reveal his true colours, reveal the distinct and salient differences in policy that will set him apart from Gordon Brown. Cameron has had an extraordinarily good time of it in the last twelve months or so, but there are some who have a lingering feeling that his success has largely been because of Brown's repeated mistakes.

Do you want David Cameron? This book aims to convince you one way or another. Written in the '*conversation avec*' format – a popular way of doing things in France – this is a conversation between a journalist and a politician, a series of exhaustive question and answer sessions that reveal – I hope – a great deal of what there is to know about the man who could potentially be Britain's next Prime Minister.

I am not a Cameron apologist, and nor am I even a real Tory. This book is not an endorsement of his policies, merely a glimpse behind the veil, and an account of a year I spent watching him and interviewing him. I wasn't sure what exactly was going on with the Tories under Cameron, so, essentially, I became sufficiently interested to go and find out.

Luckily, the Leader of the Opposition found the idea agreeable, and so for the best part of a year we spoke every couple of weeks – sometimes at length, sometimes not – in an attempt not just to chart an extraordinary year in politics (one which has seen him very much in the ascendant), but also to get to the very heart of what makes him tick.

This is not a book about politics, but rather a book about a politician, a man whose commitment to his party is matched only by his ambition. What does David Cameron have in common with me, with you, or indeed with any of us? Why should we be interested? I, like you, I think, want to know the same thing: David Cameron, are you any different? What would Britain really be like if you were in charge? And so I asked David Cameron exactly that.

Welcome to the Book of Dave.

PROLOGUE

'There is no looking back, no quarter. This is the moment. The time is now'

The coffee served at the Imperial Hotel in Blackpool is the worst you're ever likely to drink. Perhaps the Tory delegates who gathered there on Sunday 30 September, for the first day of the 2007 Conservative Party Conference were too preoccupied to notice, but if anything threatened to kill off the party during the next four days it wasn't going to be Gordon Brown, it was going to be the coffee.

The scene in the overlit lobby that Sunday afternoon was like something out of Hunter S. Thompson's *Fear and Loathing in Las Vegas*, although instead of being fuelled by martinis and LSD, everyone looked like they had just had Prozac for lunch rather than the sullen-looking roast beef still being served in the dining room. Large white cardboard placards were everywhere, all covered with the same totemic message: 'It's time for change'. Had the fractious Tories finally found something to agree on? Had they changed already? Or had they – after the unending pain of the Blair years, noses pressed firmly against the shop window of power as a string of Tory leaders imploded – finally all just flipped?

This hotel – Blackpool's finest, and once considered so grand by hardline socialist MP Dennis Skinner that he refused to stay there, choosing a nearby boarding house instead – is always party to the most telling assignations, the most venal gossip, the most gruesome arguments (it was built in 1867 and nowadays looks like some sort of ghastly redbrick wedding cake). But on 30 September the mood was positively euphoric, and MPs, councillors, secretaries, researchers, journalists and even fringe speakers were walking around with a collective Cheshire Cat grin.

I had arrived – via plane from London to Manchester, and then by taxi from Manchester to Blackpool (the trains weren't working) – expecting to find a party in ruin, expecting to see faction fighting, disparate groupings of aggrieved backbenchers whining about their lot, each and every one of them looking for the right time to twist their own knife a little further into the broken back of the Conservative Party.

But the scene in front of me couldn't have been more different: the Tories seemed to be both cheerful, and to have discovered – just maybe – the beginnings of a sense of unity and purpose. They weren't doing too well in the polls and for David Cameron, their leader of two years, his conference speech would be do or die. But there was a spring in the party's step, a feeling that things were going to improve. It was almost surreal, almost Fellini-esque. There, in the lobby, Shadow Foreign Secretary William Hague was standing triumphant, still wallowing in the applause from his opening speech; communications supremo Andy Coulson looked like a man who had had twelve cans of Coke that morning and little else, so fired up was he; Shadow Chancellor George Osborne – wearing his look of unruffled detachment – seemed for all the world as though he knew where all the bodies were buried, and so didn't need to worry about anything. Everywhere you looked you saw men and women who had come to Blackpool intent on taking away with them a genuine sense of common purpose: they believed in the project. The only other times I remembered seeing such devotion was once at an Apple simulcast in Paris in 2004 – where a cinema-full of Macoholics had come to watch Steve Jobs speak live via satellite from San Francisco – and in the queue to see *Mama Mia!* outside a London theatre. On both occasions I saw people who were determined to have a good time regardless.

In a small boardroom on the ground floor, David Cameron was hosting an even smaller lunch for New York's Mayor Bloomberg, a last-minute replacement for Arnold Schwarzenegger as that year's star attraction. As well as Cameron and Osborne, the lunch party included Shadow Home Secretary David Davis, Shadow Secretary for Defence Liam Fox,

Party Treasurer Michael Spencer, as well as the redoubtable Coulson (who was obviously only there for the caffeine). The cream of British media politely sipped water and listened to the five-foot-seven American billionaire philanthropist offer his considered endorsement of the Tory leader: Sky's Adam Boulton, the *Daily Telegraph*'s Will Lewis, *The Times*'s James Harding, ITN's Tom Bradby and Andrew Neil from the BBC, all of them seemingly relishing the week ahead, and, perhaps, wondering why the Tories were looking so damned optimistic. Many, like me, had come to witness the party's implosion, perhaps their last stand, and they were slightly taken aback by the unrelenting giddiness of it all.

One of the main topics of conversation was the Prime Minister's forthcoming trip to see the British forces in Iraq. Two days later Brown would promise that the UK forces in Iraq were to be cut by 1000 by 2008, although the Ministry of Defence soon confirmed that the figure included 500 troops whose withdrawal had already been announced the previous July – 270 of whom were already home. One senior figure at the *Ten O'clock News* was apparently 'disgusted' by Brown's overt cynicism, while Liam Fox accused Brown of 'cynical pre-election politics' for preferring a photo opportunity in Basra to keeping his promise to tell MPs first about the planned troop cuts.

An hour after the lunch, upstairs in his suite, cocooned from the rest of his party and isolated from the outside world, Cameron hunkered down with half a dozen of his researchers to establish his arguments and tinker, for the twelfth time that day, with his conference speech – a speech that would challenge Gordon Brown to call his election (while Cameron crossed his fingers behind his back, hoping Brown would do no such thing). Here he was in his 'winning' bubble, like a rock star on tour, surrounded by the party faithful; outside in the corridor dozens of young men in open-necked shirts stalked about, all of them so immersed in collective belief that any form of criticism was interpreted as disloyalty. As Coulson said later that day: 'You have to believe in the mission. If you don't believe in the mission then you're doomed. You don't ever go into a premiership game entertaining failure. The only thing you entertain is a win. The same is true today.'

'I've spent a lot of the last three days thinking hard about this speech,' said Cameron, in measured tones, upstairs in his room. 'I know exactly what I want to say, and I think I know how I'm going to say it, but I want to make sure it is exactly right. This is the moment, this is the time when the Conservative Party has it all before it. We can win the next election, I am convinced of it. Not just because the Labour government is old and out of touch, not just because people are sick to the back teeth of them, but because the modern Conservative Party is genuinely offering something new. There is no looking back, no quarter. This is the moment. The time is now.'

'It's the spirit of Gallipoli,' said a veteran of William Hague's election campaign, and by the glint in everyone's eyes you knew what he meant. They believed they were going to win, but if the opposite turned out to be true, then they would die with their boots on.

The political scientists of the future have their clammy fingers on the final judgement, but from the middle distance that speech, delivered just three days later, was not merely one of the political highlights of last year, it was a genuine political milestone. Just minutes after David Cameron left the stage, having spoken without notes for over an hour, even those who hate the ground he walks on were soon muttering grudging (if shrill) respect. Like most of the speeches Cameron has made since becoming party leader, you can still see it on the official Tory website, and it has become required viewing even for fervent non-believers. It was a speech that changed the British political landscape, a speech that marked the beginning of what would announce – it's now fair to say – a sea change in British politics: the re-emergence of the Conservative Party as a viable election-winning force.

Unlike the Prime Minister – who unequivocally hated the ground David Cameron walked on more than anyone else in this country, or indeed his own – who pointedly didn't mention him at all in his Labour conference speech, the Conservative leader devoted more than a chunk of his address to the soon-to-be-beleaguered Labour leader.

'Boy, has this guy got a plan,' said Cameron, as he roamed around the stage, trying to catch as many blue eyes as possible. 'It's to appeal to those

4 per cent of people in the marginal seats with a dog whistle about immigration here, about crime there, wrap yourself up in the flag and maybe you convince people you are on their side.'

Cameron's speech proved so successful that, shortly afterwards, Brown suffered a rabbit-in-the-headlights moment of potentially momentous consequences. During the summer of 2007 he had talked up the prospects of an election, and now, just days after Cameron's conference speech, he chickened out. Not only did Brown not take out his dog whistle at all, but he also turned the country – and the media, many of whom suddenly saw the self-delusional tendencies Peter Mandelson had been hinting at for years – against him in the space of one disastrous interview with Andrew Marr on 6 October. On Marr's TV show Brown falteringly explained that the election everyone expected would now not take place. Overnight, the Iron Chancellor, the rumbling volcano that Tony Blair had struggled to contain, became Bottler Brown. This was the biggest political turnaround since the Falklands, and proved – in case we had, because of Gordon Brown's almost unbelievably seamless coronation, temporarily forgotten – that a week is not only a long time in politics, it's often an age.

ONE

'You either carry on the same approach, or you make changes'

David Cameron's Prius, the *Spectator*, Eton, 'Trojan horse', hugging the hoodie, *From Russia with Love*, that parliamentary CV

I first met David Cameron in March 2006, in London's Victoria, not long after he became Leader of the Opposition. I was interviewing him for a *GQ* cover story, and it had been arranged by his private office that I would accompany him to his constituency in Oxfordshire for the day. Bang on time, his car pulled up to meet me outside the Rubens Hotel in Buckingham Palace Road. But instead of a stately Jaguar, Mercedes or Audi, Cameron's vehicle of choice that day was a small silver Toyota Prius, then the hybrid car *du jour*.

'Where's the Jag?' I asked as I climbed in. 'This is a pretty cheap publicity stunt.'

'Oh, stop it,' he said. 'We're trying it out, to see what it's like. Angela [his driver that day] hates it, don't you, Angela?' Angela grimaced. 'We shall have to see, won't we?' said Cameron.

And we did. I'd been planning on test-driving a Prius myself, but after two hours in Cameron's, going all the way from London to his constituency in Witney, west Oxfordshire, we both knew we wouldn't be spending our time driving – or in his case being driven – around in a glorified milk float. (When we were queuing in stationary traffic, we couldn't actually tell if the engine was on, and when we were speeding along the open road – admittedly not that easy on the M40 – it was so quiet you felt you could almost be in a car in an episode of *Captain Scarlet* or *Joe 90*, back in the days before any automated movement in children's animated entertainment was accompanied by a 5.1 thunderclap.)

That afternoon, Cameron had just come from a meeting with the Queen and was feeling cock-a-hoop (it had gone well). Earlier in the day he had been photographed for the cover of *GQ*, and that had gone well, too. He'd turned up on time, tried on the clothes without much of a fuss, chosen a Paul Smith tie to replace his own (although he was loath to exchange his Timothy Everest suit), and gurned with impunity. It was the first time he'd done anything like this, and seemed rather pleased by the result. Not only this, but Thom Yorke and Friends of he Earth had just invited him to one of Radiohead's summer concerts. 'How great is that?' Cameron asked, rhetorically, beaming like a schoolboy.

Cameron looked big, almost squashed into the back of the car. He was wearing a white shirt, no tie, a dark blue suit and had no discernible stubble. Here was a man who looked as if he only shaved every other day. A baby-faced killer.

He had agreed to our first interview with no restrictions – our office had told him we were going to talk about his 'drug past', his days at Eton, and his (at the time) less publicized years spent as a PR spinmeister working for Michael Green at Carlton – and had promised to talk about everything from process and policy to the personal and prosaic. Unsurprisingly he dodged the bullet on drugs, something he has successfully done ever since. Because he has admitted smoking cannabis at Eton, and because he hasn't denied taking cocaine, there is still a general assumption that he has, an assumption that doesn't appear to have harmed him in any way. When questioned on the subject on BBC's *Question Time* in 2006 he refused to give an answer, but he did it in such an eloquent and considered way – repeating that he thought politicians deserved a private life before public office – that he got away with it. He continues to.

In person Cameron was exactly as I had imagined him to be, without much of the well-worn defensiveness you get with most senior politicians. Confidence and breeding obviously have a lot to do with it (plus that Eton education, of course), combined with the not unimportant fact that he'd barely been in the job long enough to find the coffee machine. With only four months as opposition leader under his belt, he had yet to suffer the relentless bombardment of media, the increasingly crippling scrum of PMQs – which, it soon transpired, he actually rather loved, and turned out to be rather good at – the seemingly never-ending bureaucracy of day-to-day politics, or, indeed, the pressure of having to make a decision.

Now, as we glided towards Witney, was not the time for the 'grand statement'; now was not the time for the policy machine to be turned up to eleven. Which was just as well. In the back of the Prius, Cameron's mobile rang exactly twice, and he kept looking at it to make sure it was still working. 'It's sometimes tough being in opposition,' he said to me. 'You're often playing catch-up.' (He was so relaxed when we first met that he wasn't even wearing a watch.)

In person Cameron has a gift for conversational traction, and, like many politicians of the modern webcam-friendly era, goes out of his way to engage in collegiate behaviour. In this respect he's not a Thatcher or a Kinnock or a Prescott. He tends not to hector; instead he has conversations. But to spend time with him is to learn that here is a man who could enter a revolving door behind you and come out in front. All politicians have a repertoire of parrying techniques – some more idiosyncratic than others – and Cameron is no exception, usually using the traditional technique of suggesting a subject be looked at from another angle.

At the time, in early 2006, what the thirty-nine-year-old politician felt the need to do was quietly manage his public image, change the perception of the party, undermine the Blair–Brown succession and prove to the electorate that he actually had some policies – questions were being asked about that – without, obviously, giving away so much that his opponents could steal all the good ones.

Although he had only been on the political paternoster for a relatively short period, he understood that in today's political arena the medium is, initially at least, as important as the message. As the editor of the *Spectator*, Matthew d'Ancona, said at the time, 'People have formed an opinion on whether they like him, and they do. But they don't know what he stands for because his principles are so unexpected. To say, "Make poverty history" is a distinct shift, and he needs to repeat his aims.'

This he has done at every available opportunity; not always with the clarity that the press would have liked, but the message has largely been consistent. If Margaret Thatcher was responsible for economic revolution, then Cameron has, from the beginning, wanted to be remembered for a social revolution. He believes – passionately – in giving people more control over their lives and eradicating the top-down managerial government so popular with the Labour Party.

So what else do we know about him? Well, he drives a black Volkswagen Caravelle, he shares a tailor with Gordon Brown (the aforementioned Timothy Everest), though obviously has a fair amount of M&S, and – like a lot of young fathers these days – has changed his fair share of nappies. Cameron is also something of a James Bond fanatic, and will often reread one of the 007 books to decompress after a hard day tearing a strip off Gordon Brown (he has a collection of Ian Fleming first editions in his house in London). *From Russia with Love* is one of his favourite books (JFK liked it, too), and has professed a fondness for some of the unblinking irony in Ian Fleming's dialogue. To wit: 'They have a saying in Chicago: "Once is happenstance. Twice is coincidence. The third time it's enemy action."'

His wife, Samantha, though working for Bond Street luxury stationer Smythson, tends to wear high street brands head to toe. Cameron married Samantha Sheffield, daughter of Sir Reginald Sheffield – a baronet – on 1 June 1996 at Ginge Manor, near Wantage, in Oxfordshire. Among the guests at the wedding were Jade Jagger, the jeweller, and Samantha's sister Emily, who works in the editorial department of *Vogue*. For those who don't warm to Cameron, Samantha is an easy way in, the acceptable face of High Tory privilege, a woman who calls her husband 'lover', 'babe' and the ubiquitous 'Dave'.

The Camerons have three children. Their first child, Ivan, was born in 2002, profoundly disabled; he has cerebral palsy and severe epilepsy and needs round-the-clock care. He doesn't walk or talk, and – tragically – rarely smiles. For a long while he didn't smile at all, but when his medication was altered in 2006, his moods altered considerably, too, fundamentally changing the atmosphere in the Cameron household: 'When he started to smile it was just the most amazing thing,' said Cameron. 'It made all of us so much happier.'

But Ivan can never be left alone. Ever. Recalling the receipt of the news of Ivan's disabilities, Cameron said, 'The news hits you like a freight train … You are depressed for a while because you are grieving for the difference between your hopes and the reality. But then you get over that, because he's wonderful.' Without experiencing it yourself it is impossible to know how such a tragedy affects a parent – or a family, come to that – but it is very easy to see how Ivan informs David and Samantha's life, and how in some ways it defines it. Dominic Loehnis, a friend of Cameron's since school, has said, 'They'll never get over it, in one way. And in another way it's the steel. It gives him the ability to say "It's a job" and to think there are many more important things in life, but be happy to take risks and be shot at.'

A visit from a journalist from the *Sunday Times Magazine* in 2007 coincided with Ivan's feeding time. Cameron's son was lying across his father's lap exposing a large hole in his stomach (he had had a gastrostomy) through which a tube was delivering drugs and liquid food. 'When children visit,' smiled Cameron, 'and won't eat their tea, I tell them I'm going to put one of these in their tummy.' The journalist – fairly hardboiled – also witnessed Cameron picking up a lamb at a nearby farm for Ivan to touch. 'Can you feel the lambkin, Ivan?'

'Thankfully, we don't vote for politicians on the basis of how sweetly they minister to sick children, but when I have forgotten every word Cameron said to me,' wrote the journalist, 'and long after the next election is won or lost, that tenderness will remain.'

The first time I visited their home in North Kensington (which, as anyone who knows London can tell you, actually means Ladbroke Grove, and is far from the trendy boho paradise painted by the press), I saw Ivan's influence everywhere: the specially installed lift, his toys, the medicine being prepared in the kitchen. The Cameron household is Ivan's own little church, and everything the family do at home revolves around him. It breaks your heart, but then you get the feeling that David and Samantha's hearts have been broken a thousand times over.

The couple also have two other children, Nancy Gwendoline (born 19 January 2004) and Arthur Elwen (born 14 February 2006). After Elwen's birth – he has been called Elwen almost from day one – Cameron was urged by many commentators to mention his family less in public, and the women in my office said at the time that they wished he'd stop being photographed 'in the kitchen' (he did).

Cameron is tough. When the British press began hounding him during his drugs 'crisis', about whether he had ever taken cocaine while an MP, he refused to comment, said it was all in the past, and appeared to win the battle, if not the war, with the *Daily Mail* (which took him to task more than most). He has even done a good job of muffling the stage whispers of irritation from the Tory old guard. He's certainly the only politician in recent memory to get *Newsnight*'s Jeremy Paxman to question his interrogation technique. During the Tory leadership election he said, on air, 'The trouble with these interviews, Jeremy, is that you treat people like a cross between a fake and a hypocrite. You give no time to anyone to answer any of your questions.' Even though Cameron admitted he had planned this, Paxman also admitted it had made him think about altering his approach (he didn't).

This was pot and kettle stuff anyway, as anyone who has seen Cameron in action during Prime Minister's Questions will know. In his time he has prepared three leaders for PMQs – John Major, Iain Duncan Smith and Michael Howard – so it should be no surprise that Cameron is so good at them himself. Cameron explained his technique in an online column he wrote for the *Guardian* shortly after asking his first question at PMQs as a backbencher.

'There are four types of question,' he wrote. 'First is the "wife-beater". This is the question to which there is no answer. A typical effort would be: "What is the Prime Minister most proud of – the billion pounds wasted on the Dome or the million-pound bung from Bernie Ecclestone?"

'Next is "the teaser". This type of question looks limp and unexciting on paper, but can sometimes elicit the most interesting response by catching the Prime Minister off guard …

'Third is the *Daily Mail* special. Pick the issue that the middle-ranking tabloids are having kittens about and give it some oomph … Make it on to the front pages and enjoy fifteen seconds of fame.

'Finally there are the local issues. These are by far the most boring for everyone else to listen to, [and] easily the most effective. Unlike national papers, local ones actually report in some detail what Members of Parliament do. A short question can be followed up with a press release, an endless round of local TV and radio interviews and a prolonged burst of local stardom.'

In the past he has also written about his techniques when appearing on radio and TV. Having spent years advising politicians and businessmen how to do it, he is well versed. On preparing for Radio 4's weekly political panel show *Any Questions?*, he said: 'Don't drink anything at the dinner with Jonathan Dimbleby before the show; don't worry about the audience in the hall baying for your blood – concentrate on the folks at home. And try to sound reasonable. Michael Portillo once told me a tip he had been given: by being thoroughly rude and aggressive to the other panellists at the dinner you can wind them up into fits of indignation. They will then rant and rave on air and you will come over cool as the proverbial cucumber.' His 'tabloid tips' included knowing what was happening on TV, and to 'have some jokes'.

Tony Blair once likened the press to a 'feral beast', and it is the media who have accelerated both the erosion of Gordon Brown's standing and the ascendancy of David Cameron. The opinion polls have helped sway the editorial, but journalists have been happy to be convinced – Cameron is simply more appealing to the media than his three predecessors as Tory leader, and knows better how to handle the media. By contrast, Brown, since that fatal week in October 2007 when he lost the media's respect – following Cameron's brilliant conference speech and Brown ducking the election – has never looked like regaining it fully.

Ever since the *Independent*'s 'poll of polls' in January 2008 – which took the weighted average of monthly polls by ICM, Ipsos MORI, Populus, YouGov and ComRes – put the Tories a full nine points clear, with 41 per cent to Labour's 32 per cent, the PM has never totally got his confidence back.

A win for the Conservatives at the next general election is, of course, hardly a *fait accompli*. The Tories have fewer MPs now than Labour had during the Michael Foot years (1980–83), and they still need the biggest swing in modern times – a swing, as Broonites like to point out, even larger than the one achieved by Margaret Thatcher in 1979 with the assistance of the Winter of Discontent. But, clearly, Cameron has moved closer to grabbing power than any Tory leader in a generation. David Cameron's initial aim when becoming party leader was to make the Tories less disliked, and his task since achieving that has been to make them electable; which, although the polls continue going up and down like a battery-powered Spacehopper, he appears to have done.

For a Tory leader he is still considered rather young (born in London on 9 October 1966). A lot of people only begin to look their age when they try to look younger; Cameron easily looks five years younger than he is, which in a particular light can be a problem. And, yes, he still occasionally acts younger than his years. When the chairman of a not unimportant PR agency I know met him for dinner not long after he was appointed leader, he called me the following morning and uttered just two words, 'Chauncey Gardiner' – a reference to a rather dim Peter Sellers character in the 1979 film *Being There*, who's thrust into the limelight after the death of his boss and rises to national public prominence.

But to a lot of people Cameron looks like the first British post-Blair politician genuinely capable of leaving a legacy. He has planted his tent firmly on the centre ground and is adamant that he will not retreat to the political wasteland like his predecessors Hague, Duncan Smith and Howard. As has been said more than once, it's almost as if his manifesto is an application from the Conservative Party to rejoin the political arena. What do the Tories stand for now? I think it's fair to say the answer to that question is fundamental social reform.

'One of the things that I admire about David is that he's very upfront about where he stands on things,' said his former boss Norman Lamont. 'I'm not saying he can't be politically cunning, I'm sure he can, but he states where he stands. He describes himself as a liberal Conservative. I admired for its daring the way that he spoke about civil partnerships at the Conservative Party Conference. That was breathtaking, but quite typical of him. I think he's quite open and I think that's a great political strength. If you tiptoe around you never get there.'

One of Cameron's favourite TV shows is still *The West Wing*, and when I quizzed him about his favourite character, he said, 'If I say President Bartlett you will think I am a megalomaniac, but I like the way he cuts through all the bull and does the right thing.'

On a trip to Bradford to inspect a regeneration project in 2006, he was joined by Michael Heseltine, who immediately began to moan about the hold that Gordon Brown had on Whitehall. Cameron, who even then thought he had the measure of the future PM, said that while Brown had a 'big brain' he would struggle with responsiveness as leader, being too fastidious in his planning. 'We're quite happy Blair's going,' he told Heseltine. 'He's trying to get out of the shit and can't. Brown thinks he still can, so we have to push his face back in it.'

'I think David Cameron is not quite as nice as he looks,' said Michael Portillo in Michael Cockerell's BBC2 documentary *David Cameron's Incredible Journey*, 'and I've always said that I'm pleased to know that.'

In terms of presentation, Cameron has all the required surface smarts, yet with his Eton background he is certainly ripe enough for caricature. But then so is the oh-so-stoic Brown ('an analogue politician in a digital age', according to Cameron, who comes up with sound bites as often as his advisers). As *The Economist* has pointed out, if the real ideological oppositions – big versus small state, high versus low tax – ever become blurred, the 'cosmetic divide' of Jock versus Posh might easily replace them. If it does, Cameron will come prepared. One of the things that the

Tories have yet to seriously bash Brown over the head with is his nationality, and the PM must be thankful that there are no more Home Internationals (even though Brown rather rashly suggested resuscitating them after England failed to qualify for the 2008 European Championships). I think there are few things that Cameron would relish more than asking Brown in PMQs, the week after an England/Scotland international, which team he had supported.

In the days immediately following his 2005 leadership victory, many questions passed the lips of the constituents of the Tory heartlands: 'Who is David Cameron?' 'What does he stand for?' 'Is he a Trojan horse?' 'Is he, in fact, a real Tory?' His economic grounding says he has always been one, but for the first two years of his leadership he appeared reluctant to focus on tax, crime, immigration and all the other hoary old Tory concerns, preferring to tackle traditional Labour topics such as public service reform, fighting poverty, multiculturalism, the environment, social justice and education. He also rather neatly began to play upon Labour's obsession with civil liberties, continually referencing 'freedom' (much to the irritation of strait-laced right-wing columnists such as the *Daily Telegraph*'s Simon Heffer) at a time when the government was appearing more and more authoritarian.

But then David Cameron was a new kind of Tory, the sort of Tory no one had ever seen before. Especially, so it seemed, other Tories.

However, at every opportunity, and through every twist and turn, Cameron has invoked the long-standing Tory tradition of radical social reform, best typified by Disraeli. And while there have been mistakes along the way – some that still linger – Cameron's policies have been fairly consistent. There are still some political commentators who say that Cameron can come across as naive, although while that might have been true eighteen months ago it certainly isn't now. During the summer of 2007 his pronouncements on grammar schools (we've got enough!), and his policy review's ideas on plasma televisions (taxable!) and air travel (even more taxable!) would lend weight to that criticism, but during his late-summer assault on Brown that year, when it felt as if a new policy was leaving Portcullis House every six or seven hours, he made up for this in a major way. Cameron quite sensibly waited for his policy reviews and then bombarded us all with missives pertaining to everything from the family and the welfare state, to crime, tax and immigration.

Initially in his leadership he spent his time talking up the green agenda, and his party's New! and Improved! attitude towards social justice, which, while certainly signifying change, tended to alienate those in his party who were more used to policies involving national security and the police. Before a speech to the Centre for Social Justice that highlighted the problem of young offenders in which he called for more understanding, Cameron was reported as saying we should 'Hug a hoodie', a tag that has stuck around like old chewing gum. He actually said 'We – the people in suits – often see hoodies as aggressive. But hoodies are more defensive than offensive.' 'Hug a hoodie' was in fact coined by a newspaper sub-editor.

His big ideas from the off were social reform and the decentralization of government, which were not the sort of things to set the pulse racing. Since then, of course, things have changed, and since the end of summer 2007 regular salvos have come from Central Office on everything from crime and the war on terror to tax and the welfare state. The Tory faithful are now mostly behind him, and as one Tory grandee said after the 2007 conference speech, 'Cameron is a stray dog. But he's our dog.'

And many things have become clear: he is for fox hunting and marriage and against ID cards. He wants to overhaul the welfare state, reboot the NHS, fundamentally reorganize the education system and lower tax burdens. He wants to scrap the Human Rights Act, which came into force in 2000. Instead, he intends replacing it with a Bill of Rights, based on 'British needs and traditions'. On the West Lothian question (first made in 1977 by Tam Dalyell, the Labour MP for West Lothian, regarding the paradox of English MPs being unable to vote on matters in Scotland, Northern Ireland and Wales), he has criticized the right of Scottish MPs to vote on English matters: 'We need to make devolution work … one part of devolution that obviously doesn't work is that Scottish MPs can vote on matters that don't affect their own constituents.'

And, of course, he's fundamentally sceptical of the EU, although not in an especially aggressive way.

And – controversially – he voted for the war in Iraq. He has supported the alliance with the United States, claiming 'we must be steadfast not slavish in how we approach the special relationship', arguing that 'questioning the approach of the US administration, trying to learn the lessons of the past five years, does not make you anti-American'. Cameron also supports Israel and has described the state as being 'a lone democracy in a region that currently boasts no others'. He is a member of and has spoken for the Conservative Friends of Israel. However, he criticized the country's 2006 missile attacks on Lebanon, describing the force used as 'disproportionate'.

On immigration, he's stated that contact between different communities is essential for social integration and, as such, the government should ensure that new immigrants learn to speak English. He has endorsed the government's creation of city academies and trust schools – unpopular with so many Labour backbenchers – as a way of improving standards in deprived areas. He has called on the government to go 'further and faster' with the policy, and says that academies should be given even more freedom from central control.

When he became leader he immediately made clear he wasn't interested in trying to abolish the NHS, or bringing back grammar schools, or, indeed, focusing on Blair's ruthless mendacity (at the time the Prime Minister could easily do that for himself). Cameron was determined to present the sort of caring, sharing Tory way forward that would have been anathema to the party in the 1980s and 1990s. Twenty years ago, when there were still massive divisions between the left and right in Britain, politics by its very nature was confrontational. After three flops and nearly nine years in the wilderness, this Vigorous Young Leader (or 'Blameron' or 'Tory Blair', as he's also been called) knows that some of the traditional Tory attitudes are not going to sway a generation of even younger voters who aren't remotely aware of Margaret Thatcher's legacy. There were other surprises early in the leadership, too, involving race, green issues, foreign policy, social breakdown, equal pay, Third World poverty (working with Bob Geldof on various policies for Africa), new media and a whole lot more. Rather than firm policies – 'the other side will only pinch the ones they like' – Cameron began by espousing issues involving localism and social responsibility in place of big-state solutions. Initially he was self-consciously liberal on law and order and immigration, acknowledging that the Tories' strident tone about these topics helped ensure the 2005 election defeat.

Unlike any likely Tory contender in the past decade, Cameron stands for a 'modern', 'compassionate' conservatism, and has gone out of his way to appropriate much of the political centre ground (Labour Party's middle ground) in a similar way to how Blair climbed over the Tory barricades a decade ago. But, like Blair, as some have pointed out, he's fundamentally non-ideological, and thinks people should be left alone to get on with their lives. This is the basis of his Euroscepticism, and his genuine fear that Gordon Brown will give in even more to European rule.

Cameron has put 'economic stability ... before tax cuts', but in the early days of his leadership his Cabinet were not particularly consistent on tax. At one point Shadow Cabinet member Oliver Letwin dismissed tax cuts as a 'bribe', choosing to ignore the fact that this has traditionally been what Tory voters respond to. George Osborne once mistakenly argued that Cameron's Conservatives are just like Thatcher's Tories, and that 'The Conservatives did not promise tax cuts in the 1979 election and said they had to sort out the public finances first.' This ignored the fact that the 1979 manifesto clearly states 'We shall cut income tax at all levels', while obscuring Cameron's original pledge to 'share the proceeds of growth'. But since Osborne announced last autumn that under a Tory government inheritance tax would be slashed, there has been an assumption among press and public alike that tax cuts will eventually be inevitable.

In any discussion of the Conservatives and tax cuts, it's worth bearing in mind the words of Irwin Stelzer, director of Economic Policy Studies at the Hudson Institute in Washington DC, a confidant of Rupert Murdoch's and one of his top advisers, who once said, 'Voters know the difference between a Republican candidate (in the US) who promises to lower taxes, and Tory candidates (in the UK) who promise that at some unspecified date, if the conditions are just right, they will plan to try to attempt to keep taxes below the levels that might prevail under a Labour government.'

Welfare eventually came in for some attention, too, and at the start of 2008 Cameron unveiled a new policy that meant unemployed people who turn down offers of work will have their benefits stripped under a 'three strikes and you're out' rule (part of the Tory leader's plan to contain the £100 billion welfare bill, including trying to move a million people on incapacity benefit back into work). Chris Grayling, the Shadow Secretary of State for Work and Pensions, said at the time, 'We think it's time to take tough action against those who are deliberately staying at home and claiming benefits rather than going back to work. We think if you get a reasonable job offer, you should take it. We want to end the culture of entitlement, [as] there is no real excuse for someone saying "no, I'm not interested" to an offer of employment.'

Cameron is a huge fan of Tommy Thompson's welfare reforms, the same ones that Blair tried unsuccessfully to employ when he first got into office. Thompson was the Republican governor of Wisconsin who in 1996 enacted the 'Wisconsin Works' programme, which required the unemployed, in return for welfare payments, to undergo either skills training, or to work, in jobs supported by state subsidy or in community service activities. The idea was to end welfare dependency and to re-establish individual responsibility, and its impact upon benefit rolls was extraordinary. So extraordinary that the ideas heavily influenced Bill Clinton's own federal reforms. At the 2007 Tory conference, Cameron explicitly praised what had been achieved in Wisconsin: '... where they've cut benefit rolls by 80 per cent – and the changes we will make are these: we will say to people that if you are offered a job, and it's a fair job, and one that you can do and you refuse it, you shouldn't get any welfare'.

Writing in *GQ* in March 2008, Matthew d'Ancona said: 'So striking was Cameron's feat in delivering his speech at the Blackpool Winter

Gardens without notes, and so excited was the Tory faithful by the promise of cuts in inheritance tax and stamp duty, that very few noticed how radical was his pledge to overhaul welfare in this country. But it is by some margin the most daring strategy that the Cameroons have so far proposed, and the Tory leader's readiness to hold to his promise as the election approaches will be a key test of what sort of prime minister he might be.'

These reforms dovetailed with those suggested by Iain Duncan Smith in his 2007 policy review on social breakdown, which recommended that the balance should be 'reset' to help marriage, backing tax breaks for some married couples, trebling child benefit for the first three years and getting more single parents off benefits earlier. Since stepping down as the Conservative Party's leader, Duncan Smith had established himself as a highly respected thinker and researcher on social breakdown. Now his policy review offered up a strong range of substantial and eye-catching policies. Raising tax on alcohol to tackle binge drinking, reclassifying cannabis to Class B, a greater role for credit unions in poor communities, raising the gambling age threshold from sixteen to eighteen – with the social fabric seemingly under strain, Duncan Smith's ideas came across as sane stuff. He said the tax-break plan was not a 'golden bullet' to preserve marriage, or about 'finger-wagging or moralising'. But, he said, the current system 'penalised people who are wanting to stay together'.

Perhaps the single most important thing that Cameron understood was the fact that, for the past fifteen years, the Tories had largely been incredibly unpopular. Following the 1997 election, when Conservative MPs lost seats all over Britain – and were completely wiped out in Scotland, Wales, Manchester, Liverpool and Newcastle – it had become more or less socially unacceptable to be a Tory.

'You've got a choice when you've lost elections,' Cameron said, as the Prius hurtled silently towards Oxford. 'You either carry on the same approach, or you make changes.'

Under Tony Blair and Gordon Brown, after 1994 the Labour Party left fundamental socialism behind and became reconciled to the free-market economy. And although the party was always going to be bound at the hip to the state, New Labour became a different kind of enemy for the Tories. And Cameron understood this, too, instinctively.

The Labour Party's ascendancy during the 1990s was not just the result of a brilliant rebranding campaign – the party was also the beneficiary of a groundswell of anti-Tory disenchantment, a disenchantment that was soon to affect the party internally. However, luckily for them the Tories didn't suffer as Labour did back in the late seventies and early eighties, when a succession of very public events – the defection of the Gang of Four (David Owen, Roy Jenkins, Shirley Williams and Bill Rodgers), Tony Benn's misguided challenge for the deputy leadership, Arthur Scargill's one-man crusade to destabilize Michael Foot's leadership (Neil Kinnock called him 'the Labour movement's nearest equivalent to a First World War general') and the growing popularity of Militant – threatened to destroy Labour.

The big problem the Tories had from the mid-nineties onwards was largely one of image. Both William Hague and Michael Howard had tried tempting the public with policies based on traditional right-wing staples such as Europe, tax, immigration and crime, and the public wasn't remotely interested. And even when they warmed to the policies, as soon as voters discovered they were Tory policies they ran in the opposite direction.

Six days after William Hague lost the 2001 election, Cameron had this to say to the *Daily Telegraph*: '[The Conservative Party] has to change its language, change its approach, start with a blank piece of paper and try to work out why our base of support is not broader. Anyone could have told the Labour Party in the 1980s how to become electable. It had to drop unilateral disarmament, punitive tax rises, wholesale nationalisation and unionisation. The question for the Conservative Party is far more difficult because there are no obvious areas of policy that need to be dropped. We need a clear, positive, engaging agenda on public services.'

His speeches prior to his leadership victory advertised his determination to drag his party to the centre, although convincing the press was usually impossible: 'social responsibility', one of his key messages, was a difficult thing to grasp, and in the early days the press didn't seem too keen to grasp it at all. But since then Cameron has turned around the formerly fire-damaged party and addressed tactics, recruitment and decision-making procedures. And for someone who is immersed in one of the most cynical professions known to man, he remains remarkably optimistic: his message has always been about change.

There were, early in his leadership, concerns among the Tory faithful that what they wanted and what David Cameron wanted were two completely different things, and in the first eighteen months in charge there were various exasperated outbursts by aggrieved backbenchers and former Cabinet members, many of whom felt that Cameron was destabilizing the Tory brand instead of trying to reinvent it. The infighting wasn't all bad, though, as to be seen as a real modernizer Cameron needed to show potential voters that he really was breaking with tradition. So what if people like Norman Tebbit criticized him? As so many people knew, Tebbit was one of the reasons the country had lurched away from the 'nasty party' in the first place. Cameron had to renounce him.

David Cameron himself is as central to his project to reinvent the Tories as Tony Blair was to his reinvention of New Labour. He has – like Blair before him – tried to convince us that the party has changed because he, personally, has changed it, thus making him look strong and in control. Some might say that while Blair and Brown – and Alastair Campbell and Peter Mandelson to a lesser extent – re-engineered the product itself, Cameron has simply performed a slick rebranding exercise without doing as much heavy work under the bonnet, but it would be a fool who underestimates a man who has turned such a decrepit old banger back into an attractive roadster in so short a time. As we have come to see, while David Cameron wears his leadership lightly, he carries a very big stick.

Cameron usually comes across as being quite as self-reliant and impervious to criticism as Blair did a decade ago, when the former Prime Minister was in his pomp. Cameron certainly acts like a leader, exuding the sort of old-fashioned army officer insouciance you find at the top levels of the legal profession.

With the education he's had, this is hardly surprising. The son of a stockbroker and magistrate and the third of four children, at the age of seven David William Donald Cameron was sent to Heatherdown Preparatory School in Winkfield, Berkshire, near where he was brought up. The school counts Prince Andrew, Prince Edward and Peter Getty – grandson of the oil billionaire John Paul – among its alumni. Indeed, according to Francis Elliott and James Hanning's biography of Cameron, among the eighty sets of parents of his contemporaries there were eight honourables, four sirs, two captains, two doctors, two majors, two princesses, two marchionesses, one viscount, one brigadier, one commodore, one earl, one lord and one queen – *the* Queen.

After Heatherdown, Cameron went to Eton, following his elder brother Alex, who was three years above him. Britain's most famous public school gives its students a level of confidence and a sense of entitlement that can make non-Eton pupils quite jealous. One Etonian friend of Cameron's puts the Tory leader's inner toughness down to his schooling. Rupert Dilnott-Cooper, who worked with Cameron at Carlton, said that Eton can make its pupils emotionally 'distant'. 'I think there can be a degree of dispassionate ruthlessness that comes down to saying, "Thanks very much. Next?" I'm confident that he would be capable of being as ruthless as he needs to be.' (Whenever anyone accuses Cameron of being arrogant I always tell them he's got a long way to go before he catches up with Peter Mandelson – when Alastair Campbell saw Mandelson on television, he would say: 'There goes the Secretary of State for Smugness.') At Eton he passed twelve O levels and three 'A' grade A levels in History of Art, History and Economics with Politics, a solid achievement given his rather anonymous start to life at the school.

After that it was Brasenose College, Oxford. His time here was seemingly idyllic, too, and the story from this period that Cameron most enjoys retelling is the sort of anecdote that any undergraduate would like to own. Having invited his younger sister Clare to visit him for the weekend, she brought along a friend and fellow pupil at St Mary's, Calne, the fifteen-year-old Jade Jagger. The highlight was an afternoon spent – in time-honoured fashion – punting on the river. The following Monday, Cameron's mother Mary received a call at home, from, of all people, Mick Jagger, who wasn't exactly jumping for joy. 'What's all this my daughter's been getting up to with your son?' he said. 'You know I don't approve of blood sports.'

Admittedly there isn't a great deal in Cameron's first twenty years to explain his choice of politics as a career, but there is no denying he has found his passion from somewhere. Cameron always plays down any political ambitions he may have had as an adolescent, but while at Eton he was known to at least one contemporary as 'the guy who wants to be Prime Minister'. But not a Labour Prime Minister, obviously; he had, through his family and schooling, been hardwired with Tory values from the earliest age.

Even though his critics always claim otherwise – painting him as an inexperienced politician, having only been elected to Parliament in 2001 – Cameron has been involved in British politics for much of his adult life. He read Philosophy, Politics and Economics at Brasenose, gaining a first-class honours degree. He then joined the Conservative Research Department and became Special Adviser to Norman Lamont – in his days as Chancellor of the Exchequer – and then Special Adviser to Michael Howard, the then Home Secretary. He was also Director of Corporate Affairs at Carlton Communications for seven years.

Cameron worked for the CRD between 1988 and 1992. In 1991, he was drafted in to Downing Street to work on briefing John Major for Prime Minister's Questions. During the 1992 general election he was also given responsibility for briefing Major for his press conferences. Critics of Cameron say that he was a dilettante throughout much of his time at CRD, the Treasury and the Home Office, although on closer inspection it's obvious that not only was he ploughing a furrow consistent with that of a young politician on the make, but also that his ascent was being noticed and taken seriously.

After the Conservatives' wholly unexpected success in the 1992 general election, Cameron was promoted, becoming Special Adviser to

Norman Lamont. Although in the light of Black Wednesday (16 September 1992), when currency speculators forced the pound out of the ERM, perhaps this wasn't much of a reward.

'It was the most turbulent time I'd ever seen in government, like being on a rollercoaster in full view of everyone in the country,' said Cameron in the back of the Prius that day, as we slowed down on the outskirts of Witney. 'I was surrounded by the most intense people I'd ever seen. People's personalities changed in front of me, and then I realized what it meant to be in politics. It was then that I realized that you have to put everything into it, because if you don't it's going to consume you anyway.'

Lamont still feels he was unfairly demonized after Black Wednesday, although he didn't help himself by answering 'Je ne regrette rien' when asked whether he most regretted claiming to see 'the green shoots of recovery' or admitting 'singing in his bath' with happiness at leaving the ERM. After Lamont was sacked, Cameron remained at the Treasury for less than a month before being recruited by the Home Secretary, Michael Howard.

Finally, in September 1993, Cameron did the inevitable and applied to go on the parliamentary candidates' list. And then, having met the girl he wanted to marry – the socially smart but decidedly bohemian Samantha Sheffield – and needing to earn some proper money (to buy a house, for one thing), in July 1994 Cameron stepped down from his job as Special Adviser to go and work as the Director of Corporate Affairs at Michael Green's Carlton, which three years earlier had won the ITV franchise for London weekdays. His move into this world perhaps shouldn't have been surprising, not least because as a researcher and speech-writer Cameron was already well versed in the necessary evils of spin.

Some journalists who worked with Cameron while he was at Carlton are highly critical of both his methods and his manner, accusing him of being a patronizing bully who was more than economical with the truth. (Green is an exacting boss. One of his best friends, former *Daily Telegraph* editor Max Hastings, said that he would rather sleep with him than work for him.) He also spent much of his time defending the indefensible. Patrick Hosking, who in his role as investment editor of *The*

Times, found himself dealing with Cameron on many occasions, says, 'His PR needs were many and varied but hardly likely to instil much dignity in a future statesman: defending the dumping of *News at Ten* to make way for a revival of *Mr and Mrs* with Julian Clary; arguing the case for commercials targeted at children; defending the screening of insalutary scenes from *The Vice* within minutes of the Watershed; explaining how Carlton had come to screen a one-hour programme, conceived, sponsored and entirely funded by British Telecom.'

Of course, this is another way of saying that Cameron was simply very good at his job.

Cameron resigned in February 2001 in order to fight for election to Parliament, although he remained on Green's payroll as a consultant. Having missed out on selection for Ashford in December 1994, in 1996 he was then selected for Stafford, a new constituency created by boundary changes. But although it was supposed to have a fairly substantial Conservative majority, Stafford's swing to Labour was virtually the same as the rest of the country, and Cameron was soundly defeated. After that, he tried to be selected for Wealden and managed only to get onto the shortlists in Epsom and East Devon.

And then, finally, success. In April 2000 he was chosen as the prospective candidate for Witney in Oxfordshire, a Cotswold idyll in rural Tory England. Shaun Woodward, the incumbent MP, had defected to Labour, leaving Cameron free to ingratiate himself with a slightly bewildered constituency; he won the seat with a 1.9 per cent swing and a majority of nearly 8000.

As a new MP he landed a prestigious job in being appointed to the Home Affairs Select Committee, and in June 2003 he was made Shadow Deputy Leader of the House of Commons. When Michael Howard became party leader, he made his former adviser a vice-chairman of the party and in June 2004 promoted him into the Shadow Cabinet, initially as head of policy coordination.

With Howard's loss in the 2005 general election, Cameron broke cover as a leadership contender. His campaign was moving slowly, but then, just before the Tory conference of 2005, he was anointed by, of all people, the BBC. In a focus group for BBC2's *Newsnight* conducted by the US pollster Frank Luntz, potential Tory supporters responded far more strongly to the thirty-eight-year-old Shadow Education Secretary than any of his rivals in the leadership race – until then David Davis had been the strong favourite. 'David Cameron has reinvented politics for me,' said Luntz. (The film was so unambiguous, so fulsome, that Cameron's leadership campaign team wanted to distribute DVDs of the segment to Conservative MPs.) Like many, when I saw *Newsnight* that night I became very intrigued.

In the weeks leading up to the 2005 Conservative Conference lunchtime conversation was usually kick-started by ten minutes discussing which poor soul was about to lead the Tories into their next election defeat. The common consensus was that Cameron would be undone because he was 'too young and too posh'. And so many journalists – including, I have to admit, myself – thought that David Davis, Mr Bootstrap Council-Estate Knee-Jerk, was the man for the job (even though Matthew Parris had once said that Davis 'speaks as though delivering a managing director's report at the AGM of an East Midlands light cardboard packaging company'). After all, he was responsible for the best sound bite of the year: 'I'm a control freak for the individual.'

But David William Donald Cameron's speech at the Empress Ballroom in Blackpool's Winter Gardens on 4 October 2005 launched him into the public consciousness and set him on course for victory in the party's leadership election. He had already made a splash with key media commentators – like the BBC's Nick Robinson and ITV's Tom Bradby – at the launch of his leadership campaign on 29 September, when he also made an electrifying speech. But with the Blackpool conference speech – which offered more than a nod towards John F. Kennedy (not that anyone in his party seemed to mind) – the Cameroons were on their way.

'So let the message go out from this conference,' he said, building towards his dramatic conclusion, and pausing for dramatic effect. 'A modern compassionate Conservatism is right for our times, right for our party – and right for our country. If we go for it, if we seize it, if we fight

22

for it with every ounce of passion, vigour and energy from now until the next election, nothing and no one can stop us.'

Until Cameron's stunning performance at the Tory party conference in October 2005, another Labour election victory looked assured. But almost immediately after his speech, the media woke up to the fact that Cameron was plausible. That Cameron was serious. That Cameron, and his party – *his* party – were electable. He was young. Presentable. Moderate. Could Cameron really be the nation's saviour?

During the spring of 2006, just a few months after Cameron's election as party leader, everyone had Cameron Tourette's, and you couldn't go anywhere without being bombarded with opinions about the Vigorous Young Leader. He was all anyone wanted to talk about. I spent two weeks that April doing as much fieldwork as I could, and, having polled nearly everyone I came into contact with, 60 per cent said they wanted to vote for him. On the one hand people like John Ayton, the chairman of the jewellery firm Links of London, were saying, encouragingly, 'His world is bigger than politics', while on the other hand some people were wondering where all the policies had gone. On the last day of April one ridiculously famous actress told me, 'My problem with him is the fact he's not that sexy. Although compared to Blair he's Daniel Craig.'

I couldn't really imagine James Bond in the back of a Prius, but then, to his credit, David Cameron probably couldn't either. After all, there is a world of difference between fantasy and reality, and Cameron has already had first-hand experience of the harsh realities of British politics. But importantly – crucially, fundamentally – he is a fighter. A winner. Or, as Ian Fleming once wrote, 'The distance between insanity and genius is measured only by success.'

David Cameron is the last person to call himself a genius, although he is also a man who tends not to entertain failure.

TWO

'Reading them [Alastair Campbell's diaries] is like gulping a triple espresso'

**By-elections, YouTube, Glasnost, the *Guardian*
racing pages, Brasenose, Alastair Campbell, the
White House tennis rota**

The thirteenth of July 2007, London W3. David Cameron was on walkabout in west London, with a small army of newspaper and TV reporters shadowing his every move. He was in Ealing to lend support to a British Asian candidate, Tony Lit, who was standing in the Ealing Southall by-election in six days' time. Cameron had already been here three times in the previous two weeks, as had Shadow Chancellor George Osborne. He was taking it seriously: for the last twenty-five years the Tories had had a dismal record in by-elections, and Cameron had vowed to improve his party's performance.

This was modern-day London, modern-day Britain. Ealing Southall contains large populations of Sikhs, Muslims, Hindus, Poles and Somalis, among others, and the Leader of the Opposition was here to try and demonstrate that the Tory Party – his party – was the right place for all those people of immigrant descent who believed in the same things he believed in, namely family, religion, community, hard work, good manners, freedom, enterprise, self-reliance and social responsibility. The area was traditionally loyal to Labour, but there were beginning to be indications that many of Ealing Southall's ethnic minorities were becoming disillusioned with their representation. Lit was named on the ballot paper as a member of 'David Cameron's Conservatives', a gamble by local Tories that Cameron's personal appeal would win the party the support it needed.

Cameron darted in and out of the butchers' shops, furniture shops, cafés and newsagents on Northfield Avenue, accosting strangers on the street and giving all and sundry a healthy dose of the Cameron charm. He doesn't have the full-beam-headlights smile of Blair, but he's eloquent and genuine enough not to appear shrill, and got his points across even when being screamed at by a bunch of irate local shopkeepers whose premises in Southall High Street had been sold on by the local Tory council. They were banging a drum and gleefully trying to interrupt him, making the all-important TV coverage almost impossible. In the sixty minutes of his walkabout the animosity was at a low-level intensity, the sort of war of attrition that most MPs experience at some time or another in situations like this.

But trouble of another kind was waiting for Cameron's candidate. Two days later the press would announce that Lit had – rather embarrassingly – recently attended a Labour fundraising event, where he had been photographed with Tony Blair. Sunrise Radio, the company of which Lit was then managing director, had even given Labour a cheque for close to £5000. That Sunday – 15 July – the papers were also full of the 'Brown bounce' – the first time the Labour Party had been substantially ahead in the polls since Cameron became leader (Brown took over as Prime Minister on 27 June 2007). Five councillors had defected to the Tories during the by-election campaign, but all that was eclipsed by the news of Lit's close links with Labour – he had in fact only been a member of the Tory Party for a handful of days.

This was a total PR disaster, and, five days later, David Cameron's Conservatives trailed in a dismal third in the by-election. Party chiefs were accused of failing to heed local sensitivities, particularly among Muslims and Hindus, by imposing Lit, a Sikh, as the candidate. The results sparked fresh talk that Gordon Brown might call an early election, and Virendra Sharma, the successful Labour candidate, said that the result was 'a humiliating rebuke from Britain's most diverse constituency' to the Tories. The result was a veritable kick in the teeth for Cameron, and most of the national press were against him the day after (how could they not be). A more supportive editorial comment came from the *Evening Standard*: 'Mr Cameron must hold his nerve, clarify his message and reflect on the risks of picking candidates new to the party. But he must not move away from his core strategy of repositioning the Conservatives for 21st-century challenges.'

But as Cameron and I made our way around Southall on the 13th all of that was yet to come, and I was keen to see how he went about trying to convince a largely ethnic community that they should vote Conservative. A British Asian, Maryam Ahmed, a thirty-six-year-old NHS worker, berated the Right Hon. Member for Witney, Oxfordshire, for having so few MPs from ethnic minorities: 'You've only got two black and minority ethnic MPs – you've got two hundred seats – you've not chosen any of them. You've got a very short time to prove to me your party is not racist.'

Cameron bristled obviously at this, a statement that sounded suspiciously like a Labour plant. 'My party is not prejudiced. There's not a prejudiced bone in my body,' he replied plaintively.

A few minutes later a single mother of Asian descent accosted Cameron, denouncing the Tories' proposal to give financial support to married couples, saying, 'Why would a failed marriage stay together just because they get £20 more? That's ridiculous. I understand marriage is important and wonderful but giving people £20 to stay together is crazy.' Again, it sounded like a prompt from Labour Party HQ.

The time was up, and Cameron needed to get to his constituency, not only for his weekly surgery but also for some prize-giving at a local school, and a meeting with members of the Oxfordshire Community Foundation as well as an appointment at the Witney Buttercross Scouts. All the while he would be on the phone to Steve Hilton, the Conservatives' 'big-of-brain fleet-of-foot strategy warlord', and taking calls from the dozens of people who now felt that they had demands on his time. At some point in all of this – and this was a relatively slow day, a deliberately diary-free Friday – he would grab a sandwich and a banana.

Back on Northfield Avenue, as we both rushed for Cameron's car, he was pursued by the TV crews and the news hacks, all hoping for one last sound bite, all eager to exploit this closing window of opportunity, if only to ask another potentially embarrassing question.

And as we sat back in the Mercedes, that day's papers spilling over onto the floor, my first question was a straightforward one: why on earth does he do it?

Campaigning

David, having just witnessed the stampede out there, and the way you were set up, the way in which people attacked you, my first question is a fairly obvious one that would probably occur to anyone who's just seen what I've seen. Yes, you get enormous acclaim and satisfaction from your role, but why on earth would you do it?
David Cameron: You get all sorts of stuff on the walkabouts. Today, as you just heard, someone said to me that they thought our party was still prejudiced on the grounds of race, and it felt like that they had been primed with questions, but it was actually a good question to answer as here we have a British Asian candidate. Then someone said what about gay people, and actually we support civil partnerships with our plans – they will get the same tax treatment as married couples. Which rather surprised them. It was just interesting that today I felt as though there were people planted to ask me certain questions, but actually it meant there was a proper debate and that was more fun.

But today they were actually quite rude to you. You must have the hide of an ox …
Well, I think it's tough enough.

Do you just filter out all the bad stuff, all the abuse?
You can't, because that's why you're there, to listen as well as tell people what you think about things.

But it's not fun.

Well, actually a lot of the time it is. And when it isn't you always learn something.

The Tories haven't had a great track record with by-elections, and this is obviously something you need to counteract. How much does your presence at something like this help?

God, I don't know. I think it helps raise the profile of the campaign. These elections are really about going from door to door and getting across your message about the candidate, and this one is much more about trying to raise the profile of the campaign, which we have done well, and because of the five Labour candidates that defected [to the Tories, in the run-up to the by-election], it has been front page of the local newspaper and that probably gave it more of a rocket boost.

[We are interrupted by a call from Boris Johnson, who the next day will announce his candidacy for the London mayoral race.]

Boris Johnson

I bumped into Stephen Norris last week and he almost immediately launched into a tirade against Boris. I didn't realize there was so much bad blood between them, but he wasn't exactly fulsome in his praise.

The point is, and I am a huge fan of Boris, that he would be a strong candidate and it would liven the whole thing up.

I love Boris. I've employed him for the last eight years [as *GQ*'s car correspondent] and even though he's probably cost the company over £5000 in parking tickets, I wouldn't have him any other way. Boris is a force and I think he will be great, but he can be a bit of a loose cannon – you're assuming people like him enough to cope with his eccentricities and that he'll make a connection with them.

Exactly. He makes a connection with people, he says what he thinks, he asks questions directly. No, he hasn't run some enormous organization, but he has got the right instincts and would have good people around him and would do a good job.

What's your first memory of Boris?
I knew him at school, so I remember this dishevelled, large, beefy rugby player. He's always been quite large, has Boris. He was a giant of a man at school. I think it was probably on the rugby pitch. But he was a bit older than me …

What are the pros and cons of Boris?
Well, the pros are he's an enormously likeable, charismatic, intelligent and insightful person who has a way with people and a way with issues and I think is a great talent. The cons are that all of those things together can sometimes mean you get misunderstood. The fact that he speaks freely and openly is a great thing, because we've all got too controlled by fear of saying something politically incorrect, or whatever. And Boris has no fear about that. Of course that does sometimes cause offence and trouble, but Boris is good enough and big enough to realize that sometimes you have to put your hand up and apologize.

Okay, going back to campaigning, going door to door, meeting the public. It's not like going onstage, is it, this is real life, up close and personal … You say these walkabouts usually go well but you had a fairly rough ride in Blair's constituency, in Sedgefield, recently.
Well, yes, but I never felt at risk in any way, and I haven't yet had the full onslaught of the rotten eggs and cabbages, which you do in general elections. There is always a bit of that, pushing and shoving and all that. Generally, wherever I go, things tend to be fine.

A change of Prime Minister

Gordon Brown has only been in the job two weeks and he came out with all guns blazing this week. There wasn't just an opening salvo, this was a concerted attack.

I think he is trying to throw everything at the public and at us, trying to show that he has changed, that he is different and new. And I don't think it is working. I don't think people are waking up and thinking, I live under a new government, I think it does feel like more of the same. But he is determined. He is a very meticulous planner, and he is throwing everything into every day and there are a lot of big announcements – here is my draft Queen's Speech, and my draft constitutional programme. And I think we will look back in a couple of weeks and think, what the hell were all those announcements? I've heard it all before.

But people like him …
There's no accounting for taste.

Childhood memories

Going back to earlier on, to being on the streets of Ealing, what makes you want to put yourself in a situation like that? What sort of childhood, what sort of upbringing makes a young man want to aspire to become Prime Minister? What are the salient things about your childhood, what are the things that you remember most?
I had a very happy family home, sitting around the supper table and talking about everything and being very close, having close relationships between the members of the family. It was quite rural, a lot of time spent outdoors, a lot of countryside things …

Were you happy in yourself? You've always struck me as someone who had a relatively happy childhood, and I haven't read or heard anything different.
Very happy, and I've always been a very happy and optimistic and fairly contented person. Ambitious, of course, but quite happy with life as it is.

Ambition

Did you have a plan like Michael Heseltine's, where you had to have become Prime Minister by a certain point in your life or else you would have failed?

No. I don't have five-year plans or ten-year plans and things like that. So I don't think I can point to things in my childhood that pinpoint exactly when I decided to be a politician or walk the streets and introduce myself to strangers asking them to vote for me. My development in politics has been very steady. I was first interested in issues and problems and had a rather sort of policy wonkish entry into politics. The engagement and the communication and the meeting people came later, as that is what politicians do. And as I said, you never know what people are going to ask you. It's raw, it's live, you have no idea what these people are going to say when you ask them how they vote, why did you change this time, what are the issues, or someone harangues you over single parents and married couples. But that's politics, that's debate.

A lot of people get into politics, or, indeed, journalism because they see things that are fundamentally wrong with society and they either want to change it, or comment upon it, and you are not like that.

No, I do. I mean, that is my interest in politics, and it was driven by the things that mattered to me and that bothered me, and that I thought were fundamentally wrong with the world. When I grew up in the seventies and eighties, politically I thought that we were heading in a very kind of socialistic, state-controlled direction, and that has to change. To me my entry into politics was all about freedom and the individual, the individual versus the big state. But it's not just about that. I've always had what I would call a very liberal conservative outlook – freedom of the individual but believing in a responsible society, too. The background was always the Cold War, and what was happening in socialist states affected me deeply. What had a big impact on me was travelling through Eastern Europe and Russia between school and university. It shocked me.

Was it pre- or post-Glasnost?

In 1985, just before. Just after Gorbachev took control [in March that year]. I went travelling through Russia and it was just remarkable. You had people following you everywhere and you had to have passes to go here, there and everywhere. It was such a controlled existence.

I went in January 1986, just pre-Glasnost and probably had a very similar experience, and, to me, I could imagine it probably hadn't been very different for the last forty or fifty years. Getting into the country was like a sixties movie, and the border police at the airport were hilariously scary. We'd taken all this acutely Western stuff to trade – CDs, Levi's, dozens of copies of *The Face* and *i-D*, stuff like that. I remember being irritated that all these college kids from Fresno in California were being asked to trade outside the subway, and myself and my girlfriend – who were obviously dressed as trendy London urbanites – were being ignored. Of course, we were eventually asked to trade and even that became something out of a Cold War thriller, walking into this completely silent block of flats and being told to keep our voices down. When we got into this guy's flat, his two children were sitting on their sofa reading books, and they just looked round at us, nodded hello and then carried on reading. I remember being in the Gum department store in Moscow and joined the queue, and after about forty minutes I realized that this was a queue to look at something, not to buy something. Everything happened on the black market, which is why everyone was so paranoid. One of my most vivid memories is of no one talking on the underground, not one word out of place. We were followed from dawn till dusk, and people leaped behind buildings when you turned around to look at them following you. When we travelled from Moscow to Leningrad by train we were told we could only go at night, basically so that we didn't see anything. Of course, when we got to Leningrad and went to this guy's room in the Moscow Hotel to trade, it was like an Aladdin's cave of consumer durables – CD players, ghetto blasters, Levi's – the right Levi's – the lot ...

That was exactly the same experience I had, and it seems odd now because it was so long ago and was an old argument. But that split between East and West was one of the things that definitely got me interested in politics and in particular Conservative politics; that whole issue of the individual versus the state, that whole thing, that was what fired me up.

Thatcherism

But then politics was never more polarized, and on the one hand the old guard were dying, and on the other you had a bunch of free-market buccaneers coming over the hill with mobile phones and double-breasted suits. Thatcher spent most of the first five or six years in power dismantling the state, so what wound you up about Britain? It was not as though the socialists were taking over ...

What wound me up was that that was still a big battle, not that the Labour Party wanted to turn us into an East European state, but there were still big questions. Are we going to have a progressive amount of freedom and responsibility and independence and choice, or are we going to have a state knows best, know your place, rigid, class system? I thought that in all the big arguments Thatcher and Major were on the right side, and Labour was on the wrong side. And Thatcher won the argument.

Would you say that Thatcher was a role model for you? A hero?

I don't have any individual heroes, or role models, but obviously she was a big influence, yes. If you grew up under Thatcher, you either thought she was doing the wrong thing or she was doing the right thing and I thought she was doing the right thing. What's interesting is that the people who thought she was doing the wrong thing came to terms with what she had done and then successfully won three elections in a row. An amazing turnaround.

How did you feel about Thatcher when you met her?

I've met her lots of times, but some of the strongest impressions I have of her are the earliest ones when she was Prime Minister and I was a young researcher. The thing that strikes you most is the conviction. She is just so strong and that hasn't changed with the years. I remember being at her seventy-seventh birthday where she had a lunch down in my constituency with a neighbour, and Sam and I were very lucky to be invited. There were about ten of us, and Denis was still alive at the time. She was firing on all cylinders: any subject you discussed, whether it was the economy or Europe or civil liberties, everything from Margaret came out of a very clear sense of conviction. She knew her answer to the question before you'd even finished asking it.

The unions

You obviously approved of many of Thatcher's policies, but how did you feel about the print unions. Long after Wapping I remember working at the *Observer* in the early nineties and being told I couldn't move a filing cabinet across the office without incurring the wrath of the unions. I had to get two men from 'infrastructure' to move it for me. It would have taken me thirty seconds and took them two weeks …

I thought it was bizarre, these people at university who refused to take *The Times* because of the Wapping dispute. I remember feeling that this problem had to be confronted and defeated. It was just ridiculous that unions could hold up progress in an industry like newspapers. It was like the miners' strike. The miners' strike was tragic, but it would have been a disaster if the NUM had won because you cannot have an entire country held to ransom over producing something that was becoming increasingly uneconomic, and in the end the right of management to manage and business to invest and people to go about their lives just has to win through. I was never in any doubt about the print unions; it was always very clear-cut to me.

I don't think the miners' strike can ever be viewed as anything but a disaster because it devastated entire communities, but then there was only ever going to be one resolution. I just thought the print unions were greedy.

I saw a little bit of this in television and film, which is still heavily unionized, and it's interesting to the extent that some industries still are. I went and opened the new *Daily Mail* printing presses the other day, just outside Didcot, where we are now – a surprisingly small number of people working in this enormous building producing the *Daily Mail* for virtually the entire South East. It was just staggering.

The country's industries obviously needed to modernize, but at the time didn't you feel that Thatcher was taking a hammer to the pride of the working class?

I don't think so, because I think there were an awful lot of working-class people, an awful lot of trade unionists who realized things had to change. In the 1980s a third of trade unionists voted Conservative. Anyway, it wasn't the trade unionists she was fighting, it was the trade union bosses who were behaving in an undemocratic and unreasonable way. And sometimes that got a bit lost, and the Conservative Party needs to build back its link with the unions. And with individual trade unionists above all.

Would you address their conference?

I haven't been asked. If they asked me I'd think about it. I think it's important that we are plugged into the campaigns they're running and the things they're talking about and the issues they're discussing, in a reasonable way.

Sibling rivalry

Was there anything about your childhood that you had to overcome?

Nothing really. Although I wouldn't say that I had this completely gilded youth where I never had any problems or challenges. I suppose the biggest challenge for me was, as a younger brother, having the feeling that you're living in your brother's shadow. Are you a younger brother?

No, older, by five years.
Have you ever asked him about this?

We've discussed it, yes.
He is three years older than me, so everything I did I felt he had already done, and you feel like you're set on a track and living in his shadow. They go to a school, you start going to school, they start playing football, you start playing football, they kiss girls, you start kissing girls – and you think that you are doing everything the same, only three years later, and I think that was something I used to worry about quite a lot, that I was never going to break out of my brother's shadow.

Often when that happens the younger sibling rebels, becomes something of a renegade, but that didn't happen to you. Far from it, in fact ...
Well, a bit actually. Going to Oxford made me feel like I had achieved something that he hadn't done, as he went to Bristol. As for rebellion, I mean, wanting to break the rules and misbehave and do things I shouldn't have done was partly to forge your own path, but I don't want to get into the things I did and didn't do. I wasn't a complete rebel, but I used to like to do things that I wanted to do. But that doesn't sound like a huge bunch of things to get over in your youth.

Were you aware of politics?
Well, although I'm sure my parents voted Conservative, it wasn't an especially political household. I have a very bad memory; I think because I had a very happy childhood, I don't have a huge barrage of memories.

That could come in handy! What is your very first memory?
My parents bought this house, a really lovely house called the Old Rectory in about 1969, when I was about three, and I vaguely remember living in the house next door whilst the house was being repaired. I have

a very vague memory of that, but that is the earliest thing I remember. My first moments of being aware of politics were the Jeremy Thorpe trial. What was yours? We're around the same age. Forty-seven? So you would remember the three-day week?

The seventies

I remember decimalization, joining the Common Market, the referendum, but, yes, I remember the three-day week, oh boy do I. The power cuts, the candlelit dinners, the feeling that you were somehow living in a state of siege. This was the first time I can remember when I felt that the government weren't really doing what they were meant to be doing. Things sort of fell apart. Although I wasn't really aware of what was going on – apart from my father stomping around the house muttering 'Bloody Ted Heath' under his breath and slamming doors and that sort of thing, I wasn't really sure why it was all happening. In an odd sort of way it was actually rather bewildering, and I suppose this was also the time when, without television, and without the usual interaction with friends and family, I began retreating upstairs to my bedroom to listen to the radio. In a way you could say that Ted Heath was responsible for kick-starting my interest in David Bowie and Roxy Music.

My first memory of politics was the Thorpe trial, and I suppose I would have been about eleven, and I remember the 1979 election, when I would have been about thirteen, and I remember some of the party political broadcasts, the guy running around the track with weights around his neck. I have vague memories of those and growing political awareness from then on. We did talk about politics at home, but it wasn't a political household as I don't think my parents were members of any political party. But it was more about current affairs than politics, and we would talk about what was on the news. My father always used to say after dinner, go and warm up the television. In the late seventies and early eighties, it did take about thirty seconds to come on and he liked to watch *News at Ten*. I used to go and warm up the television, so that really does make me sound old. So there were never specific discussions about Heath or Callaghan or Wilson, just general discussions about what was going on in the world.

The daily paper

What paper did you get?
My dad used to get *The Times* and the *Express* and then he switched from the *Express* to the *Mail.*

Everyone did this, every middle-class family from Kent to Cheshire and back again. We were living by the coast in Deal at the time, and I distinctly remember that one day the *Daily Express* had suddenly been replaced by the *Daily Mail*, and it was the day it went tabloid. It was May 1971, and I was eleven. I can remember it like it was yesterday. It was like a change in government, changing schools or moving house. One day we lived in a *Daily Express* world, the next we were living in the *Daily Mail*. I can even remember where I was sitting when I saw my first copy; I can even remember the exact configuration of the living room. Odd, really. In our house it stayed that way for as long as I can remember. I can recall it as clearly as my mother buying the first issue of British *Cosmopolitan*, the one with Burt Reynolds as a centrefold.
My dad bought newspapers for racing so sometimes he would switch to the *Guardian* as they had brilliant racing. Lots of people still buy that newspaper for the sport – that's the way it is.

Parental guidance

Your mother was a magistrate; how aware were you of what she did for a living?
Quite aware because she was involved with some of the Greenham Common cases, and the Newbury bypass, and Swampy and all of that – so I was very aware of her job. I was passionately pro-NATO and deterrence and was very Conservative on that – it was one of the big things I

thought that Thatcher was right about. I was really passionate about it as a lot of people were CND. What did I think about her job? I mean, I knew a bit about it as she was always talking about it, particularly her work with juveniles.

How were your parents an influence on you?
I had a very straightforward, uncomplicated upbringing, four kids, all got on well, Mum and Dad, Mum around most of the time, Dad commuting, getting back at night, normally quite tired and having supper together. I went to boarding school aged seven, which now people think of as barbaric and terrible, but anyway, when you have an older brother it doesn't feel like that as he has already been and you are quite keen to get on with it.

Did you miss your parents at boarding school?
Yes, I did miss my parents, and I remember feeling quite homesick at the start, but it wasn't that bad.

The *Express* and *The Times* and the other papers your father had, did you ever read them? What age would you say you started reading newspapers?
I would say I started reading the newspapers at about twelve. I would say the first time I got really obsessed was the Falklands War. I really remember switching on the radio a lot at school, wanting to know what had happened, and I got very caught up in that whole thing.

The Falklands

So how did you feel about the war? You were sixteen at the time. I was twenty-two and everyone around me was radicalized, and it was assumed that I was radicalized, too. Like a lot of the country I was appalled by how callous she was being, especially over the miners, but the Falklands were different. While I wasn't exactly gung-ho, the reaction to the war in the UK among my friends made me start to become

suspicious of the left, or at least those members of the left who seemed to jump on any bandwagon just because it happened to be going by.

I thought what we were doing was absolutely right. It was only at the twenty-fifth anniversary when they played a lot of the old newsreels that it started to bring back memories from that time. The footage did look like a hell of a long time ago.

The coverage today is so very different …
I was watching something on Channel 4 last night on Iraq and it looked almost like a snuff movie, just an incredibly vivid picture of what is happening right now – footage of American solders holding up cars, and gunfights, and because it was filmed almost in real time you felt as though you were there. It is so extraordinary that this thing is now being beamed directly into our homes. I had to switch off, as [his daughter] Nancy was watching it and there was too much blood and guts and gore.

That Falklands footage is incredible, because it feels like it is another age. You're right about the quality of TV news reporting these days, as everything feels far more real. As it should. I think it's far more shocking because of the extraordinary quality. Soon we'll be watching suicide bombers and artillery attacks in HD and the whole thing will be rather sick and surreal. The quality of contemporary news footage has affected Hollywood in a major way, because without that kind of vérité quality it just doesn't look real. Have you seen the film *Children of Men* with Clive Owen? It's set twenty-odd years in the future, in a world where women are no longer able to conceive. It's an extraordinary film for many reasons – not least the trick of making something that's science fiction but only just work in a convincing way – but all the battle sequences are filmed with hand-held cameras, making it seem incredibly real. So much so that in one sequence the lens of the camera is covered in mud, but it doesn't matter, even though you're not meant to be looking through the camera. But back to the time of the Falklands, do you remember any particular columnists?

Not really, although I started reading a lot more when I began studying politics for A level. I remember Ronald Butt, who wrote the sketch in *The Times* before Matthew Parris. I thought I needed to know what was going on in the House of Commons, so that is probably my first memory. I can't remember reading old Paul Johnson columns if that's what you mean. Which is just as well, actually.

Party politics

The divisions between the parties were far more obvious back then, and differences were codified by class and upbringing and education as much as anything. Back then it was a lot easier to distinguish a Labour MP from a Tory MP. You were never going to be a Labour MP obviously, but wasn't there a hint of a Heseltine-type career arc?
Definitely not, and even at university I didn't know what I was going to do next.

Come on, I don't believe you! You must have done …
I did the usual milk round – you have to go and do interviews with banks and management consultants because everyone else is doing it. And thank God I didn't do that. Between school and university I worked for an MP, my godfather, Tim Rathbone, who was based in Lewes, in East Sussex, a very nice guy but a bit of a wet. I did some work for him on drugs policy and nursery education and really enjoyed it, and always thought that maybe I should think about doing something like that again. But I hadn't made up my mind at all until right at the end of my last year and then I saw an advertisement in a careers bulletin for a job in the Conservative Research Department, and thought, I can give that a go, and that was the job I got. So I didn't have a career plan; certainly when I went to Central Office I wasn't thinking I definitely want to be an MP. I just thought, I'll give this a go and see what happens, although the more I was there, the more I thought I wanted to get out of the back room and into the front room and do this myself. I am sure I probably said once or twice at university that I would like to be in poli-

tics, because I was interested in politics, but I definitely hadn't made up my mind.

I remember once seeing David Bailey on *The South Bank Show* back in the early eighties, and he said something that's stayed with me ever since. He said that just because someone is dedicated and passionate about their work, and just because they're well suited to it, doesn't mean they're necessarily any good. Sounds obvious now, but it impressed me as an adolescent. But Gordon Brown has wanted to be PM since he was fifteen, and you appear to have sort of discovered the idea by chance. Surely you can't deny he's a committed and talented politician …
But that has always worried me. I think people who have wanted to be PM since they were fifteen should be automatically disqualified. It's ridiculous, and is not a good qualification for the job. Of course you want someone who is passionate, who has drive and ambition, and gets things done, but also you want someone with balance, judgement and consideration and scepticism.

You don't often come across as particularly sceptical.
I think in life it pays to be sceptical about everything. I don't like grand plans and grand visions. I think, in the reassessment of Blair in years to come about his foreign policy, there will be a worry that there was this unbridled liberal internationalism, and a desire not to question his grand plans and vision; there is already that worry and there will be a lot more to come. I was talking to a senior official, who really said some very chilling things, that Blair lived in a fantasyland and didn't want to listen to anything, and that he didn't accept what was going on in Iraq, and had a refusal to engage in reality. I think scepticism and practicality may not be romantic qualities, but they are very important qualities and you do need that in leaders.

And you have these qualities, do you?
Yes, of course I do. I'm a Conservative.

Moving into politics

When you finally alighted on a career in politics, at what point did it occur to you that you might want to go for the big job? How old were you when that notion arrived?

That's a very good question, and I'll have to examine my memory and try to get it right. Really quite late on, actually. You're always asked when you become an MP, do you want to become PM, and I always said no in a pretty genuine sense, in that I just thought that being a Member of Parliament was something I wanted to do and, the more I saw of Parliament I thought, this is something worthwhile and something I want to do; anything after that would be more interesting and more worthwhile. One of those senior jobs would be really fascinating and fulfilling and you could see and change things, but I must say at that stage I did see the PM's office as a place apart. Even after the 2005 election, my instinct was 'I'm not going to get involved and this is not for me'. But then I changed my mind.

John Major

Okay, so you're working in John Major's office, and you have a fair bit of contact with him, in quite close proximity … at what point did this world seem like a world that you could be part of in a more meaningful way? You already had the brain and the surface smarts, but when did the ambition kick in?

I did see Major's office quite often, and was in there about twice a week between 1990 and 1992 with Prime Minister's Questions. But at that stage of my life I just didn't think that this was something that would be for me. I certainly felt that politics was for me, and that I wanted to be an MP, but I really didn't imagine that I would ever be in the running for becoming leader of the party and Prime Minister. I really didn't. I thought I could have a successful career, and could contribute something. But the interesting thing about my decision to stand for the leadership is that I remember very clearly making it on the basis that it was the right decision at the time. And there hasn't been a moment in the last eighteen months when I have thought, 'Oh my God, what have I done, is this a mistake?', or even a night when I have thought, 'Can I really manage all these things?' I did at first think there are an awful lot of things I'm going to have to manage and make sure I am up to doing, and there were all sorts of questions like, 'How are you going to handle sending troops into places like Afghanistan?' 'How are you going to talk to mothers who have lost children?' But what I found is, each time a difficult hurdle has appeared, I've always felt, 'Yes, I can do this.' And I have done it, always knowing I can do better next time.

What did you learn from John Major?
That maybe you didn't have to be a certain type of person to do this job. That you didn't have to come from a particular background to do well in the Conservative Party.

Self-confidence

I find your self-confidence fascinating, but then I suppose a sense of belief is the second most important quality to have as a politician, after some sort of moral compass, that is. Peter Mandelson used to write a political column for *GQ*, and although he did it for some time, after a while it was subject to the law of diminishing returns. He started off well enough by writing a column at the end of 2001 about how Gerry Adams might see a united Ireland in his lifetime. The story made the front of the *Telegraph*, there were questions about it during PMQs and it generally caused a bit of a fuss. But after about six months or so the columns were beginning to tail off, so I took him to lunch to see what we could do. We were sitting in this restaurant, as his two security guards looked on from a nearby table, and I started suggesting various topics that he could pick up for his column. I said that he should write more about his relationship with the press, as that was one of the topics that he was rarely circumspect about. He tended not to pull his punches. 'You should really think about this,

Peter, as you're always good at kicking up dust, and it's good to get your own back every now and again,' I said. 'I mean, you're always being hounded by the press, in fact you've been vilified. Just imagine what it would be like if you were a celebrity instead of a politician.' At which he stopped eating, looked at me plaintively and grabbed my arm and said, 'But I *am* a celebrity.' Fifteen-love. That taught me a lesson ... Do you consider yourself to be a celebrity?

The attention has certainly surprised me. I don't think that the Leader of the Opposition is a celebrity, and I would have thought that even though you have a certain profile it is just a job; I didn't realize quite how much you get approached by complete strangers wherever you are. I don't mind as I am quite a social person, and I don't mind people chatting. I just didn't realize how much publicity you get. But again, all the things that happened to me in the last eighteen months have strengthened my belief that I have got what it takes to do it, rather than making me think that I can't manage that bit. I feel very comfortable about it all eighteen months in.

It fascinates me that you've said twice now, that in the time you have been leader, you haven't had a moment's doubt, that you haven't had a dark night of the soul and woken up in a sweat.

I have had moments where I thought, I should have done that and not this, and that didn't go well. But I haven't had a moment of thinking this was a mistake and I shouldn't be doing this, this bit of the job is so unpleasant I can't bear it, I can't stand the press intrusion etc. I'm really quite even-minded and stable about the whole thing.

Your self-confidence is blinding, but that's Eton for you ...

I think it does give you a self-confidence, a strong sense of independence. From the age of thirteen you have your own room and it does have a university feel to it. And because you don't have to be excellent at sport or academically in order to be a success, it is big enough for you to find your own mixture of things that make you content and happy.

How confident were you at university? What I remember from those days is the endless midnight conversations about just about everything – big ideas, small ideas, pop music, ambition, ill-informed conversations about politics, the lot ... Was this the same for you?

The best bit of university was sitting around drinking and chatting. In Brasenose we had a really good mix of people from different backgrounds who liked sitting at the bar, going to each other's rooms, drinking and chatting, playing music and having a laugh. It wasn't heavy, it could get heavy, but it was also a lot of jokes ... in fact my happiest memory of university was drinking and chatting.

If you weren't driven by politics, what were the things that obsessed you at the time?

Mainly, girlfriends! I worked quite hard and I wanted to get a good degree, and I really enjoyed what I was doing at university. I loved my course, and I used to work three very hard days a week, and the other four were very free. So there were parties and drinking and I had a good time. My friends at Edinburgh, Bristol and Newcastle worked about three days a year, so I thought I was working incredibly hard. I do often feel very nostalgic when I go back, which I do from time to time, as my constituency is very near. When I walk round Radcliffe Square, I'm reminded that it's a rather lovely existence, because, you know, you have three years to learn but also to broaden yourself.

There is a very particular sort of self-righteous Conservative, the kind we see everywhere, who, because they didn't have a good time when they were young, want to make sure no one else does. You know: why should anyone else have a good time if I didn't?

Conversely there is a situation with people who had a very good time when they were young, pull up the drawbridge as they get older. It's like that old joke: What's the definition of a conservative? It's a libertarian with children. And there is some truth in that – that is one of the things that can change you in terms of your political view, and you can switch, particularly if you started out being very interested in the economic side of politics, you can become very interested in the social. I suppose I was very much in danger of becoming a sort of typical Conservative. I went to Eton, to Oxford, to the Conservative Research Department, the Treasury, everything apart from being in the Guards.

George Osborne

What have you learned about the tensions between Number Ten and Number Eleven?
I've learned they are endemic. But then they always were. I worked for Norman Lamont when relations between him and John Major weren't good. The fact is, the relationship between the First Lord of the Treasury and the Chancellor is an incredibly important one because nothing can happen in government without the finance director agreeing to it. And so that relationship has to be based on trust and mutual respect and you've both got to want to do the same sorts of things, and you've got to talk them through and plan and make it work. Otherwise you end up like Blair and Brown, hating each other. The good thing with George [Osborne] is the fact that we're friends, which obviously helps, but we just have a very clear, shared analysis of what's wrong with the country and what the Conservative Party ought to be doing, and what a Conservative government would do.

What are the salient differences between you?
Of course there are differences, but the hare/tortoise thing is rubbish.*
It's just not true. If you look at the two of us, I think I probably have a more rural outlook on life, having been brought up in the country, and George is more metropolitan. But the differences are differences of emphasis. We have a genuinely shared view of what was wrong with the

---

* *In the spring of 2008, the Conservative activists' website, Conservativehome, argued that the party leadership ought to be more radical and bold on things like tax cuts and suggested there was an intense debate going on between the 'hares', led by George Osborne and Andy Coulson, who allegedly wanted to go faster, and the 'tortoises', led by Cameron and Steve Hilton, who advocated a more steady approach.*

Conservative Party and what is wrong with the country and what we'd like to do to put it right.

What did you and George Osborne say to each other when you both decided which of you would run for the Tory leadership? What was the deal?

There was no deal, there was no pact. We talked a lot about it, all the time. We used to bicycle back home from the House of Commons and we talked about it all the time, throughout the 2001 and 2005 parliament. Our analysis of what was wrong with the party was something we talked about every night as we cycled home, and we learned from each other. He was very sharp on some things and I hope I was sharper on others. It was great to have that sort of relationship. Then when it came to the leadership we decided independently, separately. I decided I was going to run and George decided he wasn't going to. And then we met and spoke about it.

Why didn't he want it? You must know …

You'd have to ask him, but what he said to me was, he'd been given the job of Shadow Chancellor by Michael Howard and he was delighted with that, as it was a huge job to do up against Gordon Brown, and I think he just felt that this time he wanted to focus on that. He's a bit younger than me, and I think he thought this was not the right time, and that he should wait. He said to me that if I was going to go for it then he'd run my leadership campaign, which he did. And it was lovely to know that my friend and colleague was supportive.

But was there an agreement? Are you going to step down after a certain time? Or, rather, lie about when you're going to step down and be dragged kicking and screaming from Downing Street?! There was no hint of a deal?

There was no hint. I'm sure that whole thing was in his mind because the Blair/Brown Granita thing has become such a famous part of the political folklore, but there was no deal between us, no, there was no deal.

Is he your successor?
I don't pick successors.

You know what I mean. Is he [someone] who you would choose to lead the party after you've stepped down?
I think he is extremely talented and I think he would do the job extremely well. And I think he's been incredibly impressive over the last two years. A lot of people said he couldn't hack it, and that going up against Gordon Brown at the age of thirty-three was too tall an order, but he's been brilliant. People wondered if he'd be convincing to the City, to business, will he take his colleagues with him. He has answered all those questions with a very convincing yes. So I think he would do the job extremely well, but I don't want to blight his prospects by appointing him now!

Steve Hilton

Tell me about your first meeting with Steve.
When I was working for the Conservative Research Department back in the 1980s he came to do a holiday job with us from university. He was brilliant, and had this natural flair and ability for politics and was great fun and we got on very well. Then I was very keen to hire him when he came out of university, which we did, and then we worked together quite closely during the 1992 election. He was point man at Saatchi's during that period; he was embedded with them, while I was doing the early morning briefing for John Major before the press conferences and running the political section. He's a very good friend and we work very, very closely together.

Meeting Samantha

And then you met Samantha. Who grounded you.
I was lucky in that Samantha – as much as the papers keep writing that she comes from a very blue-blooded background – is actually very

unconventional and is hard to put in a box. She went to a day school, was a Goth at fourteen, had quite a wild childhood, is unconventional and challenging and that is very good as it stopped me from being too straight down the line. She is not very interested in politics, but she has very good judgement.

Alastair Campbell

What did you think of Alastair Campbell's diaries?*
Someone gave me a copy, and I dipped in just to have a look, and you can tell if you are going to like it, and I thought I am going to hate this. It's frenetic but not very interesting. Alan Clark's diaries are very funny and rather under-read and very insightful. Campbell's are not. Reading them is like gulping a triple espresso, it's all so frenetic and I didn't think I would enjoy it. But someone in my office said you should read it as they went through so many of the same issues that we did.

They are totally fascinating, rather brilliant, even though everyone and their mother has queued up to take a kick at him. They are just written in a very fast-paced tabloid manner. You don't warm to him, not at all, but they are obviously fascinating. One interesting thing is the sudden way he manages to switch from being a journalist to a public relations officer instantly. I was speaking to Andy Coulson about this the other day and he said it's remarkable how easy it is to switch from one to the other, from Church to state.
I knew Campbell when he was at the *Mirror*; he was a political hack. In the press conferences during the 1992 general election it was like having a member of the Labour Party come and try and disrupt your conference, and afterwards he would pin you against the wall and ask you all the hostile questions. He was a partisan, he was not a political journalist. So he was much better in the partisan job than he was as a journalist, but

---

* *Alastair Campbell and Richard Stott, eds,* The Blair Years: Extracts from The Alastair Campbell Diaries *(Hutchinson, 2007).*

I think he pushed everything too far, the bullying, the hectoring, and the David Kelly episode was just tragic.

It was shameful. A man died. For nothing. Not even for national security. It was just shameful.
Andy Coulson is tough, but he is not an Alastair Campbell and I would not hire an Alastair Campbell. Campbell never got the balance right between policy-making and communication. I think he was trying too hard to be a politician. Also I think being an editor is different from being a journalist because you are managing an operation, and managing a newsroom is quite like managing a political party – you have people on different desks with different issues … I think that was why I was so keen to hire him [Coulson]. What he did in terms of a management role, as far as firing people up, getting people going and leading a team, is quite similar to what he needed to do for us.

Why was Andy Coulson the man for the job?
It just sort of emerged. I met him and liked him when he was doing his job, and then obviously he had some difficulties. I think I may have had a cup of tea with him about things and then we started thinking that maybe he could do something for us. We have always wanted someone on a very senior level in that sort of communications role. I just think he is very confident, clear-headed, gets straight to the point, and I think he will be good because he will be very tough with us; that was good, that was bad, that was a problem, you will have to resolve it – we won't be able to run away from things. In politics you have always got the positive and the negative and you have to address the negative. We needed to get smarter and cleverer and I think we have a better media operation than we used to and getting our message across and all that … The funny thing about people like you and me, although quite young, we have been knocking around in politics for quite some time. So you do need ideas and fresh thinking.

Media diet

The current US election is the first to be fought online. Have you seen the citizen ads? There are a lot of them, and they are getting millions and millions of hits, far more hits than the ones that are actually put out by the candidates. The Obama Girl clip did wonders for Barack Obama's campaign. This could be remembered as the YouTube election.

I have seen the 1984 Hillary Clinton one. I love the 'Changes' video with me and Blair using the same words, which is hysterically funny. Really well put together. I don't know who did it, but someone sitting in their back room. This is going to be a big thing. We are doing WebCameron; you could see today I had a microphone on and had someone filming me, which will all go online. Some of our videos are very good, some are very bad, I write a blog a few times a week, but we could do more.

Also considering how difficult it is to reach young people, who don't watch the news and who don't buy newspapers, could the Internet play a part in the next election here?

It will be a huge influence. Millions of people look at the BBC website every day. I still think the big message in the television and the newspapers is very important but they may start reporting what is happening on the Internet and that may influence mainstream news.

In your free time, what little there is of it, what do you do online? And how long do you tend to spend looking at the newspapers in the morning?

I tend now to read the newspapers online and have a quick flick at the *Guardian* and *The Times* and the *Telegraph*. These papers on the floor here, I've literally spent five minutes looking at them. I don't always do it, it depends on when the children are getting up and going to school. If I don't leave the house before 8.30 a.m., I will have gone to school and helped look after the kids and then quickly flicked on the computer and seen what they [the papers] were up to. I wouldn't say I experiment online; I mean I don't have a Second Life or whatever. Sarkozy did apparently. I don't have a MySpace profile either. I use iTunes, but not that much recently. I'm good on weather, too. Samantha is obsessed that when we go on holiday it will be too cold; we were going to somewhere in the Gulf and she was convinced it wasn't going to be hot enough, and while I don't quite hack into the NASA space station I spent hours trying to prove that it was going to be 26 degrees. There is such a huge generational gap between us and my sister-in-law, Alice, who works in my office. They all do MySpace and their instinct is to search online for everything; so if you ask what is on the telly, they will look it up whereas I would look at the newspaper.

Quite a few people have said that the job of being PM won't send Brown mad: it will be everything else, it will be all the meet and greets and the endless paperwork that he is not interested in; the intellectual part of the job and the cognitive part he will rise to, but the rest will swamp him.

I think that all PMs feel like that, as there are so many things you have to do that are not part of running the country. As Leader of the Opposition you can try really hard to focus on what matters in terms of sorting out your party problems, making sense of the big issues and getting elected, but there is a lot of other stuff to do, too. Someone said that Jimmy Carter even got involved with the rota for the tennis courts at the White House. I'm determined to avoid that kind of micro management. Part of it is your attitude. I have a really good private office and you have to be prepared to trust people.

Brown is untested as PM, and I wonder if things will look so rosy in a year's time.

We shall see …

THREE

'Why am I going to Rwanda? Because I think it's a good idea'

**Robert Harris, Gordon Brown's coronation,
Michael Green, a PR disaster, William Hague,
cannabis, casinos, IDS**

The twentieth of July 2007, London N1. I was sitting on a train bound for Nottingham with a battle-weary David Cameron, who was coming to terms with two huge by-election defeats the previous night – at Ealing Southall and also at Sedgefield, where the seat had been vacated following Tony Blair's decision to stand down as an MP. In Ealing, the Tories had limped in in third place, increasing their share of the vote to just 14.6 per cent, from 14.4 per cent in the 2005 general election. Gordon Brown had passed his first major test since becoming Prime Minister. And Cameron was exhausted.

The fallout from Ealing Southall was already under way. Francis Maude – the recently ousted chairman of the Conservative Party – and the Conservative campaign manager Grant Shapps were blamed for leaving Cameron dangerously exposed after allowing his name to be so closely associated with the campaign. This whole unedifying episode was perhaps best summed up by the *Spectator*'s spoof Tory insider, Tamzin Lightwater, months later in her end-of-year review: 'Terrific excitement in Ealing where we are on course to win an historic by-election victory. Unfortunately our campaign chief, Little Mr Shapps, gets carried away.

Plans for a herd of elephants to parade down Southall Broadway carrying our candidate Tony Lit have to be cancelled amid animal welfare concerns, and we never regain momentum. Mr Lit doesn't help himself by joining the Labour Party.'

In Sedgefield, Labour's majority had been halved – turnout was low compared to the 2005 general election. But in another considerable setback for Cameron, the Conservatives had slipped back into third place behind the Liberal Democrats, whose candidate, Greg Stone, polled 5572 votes, compared to the modest 4082 recorded by Tory Graham Robb.

The Tories were never going to take Sedgefield – but perhaps it was foolish of Cameron to imagine that he could move from third place in Ealing Southall to take the seat. The two by-election results made for a serious wake-up call, just in case he hadn't heard one coming. 'Cameron's judgement is now the issue,' said the Lib Dems' election guru, Lord Rennard. 'His honeymoon is definitely over tonight.'

Certainly, since winning the leadership Cameron had never been in a more fragile position. Having had an eighteen-month free ride, with these two results – as well as Brown's coronation – the world had suddenly turned upside down. Why hadn't he managed to unite his party? And, crucially, where were his policies? Where were the meat and potatoes we had been promised, the ones we had always hoped had been there, sitting on the service trolley waiting for the starters to be gobbled up?

I was feeling let down, too. Cameron was my man, his ascendancy coinciding with my own political shift. He was the man who was going to carry the great blue flame into a bright new tomorrow. But why was he abandoning grammar schools? Why was he sending out confused messages? Why was he buggering things up so soon after convincing a healthy number of undecideds that he was the man to tackle our lawless streets, curb the runaway expansion of the public sector and sort out unpoliced immigration?

George Osborne once claimed that Blair was on the right track, but stranded in the wrong party, although no one would ever accuse Gordon Brown of that. One of his first pledges since becoming Prime Minister was a promise to reform city academies, which were to become subject to greater central control by local education authorities. It looked like the public sector reforms rolled out by Blair were, more than likely, going to be – stealthily – rolled back by Brown. Maybe he really was the old-fashioned socialist we all secretly thought he was. More than ever, I felt, a more than roadworthy Conservative leader was needed to take him on.

But, following Ealing Southall and Sedgefield, I felt I was seeing the Cameron Construct crumble before me. I was reminded of how optimistic DC's admirers had felt a year earlier. And as we took our seats on the train to Nottingham, I had another reason to feel doubtful about the Cameron project. Why, a couple of days hence, was he taking a whole bunch of his team to Rwanda – especially as most of his own country seemed to be six feet underwater, including parts of his own constituency?

Throughout June and July, widespread flooding had affected nearly a million people, along with tens of thousands of homes and thousands of businesses. Eleven people had died, while the estimated damages ran into several billion pounds. Dozens of counties in England, Scotland, Wales and Northern Ireland had been struck. Flood waters entered Tewkesbury Abbey for the first time in 247 years. It was a truly wet and miserable summer for a lot of people. Yet just as the floods in his constituency were reaching record levels, the Tory leader was about to go off showboating in Africa, looking as if he just didn't care.

Organized back when God was a boy, the African trip was designed to highlight the party's plans to combat world poverty as well as to support Conservative volunteers who had been helping with a range of development projects. But did he have to do it now, I asked him as we rattled towards Nottingham? 'It is about learning the problems of that country, making sure we get our policy right,' he replied. 'And I think that's a damn good thing for an opposition to do.'

The Rwanda trip played badly in the press. Former Home Office minister Ann Widdecombe, who could always be relied upon to be as unhelpful as possible, was even quoted as saying that she wasn't sure how many voters there were who actually knew where Rwanda was. But as almost every newspaper chose to ignore, Cameron actually visited the flooded areas in his constituency before he flew. But that wasn't the story. The narrative in the papers was 'Cameron flies to Africa as Brown comforts flood victims', which, while not exactly true, was true enough for most of the nationals. Cameron was unrepentant, and brushed aside the press criticism of his trip, and the supposed dissent against his leadership as a 'non-story'.

This press frenzy was then compounded by the one true litmus test of political popularity, the poll. A couple of days after our Nottingham trip, a YouGov survey for the *Sunday Times* put Labour on 40 per cent – up five points on a similar poll a month previously – the Tories 33 per cent (down four) and Liberal Democrats 15 per cent (up one). An Ipsos MORI poll for the *Observer* had Labour on 41 per cent, the Tories on 35 and the Lib Dems on 15.

As we travelled to Nottingham that day, we discussed the political rollercoaster, and his own particular place on it – which at the time felt as though it were about to descend with some force. But although the 'Brown bounce' (copyright all newspapers) had taken everyone by storm (not least the rubberized PM himself), I referred people to the opening chapter of Robert Harris's *Imperium*, where Apollonius Molon is instructing our hero, Marcus Tullius Cicero, in the art of public speaking. '"What about the content of what I say?" Cicero asked. "Surely I will compel attention chiefly by the force of my arguments?" Molon shrugged. "Content does not concern me. Remember Demosthenes: 'Only three things count in oratory. Delivery, delivery, and again: delivery.'"'

Brown was certainly delivering a lot of oratory, but could he actually follow through?

The Ealing by-election

The last time we saw each other was last Friday when you were campaigning in Ealing, and not doing too well. It's been a fairly terrible week for you.
A week is a long time in politics.

For the Conservatives this has been one of the longest of all time. You could say it's been fairly eventful.

I had the Ealing walkabout and then I went off to my constituency, and did all manner of things. I did a really nice prize-giving event, Scouts, Brownies and Cubs, all the usual things. I had a very good weekend. I scored fifty-eight in the cricket match. That was where I thought it could probably go wrong. And, boy, it certainly went wrong ...

When did you first hear about your candidate Tony Lit making a donation to Labour? Before you saw it in the papers?

Well, the team knew about him attending the dinner. He didn't make a donation himself, but Sunrise Radio did, which takes tables at lots of dinners like this, and took a table at the England/Pakistan fundraiser the week before. I don't think it's a particularly big deal, someone who went to a Labour dinner, who is a lifelong Conservative voter. But the press obviously did.

Of course they did. It wasn't a great PR move.

Well, I don't think it was as bad as all that, to be honest with you, I just don't.

It was obviously bound up with the Brown bounce and both stories were sold very hard, and I think you were very unlucky. The media narrative has been fairly predictable, and it almost doesn't matter what Brown does at the moment because he is being given a free ride by all and sundry. But that will change; it always does.

Yes, they made a big deal of those stories, that is definitely true.

Can we talk about last night? You must have been devastated, as you didn't so much lose, you were pummelled. It was a pretty awful defeat. I must admit your resilience is impressive, although you must feel terrible right now. At times like this, do you feel like giving up, do you feel as though things could be slipping away from you? You've been kicked all over the papers today.

We put a lot of effort into the campaign, particularly into the Ealing side. It was interesting – we had five Labour councillors defect to us and so we left the campaign with five more councillors than we started with. There is a very large ethnic minority there, and I do think there is a change taking place where we have far better links and relationships with those communities. But it wasn't enough. Tony Lit is a very good candidate, but we obviously didn't do as well as we would have liked. The Liberals took too many of our votes.

But you must admit it was a disaster.
Of course it wasn't a disaster; we actually improved our share of the vote. Now, we didn't win, and that is a disappointment, but people who say it was a disaster are completely wrong.

You can rationalize that yourself, but how important is the effect of today's newspapers? What they are saying is damning, and this will be very damaging for you, at least for a while. You must be hurt by this, and your pride must have taken a battering, surely?
You know what? I don't think by-elections change the world, and you know that. They change the views of the MPs, particularly if you start in third place, as it is very difficult to get up from there, but I don't think in a few weeks' time we will be talking about the by-elections.

Of course not, but, strategically, this is a massive blip. And the press will get worse for you, as it has done over the last few months …
Well, we would like to have done better, of course we would. But we are in the middle of Brown's honeymoon period, and this whole phase, this whole period of Brown taking over as Prime Minister, was inevitably going to result in the sort of press he's getting right now. Inevitably there will be a period where he will get ahead and we are behind for a while, and we always thought that might happen, and it has. But we have to stick to the plan, stick to the strategy and not tear everything up and start going in a different direction.

Obviously that would be a bad thing, that's a given. But you will now be bombarded by salvos within your own party, those who will berate you for not following a more traditional path, those who will try and steer you to the right. And you're going to sit there and deny that there is a problem, that there is no sense of urgency. Shouldn't you be more worried? You must at least be tempted to shift your party slightly more to the centre ground, because I think even the floating voter now wonders exactly what it is you stand for.

I wouldn't describe our policy as sitting back, and I don't think that's fair at all, but the idea of going off to the right, that is completely the wrong response, and I think that is what Labour would like us to do. It's what we've done in the last three parliaments, and on each occasion it has ended in tears. It is also not where the British people are or what they want us to do. I just think inevitably when a new PM takes over, you can't command the agenda in the way that maybe we have done previously. But we're not doing too badly right now, and we did have a week when the Iain Duncan Smith report was published [Duncan Smith's Social Justice Policy Group recommended major changes designed to fix Britain's 'broken society'] when we were setting the agenda rather than following it. But you can't do that every week.

Gordon Brown's coronation

The press are giving Gordon Brown an easy ride at the moment. That must be hard.

Do you know what? We expected it. He will have a very easy couple of months. After that, who knows?

The sectarian violence in Iraq seems exponential, and all of us who thought we'd end up with another Vietnam have more than been proved right. We've already lost more than 150 troops, yet Gordon Brown is treading extremely carefully with this one. He can't be seen to have a knee-jerk reaction against the coalition policy, not least

because of his as yet untested relationship with George Bush. But he has just announced he's bringing 500 troops home.
That's true, but he's had to do something. Recently we've had announcements about cannabis, casinos, as they want to try and create that impression of change. My view is that a few months down the road people will start wondering if anything has really changed: are the hospitals that were to be closed staying open, are we not going to have ID cards, has the government changed the way it behaves? I think the answer will be no.

How do you begin to move up through the gears when your support is so low? You initially won so much support and acclaim and general goodwill because there was the impression that you were someone who would be keeping his drive, but where is the passion now? How do you display that passion now? The media is against you, the public are against you, so how do you make a noise in a vacuum?
I think where we have been successful is by setting an agenda and getting on the front foot and being positive. I think that if you take the things that marked our first eighteen months, it would be the campaign on the environment, the NHS, the women candidates, it is the positive things that actually define you in politics. On Monday in Rwanda I will be launching our report on poverty, then on Thursday our report on national security, and then I go on holiday and then after that we have reports on competitiveness and the quality of life. I think that is the way to regain the initiative. By going forward, by being positive, and by not worrying about a lot of spin from Downing Street.

There is another school of thought, though, isn't there? The Michael Heseltine approach where you don't worry so much about policy, you just batter the opposition as forcefully as possible and when it stops you start again. And hit them even harder. He always used to say that whether you were in Prime Minister's Questions, or on television or on the radio, or indeed anywhere, at any press conference, you just

bludgeoned the opposition into the floor. And then started all over again when they got up. If they got up, that is …

No, I don't think that is enough. I think it is right that I'm robust and tough with Brown in the House of Commons as I was at Question Time this week over prisoner releases, as we do need to puncture this puffed-up idea that this is a new PM when he has actually been there for the last ten years. So, yes, we need to be tough, with rigorous questioning and point out the government's failures.

You don't think Brown's up to the job?

I'm not sure that he is. But I don't think that's enough, I don't think oppositions win by attacking government; they have to set up a positive alternative, set up what they want to change. People will vote for change, not just if they think there is something wrong but if they think that we can put something right. I think the big theme for the Conservative Party is that spirit, mending Britain's broken society – that is what is wrong with our country. People can see that society is generally getting a lot poorer, there is family breakdown, drug abuse, alcohol abuse, persistent unemployment, sometimes three generations of families being unemployed.

Brown has done a more than capable job of presenting a very particular image to the public, one that they seem to like right now. He's coming across as assured, contemplative yet decisive, and – crucially – strong. The volcanic element that we all know is there has yet to come to the fore, and although you occasionally rile him at Prime Minister's Questions – and at times you are fluently contemptuous – at the moment he's coming across very well. Tell me about your relationship with Brown. What's it like?

It is pretty non-existent, to be honest with you. I have met him a couple of times in my life. I met him before I was an MP when he came and had lunch at Carlton once, but as an MP I have met him literally just a couple of times. He is not a very social man at all. Some MPs do have friends, or at least acknowledge people from across the divide, but Brown has never really been one of those. He rang me on the day he became PM, and I obviously congratulated him, but I haven't really had a conversation with him since then.

It must be extremely odd, in that gladiatorial way you are continually shouting at each other. It's incredibly funny sometimes.
Speaking firmly is how I prefer to think about it.

But it is like you are two breastplated sportsmen, battling it out in front of an invited audience. You look like you enjoy it, too, you look like you enjoy playing with him as though you were a cat and he was a mouse. He's imposing both physically and intellectually, but you tend to win most battles, probably because you're quicker on your feet. But he always has a script, and even when he has a gag that's been written for him, so he can end a particular passage about something with a joke, it falls flat. This is usually because the conversation has gone off on another tangent but he uses the joke regardless of its suitability. He also looks incredibly cross when he doesn't get his own way, almost as though by dint of the fact that he's the PM, you should just roll over and do as you're told.
You're not attacking him for what he is, you're attacking him for what he's done, or more usually what he hasn't done, so it doesn't necessarily matter that you don't have deep insights into his character. What matters is his policy, and that is what I take him to task over. That is why I am robust over prisoner releases, NHS cuts or whatever, that's my job.

There is a great sketch by Matthew Parris from 1997, where he says that Brown's presentational skills have been transformed since Labour came to power. 'He used to be boring and deafening,' he wrote. 'Now he is just boring. He used to thunder; now he just rumbles. He used to sound positively suicidal; now he just sounds faintly grumpy. He used to seem gripped by some black and fathomless internal rage; now he just looks cross.' Seriously, what do you make of him?

I honestly don't really know. What I don't like is this awful arrogance of power and the arrogance of central control and I think he is a great believer in central government pulling levers, telling people what to do, controlling everyone and everything around him, and I think he is wrong. His approach to everything seems to be centralized, whether it is crime, ID cards, the health service, wanting everything to be sorted out by an incredibly complex central system. Our view of politics is incredibly different, and the real thing you need to do is empower the people. He talks about this a little, but even when you listen to what he says it doesn't sound as though he means it. He is a man who wants to control as much of people's lives as possible, and that is completely the wrong kind of approach for successful government, and especially wrong for the times we live in where technology and innovation mean you can actually give people much more power and control over their lives than ever before.

Party cohesion

When you became leader, one of the first things you tried to do was make the party cohesive again, and to present a solid front to the electorate.
This is the first part of the plan, and to a large degree it has worked and we are very happy with where we are.

So how annoying and how irritating is it when you see things like the piece in the *Telegraph* today, a day after your by-election disaster, when you've got the details of a supposedly private 1922 Committee meeting splashed all over its pages – the central tenet of which is harsh criticism of yourself?
It is irritating when you have a private meeting and say what you think and then you see it all over the newspapers. It's frustrating as it leads to a situation where meetings become a formality rather than a genuine discussion and that is rather sad. There are situations where you can't have meetings because you know what you will say is going to be leaked. But I have cracked down and I will continue to crack down.

I know I've asked you this before but do you ever feel like giving up?
Of course I don't. This is what I've chosen to do and I'm going to do it to the best of my ability.

Tony Blair succeeding John Smith

Can we go back a bit and talk about how you felt when Blair took over the Labour Party in the early nineties? What did you think of that? I was working at the *Sunday Times* when the news broke that John Smith had died of a heart attack [May 1994], and after the shock and the aftermath there was incredible excitement surrounding Blair's victory, because he was even more of a modernizer than Smith, and so many of us thought that things would change for the better – which they did, initially. The Conservatives were moribund at this time, and you must have sensed a certain inevitability about Labour's rejuvenation. I was as excited as anyone … Patrick Rock, a colleague of yours when you both worked for Michael Howard, says that when he heard the news he went round the corner from the Home Office with you for a drink: 'We both agreed that Blair coming meant that we would be fucked.'
I thought it was a) inevitable, and b) deeply worrying for the Conservative Party. I remember exactly going for that drink with Patrick, standing outside the Two Chairmen pub, near Old Queen Street in St James's, and it was just after John Smith had died, and we said it will be Blair and that will be disastrous for us as he is a deeply intuitive politician, and certainly had an understanding of what makes people tick. He was never instinctively of the Labour Party and always had a much more centre right sensibility and mindset, but I thought he would be very effective and he was.

They were obviously a fantastically effective team in the early days, and when they were first in power no one can say they weren't impressive. If you read the Alastair Campbell diaries you are taken back to that period when Blair succeeded John Smith, and you see a portrait of

four men – Blair, Brown, Campbell and Peter Mandelson – so committed to the project, so devoted to the cause that it would have been impossible for them to fail. Even though they all had personal issues with each other, they worked together as one. They were just four men in a room working amazingly hard for one common goal. The remarkable thing about the diaries is that every day is a battle, every day there were battles to be fought, wars to be won, fires to be put out and fires to be started. When you understand the level of commitment that they all had, the seven-day-a-week, eighteen-hour days, you understand how the Tories never really had a chance at the '97 election. The way they set out their stall, the way they planned every day as though it were a battle, in hindsight it makes for fascinating reading. I would have thought there is a lot there that would make very interesting reading for a party in transition like yourselves ...

I am trying to remember what I really thought. I suspect beneath the veneer there was quite a lot of fast pedalling, both forward and backwards. I thought in ninety-seven, when they won, I was not particularly focused on politics at that time, that they were very good at creating this aura of change and excitement – every day there was some new announcement. But the more you saw of this, the more you started to realize they were operating in a virtual world, that they were still behaving like the opposition and I think they have admitted it now. You had this stream of things being announced; but was anything changing and was anything really being done? I think that was their problem. Having worked in government I know how difficult it really is to change things and how long it takes – and they didn't take many difficult decisions early on, and you have to in order to effect change. It was impressive, how they created a mood that the whole country was changing, but if you look back I think it was the time of their greatest failure.

Why was that?

There is a dreadful but rather insightful book called *The Spin Doctor's Diary* [a fascinating book published in 2005, subtitled *Inside Number 10 with New Labour*, by Lance Price, who was Alastair Campbell's deputy for three years, making him the sidekick to the control freak's control freak], which gives you an indication of the thoroughly depressing way they were running the country, as though there was a general election every day, and that is a terrible way to run a country.

But you would say that. You're right that the Labour Party were masters at making us all feel as though we were moving towards a bright new tomorrow – something that was obviously helped by the mid-nineties acclaim for Britpop and Britart and all the other cultural movement in the country – but while the perception might have worked fantastically well in their favour, the reality for lots of us at the time was that we were doing quite well. We enjoyed having a Labour government; they'd only been in for five minutes so we were excited by the idea of change, and the Tory stink had died away.
But I don't think that's strictly true …

Trust me, that was the popular view. So why was this such a terrible time for the country? Surely it was just a terrible time for the Conservative Party?
Because to make decisions in the long-term interests of the country you have to take quite tough decisions quite early on so that you can get things done within the life of a parliament. But they didn't take any of those big decisions early on, they didn't really carry out any of the fundamental social reforms the country needed, and, as a result, ten years on they are still grappling with the failure of the health service, the education system, family breakdown, because they didn't necessarily do the hard work at the beginning. One thing they did do was make the Bank of England independent; that was a fundamental shift and that made a big difference. It's a pity that there weren't other things that were done on the same basis.

The Conservative Research Department

Let's go back further. After you graduated, you almost immediately started working for the CRD. In hindsight was this a job you did because you got it? After all, as we've already discussed, you were fairly ambivalent about politics at that age.

I was actually offered a job at an accountancy practice doing some kind of consultancy but I decided not to do that, and then I saw this job for the Conservative Research Department, and, having worked for an MP between school and university and having quite enjoyed it, I went for the interview and got the job. It was quite a nice bridge from university as it was still academic in a way.

You were there from 1988 to 1992, initially covering trade and industry and energy, writing briefing notes on legislation for the House of Commons for backbench MPs. You were doing campaign guides and policy pamphlets and stuff like that. It was mostly writing and then you got into the job of briefing people and preparing them for Question Time, and then eventually political strategy. You also had the job of briefing John Major before the press conference for the 1992 general election. But what were you really learning about the business of politics? This was your first proper job and rather through luck than judgement you ended up advising the PM. That's a pretty extraordinary place for a man in his early twenties to be, no?

I suppose I learned a lot about how Parliament worked and parliamentary processes, the roles of the various offices – Central Office, the whip's office, backbench committees. You got a feel of what the Prime Minister's office is like, which was extraordinary. I was drafted in to help the PM with Question Time, and so I got a good feel for how a political party in Westminster works and probably less of a feel for how the rest of the country worked.

It was around this time that you started thinking about becoming a journalist. It's extraordinary to think that you could have ended up as a Simon Carr or a Steve Richards or a Simon Heffer or a Dominic Lawson.

I was thinking about it, yes. I thought I'd be quite good at it. At university, in 1987, I had an interview with *The Economist*, but I didn't get the job. I really enjoyed writing, but I don't think I am by nature a journalist; I think there is a big difference. I sometimes think that there are people in politics who ought to be in journalism, and there are people in journalism who should be in politics, but I'm certainly not going to say who. I am definitely a politician.

Black Wednesday

In 1992 you went to work for Norman Lamont. How was that?

It was fascinating, I was twenty-six and I was relatively junior; there were three special advisers at the Treasury and I was very much the one who was involved in speech writing. The Treasury was much more fun than the Home Office, as you were encouraged to chip in during meetings, and to debate and to argue, and it was a brilliant experience. Obviously it was a very stressful time, and there was incredible strain, and in the second part of the year it was very difficult and Norman was having a pretty miserable time.

Tell me about Black Wednesday. It must have been incredibly stressful but it must have proved to you that when you're in politics the world revolves around you, that this is where you affect the world as you know it, this is where you make the papers. It must have been quite addictive.

The Treasury was acutely conscious of the problems but couldn't do anything about them. Germany needed high interest rates to reduce inflation after unification, and we needed low interest rates to reduce unemployment after the recession, and there was this incredible strain and in the end that was what broke it apart. It will always go down as a bad period in British economic policy, there is no doubt about it, but what matters is that you learn the lesson from it and the people who were there by and large did. I learned so much from just being there, seeing everything that went on around me.

How did that affect your career, because after that you decided to move out of politics for a while? Were you battered and bruised?
It didn't really change. I probably would have stayed in the Treasury for longer, but when Norman was sacked, even though Ken Clarke asked me to stay on eventually I was moved on and went to work for Michael Howard as his adviser at the Home Office. I was already thinking that it might be fun to do for a year, but thought I should start thinking about getting a job outside the world of politics and there were one or two avenues I was exploring.

Carlton

Why did you think it was necessary to go out of politics for a while? In July 1994, you left your role as Special Adviser to work as the Director of Corporate Affairs at Carlton Communications, where you stayed for seven years. You were forging a significant career in politics and then decided to jettison it in favour of a life in the private sector.
I always thought it would be good experience to have spent some time in the commercial world outside of politics. I think it is good to have done something different. Waking every day and thinking: I've got to sell television packages, or market shares to Japanese investors, it was just a totally different thing to think about. Obviously it was going to be a bit of a wrench leaving politics, but money was an issue, too, and at the Treasury I was earning maybe £26,000, which wasn't bad, and I was earning my age, but I was buying a flat and money was a concern. I was conscious of the fact that at the age of twenty-six I needed to go somewhere and learn more about the world. So having met Michael Green I thought it would be a good idea to take my understanding of politics and

regulation and legislation and add to it a knowledge of business. Media is a relatively regulated business, so I thought it was a good place to go.

But why Green? And why Carlton? It wasn't exactly renowned for great programming.
What I liked about Green was that he was very unstructured, in as much as if you were good you got more to do, and if I had gone to some bigger company I might have been hidden away. Basically I got to know the City.

Michael Green is an extremely enigmatic man, isn't he? Was he difficult to work for?
There are some people who are rather more corporate types, who have worked their way up the ladder, and there are the more swashbuckling, entrepreneurial, unconventional types like Michael, and there is a lot more excitement about the latter. There is also a lot more pain and problems as you are dealing with someone who has their own way of doing things and is rather emotional, but he was a great guy. I learned a lot and had a great time.

Well, you were there for seven years, which is a career in itself for many people, so how did your job grow from that? How did you progress in the company? You must have felt that it was unlikely that you would go back into politics.
He offered me a job on the condition that I didn't fight the next election. He didn't want to have me trained and then for me to bugger off. I said no, told him I had to be absolutely free to fight the next election as, I said, politics is my first love. So he said the job was off. Then he came back a week later and said here is another job, with lower pay, and I jumped at it, so I paid for my love of politics with a pay cut before I had even started. I went there in 1994, and started with rather regulatory affairs – restrictions on the ownership of ITN, and cross-media ownership rules. But after that I started to broaden what I was doing to include maintaining our relationship with shareholders and explaining

our business to analysts. You had to be at your desk at 7.30 a.m., every day, and anything happening in the markets that day or with the business that day I had to be able to explain the impact on the business. I was the front man in terms of talking to brokers and understanding the markets.

You must have met some serious people in that time, including many people in the Murdoch organization.
I spent a lot of time with other media companies, but much more time with highly paid analysts at Goldman Sachs and Merrill Lynch and a lot of travelling to America. We owned Technicolor in California and so went there every year and made quite a lot of trips around Europe, to Spain and France and Germany, talking to shareholders. We were competitors to Murdoch, and media companies are always talking to each other – there is some terrible word 'co-opetition', where you cooperate and compete at the same time, so one minute you are saying let's merge Sky News and ITN and the next you are beating each other's brains out trying to sell satellite boxes and dishes. In the end they were the ones who won that battle, and it wasn't an especially successful endeavour for Carlton.

What did you learn about presentation, about selling, about PR?
Fundamentally I learned how to explain difficult and complex things. I also learned that spin and PR will not get you where you want to go, and that truth is the most important commodity.

It's ironic that your PR background has been used against you in a sort of post-Blair, anti-spin way.
It was a fascinating experience and only did me good.

And when you moved into the private sector, you still weren't sure if you wanted to move back into politics, still weren't sure if you wanted to give up a relatively cushy life of international travel, good money, perks, and getting up late in the morning … for a life of potential

drudgery, and people shouting at you in the press every day. What was going through your mind during your last year at Carlton?

I was earning really good money by the time I left. I was Director of Corporate Affairs, on the management executive; it was a very good job. I was being headhunted to do the same thing with other companies. But my love was politics, so I started to think about looking for a seat, and finally got selected in 1999.

Back into politics

Tell me about your re-entry into the political world. You'd been looking for a safe seat for a while, and when Shaun Woodward defected to Labour in 2000, you went for his Witney seat in Oxford-shire. A few other seats came up at the same time, didn't they?

That's right. East Devon, Wealden and Epsom, but Witney selected first and that was definitely the one I wanted as it was the right seat. It was forty miles from where I grew up, it was an area of the country I knew, it was rural but also connected with London, where I just felt an affinity with the place and an understanding of the people. I absolutely love it, and it is still my favourite bit of the week, when I turn off the A44 and see what is really the gateway to the Cotswolds. It was a stroke of luck really that Shaun Woodward decided to cross the Commons and make the seat available.

How did your life change?

Quite a bit, because the local Conservatives felt incredibly let down by Woodward, and the whole thing was a bit of a mess. The association was fractured and short of money, so I immediately rented a cottage in the same village where we now live. I was there every Friday, there every weekend, and really worked hard at getting the show back on the road. It was the usual thing – raising money and getting involved in local issues. It became more hectic as I was also doing the Carlton thing at the same time, so it was a busy time. It would have been a disaster if I had lost, put it that way.

After the 1997 election the Tories began to hollow out and disintegrate. It was the end of an era and a shock to so many people who had been in power for such a long time. It was inevitable, though, wasn't it, as after a while the public just get sick of a party, and after 1992 there was a sense of inevitability about the end of the Thatcher/Major era? Your grass roots started dying, people started leaving and the party felt all washed up.

That's true to a certain extent.

William Hague's Tories

I know you weren't there in the eye of the storm, but how did it look and feel to you at the time? You must have had the sense that your party was about to wander off for a rather long walk to obscurity … People are always saying that William Hague was the right man in the right place at the wrong time. Everyone knows he has a big brain, but, having tried to make the Tories inclusive and 'modern', he panicked in the face of poor poll ratings, lurched to the right and the Tories went to hell in a handcart.

I knew William Hague, we had worked together at the Treasury, and I was a great fan of his, and still am, and I thought the party originally set out on a modernizing programme under him. He was a great leader. If you go back to 1997, 1998, Hague was saying then that the party had to modernize, had to shake off the dust of the previous twenty years, and he really did try and set off down that path. But he had an impossible task because not only was Blair carrying all before him but Hague was surrounded by people who were saying that Blair wouldn't last five minutes, and that the whole thing would fall apart. I was very pro-Hague at the time, but then he changed tack, and, as I have discussed many times, he was stuck and nothing was working for him, and I think it was the wrong decision and he regrets it. It was the wrong decision, but I think it is easy to see why it was made as he wasn't getting anywhere and there was no traction, no movement.

Hague didn't so much lurch to the right as leap at it, get it in a headlock and strap himself to it. This was kick-started by the Tony Martin affair. [Martin, a Norfolk farmer, was convicted of the murder of Fred Barras, a sixteen-year-old burglar whom he caught in his house. He was sentenced to life imprisonment, but on appeal this conviction was reduced to manslaughter on grounds of diminished responsibility, as the Courts accepted that Martin was suffering from a paranoid personality disorder. His sentence was reduced to five years, of which he served three.] Fast-forward a number of years and you could be moving into a period of time when there is an awful lot of pressure on you to make similar moves. And the Labour Party can smell it – anything you do that suggests you might be reverting to type will be jumped on. They've even started to do it already, and in a way it's something that will dog you forever, in much the same way that, if you want to be pejorative about it, their relationships with the unions will forever dog them.

Yes, exactly, and what is good about having William Hague there is that he is a very good reminder of that, both in body and in spirit. He always says don't make the same mistake.

But were you never tempted to run on a more right-wing ticket when you went for the leadership?

No, not at all. It would have been totally wrong. The interesting thing about the 2001 election was that, having knocked on a lot of doors, the public were adamant that they wanted to give Labour another chance. The gist was, I don't think they have done that well but I am going to give them a proper chance and vote for them again. So you sensed you were heading for a very similar result, and there was no big swing taking place. In a way, what the Conservatives did instead was irrelevant as people didn't want to change; they wanted to give the Labour Party a proper go, so the 2001 election was a bit of a non-event. For us at least.

Iain Duncan Smith

What did you honestly feel about IDS, the so-called quiet man who no one was remotely aware of, let alone scared of? Obviously he is still working for you, but he wasn't a great success, was he?

I got into Parliament in 2001 and we were immediately thrown into an election. I pretty quickly declared for Portillo because I thought the party needed a change, and the problem is that he didn't win, so we wound up with a contest between someone the party didn't know [Duncan Smith] and someone they knew, in Ken Clarke, but didn't get on with. And the rest, as they say, is history. I just didn't think Ken would be able to lead a united party. I think there would have been a squabble about Europe for ever and a day, so I voted for Portillo in each of the three ballots. But Duncan Smith won easily. I voted for him in the membership ballot, although Samantha favoured Clarke. No one really knew much about him really, and, as you say, it wasn't a very happy period, we weren't making any headway. However, Iain was making very strong points about social breakdown, which is something he's been working on ever since and is doing work on that now for us – it's right at the heart of our plans. He is very passionate and committed to dealing with the problems of entrenched poverty and social breakdown. The problem was that in 2001 it came slightly out of the blue. The thing about politics or leadership is that you have to hit all the buttons, do well in the Commons, do well in Question Time, handle your party, develop good strategy, get on well when you go round the country – you have to tick all those boxes.

There must have been a point, pretty soon after Duncan Smith got in, where the consensus was that the only way that Labour would stop winning elections was if they imploded like the Tories did in the early 1990s, because the media was so relentlessly anti-Tory at that time. There was a real sense that we were a one-party nation, and that whatever the Tories did was met with blank stares and shrugs. I remember going to dinner parties at the time and people simply laughing

whenever the word Tory was mentioned. It didn't matter what you said about them – didn't matter if you wanted to launch into a tirade about them because you weren't given the opportunity.

It was a terrible time for the Tories.

You whispered 'Tory' and it was as if you had mentioned some ridiculous pantomime figure. Like saying the words Hale & Pace …

It seemed to be all about Tories in turmoil, rather than Tories steadily recovering, which we obviously would have preferred. And we couldn't seem to break out of that. Remember, I was a new backbencher, I was on the Home Affairs Select Committee and I was incredibly loyal. I am an instinctive loyalist, I have always been loyal to all the leaders of the party and I think politics is a team game. You owe loyalty to your team leader or else you are doomed. May as well give up. However, the party did behave appallingly at the 2002 conference. There was some open plotting and it was really unattractive. I was only at the 2002 and the 2003 conferences for a day, as I had to go off to hospital and was sort of saved, and watched these conferences on a rather cranky NHS television.

Surely you must have felt a terrible sense of disappointment at the fortunes of your party. Here you were, a young man who had started out in government, energized by working in the private sector, coming back into politics and finding that your party of choice was disintegrating before your very eyes. The whole construct was falling to bits. Did you ever have a dark moment when you considered jumping over to the other side? I mean, here was a fabulously sexy, modernizing Labour Party. Strong, not the same party they were fifteen years previously; did that ever cross your mind?

No, I am an instinctive Conservative.

Not ever? After all, they were in the ascendancy …

No. Labour is about the state and we are about society. I grew up in the eighties when all those arguments of protectionism versus free trade, of privatization versus nationalization, trade union power versus consumer power were uppermost in people's minds. They were certainly uppermost in mine. You don't just go jumping over fences because your party has nowhere else to go, and the Tories were rather outside those arguments. I find it appalling what Shaun Woodward did, where five minutes beforehand he is slagging off the Labour Party and then suddenly he has changed teams.

This is the politician as footballer, mercenary rather than ideological, always looking for a better deal and a better home.
In a way that's exactly right, because unless politics is about principle it's about nothing. When you see someone change teams like Woodward did it makes you incredibly angry. Look at all the people he was letting down!

Okay, but you must have thought, here I am, back in the middle of this moribund party, what on earth am I going to do now?
Trust me. No one ever believes this, but I think being an MP is a wonderful, fascinating, fulfilling job and anything beyond Parliament is a bonus. You can get things done, you can make progress on an issue, you can campaign and really see the results of your work.

Michael Howard

And then, of course, you were lumbered with Michael Howard, Dracula of the parish. There was a vote of no confidence in Iain Duncan Smith, and suddenly we had a man of the people who couldn't even pronounce the word properly.
You mean Michael Howard? That's certainly not how I'd characterize him, but yes. Well, it all happened very quickly really, didn't it? Howard emerged very quickly, which in hindsight I think was the right thing because the party needed shoring up. You definitely felt that the professionals were back in charge, and he was good in the House of Commons, he knew what needed to be done in terms of organization, but again he made the same mistake that Hague made. After making

some modernizing announcements he lurched to the right. I admire Michael a lot, and some people's public image is so different from their private lives. Michael is one of the nicest and kindest people you will ever meet. He has an incredibly clever mind, one of the sharpest, but sometimes it's too sharp. Often he will win an argument even when he is wrong, which is just the most frustrating thing when you're a politician. I had several occasions like that. But I think the difficulty is that in politics you have to be what you are, and he was a believer in tough law and order, open markets and choice, and is quite a traditional Tory in that respect.

I only heard him speak a few times in person, and, while he can be incredibly charming when he puts his mind to it, you only have to give the slightest indication that you don't care about something in order to give off a bad smell. A few years ago I was chairman of the British Society of Magazine Editors, and one of the many things you have to do as chair is organize some sort of event each month – that's twelve high-profile events a year, all with a heavy-hitter as the main attraction. Anyway, that year we'd had Tony Blair, Jeremy Clarkson, various newspaper editors such as Roger Alton [in his previous incarnation as editor of the *Observer*], and it made sense to invite Michael to speak. And, frankly, he was a disaster. We held the event in the lecture theatre at the Soho Hotel, and we had a full house, over a hundred magazine editors as well as a bunch of people from the papers. But Howard spoke as though he was waiting for his taxi – which he probably was. He gave us a yard of typical non-speak, topped and tailed with a bit of material relevant to the print industry. And absolutely no one bought in to him. One very much got the feeling that here was a man who was filling in, who had no conviction that he could hold his own party together, let alone win a general election. Here was a twenty-minute window of opportunity to ingratiate himself with a hundred of the most influential journalists in the country – and some of these men and women were editing publications which had readerships in their millions – and he barely turned up. And if he did that once, he must

have done it a hundred times. Perhaps it was the residual arrogance of once being in power. He was just going through the motions.

Politics is about building a team and getting things done, and Michael certainly has those capabilities. But one of the things he said to me was that his diary got incredibly packed, and so it's lunchtime with magazine editors, evening with somebody else and before you know it you're stuck in a situation where you are going through the motions. You lose the freshness, and I am permanently aware of this. Of course I'm worried about these things myself, about appearing as if I don't care. You can go to all these things with a perfectly scripted speech, and it is perfectly adequate but flat, and what you really need to do is engage directly with people. If people don't believe what I'm saying then I'm doomed. Some of the people who work for me worked for Howard, and they tell me that this is a really important thing, to keep the diary open so you do have time to think things through and to do things thoroughly. There are days when I feel I am going through the motions myself as there are too many things you are trying to do and too many speeches to make. Obviously it is much better to cancel some things and do what you want to do well.

How far into his leadership did you begin to think to yourself, I ought to be doing this, I can do it a darn sight better. This could be the David Cameron Show! When did you start to think that if you're going to do this thing, then what you really ought to be doing is trying to be the leader of the party, and then ultimately Prime Minister? You didn't get into politics to sit on the back benches; you didn't get into politics to scurry around Parliament without anyone noticing you. When did you begin to think that it was time for some me time?

Honestly, I really wasn't thinking like that at all. I was part of the team and liked working with him, but I would cycle over to the Commons with George Osborne, and all we would talk about would be how we would do things differently. Nothing else, just that. There wasn't an assumption that either of us would be running the Tory Party, and certainly after the 2005 election my instinctive reaction was not to go for the job. But I was definitely thinking about it then. We discussed me going for the job, but not in a clinical way. This wasn't a Granita moment. There was nothing dark and Machiavellian about it. I think what many of us felt was that things needed to be a bit more modern and forward looking.

The 2005 speech

Where did your 2005 conference speech come from? This was a turning point for the party, and it was make or break time for you …
It certainly was make or break time …

It was one of the most dynamic speeches heard at a Tory conference for years. You delivered it largely without notes. How long did you spend practising? Where in fact did the speech come from?
Actually, the key day was a few days before, when I launched my leadership campaign, and that was when I gave my first no-notes speech in front of a national audience, and that was the moment my leadership campaign took shape. I think the journalists who came thought, hey, this guy's got something really quite interesting to say about the Conservative Party and what needs to change and he's telling it exactly like it is. It was a great moment, I think, and the whole campaign took off, and people started to see that, actually, the person with the clearest message in the leadership campaign about the need to modernize, the need to change and what needed to be done, was me. So the conference speech followed quite naturally from that.

How did the launch speech end up that way?
I remember going to practise the speech, and I really didn't like it. It just didn't feel right. I said, I'm going to give up the speech and just say this. And it went down really well.

Who was there?

I think Steve [Hilton] was there, Catherine Fall was there. They just thought it worked, and so I went with it. I love engaging with an audience in that way and it just seemed to work in that format. Casual, natural, without notes. It was genuinely unscripted, it wasn't learned, and contained exactly what I wanted to say. And I think the speech at the launch is by far the better speech, although everyone always focuses on the conference speech, for obvious reasons. And then I had a few days to prepare for the conference speech and decided to use the same method. I hadn't written anything until that weekend, and I remember a whole bunch of us went out to lunch – Danny Finkelstein, George [Osborne], a few others – and we talked about what I should do, and then I went home with Steve and we wrote the speech together.

How long did it take?

It took a couple of hours. It was quite similar in content to the launch speech, so a lot of the groundwork had been done. And then I just rolled it around in my head a lot, and decided to do it without notes. I just needed to make sure I was familiar with it. I didn't learn every line, but it was very similar to what I planned to say. I had a structure …

Did anyone else help you with the speech?

Actually, I bumped into Matthew Parris before making the conference speech and he said you need to understand people's respect for the history of the party, and the contribution all the previous leaders have made. And that made me think about the context of the speech, and so I rewrote the beginning, and actually it worked very well and I was very grateful. Matthew has a wonderful understanding of the Conservative Party. He loves it, but at times he gets incredibly frustrated with it … but he gave me a lovely tip.

Even you must have been surprised by the reaction. You told us all you wanted to make us 'feel good about being Conservatives again', and

**said you wanted 'to switch on a whole new generation', and people
stood up and took notice ...**

Yes, I was. I was incredibly nervous beforehand. It was a hugely exciting
conference, Blackpool was packed, there was a lot of expectation, and
people seemed very excited by all these leadership contenders all making
speeches. But it was a big roll of the dice to do it without any notes. No
autocue, no funny business. There was a moment when I lost my train of
thought, but no one really noticed.

You were pausing for dramatic effect, obviously ...

Maybe that's what it looked like. A pause feels like an eternity to you
when you're up there, but the audience doesn't think so. I remember that
day very well, as the audience was very buzzy. I certainly got a buzz from
it. There was a leadership campaign party that had been organized for
me, in a fairly small room with the usual Blackpool warm white wine,
and it was absolutely packed. I'd never seen so many people. Literally
hundreds of people had obviously decided that this was the leadership
contender they wanted to get behind. It was really exciting.

**Before the conference, did you think that David Davis had it in the
bag? I remember writing a story in the *Spectator* the week before in
which I said Davis would get it. At the time he seemed the obvious
choice. But you blew him out of the water.**

Oddly enough, I didn't think he was the obvious choice. Nobody will
believe me but I always thought, right from the beginning, that I had a
really good chance. No one really had it in the bag, and I genuinely
thought I had the clearest understanding about what needed to change.
The Conservative Party was fed up with losing, and was more ready to
listen to someone saying we had to tear up the rule book and do things
differently. I remember thinking I've got to be absolutely prepared to do
this job and to be Prime Minister if we win an election, because entering
this race could mean both.

The aftermath

How did you feel the morning you woke up as leader of the party? What emotions and sensations went through you?
Fear, first of all, because if you remember it was Prime Minister's Question Time that day.

So you had twenty-four hours' grace and then straight into it.
Yes, I had twenty-four hours' grace and then it was all systems go. I went to bed after the party feeling very excited and then started worrying about PMQs, wondering what on earth I was going to do. So it was a real baptism of fire. It was a shock to suddenly become leader because you're doing all sorts of things and you have pressures and a profile that you didn't previously have, but it's been less of a shock than I thought it might be.

What did you notice about how differently people treated you? When did the brown-nosing start?
It's not as big a change as you think. You have to make sure immediately that people are telling you things that they need to, because there's a lot of miscommunication in Parliament, at least there can be. My friends didn't treat me any differently; my wife certainly doesn't treat me any differently. A lot of people you've never met before come up and say hello and they tend to be quite friendly …

No, in the party, the greasy polers …
That's a very good question, and I haven't spent an awful lot of time thinking about it. I would say there's no doubt that because you've been elected and you've got a mandate, people do, I hope, treat you with some respect, but there's not suddenly undue deference. People tend to be pretty reasonable.

How easy is it to gain respect in politics, among your peers? It strikes me you're even more cynical than journalists, and that you have a

pretty good radar … You've spent a lot of time around journalists, you know what's going on …

The truth is that political power and influence and the ability to get things done come much more from success than from the office you hold. The truth is, if things are going well, you've just won some local elections, you're doing well in the polls, it's much easier to get things done. That's always worth remembering. I think it's the same if you're Prime Minister or the Leader of the Opposition. When times are tough you have to work a lot harder to take people with you. Power comes with success as well as office.

Rwanda

Today we're off to Nottingham for a regional fundraiser but in two days you're off to Rwanda. Given what's going on at the moment with all the floods, and your low standings in the polls, is this really the best time to leave the country and wander around Africa? No one seems to think it's a good idea, including rather a lot of people from your own party.

This weekend as well as the fundraiser I'm also visiting one of the flooded areas to see for myself some of the problems people are having. I went to have a look at the floods in Leeds just after it had happened and I need to see more. I've met loads of people who have been forced out of their homes and it's a terrible situation. And then on Sunday I'm flying to Rwanda where for the last two weeks there have been about forty Conservatives taking part in a range of development projects. It is incredibly frustrating that the media are painting this as some glorified PR opportunity. There is a team of people helping to build an orphanage, which is a key project. There is an orthopaedic surgeon carrying out operations and there's an expert in finance helping the finance ministry and there are genuine projects that, hopefully, will have a lasting effect. So I am going out there to meet the President, make a speech in Parliament and see what the projects are, and, vitally, to publicize our policy group report on poverty – which has been a year and a half in the making.

But it doesn't matter why you're going or what you're going to do when you get there. The media don't want you to go so they're going to make your life a misery by telling you so. You know that, so why are you still going?

Why am I going to Rwanda? Because I think it's a good idea. Because I think it's the right thing to do. In politics fast-changing events mean you have to switch from one issue to another, so to spend two weeks focused on something and be involved with a project like this is a really good thing. I think it is absolutely true that international poverty is a mainstream issue and how we heal the enormous divide between the rich and the poor countries is one of the big challenges for the twenty-first century. If we cannot help the economic development of these countries, then we will continue with problems of migration, starvation and poverty. These are problems that not only affect the people of Africa, but also us at home, and this is one of the big challenges of our times.

FOUR

'It is amazing what a new Prime Minister can get away with'

Elton John, the 'big clunking fist', a turnaround in the polls, the Prime Minister lying on television

In early September 2007, six weeks after the Ealing debacle, I was standing eating sandwiches and drinking beer at the O2 Arena down in Greenwich ('the tent in Kent') waiting for Elton John to perform his Red Piano show, along with half a dozen national newspaper editors, a similar number of magazine editors, a smattering of celebs and every gossip columnist worth their organic sea salt.

Having dispensed with any polite conversation regarding what we may have done over the holidays – where we went, what we read and who was lying by the pool with us when we read it – all anyone wanted to talk about was Gordon Brown and David Cameron: in particular, how well the former was doing in the press, and how disastrously the latter was doing in the polls.

'Cameron is a busted flush,' said the former editor of one national daily. 'He's had it. Toast. Kaput. Vamoosh. He may as well give up and crawl back to the private sector, because Brown's got him by the balls and he's not going to let go. Not until after the election, anyway, which if he's got any sense he's going to call on the second day of the Tory conference.'

Worryingly for any Tories present, his sentiments were echoed by many that night.

'The problem is, well, the problem is a simple one, and one that Cameron probably couldn't do a lot about even if he wanted to,' said another editor. 'For most people politics is something they think about for fifteen seconds a day. They glance over at the TV and see this guy who's not Tony Blair. But he looks like he knows what he's doing. And then we turn away from the TV and get back to whatever it is that we spend the rest of our lives doing. That's what Cameron's up against. No one really cares if he exists at the moment. That's his problem.'

Cameron had only just come back from a bucket and spade holiday in Brittany, where he'd had more than sandcastles to think about. Just three months previously the Conservative leader had enjoyed record gains in the local elections, winning more than 800 seats in a nationwide test of public opinion – and, as the *Spectator* said at the time, recording general election-winning levels of support. That success was the result of an intense eighteen-month period during which Cameron had changed his party almost beyond recognition, modernizing its policies, presenting a Fresh & Wild face to the electorate, keeping a firm hand on the tiller and keeping a steady lead over Labour in the polls.

Since then, however, Brown's coronation – he became Prime Minister on 27 June – had been welcomed by the country with open arms, seemingly unanimously. And while those in the gallery of the chamber had expected the Stalinesque control freak to explode upon re-entry, actually he had simply stood in a corner and looked important. Having spent over a decade saying he lacked what was needed to become a leader, the press suddenly decided to revere him, even those papers which had traditionally despised everything he stood for. The 'Big Clunking Fist' (copyright Tony Blair) was stoicism personified, giving interviews as if the fate of the universe depended on how emotionless he could be.

To paraphrase Robert Harris, Tony Blair wasn't so much a politician as a craze, and this was exactly the sort of thing that Gordon Brown had set out to distance himself from. He wasn't interested in being a 'craze'. Brown was stoic. Dull (really dull). A little older. A little more considered. Or so we all thought. If Blair elevated political clichés by the sheer force of his personality, then Brown wanted us to feel he was doing exactly the opposite. What Brown did Brown had to do, simply in order for us to carry on with our lives. That's the message the PM wanted to get across. And, perhaps surprisingly, it was working. The number of dyed-in-the-wool Tories who stood in front of their TVs on 30 June, after the terror attack on Glasgow Airport, whispering, 'Actually he looks good. Maybe he's going to be okay', was alarming. Even those Tories for whom Margaret Thatcher had been some sort of Florence Nightingale figure, even they were being swept away by the PM. The Brown bounce wasn't just big, it was Meaty Beaty Big and Bouncy.

Faced with a string of crises – a terrorist attack, nationwide flooding – Brown reacted coolly and sensibly. Could it be that the Conservative leader's popularity was only viable when he had a lame-duck Blair as his opponent? As Brown began radiating a newfound prime ministerial dignity, all of a sudden Cameron started to resemble Downing Street's previous incumbent, a PR lightweight in a shiny central heating suit and a 'Hey guys' open-necked shirt.

For Cameron, the fallout from Ealing had been immense. Few doubted that the Tory leader was determined, brave and capable, but the concerns remained that all his hard work didn't appear to be adding up to much. Cameron was mostly saying the right things, but where was the desperate passion needed to overturn a government? Where was the spice? And why did he and the rest of his Shadow Cabinet seem to take things so easy? Neither Cameron nor those around him appeared to be taking things as seriously as his supporters wished he would. Why wasn't he demonizing Brown in public like he did in Prime Minister's Questions? Why was he being so soft on the whingers in his own party? Why did he never wear a tie?

To some Tory supporters it was beginning to look as if Cameron, far from being the solution, was the problem. As Janet Daley said in the *Daily Telegraph*, 'Mr Cameron and his friends must not delude themselves: their modernisation mania has come irretrievably, irreparably unstuck …'

Cameron's ungainly stumbling during the summer was the stumbling of a man who looked like he didn't know where he was trying to fall. Where Cameron had once painted himself as the 'new' Blair, now, with

Brown on the throne, voters wanted nothing to do with any sort of Blair, either old or new. They wanted someone as different from Blair as possible. Old Mr Brown, in fact.

But, like all political pictures, it wasn't entirely black and white. One promising sign of a new depth to the Cameron project had been midwifed by Iain Duncan Smith, whose Social Justice Policy Group published its Breakthrough Britain report in early July. It recommended fiscal incentives for marriage – which Cameron endorsed, to rapture in Tory-leaning newspapers – and, at the same time, Cameron had started to talk more about Britain's 'broken society', and in particular about welfare reforms. Cameron said, during July, that Margaret Thatcher had won her elections because she had the answer to the question of the day, 'How do we fix the broken economy?' whereas now the question was 'How do we fix the broken society?' Here, in tackling deeply entrenched social problems and championing marriage, was the seed of something, something that seemed to be about day-to-day life in Britain in the noughties – something that got people's attention, too. Here was the first tangible evidence of Cameron's pledge in his spring conference speech earlier in the year, to put social revival, as distinct from economic revival, at the heart of Tory policy.

But still, Cameron had been well behind in the polls since Brown's coronation and looked stuck there. And as if this wasn't bad enough, Brown had reached for his collar, checked the label, and stolen his blue shirt. Instead of swerving to the left after his coronation – as most political commentators had predicted – Brown had moved to outflank Cameron on socially conservative issues. Ditching the Manchester super casino, signalling that cannabis was to be reclassified as a Class B drug, making speech after speech espousing the 'British way of life' and the anxieties of 'British workers'. What could Cameron possibly do now? It was apparent to everyone that the Tories had somewhat mishandled Brown's succession, and had ended up looking 'cheap, carping and churlish', at least according to Tim Hames in *The Times*.

Not only was he getting a battering from the press, but during the summer Cameron had even had to brush off a minor leadership challenge – the first formal evidence of internal dissatisfaction with his leadership. At least two MPs – and possibly up to half a dozen – wrote to Sir Michael Spicer, the chairman of the notorious 1922 Committee of Tory backbenchers, to call for a vote of no confidence. As was noted at the time, that nothing came of this initiative says much about Cameron's ability to at least privately control his troops – even if marshalling wayward backbench Tories is like catching frogs.

The sense that Cameron needed to work harder to bring his party with him was compounded by the resignation, the day after the Ealing Southall debacle, of George Bridges, Cameron's campaign director. Bridges said he stood down because he was getting married and did not want to juggle a political position, although it didn't take long to work out that perhaps Bridges was jumping before the ship began to take on water.

When Cameron took over the Conservative Party, hopeful Tories thought they had finally found their Tony Blair, a young, energetic modernizer who would lead them out of the wilderness. But after Ealing, as the *Observer*'s Andrew Rawnsley hinted, some Tories began to worry that he might turn out to be their Neil Kinnock, a leader who did much to rescue and rehabilitate the party, but who couldn't actually deliver power. 'Kinnock saved the Labour party, but his public reputation always suffered once he had been branded as the Welsh Windbag,' wrote Rawnsley. 'Ominously for the Tory leader, the phrase Sham Cam is becoming a headline. If that sticks, this will not be the worst of his troubles, merely the beginning of them.'

And when it came to headlines, in the weeks following Brown's coronation the Tories were finding it really difficult to get their side of things into the media. When Andy Coulson, the former *News of the World* editor who had been hired in the summer as the new Conservative head of communications, phoned the BBC over the weekend before Cameron's Rwanda visit and reminded them that his boss was in Witney visiting constituents caught up in torrential weather, he was told the broadcaster wasn't interested. As, indeed, were none of the papers. For Coulson this was something of a baptism of fire, and it taught him –

immediately – that his team would have to move up a gear and start going on the offensive, rather than simply being reactive.

As summer wore on it seemed Cameron couldn't do anything right. Napoleon is said to have judged a general's practical value by the answer to a single question: 'Is he lucky?' In the case of Cameron it has to be said that he was anything but. Some of it was his own doing, but a lot of his luck was determined by his friend Gordon. Even in PMQs, traditionally a place of some comfort for Cameron, he was coming unstuck. During some of his worst displays, when his salvos failed to find their target, Tory MPs took to texting each other: 'PODWAS', they would write … Poor Old Dave, What A Shame.

Slowly, however, Cameron began to fight back, and tentatively started to acknowledge that, as the Tories had once stood for law and order, so they might again. In July he scored a hit with an article attacking the government's record on crime and promising that the Tories would build more prisons. 'It is amazing what a new Prime Minister can get away with,' he wrote in the *Sunday Telegraph*. 'Due to Gordon Brown's decisions as Chancellor, more than 2,000 prisoners – over 300 of them guilty of violent crimes – have been released from prison before the end of their sentence. The concerns of probation officers have been overruled. Some of those released have already committed new crimes … So I earnestly implore the Prime Minister not just to steal our prison policy, but to implement it. That way, the current crisis will be a short scandal, not a permanent feature of Brown's Britain.'

And a few voices began to challenge the public's endorsement of Brown. 'Any sort of argument that the Brown government has broken with the era of spin is increasingly difficult to sustain,' wrote Matthew d'Ancona in the *Spectator*, before going on to explain that Brown's much-trumpeted creation of a new border force was simply cosmetic rebadging of existing agencies, rather than a substantial new force. D'Ancona went on: 'There have been any number of other examples where announcements made by Mr Brown and his colleagues, which have been trumpeted as breaks with the past, amount to little more than a reheating of Mr Blair's leftovers. This bubble-and-squeak politics can only lead to public disillusion.'

But it was a sign of how bad it had got that even the *Daily Mail*, often Cameron's fiercest critic, had felt it right, in the dark days of late July, to come to his defence: 'The *Mail* has never shrunk from vigorously criticising the Tory leader's mistakes – such as his spectacular own goal over grammar schools and his weakness for empty publicity stunts. But overall, hasn't Mr Cameron worked wonders for the Conservatives in his first 18 months – making them electable again when many had written them off? The party leader's Tory critics should accept that he remains by far their best hope for the foreseeable future.'

Still, by the end of July Cameron's YouGov ratings were getting worse. Asked what they thought of Brown's performance, 22 per cent of those polled said he had exceeded their expectations and only 6 per cent thought he had done worse. Most of those polled – 54 per cent versus 32 per cent – thought he should call a general election to get his own mandate to govern. Brown also scored a clear lead over Cameron on a range of personal attributes, outscoring the Tory leader by 44 per cent to 12 per cent for 'sticking to what he believes in' and by 35 per cent to 8 per cent for being 'strong'. Cameron's only advantage over Brown was that he was seen as being more charismatic, although it was plain to see that – gulp – Cameron obviously wasn't turning out to be as convincing as many had thought he would be. And, more importantly, Brown had surprised everyone. Maybe the dour Scot was a half-decent snake oil salesman after all.

By the beginning of August, Labour were a full eight points clear, and the Brown bounce was lasting a lot longer than anyone had anticipated (it was goodbye Teflon Tony, and hello Gore-Tex Gordon!). Consequently, in August, the Brownites began talking about an early election as a way for Brown to move his boots under the table, as a way to swat Cameron away forever. On 25 July, the day that Cameron returned from Rwanda, the *Guardian* ran the headline 'Tory voters turn against Cameron' – and a call to arms was sent, in the form of a letter, from Ed Balls, one of Brown's closest Cabinet allies, to all Labour MPs: 'This has been the worst week yet for David Cameron.'

The same day Brown attempted to ring-fence the security agenda, stealing a Conservative proposal for a new kind of integrated border agency as well as suggesting that 'detention without charge' be increased to a whopping fifty-six days. The announcement was bold, it was brash, and – as it was impossible to disguise, not that Brown even attempted to do so – totally Conservative in construction. However, Brown's attempts to usurp the Tories came unstuck when it was discovered – after the very slightest scrutiny – that this new element of Britain's counter-terrorism strategy would be weakened because it wouldn't involve the police.

But what was DC going to do now? What line was he going to take, now that Brown was going all out to marginalize him? Perhaps it didn't matter, as Cameron knew he was about to be overtaken by events. The forthcoming election, basically. On 18 August Cameron ordered an emergency election manifesto to be written and warned Tories that they had to be prepared to fight a general election in just three weeks. A leaked memo from the Tory chairman, Caroline Spelman, revealed the true nature of the worries inside Conservative HQ. The memo said that the election 'could be called at any time from the beginning of September … George Osborne has chaired the first meetings of our general election planning team which continues to meet through August. Work has commenced on developing a manifesto.'

They were hardly alone in thinking this, as internally the Labour Party had been primed for an election for several weeks, with advertising campaigns being commissioned and poster sites booked. An autumn election wasn't going to be a surprise to anyone. Martin Salter, a vice-chairman of the Labour Party, was quoted in early August as saying the PM had put them on notice for a poll as early as October. 'I can confirm that the party has been put on alert for an early election that could take place as soon as this autumn.'

If Gordon Brown needed any more encouragement to go for gold it was right there in the *Sunday Times*. On 12 August a YouGov poll put Labour ten points ahead of Cameron's Tories, enough to deliver a landslide election victory with a Commons majority of over 150. 'Politicians take no notice of opinion polls, or so they tell us,' said the leader in that

Sunday's paper. 'The truth is that they pore over them with the intensity of a palaeontologist with a rare find. The bounce in Mr Brown's poll ratings shows he should have nothing to fear by going to the country. We shall see in the next few weeks whether he has the nerve to do so.'

Even in his wildest dreams Brown could not have imagined his first weeks in power would have gone this well. I'd expected to see him engaged in a long-running battle to overcome public suspicion of him as a tax-grabber, what with all those years in the Treasury devising ever more sneaky ways to lift the cash from our wallets and purses. But in fact he appeared regal and self-assured.

From a Labour perspective, the reasons against an early election were few: there was the possibility that Brown could look less impressive under closer inspection, as well as the possibility of the Brown bounce flattening. On the plus side, it would cost the party a lot less to go now, with such a short run-up (in August they were still £25 million in debt) – and with Brown setting the policy agenda, and Cameron riding so low in the polls, what was there to lose? Cameron could bleat all he wanted about the government's paltry record in Afghanistan – where the Tory leader went on a two-day fact-finding mission at the start of August – but it was largely falling on deaf ears.

It really was backs-to-the-wall time for Cameron, and, unless he came up with something to win over the electorate in the next few weeks, he was probably going to go down in history as just one more name in a string of Tory leaders who were seen off by New Labour. Seriously big guns were needed at this point if he wanted to put some dents in Fortress Brown, and they needed to fire off heavy, well-targeted shells in quick succession. So, during August, Cameron took the decision to bring in the heavy artillery: crime, social breakdown and the family – plus strong hints from George Osborne of at least one tax cut and maybe more to come.

On 17 August came a report from the Tory economic policy group, headed by John Redwood. The report called for lower taxation and more deregulation – and Osborne's presence at the launch looked like a broad endorsement of Redwood's tax-cutting ideas. Osborne was playing his hand fairly closely – so no one was 100 per cent sure what it all meant –

but it generated headlines like 'Tories signal tax cuts' and it looked like inheritance tax would be in for a big trim from a Tory government.

Then – miracle of miracles – on 23 August Cameron was awarded a double-page endorsement in the *Sun* after he backed the newspaper's campaign for a crackdown on hoodies and yobs. Echoing the old Sex Pistols anthem, he said there was 'anarchy in the UK', and laid the blame firmly at the feet of the PM. He claimed the country had been left reeling by 'family and social breakdown' under Labour, and called for greater discipline in school and tougher penalties for hooligans. And though some carped that this was a mini lurch to the right, all Cameron was doing was reacting to the appalling crime wave that swept over Britain in the summer of 2007, where gangs and gang culture seemed to have taken over much of our inner cities as well as many of our once idyllic market towns.

The same day, Cameron was on the offensive again, promising a 'bare-knuckle fight' with Brown over threatened hospital cutbacks. He also said he was determined to nullify Labour claims that he was about to lurch to the right with a tax-cutting manifesto, saying that, while he wanted tax cuts in the long run, he would only do so when the country could afford it, repeating a mantra he'd initiated two years previously.

And if that wasn't enough for one day, that same evening he repeated his call for the Human Rights Act to be scrapped, amid mounting anger that the controversial law had allowed Learco Chindamo – the killer of the head teacher Philip Lawrence, who had been murdered outside his school in 1995 – to avoid deportation to Italy. Cameron accused the government of being 'blind' to the Act's weaknesses as it emerged that Chindamo's lawyers had argued that deportation would breach Chindamo's rights to a family life, despite the fact that the Home Office regarded him as a 'genuine and present' risk to the public. In his most explicit remarks yet on the legislation, Cameron said: 'It has to go. Abolish the Human Rights Act and replace it with a British Bill of Rights, which sets out rights and responsibilities.'

Things had changed in the Cameron camp, and having been hauled over the coals by the press during the floods crisis, he wasn't going to stand idly by and watch it happen again. Having promised to fight Brown on the NHS, he was now going on the attack regarding every domestic news story and Labour policy announcement. His approach to the outbreak of foot and mouth in early August was markedly different from his handling of the recent floods and attempted terrorist attacks. It was not just that he postponed his holiday; it was more to do with the fact that he was beginning to be far more aggressive with Brown than he had been with Blair. And with good reason: Cameron soon learned that Brown couldn't take his body punches. Brown, the 'Stromboli of Downing Street' (coined because he was in a state of continuous eruption), simply could not cope with Cameron's relentless sarcasm, or his instant retaliation to any policy announcement. Even for those MPs conditioned to the tricks of oratory, Cameron was something to behold.

But would any of this work?

Cameron's promise to mend our 'broken society' was given more amplification in the aftermath of the 'accidental' killing of eleven-year-old Rhys Jones in Liverpool. Cameron didn't want to be thought of as scoring political points over Rhys's murder, but his messages about mending society were just what a lot of people wanted to hear. Cameron advocated letting police and head teachers go about their jobs without top-down interference, thus strengthening communities. He talked about using the tax system to encourage family life – and, given the choice between family life and gangs of feral youths, most people knew what they preferred. As well as doubling the time an average policeman spent on the beat, he reiterated that he wanted officers freed up so they could be more responsive to local demands ('The whole focus of the police [should be] "how best do I serve the communities" rather than "how do I meet this target from the Home Office?"'). In an attempt to keep the pressure on Brown, and ever mindful of a potential autumn election, he unveiled plans for minimum jail sentences, an extension of stop and search powers for police and, crucially, more prison places and less tolerant attitude towards crime.

Cameron accused the government of being complacent and 'in denial' about gun crime, dismissing as 'feeble' Home Secretary Jacqui

Smith's response to Rhys's killing – which was to propose the setting up of 'drop-off zones' where guns could be handed in anonymously to a third party.

This was indeed a fairly pathetic idea, and it was said that if there had been a nationwide poll based on this initiative alone, Brown and his Cabinet would have left Downing Street that same night. Even the *Sun* ran a leader column backing Cameron's moves: 'Labour promised to be "tough on crime, tough on the causes of crime". The shocking explosion in knife and gun violence suggests they have failed on both counts. Police are drowning in paperwork. Troublemakers are let off with a derisory warning or a meaningless ASBO. Serious offenders get soft sentences and then get out after half time. Now at last the Tories are moving on to vacant ground.' Three days later, the *Daily Mail* – another right-wing paper that had been ambivalent towards Cameron – came out in favour of his zero-tolerance approach to crime, and on 29 August rewarded the Tory leader with a 100 per cent endorsement on its front page – 'CRIME: TORIES FINALLY GET TOUGH'.

That night on television Cameron was asked a question on *Newsnight* about immigration, a subject guaranteed to risk accusations of a 'lurch to the right'. Saying that immigration 'has been too high', he added that it was right to be concerned about the pressure immigration put on schools, hospitals and housing. 'We have put too great a burden on public services and I think it needs to be better controlled,' he said. 'What's required in the whole debate about immigration is a careful use of language but actually some fairly tough and rigorous action.' The *Observer*'s Andrew Rawnsley and others in the press over the next few days claimed that, like many Tory leaders before him Cameron, was trying to win over the public by elaborately drawing an especially grim picture of a country overwhelmed by the criminal immigrant. However, this time it appeared to be working.

But any thoughts that DC may have had about his successful realignment of the party in light of Brown's unprecedented bounce were temporarily forgotten when the *Daily Telegraph* published the results of its YouGov poll on 31 August (never had a polling company had so much business). The survey showed Labour maintaining an eight-point lead over the Tories as Brown entered his third month as Prime Minister. Despite Conservative hopes that David Cameron would be able to gain ground once Brown took over as leader, the poll put Labour on 41 per cent (unchanged since July) with the Tories on 33 per cent (up one point). The Liberal democrats were down two points on 14 per cent (not that anyone was really paying any attention). If replicated at a general election, the results would have given Brown a Commons majority of more than 100 – up from the 69 he already had. Even though the Prime Minister was refusing to offer the British public a referendum on the EU Constitutional Treaty (implication: referenda are for wimps), the public didn't appear to be that bothered.

But still, the signs were that there was still plenty of life in Project Cameron. On *Newsnight*, prior to his remarks on immigration, Cameron found himself being taken to task by Stephanie Flanders, the show's economics editor and an unmarried mother. She asked him, curtly, if the Conservative Party would prefer it if she were married. Even the dispassionate agreed that he gave an extremely good account of himself. Cameron won the argument, and made Flanders – and by dint of the attack, the rest of the *Newsnight* team – look rather silly.

But Brown – whose advisers were igniting election fever – stole back the spotlight in the early days of September with a pledge for a more inclusive form of government that would include Conservatives within it and take heed of Tory concerns. And on 3 September, in a bid to destabilize Cameron, and to show he meant what he said about a 'new type of politics', he appointed two Tory MPs (Patrick Mercer and John Bercow) as government advisers.

Things were moving quickly. A Populus poll for *The Times* on 4 September put Labour on 37 per cent and the Conservatives on 36 per cent (with the paper announcing 'Brown Bounce Wanes Under Cameron Attacks' and 'Times Poll Puts Tories Ahead in Key Marginals'), yet still the impression within the Labour Party was that they were going to the polls in early November.

Later that month Brown offered an even bigger olive branch to the Tory faithful by not only labelling himself a conviction politician, 'like Lady Thatcher', but also by inviting her – with great fanfare – to Downing Street.

Who said spin was dead? On 13 September, in a PR stunt worthy of his predecessor, Brown welcomed Baroness Thatcher to Downing Street for tea (and photographs). This was a deft move, and, although it irritated many on the hard left (there was a constant dialogue at the offices of the *Daily Mirror* concerning what they should do in the event of Thatcher's death – some on the paper still thought the head-lines on the front of the paper should quote the venomous anti-Thatcher song written by Elvis Costello, 'Tramp The Dirt Down'), it played well in much of the country, especially among those who had prospered under the Tories in the eighties. (If it was a strange sight seeing Brown and Thatcher behaving like old chums, then Cameron's own relationship with the former Tory leader had been pretty surreal, too. In December 2005, immediately after he became leader, Cameron found himself at a party with the baroness. When Cameron was presented to Mrs Thatcher, she assumed he was a young candidate in search of a seat. When told of her mistake she looked rather mystified, compounding Cameron's embarrassment by expressing astonishment that any Conservative leader would elect to wear an open-necked shirt.)

In the second week of September I had dinner with the editor of a national broadsheet, the editor of a Sunday broadsheet and the former editor of a tabloid, and not one of them thought that Cameron had a hope in hell.

'He is fucked,' said one. 'Double fucked,' said another. 'Fucked squared,' said the last.

And while a *Sunday Times* YouGov poll on 16 September suggested that Labour's lead was on the slide, an ICM poll published in the *Guardian* on the nineteenth happily said that David Cameron was Britain's least popular party leader, liked less than Gordon Brown or Menzies Campbell. Not only that, the paper suggested that Cameron's efforts to revive Tory fortunes were suffering in the face of recovering respect for Labour's current administration.

It looked as though Labour were going to go for it, to call the election. All the junior ministers were pushing for it, as were the Labour stalwarts in the press. Crucially, on Wednesday 19 September, Brown took advice from various Labour MPs in marginal constituencies, hoping to get a feel for the expected levels of success, should he choose to do it.

Election fever was at boiling point throughout the Labour conference in Bournemouth, held in the last week of September. It was the Gordon Brown Show – the new Prime Minister had airbrushed Tony Blair from history and barely mentioned him – and four out of five ministers were predicting a snap election. Labour were a healthy eleven points clear in the polls, which was almost a mandate in itself.

Could Cameron do anything but die a swift and brutal death? The cover of the *Spectator* in the week before the Tory conference in Blackpool pictured the Tory leader on a horse with a noose around his neck. The cover line? 'GET OUT OF THIS DAVE'. Presciently, Fraser Nelson's piece inside bore the headline, 'This will be Cameron's finest hour – or the scene of a lynching'.

And, boy, was he right.

That week's leader column said the following: 'Two years ago, Mr Cameron won the Tory leadership in Blackpool with a speech of panache, sincerity and courage. Now, in the same seaside resort, he must dig even deeper to show that he deserves to be Prime Minister; that he is, truly, made of the right stuff.'

And a few days later he proved, once and for all, that he was. Three days before that momentous speech, I asked him a few questions.

Character, ideology and vision

What, in a sentence, should be a prime minister's first goal?
To keep the country safe.

You told the *Sunday Times* that 'character is far more important than policy' ... You also said, in the same interview, that you distrust people with 'too much of a mission'. Do you still stand by those statements?

Absolutely. To address the character point, whatever you put in your manifesto, and they're absolutely vital documents because they give people the best possible guidance as to what you're going to do, in the end the real test of being a prime minister, or a president or a cabinet minister, is how you will respond to the difficult crises that are put in front of you. That is when character and your reaction come to the fore. Can you build a good team, can you listen to people, do you think before making decisions, do you basically understand the instincts of those you're trying to govern? That's all about character, and in the end I think that's more important than any one particular policy.

And people on a mission?

What I meant by that is I have a fear of people who are so messianic about one particular goal that nothing's going to get in their way. In the end, being an effective government or being a good prime minister is about making the right judgements. And I want to know that the person making those judgements is balanced, and I'd rather be governed by someone who understands the importance of making balanced judgements and getting to the right decision rather than someone who was driven by some sort of messianic cause.

In 1903, former Liberal Prime Minister Lord Rosebery described his party as a 'caterpillar in search of a leaf' – in other words, searching for a policy that would attract public support. I remember seeing Mariella Frostrup on *Question Time* not so long ago talking about political commitment, saying that in days gone by someone decided what policies they liked, and then tried to get elected ... and that these days it happens the other way round. Would it be fair to say that this Trojan horse sensibility was used by yourself to try and make the Tories electable again?

I don't think that's true at all. Here policy is driven by principle and what we want to do and what we believe in, rather than, let's listen to the focus group and look at the polling or whatever. Everything we're saying now – it was all set out in the speeches I made in the summer of 2005, in the leadership contest. There were no focus groups then, no polling – it was just me and a handful of supporters, and in those speeches I was just setting out what I believe. And that's the foundation we've been building on ever since. Of course you know what you want to do and you want then to work out how best to explain it, as it's important to use language that people understand. But I don't ask people what I should do; I know what I want to do. I think it may have been true with New Labour, who knew that all the things that the Labour Party had wanted to do in the past – nationalize industry, give power to the trade unions, put up your taxes, get out of NATO – they knew all those things were unpopular so they had to completely change what they believed, and I think they were very marketing driven. I really don't think the Conservative Party is.

In terms of ideology, you can appear to be fluid. I recall one question you were asked about conflicts with previous Tory policy and you said, and I quote, 'In elections, you fight as a team and you win or lose as a team. When you lose, as we did in 2005, then you learn as a team.' How would you describe your ideology?
Giving people more power and control over their lives. Trusting people rather than big government. All else follows from there.

Tell us a piece of wisdom to live by.
Learn from your mistakes.

When a party is in opposition, they perhaps are more inclined to align themselves with the mass. Are you a man of the people?
I think that's a rather presumptuous thing to describe yourself. I hope I'm a man who people will get to know and vote for and support. But the idea of me trying to describe myself as a man with a hard-luck story is pretty ridiculous.

What have been your three, say, biggest mistakes?
Since becoming leader of the party, well obviously I regret that my government driver took some of my papers home while I was on my bike. I regret that. It only happened a few times but I suspect I will be reminded about that for a few years to come. Sometimes I've put off making decisions that maybe I should have taken earlier … But I'm not sure I've done anything too terrible.

Armando Iannucci says that he originally wrote a scene in *The Thick Of It* where a minister decides it would look better walking to the House of Commons instead of taking a car, although his civil servants say that his dispatch boxes would have to follow in a car. Iannucci says he didn't use it because it sounded so silly. And then you did it … Anyway, in terms of the working class, there is a world of difference between the Robert Frank photographs of Welsh miners of the 1950s and the post-industrial landscape of the twenty-first century. But still the message persists that the Labour Party is for the workers, and the Tory Party is for the owners. Considering that after the 1997 election there were suddenly no Tory MPs in Scotland, Wales, Manchester, Liverpool or Newcastle, what message are you sending out to traditional working-class families in order for them to switch their vote?
I think there are two vital things that the Conservative Party have that should appeal to people right across the board but particularly to people who think of themselves as hard working. Firstly, we believe in giving you more control and power over your life. Just as Thatcher said own your council house, so we should be saying have more choice over the school your kids go to or the hospital you get treated at, or own shares in the firm you work for. There is still that aspirational side to us, because we're on the side of striving people. That is a very important part of the Conservative Party. The second thing is a very clear set of values, understanding that society is built from the bottom up, it's about individuals and families and neighbourhood organizations and we want to strengthen those ties that bind, that help families and help couples. And I think that is a very appealing idea for people of all backgrounds, classes,

ages, races, and all the rest of it. I think everybody knows that families are such an important thing.

What would you most like to be remembered for?
Making the country stronger and improving people's quality of life. In the end, if you put yourself up to be Prime Minister you want to do the job and at the end of it people look back and say you took good decisions to make this a better, stronger country to live in.

What conviction has stayed with you the longest?
That in the end if you trust people to make the right decisions they do so. That's what makes me a Conservative, the belief in people rather than big government. That's what made me a Conservative and hopefully what will make me a good prime minister.

Do you have a favourite philosopher?
I read a lot when I was studying it but I haven't so much recently. I like the sort of sceptical British philosophers because I think a healthy dose of scepticism is both important in life and important as a Conservative. Because we are sceptical of great utopian schemes and great plans. My favourite political quote, which I came across again the other day, and thought that is brilliant, is by Disraeli: he said the Conservative Party should be the party of change but change that goes along with the customs and manners and traditions and sentiments of the people rather than change according to some grand plan. That so sums up why the Conservative Party succeeded over the years, and what I think a Conservative government ought to do. And it is so much about what Labour is not about, because they just don't get the importance of change that goes with the grain of human nature.

Which are you instinctively – a conformist or a rebel?
I don't like the word conformist but I'm not a rebel. I think this is a great country, I think we've got great institutions, I think there are some that need reform and shaking up, but I wouldn't describe myself as a rebel.

What's the most left-wing thing you have ever done?
That's a very good question. I voted to abolish the blasphemy laws, so I suppose that's taking down a tradition. But that's not left-wing.

You've been described as calculating and feline. Are you?
I think I'm canine rather than feline. I like company, I like people, and that is much more dog-like than cat-like. And I'm more of a dog lover than a cat lover. Calculating? All politicians calculate. You think before you stand for a leadership election, you calculate about whether you have a prospect of winning. But calculating in that cold sense? I hope not. My style in the Shadow Cabinet is more like a chairman rather than chief operating officer. And I enjoy the success of others. I enjoy devolving power. I think calculating implies just sitting there permanently worrying about someone coming to take away your job. I don't.

You've also been described as a cautious man. Are you?
Well, I'm a mixture of sometimes being quite radical and wanting changes, and on the other hand being cautious and thoughtful about how to bring it about. I don't see how anyone who stands up and makes a speech for an hour without a note and insists the Conservative Party select more women could be described as cautious.

People have said you seem a bit pleased with yourself. Is that true?
I'm aware that people have said it. I hope not. The fact that I'm basically an optimistic and happy person who enjoys life and friends and family, and the fact that I'm relatively contented, I'm sure to some people that can sometimes look complacent. But I'm not like that at all because there are lots of thing I want to do in government.

What is your greatest fear?
Failure.

What is your greatest hope?
To do a good job, and to be able to think afterwards that I've achieved something worthwhile, and had a happy life at the same time.

What is your greatest regret?
That you only have one life, really. I sometimes think it would be lovely to work overseas, or have done this or that. But I don't look back and think, if only …

How have your ambitions changed since becoming leader?
I think they're beginning to get more specific, in that the challenge in becoming leader of the Conservative Party was to get us to a position where we could challenge for government. And I think my ambition now is much more about really thinking through the things that I would like to achieve in government, and the more I think about it the more education becomes the thing that I really care about. The state of some of our schools is so far from what it should be. We're never going to achieve all the things people want for the country, whether that's in terms of the economy, or giving people the opportunity to get on in life or whatever, unless we are seriously radical in reforming our school system. You have to have a very clear idea of what you want to do early on in government and I think in education we've got some really exciting ideas.

Describe yourself in three words.
Optimistic. An optimistic person who works hard and loves his family and his country. That's more than three words but it will have to do.

There are politicians who reinvent themselves, and politicians that come fully formed. Which sort are you?
I don't think reinvent, but I believe politicians develop. And I think the best thing to do is to have a set of principles and beliefs that drive you but to think and argue and develop and not get yourself stuck in so much of a rut that you can't develop your thinking. Samantha was telling me this last night, that when she talked to her bank manager when she first set

up her business, the bank manager said we love women who set up businesses because, if it doesn't work, you develop the business plan, you develop the model, you think afresh. He said the problem with men is that they have an idea and they just keep driving it, and it doesn't matter if it's the wrong idea, until they go bankrupt. I think the best politicians are the ones with clear principles who are pragmatic.

Stress

You stand up to criticism well, that's obvious, and you appear to be fairly stoic in the face of some fairly serious media attacks. You don't seem in the least bit surprised by this. What has surprised you about being leader? Bono once said that having gone backstage and seen the laundry room and all the wires that are sticking out of the back, he realized that politics was a lot like sausage making, and that if you knew what went into it, you wouldn't eat the damn thing.

That's true, it can be an exceptionally duplicitous and cynical world to live and work in. But I do believe that most people who go into politics go into it for the right reasons. I certainly did. Unless you think you can genuinely make a difference then there is absolutely no point continuing. And I firmly believe that. But there is a different backstage, too, where you see incredible drive and passion. When you go to a by-election, or a conference, or a fundraiser or any sort of party event, you see so many people working so hard. I do have a sense of responsibility to do my best for them and the cause we all believe in. I sort of knew what the job involved, the different bits. I was surprised that you had to do a lot more fundraising than I thought, and that is quite a big thing. I think I knew what the job involved, managing the party, making speeches, developing policies, attacking the government, campaigning, dealing with people, going on the telly. I knew what being Leader of the Opposition involved, but I didn't know how I would feel about doing them all and whether I would be able to manage all the balls in the air. But I can. And I will. Until we get rid of this government.

On a fundamental level it must be extremely tiring, both physically and mentally …

But manageable. I wake up in the morning and think this is okay, I can do all of this. It is sometimes quite unrelenting and you get to Wednesday and it's PMQs, followed by a statement to Parliament and you get through that, and then you think it's Thursday and then I have to do this speech and then it's Friday and I have to do this thing and on it goes. And if this is what it is like as the Leader of the Opposition then becoming Prime Minister – it is another massive step up. But you never really know until you do it.

You mentioned Samantha having good instincts – and not like those of a politician. What are your instincts like? What's your judgement like? Have you always chosen the right people to work for you?

I like to think that they are pretty good, but there are times when I look back and think if only I had trusted my original instinct. I think you should always trust your gut feelings about everything. We probably all feel that and think, of course I knew all along. Generally I am pleased with my instinctive reactions with people. Quite a lot of people who work for me I have known for a while. Steve Hilton I have known for quite a long time. You know how you work together. And if you look at our Shadow Cabinet, it beats the pants off the Labour Cabinet. Nancy Cameron could handle the economy better than Alistair Darling.

When you're choosing candidates, looking through a list of people who might be good to stand, it's a lot like publishing books. Yes, you'd like a good one to make themselves available, but to be brutal you're simply choosing the least awful one you can find. Because they're not all cherries, are they?

Yes, but the difference is that if you publish a book that doesn't work out that is not the end of the publisher's world. In politics you are judged by your decisions, so you have to get them right. I think I am a reasonable judge of those things.

You have to be on your guard all the time, surely. You have to watch your back ... Someone once interviewed an ex-Cabinet minister who said, when you're at school there tend to be approximately three groups of people – some are just obnoxious; some are clever and quite able; but most are just dull and wait till it's over. He said that when he joined the Cabinet, the distribution was exactly the same. Do you have to watch your back?

I generally tend to have an open style, and [if] people like David Davis, Caroline Spelman, Andy Coulson or George Osborne or Michael Gove or indeed anyone wants to come in and talk something over, then that's fine. I like to have a chairmanship role, to behave more like a chairman. I am a great believer in hiring good people because you trust them. I'm very inclusive – I will chair a meeting and listen to views and then make a decision rather than steamrollering it through. And that is where good judgement comes in; you appoint good people, and trust their decisions, but you have to know when to step in. William Hague has really helped me, because he made all the mistakes the first time around. And I don't say that lightly, as he says it himself. He really has been enormously helpful.

The Shadow Cabinet

How ruthless are you? I would hope you're exceptionally ruthless. You have to be, don't you?

I don't think it is a natural character trait of mine, but yes of course you have to be ruthless. A while ago in a Shadow Cabinet reshuffle I had to lose an old personal friend, but I thought it was the right thing to do. And you just have to keep thinking, am I doing the right thing? And if you think you are, then you have to get on and do it. So, yes, I think I could do that awful job as PM of firing people. I will probably have to fire many friends.

I've fired enough people to know that I should have got rid of most of them sooner. You usually have a gut instinct about someone, especially when you arrive at a job, and whenever I've given someone the benefit

of the doubt, I've always been proved wrong. I don't have to bawl people out very often, but when I do, one of my favourites is: 'When my boss says, "Jump," I say, "How high?" – and that's what I expect from you. You don't like it, you get out. Now.' But of course legislation makes the process of getting rid of someone extremely drawn-out these days, sometimes impossibly ... But in politics you have to be circumspect because people never really leave, do they?

You're right, and politics is slightly different in that respect. When someone has to leave the Shadow Cabinet, for whatever reason, they are normally an MP and part of your team, so you are not saying goodbye to them completely. In other walks of life they are gone and that's that and you wish them the best for the future.

Or not.

Or not, but in politics you always have to tread more carefully because you might need to work with this person again in the future, and you're often left with an MP who is still part of the team. I've seen it happen time and time again.

In Alastair Campbell's diary there is quite a lot of stuff at the beginning of the book about Blair getting used to the idea, or not, of moving people around. He seems to have found it quite difficult moving people in and out of the Shadow Cabinet. Obviously it's difficult putting all these pieces of the jigsaw together, but he appears to have wanted to be consensual about the whole thing, or at least in the early days anyway, before he became presidential. Campbell says, 'I'd only ever seen reshuffles from the media side of the fence, and could never understand why they always took so long. Surely the PM or the Leader of the Opposition just did the list and told people what was what. Er no. First he had to decide what HE wanted. Then he had to find out whether that is what THEY would be prepared to do. And he had to get buy-in from the other big beasts, and if anyone said no to something, or started to negotiate, it was back to the drawing board ...'

He wasn't tough enough with his team. They kept saying, I am sorry I am not going to accept this, I don't want to go. Well, I'm sorry but in my position when I want someone to go I simply tell them, and then that's that. You have to be tough about it. You can't get into a negotiation or anything ridiculous like that. I think that Blair was very dictatorial over other things. You must get people into the places that they should be in. If you really think you have thought through their abilities and have put them in the right job then you need to be firm and not let them negotiate their ways into other things, and then having done that you have to trust their judgement. That is the way I like to do it.

Sell me your Shadow Cabinet. What's so brilliant about it?
Our Cabinet is so much stronger than theirs. David Davis [Shadow Home Secretary] is quite clearly so much stronger than Jacqui Smith. Or look at Liam Fox [Shadow Secretary of State] against Des Browne. There's just no comparison. Andrew Lansley knows more about the NHS and how it works than any Labour Health Secretary. Michael Gove [Shadow Secretary of State for Children, Schools and Families], a very bright guy with two kids, is clearly the right guy for that job. Up against Ed Balls. Balls has an incredibly high opinion of himself but he really isn't as good as he thinks he is. Not by a long chalk. Party chairman Caroline Spelman is clearly the best woman for that job. George Osborne is a better Chancellor than the tragic figure who is performing the same role for the Labour Party. William Hague is one of the most dedicated, most intelligent and one of the most experienced politicians in Parliament. Every member of the Shadow Cabinet has something to offer, and I would put any of them up against their opposite number in a flash.

Are you tough enough to beat Gordon Brown?
Of course, the whole team is. It's going to be an incredibly interesting autumn, and we're going to fight the government with everything we have. I think we've actually shown that we're tough enough to beat him.

FIVE

'I love you, David Cameron!'

**'Hollywood black tie', Mr Bean, the election that never was,
twenty-four-hour drinking, social responsibility,
stop and search**

Trying to control the press at the party conferences is like herding cats, and the Conservative Party's 2007 conference, which began on 30 September, was certainly no different. Although the press spent most of their time looking for stories where there weren't any, one real story was the non-appearance of Arnold Schwarzenegger (the erstwhile star guest, unavoidably detained but strangely available via satellite), and the very public appearance of the mayor of New York, Michael Bloomberg, accompanied by deputies, aides and a phalanx of press principals. Having flown in by private jet from a city where Nicolas Sarkozy was more famous than Gordon Brown, a place where the new British PM was as invisible as Angela Merkel, landing in Blackpool gave the Bloomberg posse a real taste of the fervent nature of British politics before an election.

Here was David Cameron, unflappable and focused, concerned with what everyone knew would be the defining moment of his career (one way or another), hunkering down and surrounding himself with his able-bodied army of big brains and eager beauties (why is it that the Conservatives always have the most attractive administrative aides?).

Here he was, sleeping in a bed once used by Churchill, and – judging by the service standards at the Imperial Hotel – probably in the same sheets.

And to witness the world that Blair and Brown built (kick-started by the Tories), they only had to step outside to see not only the rows of B&Bs full of unfortunates living on benefits, but also the rank and file of hen-party revellers, dressed up and ready to drink their bodyweight in cheap imported lager. 'I saw a gang of extremely drunk doctors last night as we went to get on the Ferris wheel,' said one Bloombergian as we waited in the lobby. 'And you know what? I don't think they were real doctors.'

The most remarkable thing about the conference was the almost palpable sense of companionship, as though everyone in the Imperial Hotel – in fact every Tory in Blackpool – had decided that this year – for one year only! – they were all going to pull together, sing from the same hymn sheet and act as though they all liked one another. It was astonishing, and the air was full of optimism.

The contrast between the mood in the conference and the gloomy press headlines could not have been greater. On the first day of the conference, the *Observer* carried the headline 'Cameron in meltdown as public urge early vote', giving Labour a seven-point lead in an Ipsos MORI poll. The *Sunday Times*, though, praised the Tory leader for telling Brown to 'quit stalling and call an election'.

Not only did William Hague's opening speech rally the troops, in his address the next day Shadow Chancellor George Osborne drew a rapturous response from the Tory faithful when he announced that under the Conservatives the burden of inheritance tax would be reduced by raising the death duty threshold to £1 million. It was a brilliant initiative that understandably played incredibly well, maybe even better than expected. On the same day, the fashion designer Vivienne Westwood said she was going to vote Tory at the next election. 'I've never voted Tory in my life,' she said in Paris. 'But I would do anything to get this bad lot out.' Elsewhere Michael Gove promised 'pioneer schools' based on the successful Swedish model, allowing teachers and parents to set up their own schools; and David Davis pledged a New York-style zero tolerance strategy towards crime.

And then on the last day of the conference, just a day after Gordon Brown had given his strongest hints yet that he was about to announce a 1 November election, Cameron made the biggest speech of his life, bigger even than his 2005 party-winning address. It was billed as a make-or-break speech and that's exactly what it was. To growing applause, the Conservative leader declared: 'Call that election. We will fight. Britain will win.' As Steve Richards pointed out in the *Independent*, it was a sign of the success of his party's conference that in the heady atmosphere that surrounded his speech the declaration of war sounded more than credible. Speaking for over an hour, with only a few scribbled notes on a nearby table, he delivered his message with style, and proved calm under fire. Even the *Guardian* called it a virtuoso speech.

Two days later Cameron was rewarded by an eight-point bounce, making the Conservatives level with Labour on 38 per cent, even though there was still wild speculation that Brown was going to call the election the following Tuesday. Nearly every political analyst and journalist was convinced it was going to happen. After all, why would Brown call it off? He couldn't lose.

But lose is exactly what he did. Every British newspaper on Sunday 7 October carried the same news: Brown had bottled it, and was now not going to call an election. Having studied Labour's private focus group research and opinion polls, he thought it was simply too risky to call it, hinting strongly that he wouldn't do so until 2010, or 2009 at the very earliest. At noon on Saturday Brown had summoned Andrew Marr to Downing Street to try and explain his bizarre decision, using the line that he wanted to get his 'own programme of reforms under way before going to the country'. Disingenuously, he said his decision had nothing to do with the polls, even pointing to problems with the electoral register, suggesting that because over a million voters were not currently listed, an election would have been unfair.

Brown told Andrew Marr, who conducted the interview for broadcast the following morning, 'I'll not be calling an election and let me explain why. I have a vision for change in Britain. I want to show people how in government we are implementing it. Over the summer months we have had to deal with crises. We have had to deal with foot and mouth, terrorism, floods, the financial crisis. And, yes, we could have had an election on competence and I hope people would have understood that we have acted competently. But what I want to do is show people the vision that we have for the future of our country: in housing, health, education. And I want the chance in the next phase of my premiership to develop and show people the policies that will make a huge difference and show the change in the country itself.'

And then Brown's world collapsed. The following week, three opinion polls put his party between three and six points behind the Tories, and the press were united in their condemnation of his decision. If he had called the election, he probably would have won. But not only did he encourage the press – and therefore the public – to believe that he was moving towards an election, he then went on national television and lied about his reasons for not doing so.

'British politics has only very rarely been the scene of such an astonishing turnaround in fortunes as we have witnessed in the last seven days,' said Peter Oborne in the *Daily Mail* on 8 October. 'This time last week, conventional wisdom held that David Cameron was almost finished. Labour enjoyed an eleven-point lead in the opinion polls. Gordon Brown seemed on the verge of calling a general election that would annihilate the Conservative Party and destroy David Cameron for good. Today the story is utterly different. After a week of drama and remarkable moral courage it is Cameron who is in the ascendant, while Brown looks weak, indecisive and in trouble.'

In a matter of days this became the biggest political turnaround in public opinion since the Falklands War in 1982. Then, with Margaret Thatcher's administration having been in power for three years, the economy was in trouble, there was mass unemployment, and urban riots were dominating the evening news. Yet victory in the Falklands dramatically improved the Conservative government's popularity, and they went into the 1983 election 13 per cent ahead of Labour. The shift in public opinion since Brown's TV appearance was no less dramatic. His pitch on arriving in Downing Street was that he was strong, statesman-like and decisive. The reality was that, in the time it takes to collate an opinion poll, Brown looked weak, petty and 'dithery'.

At a press conference on Tuesday 9 October the PM said he would have won an election, had he run. Yet the cameras picked up his hand-written notes reminding himself of what he wanted to say: 'considered election', 'could have won', 'first instinct set out vision and delay', 'wanted time' and – most importantly of all – 'not the polls'. But despite his rehearsed excuses, it was clear that it was the fear of losing – and the possibility of a hung parliament – which had led him to duck out.

He had bottled it.

For those who chose to remember, this reminded them of the non-election of 1978, when Prime Minister James Callaghan had allowed various 'authoritative leaks' – suggesting he was about to call an election – to find their way onto the front page of every Fleet Street paper. When Callaghan denied contemplating an election, he lost the support of both the unions and the public, and with the country in disarray due to his inability to control public services, lost the election he was forced to call the following May. This was hubris writ large, as it was for Brown.

Following the fiasco of Brown's non-election, the polls swung so far so quickly that three weeks before Christmas there were already whispers about the likelihood of David Miliband, Alan Johnson or even Jack Straw rather than Gordon Brown fighting the next election. Brown had only been in power for five months and already there was gossip about succession. Suddenly, kite-flying was back in fashion.

There were plenty of advisers who let it be known that they had 'suggested' to the Clunking Fist that an election would be unnecessary, but then as more than one commentator pointed out, advice after injury was like medicine after death. And in the polls, Brown was dead.

How Alistair Beaton's satire rang true. In January 2007 the BBC had broadcast *The Trial of Tony Blair*, a comedy set in 2010, just after Blair had finally stepped down, and just before he was about to be prosecuted for war crimes. The programme hit a nerve, and as it was being endlessly repeated on what seemed like every digital channel, everyone in the Commons was still talking about it – especially now. In one scene Robert Lindsay, playing Blair with unerring accuracy, mocks Brown for putting off a general election until the last possible moment. 'He's scared. Yes, Gordon scared … Honestly. That man has got all the daring of a church mouse.'

And then everything started going wrong for the PM. Cameron continued battering him in the Commons; in his pre-Budget report Chancellor Alistair Darling was accused of stealing Tory policies regarding inheritance tax, non-domicile tax and air passenger duty; then Andy Burnham, the Chief Secretary to the Treasury, was fingered for stealing the Tories' policy on tax breaks for married couples; Brown was personally attacked by Tony Blair for being 'empty'; Irwin Stelzer suggested that the *Sun* might dump Brown in favour of Cameron; ministers were forced to apologize after revealing that 300,000 more foreign nationals – equivalent to the population of, say, Coventry – were working here than previously thought; a Labour donor was found to be giving money via third parties; the details of twenty-five million British citizens went missing when a computer disk was lost in the post; the Northern Rock Building Society crisis continued to dog the government; and everyone with access to a pen or a computer lambasted the PM for signing away our rights with the dreaded EU treaty (Brown wasn't interested in a referendum – as far as he was concerned we were going in). On 5 December even the *New York Times* weighed in with a piece detailing how Brown's government had lurched from crisis to crisis.

By the middle of October the Conservatives were enjoying their best poll results since 1992.

As if this weren't enough, the year ended with Brown's Lord Chancellor and Justice Secretary Jack Straw admitting that Cameron's 'messages have been resonating' with voters. 'Politics is about change and governments, if they want to stay in government, have to adapt to changing circumstances.'

And circumstances were changing all the time. Ten days before the end of the year I found myself at the birthday parties of two national newspaper editors. At both events Cameron was discussed at length, and on each occasion he was honoured with a new soubriquet: 'Britain's next Prime Minister'.

* * *

If anyone needed any further examples of how far the fortunes of the Tories had come since David Cameron became leader, all they needed to do was to have a peek at the committee for the party's annual fundraising knees-up, the Black & White Ball. Whereas in the past these sort of events would have been peopled by the likes of Jim Davidson, Gary Numan and the sort of no-marks who read the weather on TV channels that end in an exclamation mark, the 2008 extravaganza had the following on the committee: TV frock doctor Trinny Woodall, celebrity chef Tom Aikens, sandwich king Julian Metcalfe, trendy architect John Pawson, handbag queen Anya Hindmarch – who chaired the committee as well as organizing the event – film director Matthew Vaughn and model Saffron Aldridge. This was no approximation of Cool Britannia, and these people had not been invited to meet the party leader in order simply to generate photo opportunities; they were involved because they were committed to the cause.

In certain celebrity circles, admitting you were a Tory would once have been social suicide. But not in 2008. Kirstie Allsopp, the co-presenter of the Channel 4 property hit *Location, Location, Location*, said, that February, 'Tories like me had kind of got used to the isolating experience that voting Conservative entailed. In my own small way, as the girl who never wore 501s or Dr Martens, it was my little act of rebellion.' But in 2008 there was nothing rebellious about it. Being Tory in 2008 was less to do with being staunch and more about embracing choice; less about the past, all about the future.

The ball took place on 6 February, in a huge temporary construction in the middle of Battersea Park, south London. There was champagne (good champagne), designer food (proper designer food – none of your mass-catering rubbish), a silent auction (so much cooler than the real thing), and a guest list of the glamorous and the notable, the great and the good, and the sort of bold-face celebs who rebel against nothing but personal discomfort: lounge lizard and Roxy Music frontman Bryan Ferry, former Formula One boss Eddie Jordan, Viscount Linley, the hotel and gambling magnate Sol Kerzner, leather designer Bill Amberg, Cartier bigwig Arnaud Bamberger, *Top Gear*'s Jeremy Clarkson, Condé Nast vice-president Nicholas Coleridge, *Spectator* editor Matthew d'Ancona, concierge service maverick Ben Elliot, fashion entrepreneur Joseph Ettedgui, Lady Helen Taylor, Giorgio Armani PR Victoria Gooder, socialite-turned-activist Jemima Khan, the Earl of March, Pink Floyd's Nick Mason, *Vanity Fair* contributing editor Kate Reardon, Sir Tim Rice, crystal queen Nadja Swarovski-Adams and fashion designer Amanda Wakeley. As far as David Cameron was concerned, this wasn't so much a guest list as a statement of intent. Men wore 'Hollywood Black Tie' (i.e. lazy black tie, or wearing anything you like), women wore rocks, and the paparazzi pictures filled the pages of *Hello!*, *OK!* and *Heat*. Cameron's speech that night was not vintage – the corners of the room were difficult to reach, and there was a sense that he was preaching to the converted – but it worked, and by the time he'd finished every woman was nodding metronomically, as though they were all sitting on the rear shelf of an old Mondeo. Since becoming leader Cameron had occasionally had a problem with women, who could find him smug, but tonight any trace of smugness had evaporated, replaced by genuine concern, and genuine passion. 'Do you know what?' Cameron said towards the end of the evening, 'I can feel it all coming together ...'

Three weeks later and David Cameron was standing in the Camargue Room in the Great Victoria Hotel in the centre of Bradford, chairing a meeting of the Shadow Cabinet. Cameron was targeting the North, where Tory voters had been thin on the ground for a decade, and was taking the Shadow Cabinet on a tour to get their faces known and to meet community leaders. That morning Barack Obama had been all over the papers, revelling in winning yet another state in the presidential primaries, Sir Terry Leahy, Tesco's chief executive was calling on Gordon Brown to introduce new laws to ban the sale of cut-price alcohol amid growing concern over the level of drink-fuelled crime and disorder, and the local papers were full of the police search for Shannon Matthews, the nine-year-old girl who had gone missing on her way home from school in Dewsbury, West Yorkshire, two days earlier. Ever since 1997 the north of the country had been an issue for the Tories, and so far since Christmas Cameron had been to the area three times, to add to the seven times he'd visited in 2007. After the meeting it was lunch at the 'world famous' Mumtaz Indian restaurant on Great Horton Road, for some karahi chicken masala, aloo paratha and vegetable pakora with Sayeeda Warsi, the Shadow Minister for Community Cohesion and Social Action who famously participated in the successful mission to the Sudan to secure the release of the British teacher Gillian Gibbons in December 2007. The previous evening, at another, less celebrated Indian restaurant, the Shadow Cabinet had enjoyed a Cobra-fuelled dinner, but the Mumtaz was famously dry, which is why Sayeeda had chosen it. 'It's a rare example of someone taking account of their community,' she said, encouraging Cameron to put down his mobile (he was desperately trying to get in touch with his wife Samantha, who was about to touch down after flying in from South Africa) and try everything on the table. 'The atmosphere would be totally different if everyone was drinking. It's quiet, you can bring children here, no one is fighting … This is a vibrant part of the country and we need to articulate that, need to attract business here, and make sure that Bradford doesn't just turn into a satellite of Leeds. There is a lot of work to do here.'

Having dropped Sayeeda off at the railway station – she was due down in London to receive an award – we drove across town to Mary Seacole Court, a refuge for Afro-Caribbean elders, where Cameron was to chair a discussion on forced marriages with twenty Asian women, a representative from the Vulnerable Persons department from West Yorkshire police, representatives from the Anah Project (which provided support for Asian women who had become the victims of domestic abuse), Jasvinder Sanghera (author of a book detailing her own experience of a forced marriage) and Theresa May, Shadow Leader of the House of Commons and Shadow Minister for Women. Then it was back to the Great Victoria for more media interviews, with Cameron eagerly offering tea and coffee to the local journalists. At one point he stood staring forlornly at a tray of chocolate brownies, before being told by his press secretary, Gabby Bertin, to leave them alone. 'It's become Gabby's job to watch my calorific intake,' smiled Cameron. 'She's regularly on bun watch.'

Cameron's interviews that afternoon contained much of the information he'd gleaned from the meeting at the refuge, information he'd managed to weave into his own policy thoughts. 'There should be no place in Britain for forced marriages,' he said. 'To eradicate this practice we need to tackle the deep cultural issues that surround it, as well as enforcing and strengthening legislation. This can only be done through joint work by the government, local authorities and communities. Two hundred and fifty Muslim girls under the age of sixteen disappear every year, many of whom are simply kidnapped and taken back to Pakistan. This is not part of our culture, it's not part of anyone's culture, and it's a situation we should do something about. The issue of forced marriages has been ignored by this government, and this is something that Gordon Brown just doesn't seem to understand.'

Since failing to call the election at the end of 2007, Gordon Brown had begun to resemble George Harrison. Like Harrison, Brown had spent a decade in the shadows, only allowed out for the very strictest amount of daylight. And like Harrison when the Beatles split up – he released a triple album almost immediately – as soon as he became PM Brown came lurching out of the gate, spewing out policies as though his career depended on it. Which it did. Having been kept on a tightish rein for the previous ten years, Brown spent the first few weeks of his premiership releasing singles from his dusty, regularly updated and annotated triple album of treats (known and referred to in his inner sanctum as Policies To Introduce After That Bastard's Gone). And then? A lot of stern looks, some carefully organized photo opportunities where he would practise his smile, and a fair amount of shuffling about outside Portcullis House, mugging any Tory researcher who looked like he might be carrying anything interesting (i.e. anything involving law and order or drugs).

One thing appeared to be certain, however, and that was Gordon Brown's almost irrational hatred of the opposition leader. One visitor to

Downing Street shortly after Christmas told me, 'A dark mood takes over Gordon whenever someone mentions Cameron. He just hates him, hates the privilege, the fact that he went to Eton, all of that.' Brown's biggest chip, however, was Oxford; he had a perverse and rather unhealthy attitude towards anyone with an Oxbridge education, and loathed Cameron even more because he was successful at Oxford. Members of the lobby were beginning to find this hypocrisy quite irritating, not least because Brown was obviously enjoying the trappings of power almost as much as his predecessor, entertaining at Chequers on a regular basis. One night in the autumn, the BBC political editor Nick Robinson told me: 'The thing that no one can quite understand is why Brown is so obvious in his disdain for David. Whenever he stands up in the Commons to ask him a question at PMQs you can see a sneer begin to creep across his face.'

After the interviews in the Great Victoria Hotel, and thirty minutes writing his blog, it was time to drive off to Granada in Manchester for a pre-recording of a popular chat show. Cameron's schedule was incomparable to what it was two years earlier, with every five minutes of his day filled with something or other: a Shadow Cabinet meeting one day, a prison visit the next; a trip to Washington one week, three days in Afghanistan the next. Plus policy meetings, City talks, media interviews, walkabouts, speeches, prison visits and photo calls, all over and above the actual day-to-day minutiae of being a parliamentarian. In his black suit, white shirt and pale blue tie, looking more statesmanlike than ever, striding into the lobby with his right hand in his trouser pocket, Cameron managed to appear senatorial and casual at the same time, which is never an easy thing to pull off on a miserable wet February evening in Manchester. At the Granada Studios he was steered towards another sofa, attached to another microphone, and left to fend for himself as the presenter worked out his cues and his marks. And then the studio manager dropped her arm and we were live. 'And now the man who wants to be Prime Minister. Are you ready to vote Tory?' Attacked with various lines regarding his inability to convince the North West of the Conservatives' new values, DC fought back in the only way he knows how: tough, articulate and conciliatory.

Later on, as the car stopped I took a call from my office in London telling me that the cover session in Los Angeles for our next issue of *GQ* had gone particularly well. The subject was Cameron Diaz, and she had enjoyed the sessions so much that she accepted an invitation from Paul Solomons, the magazine's art director, to go for a drink that evening with him at the Sunset Marquis Hotel. When I relayed this to Cameron, he looked out at the teeming night-time northern rain and said, 'Well, you sure picked the wrong Cameron, didn't you?!'

Later that night, Cameron and I went out for dinner for some corn-fed chicken and Amarone at Albert's Shed, a noisy Anglo-Italian restaurant in the Castlefield area of Manchester, deep in *Corrie* country. As he was giving a full and frank description of the New Year's Eve party he went to, asking me about the iPod DJ terminal that kept the party buzzing until the small hours – 'It was the first time I'd stayed up till three o'clock for a very, very long time' – he was approached by an enormously pretty twentysomething girl on the next table. 'Can I buy you a drink?' she asked, as though she was asking directions to the town centre. 'I thought she was going to buy me twelve Flaming Sambucas,' said Cameron after he'd politely declined. Later, as we were leaving the restaurant, he was approached again, this time by a former Conservative volunteer who wanted his autograph and a picture. Again, she was young, and very attractive ('He's a hottie!'). As we left, padding across the cobblestones back to the Great John Street Hotel (one of the great examples of local urban regeneration, although unfortunately my room smelled as though someone had put prawns in the hems of the curtains), he got a shout-out, too, from half a dozen lads in polo shirts drinking bottled beer, braving the February chill: 'Hey, David Cameron! Respect!'

We spent the evening discussing the changing fortunes – and the changing editorships – of various national newspapers, and the misfortunes of Michael Martin, the Speaker of the House of Commons, while also gossiping about Westminster. We also chatted about David Bailey, who I'd asked to photograph Cameron for a political gallery for *GQ* just before Christmas. Unsurprisingly, Cameron had loved the experience – who wouldn't want to have their portrait taken by Bailey? – but was flabbergasted by the photographer's swearing. 'I mean, I know I can swear, sometimes a little too much,' he said as he sipped his Amarone and tried not to catch the eye of any flirtysomething waitress, 'but Bailey swears every other word. It was "fuck" this and "fuck" that and "fuck" everything. He is, though, an utterly charming man. Even if he does have this disconcerting way of holding your shoulder when he's talking to you.'

We also discussed Bailey's session with Gordon Brown, for the same portfolio. 'Bailey was great, and he told me how he baited Brown. Apparently Brown said that he thought all photographers used digital cameras nowadays. And Bailey said, "I hate digital photography. It's like socialism – it makes everything look the same."'

As well as chit-chatting, throughout the day and the evening I'd been questioning Cameron for this book. There was a lot to catch up on, especially his dramatic comeback following the October 2007 conference speech.

The election that never was

In the months since the conference you have gone, in tabloid terms, from zero to hero.
It's been an extraordinary couple of months, there's no doubt about it. It shows that things can change very rapidly in politics, and they have.

And not only have your fortunes changed, and the fortunes of your party, but the fortunes of the PM have changed, too. He's gone from being depicted as Stalin to being portrayed as Mr Bean. You are now back riding fairly high in the opinion polls, and you have more of the country and the media behind you.
It's been a really exciting period. The conference was very dramatic and very exciting, and it's a week I won't forget. Our backs were very much against the walls, everyone was saying, they're on their way to Blackpool, it could be a disaster, the party might turn in on itself.

How do you feel? After all, there was a danger there that some people thought you were going to turn out to be all gong and no dinner …

But we just had this fantastic conference, and there was an amazing atmosphere there. Partly because there was a sense that an election could come any minute so the party wanted to unite, it wanted to fight, and also partly because I really do think we had our act together. The team was brilliant, we were all up for it. Compared to the Labour conference, we had great speeches from [William] Hague, from [David] Davis, [Caroline] Spelman, [Liam] Fox, [George] Osborne … The team was good but also we were setting out such a clear vision. We had really worked out what modern Conservatism should be about and how we were going to articulate that. It all came together and I think people could see that. I've always known what we were aiming to achieve but we needed to set out clearly how it applied to the full range of policy areas, and that has now been done. Power and control over your life, a more responsible society and a secure country, and we were really putting out some proper, interesting policies that were all linked to that. And then I had this interesting idea of making a speech without any script. It was a huge risk but it worked I think.

The 2007 conference speech

It was incredibly impressive, but, more importantly, it worked. It was convincing. It very much had the feeling of something you'd worked at and then junked a lot of stuff you'd spent weeks preparing.
There was an element of that, but the truth was, I'd been working on the speech for weeks, as you always do, but at the same time I was thinking, maybe I won't do it like this at all, maybe I'll do something completely different, something that was forming in my mind. The two things weren't unrelated.

Where did it come from?
About four or five days before the conference I thought I was going to stop developing it and just think in my mind how I really wanted to say the things I wanted to say. I basically had five days to do it from scratch. I had some notes on the table but I actually didn't need them. Once I got

going it was all there, and it really shows how clear our argument was that it was possible to do it like that. It's a wonderful hall to speak in, and even though we're not going back there, that hall has some great qualities. And it was a dramatic moment, because the Prime Minister was preparing for the election, I was really up for it, I thought the party was getting into shape, and I really like the opportunity you have at the conference to get out there with your window of ten minutes on the nightly news to tell the nation what you really want to do and what you believe and what it is you want to achieve.

And although you were calling for an election you must have been unbelievably relieved when Brown bottled it?
No, I really wasn't, and I know that people don't believe me but I really wasn't. I believed then and I believe now that when you have an election and when you have that chance to explain to people what you stand for, I think, yes, we can win! Because a lot of the time in opposition you just can't get across to people what you're on about. The government's got the big guns and they're on the media every night and you struggle to get anything more than a thirty-second sound bite on the news. At your conference or on a general election campaign you can really get your message out. That's when we do well …

Come on, when you discovered he'd been on *Andrew Marr* and called it off you must have punched the air!
The thing is, I was at home watching him on *Andrew Marr* on the telly and my mobile phone doesn't work that well in Oxfordshire so I had to keep running between the garden and the television, so it was rather farcical. I'd actually found out the day before, but still it was fascinating to watch. In one sense there was a feeling of, yes! Because he had blinked in the face of our conference and our success, but on the other hand the reason he called off the election was because we had gone up in the opinion polls. We saw this incredible surge in the polls during the week before. This is something that has been misreported. It's been said that he bottled the election and therefore the Conservatives started to do

better. Wrong. We started to do better and he then bottled it. But of course when he did bottle it there was a sense of 'We've won that round', and we'll have more time to prepare for the election. On the other hand I was really up for it.

Come on, David, honestly?
Honestly. I got the troops together in Central Office on Thursday night and told them to prepare for the campaign. Cancel your holidays, kiss goodbye to your loved ones because you're not going to see them for three weeks. But I was mentally ready for it. I thought, yes it's going to be tough, and we may not win every seat we need to form an overall majority but I absolutely believe that if we'd have had that election that Gordon Brown would no longer have been Prime Minister and that the Conservatives would have been the largest party in a hung parliament. And some of the polls back me up on that. It may have been a hung parliament but Labour would have lost their right to govern. Plus the momentum was with us and people liked what they were hearing.

But Brown lied on national television and the political landscape turned upside down. I can't remember such a turnaround in public opinion since the Falklands, when Thatcher had her resurrection. In the space of a week, with the inheritance tax announcement, your speech, and the Brown bottle, the landscape changed …
That's true. And Brown compounded calling off the election by then saying it was nothing to do with the polls, which was a massive mistake. It was a lie and it was treating people like fools, which is something he does. He's sort of doing it over Northern Rock, too, saying we took the right decisions at every moment, at every turn, but people know that's just not the case. And I think that was the most egregious example of Brown's behaviour. I remember that in the Commons actually, some weeks afterwards, and I asked him to look me in the eye and tell me that calling off the election had nothing to do with the polls. And when he said it didn't the House collapsed in laughter. But you're right, it was extraordinary.

Brown's effect on the Tories

How did Brown's failure to launch affect your party internally?
We have to rewind a bit here. Back in August William Hague said to me, if Labour are going to call an autumn election, and I think they will, they should have it on 4 or 5 October, and they should write off the conference season altogether. If they're going to do it they're going to do it. So ever since then, when I broke off my holiday, we've been preparing for a general election. We weren't spending buckets of money but we were getting ready. We delivered millions of leaflets around marginal seats around the country. So what happened when it was called off was, we thought, okay, plan B. You know, the football match is off. But there was a great sense within the party that we were back on track again.

You'd been vindicated ...
Yes, but there's no complacency. You can see it at the moment. We're doing okay, but the government hasn't collapsed, crawled into a hole and shot itself. It's real trench warfare this. They're rolling out all these policies that they won't be able to implement. Every day there's another three missives from Camp Brown. What children are going to be taught in school, what's going to happen to illegal immigrants, they're just throwing all these things over the top.

How has your own opinion of Brown changed since then?
I still don't know him really, because we don't see each other very much. But in terms of him as a politician and a leader, I do think that when he said that not calling an election had nothing to do with the polls was quite a big moment for me because I just thought that was such rubbish. And I thought Blair would never have done that. Blair would have come into that Downing Street press conference and gone, 'Yes, of course we looked at the polls and, you know what? We've got to do better.' And he would have got away with it. Instead there was this sort of 'black is white' routine. He's also been lying about not getting his ideas about inheritance tax and non-doms off the Tories.

131

So, essentially, Gordon Brown is a liar.
On this he lied.

How do you think Brown's attitude towards you has changed?
I hear all sorts of things. I don't know and I don't really mind. I think we
have a very different outlook on politics and on life and I think we both
want to achieve different things. I am very much a believer that if you
give people power and control over their lives, they will create a better
and stronger society. And I think Brown is very much 'I am going to re-
order the world from above'. The Supreme Leader portrayal in *Private
Eye*, there's actually something in that. Just look at this week; we've had
doctors now issuing well notes instead of sick notes, you're going to go to
school and you're going to have four hours of culture, and your children
will be fingerprinted on the way to school, and, on the way back, you'll
enter your details into the national database etc. There is a sense that so
much is being determined and driven from above. I've always thought, if
you look at Brown's history in the Treasury there was always lots of direct
intervention, lots of fiddling with the budget, lots of opaque accountancy, it was all very much top-down, interference, I know best. And I
think we're just seeing that writ large.

**I think one of the fascinating things is the way the press have changed
towards him, because for the first few months of his tenure they
handled Brown with kid gloves, never annoying him. But now they're
far more inclined to delve into his inner life, to explore the psycholog-
ical flaws and the temper tantrums. Essentially because he lied and
now looks vulnerable.**
That's true ... his honeymoon period is certainly over. I had one when I
took over, but that went. Oh, you're new, what are you going to do, everything you get up to must be more interesting than what everyone else is
up to because you're new, even if it's not very interesting at all. But it
never lasts.

It reminds me of that famous Dr Johnson quote, when talking about one of his contemporaries: 'He may do very well, as long as he can outrun his character. But the moment his character catches up with him, he's all over.'

People have given him the benefit of the doubt and then it came to a crashing end. But these things always do. Then you get down to the fundamentals. Which is why the period from now until the election is going to be so interesting.

Your success in the polls is as much to do with the results of your policy reviews as it is Brown's incompetence. What have you been most pleased with?

Well, I'm always dissatisfied. But I think the most pleasing thing is that a lot of people now know what the modern Conservative Party stands for. And you're right: politics is so important, and over the course of the last six months everything has come together. What we said about welfare reform was very important and I think has resonated with the public. There are nearly five million people on out-of-work benefits, many of whom could work, many of them want to work, but we leave them sitting on the sofa watching TV, not just week after week but often generation after generation.

The Labour Party appear to have accepted this.

Of course they have. And I think our quite tough package, saying that of course we'll give you help with the training and the education but at the end of the day if you don't accept a job you won't get the benefit. Also, what I said about immigration and the need for controlled immigration was welcomed by Trevor Phillips, Chairman of the Equality and Human Rights Commission, and I thought that showed that people are now much more ready to listen to difficult and quite robust messages from the Conservative Party, because they now see us in a different light. They see us as a reasonable bunch of people who want the best for our country and we're going to listen to what they have to say rather than dismiss them.

The Welfare State

I've become rather obsessed with Tommy Thompson's welfare reforms – the so-called Wisconsin Miracle, where people had their benefits taken away if they didn't look for or accept work. So successful was he when he was governor of the state that the ideas were adopted by Bill Clinton, and even Blair tried to employ them until he experienced a Cabinet revolt. When were you first aware of them, and when did you begin to think they could work in Britain?

Blair never went for it. There's always been an argument that the left can't do welfare reform because the trade unions won't allow it, and the right can't do it because they're seen as too mean. And a lot of people thought Blair would do it because he'd face down the unions, but in the end he never did. And I think we've shown that we can do it because we're showing that this is motivated by the interests of the people sitting on the sofa who aren't working, and getting more ill and poorer and whose children are suffering, and we want them for their own benefit to get off the sofa, off welfare and into work.

So how does your scheme differ?

Now, there are two key elements that Labour wouldn't do that we will do. You say first of all, like in Australia, like in America, you've got to get the voluntary sector involved in the delivery of this programme. They are better than many state organizations because they understand how to do it. And the second thing is you have to be tough in terms of some form of time limit. If you've been on welfare for two years then you have to work for your welfare. This is a step change that could actually get over a million people off welfare and back to work. That would have a transformational effect on them. But I think if, two years ago, I'd made that the centrepiece of my conference speech people would have said, 'Oh, it's the Tories again bashing the dole scroungers.' We needed to show that we understand the needs of the poorest first.

One of the reasons that people fell out of love with the Tories last time was because they thought they were unnecessarily greedy. One Thatcherite lieutenant even suggested privatizing the Royal Parks, so they could bring in more revenue ... One of the most important markers must be the recent publication of the report from Progress, the Labour think-tank, in which they acknowledged that the Tories were no longer being seen as the 'nasty party' and that the Labour Party now has to fight for the centre ground with a party which is socially more liberal and constantly engaging in counter-intuitive positioning. You are now more socially liberal than you've been. But then you have changed the party as dramatically as Thatcher did.

That was a great moment, for when your opponents say that about you then you realize that the argument has really got through.

The thing that many people forget is that Thatcher wasn't a traditional Tory either, and in many respects she was a radical. She was distrustful of the Establishment and went out of her way to remake the party in her own image. Which is what Tony Blair did. Which is what you've done.

Margaret Thatcher in her time realized that the big challenge was reviving Britain's economy, and we should recognize that the challenge for the modern Conservatives is reviving our society. And that's one way of putting it. But there's another way of looking at it – and I think this is crucial, fundamental, to what I'm trying to do – and that is that there is a generational argument here, which is that I think a new generation of Conservatives have a real opportunity to grapple with and solve some of the big problems facing our country. Because we're not encumbered by the baggage of the past.

Give me some examples ...

Recently I said let's make it easier for the police to stop and search people, and let's not worry about what different communities might think because actually it's young black and Asian people who are being shot and stabbed and dealt drugs and dying on our streets and they will welcome the change. And you know what? They did welcome that change. We don't see this argument through the eyes of the 1980s.

So what have you learned?
I think you've got to trust your instincts. In the end, as the leader of an opposition party you have an enormous opportunity to set your own stamp on things, set out your own stall, and do it your own way. The difficult thing in politics I've learned is the daily battle you have to fight to try and stay ahead. While all the time thinking of the big picture you've got to paint. And you've got to do both. Plus the team, choosing a good team, trusting them to make the right decisions. You have to give them their head.

You seem more confident than you've ever been, principally I think because your message is getting through, and you've begun to articulate it in a way that is resonating with the public and with the press.
Yes, the problem with politics is that when you're ahead, people listen to you and success breeds success. But when you're behind then all the difficulties emerge and rise up to annoy you. That's why you have to win the short-term battles as well as the long-term battles.

Okay, can you briefly tell me what we've been doing today and why it needed to be done?
One of the big challenges I think that faces the country is what in Conservative terms we would call building one nation. We have a problem with lack of cohesion – failure of what I would call state multiculturalism, treating different people in different communities differently. The attitude has seemed to be that we should focus on the things that separate us rather than the things which unite us. Which I think is a profound mistake. There is a huge pressure to bring it to an end, and even the Prime Minister has started to talk about the importance of encouraging Britishness.

Multiculturalism

There is a growing consensus that state multiculturalism has failed.
It is seriously failing. But it's no good just saying that; you have to work out the things that really have to change. For instance I think the statements made by the Archbishop of Canterbury about Sharia law were completely wrong, as they advocate a sort of parallel society, and nobody wants to live in a country like that. It was wrong-headed to say that we should have different sorts of laws in different sorts of communities. And today was a specific example of the particularly horrendous problem of forced marriages, where thousands of young girls in this country, and some young boys, are taken halfway round the world and married against their will and often locked in unhappy and often violence domestic situations. For too long we've said, as a society, these things happen in different cultures and we should just accept them and be careful not to intervene in case we offend people. And I think that's completely wrong, and we should be intolerant of forced marriages. They involve a huge amount of law-breaking and suffering and trampling on people's rights, and we need a cultural change as well as a legal change to stop it. That was the point of today. But this is part of a bigger picture of saying we need to scrap the out-of-date state multiculturalist model and build a stronger, better, more integrated country.

Bradford is one of those places that has largely always been a Labour stronghold, and, regardless of the new boundary changes, it probably will remain one. What can you do to woo them? Why should the good people of Bradford vote for you at the next general election?
Bradford has always been a politically exciting place, and the Conservatives ran it in the 1980s. Eric Pickles, who's a member of my Shadow Cabinet, was the leader of Bradford City Council. And I think we could win here. If the Conservative Party cannot appeal to people in the heart of our great cities then we are failing. If you look at what people who live in the cities care about – and that's crime, education, the ability to move

about safely, the quality of life – then they are all things the Conservative Party has a lot to say about. I refuse to accept that we're going to be locked out of the inner cities. The Conservative Party has become too rural and too southern and we need to change that.

Economically there is no magic wand you can wave in places like this, is there?
There's an important branch of Conservative thinking that understands that you will only build a strong society if you build strong civic institutions, whether that's the family or neighbourhood and community institutions. The strand of Conservatism has also always understood how important it is for politicians to focus on what I suppose today we call the quality of life agenda, or the well-being agenda. Really, this is nothing new for Conservatives, if you look at the pioneering work that previous Conservative leaders, whether locally or nationally, did on things like slum clearance and urban regeneration.

There's a rich multicultural mix here – Muslims, Sikhs, Hindus. Twenty years ago Muslims publicly burned copies of *The Satanic Verses*, eight years ago there were riots. It's a hotbed, and far more multicultural than it was twenty years ago.
Look at our candidate in Bradford West, who is a British Muslim; there's no reason why they can't win that seat. Sitting next to me at the Shadow Cabinet meeting this morning was Sayeeda Warsi, the first British Muslim woman in any Cabinet or Shadow Cabinet, and I think you see a Conservative Party that has gone a long way to reach out into those communities. Not out of political correctness, but for a really important reason, which is that if you really believe in building one nation then you have to have everyone included. Also, role models are incredibly important. If you think about what [the boxer] Amir Khan has done for British Asians, it's amazing. His example says you can achieve extraordinary things through your own talent and aspiration and application, and you can represent your country and be incredibly popular. Look at Sayeeda. You should see her in mosques and community centres, switching from

English to Urdu in a matter of seconds, talking to some of the elders as though she has known them all her life.

She's a brilliant broadcaster, and has the ability to talk in perfect paragraphs.
I remember when Michael Howard first met her. George Osborne and I went to brief him for PMQs in the normal way, and he said, 'You boys are completely finished, you have not got a chance of leading our party because I have met the star of the future and her name is Sayeeda Warsi. You may as well pack it in.' That's why I put her in the House of Lords!

Community and youth

What's your definition of community?
Good question. Community is something that people actively want to be a part of. And it's all very well saying that there is an Asian community or a Muslim community or a Pakistani community but it's very important there is a British community.

How can we control drinking on the streets? Would you stop twenty-four-hour drinking and supermarkets selling cheap booze? In small towns, in cities, on a Friday or Saturday night you regularly see people throwing up in the street by seven o'clock in the evening, fighting, pushing over cars, acting as though they were auditioning for a Hogarth painting. It's even worse in the summer months when all this happens in broad daylight. It's a sort of brightly lit nightmare.
This is a very complicated issue and a very important one and you have to unpick it extremely carefully. Binge drinking is taking over our streets, and it's linked to crime and to antisocial behaviour and it's making some of our towns and cities uninhabitable. It's like the Wild West. I've seen some terrible things, but then you have to ask yourself what it is about our culture that encourages and allows this. Who has given the green light for people to go and get drunk and get into a fight?

Presumably the occupants of Ten and Eleven Downing Street.
A lot of this is the result of underage drinking and buying from shops, rather than what happens in pubs and clubs. And there the police can shut down shops that sell alcohol to young people. There should be a zero-tolerance approach to that. As well as to selling alcohol to underage people in pubs and clubs. But I think there's a danger on the whole crime and law and order front of thinking that unless we pass another law then this will continue forever. But we need a more hands-on approach – we need the police to get in there and sort things out, and arrest people selling drink to people under the legal limit, and arrest those who cause trouble in those places when they're drunk. Off-licences, shops, convenience stores, supermarkets, pubs, clubs, the lot of them. We shouldn't underestimate what could be done by the police if they were freed from doing all this paperwork.

After retreating from Vegas-style casinos, Brown has sanctioned sixteen new smaller casinos to be built. What do you think of this?
This was a classic piece of spin by Labour, with Brown saying he wasn't going to be burdened by Blair's casino legacy and then we find out he's going to build sixteen more somewhere else. We were always sceptical about super casinos. There was a need to liberalize the law but I think the government's gone about it in the wrong way.

You talk repeatedly about social responsibility. How would you explain social responsibility to someone from another planet, albeit someone from another planet with a good command of the English language?
If we want to achieve any of the things that we want to achieve in our country it's not enough for the government to pass another law. Social responsibility has to be part of everyone's life. Everyone has to play their part in building the country we want. In education you just can't publish a great curriculum, you need parents to get their children to school on time, you need teachers controlling the classroom, you need businesses recognizing they can't endlessly promote sex and violence to children

without them being affected. Everyone's got their role to play. Responsibility is the most important word in politics.

How do you plan to engage with apathetic youth, bearing in mind that more people vote in *The X Factor* than vote in the election?

I'm not sure Britain's youth is that apathetic, actually. And there is a danger of damning an entire generation of young people, and that's wrong. There is a gap between adolescence and adulthood where we don't have any sort of rite of passage.

Can you expand on the National Citizen Service a little? Where did it come from, why do you want to do it?

This is something I first spoke about in the leadership election. The idea came to me through conversations I had with people of my father's generation, who all said how much they had enjoyed National Service because it was something that they all did together. It didn't matter if you were from the north or the south, or a Protestant or a Catholic, rich or poor, they were all in it together. They lived together, learned together, and it was something that marked the passage from adolescence to adulthood to citizenship. I don't want to bring back National Service, because I don't think it would be good for the armed forces, and I don't think it's what's required today. But I think that idea, that there's something we could get young people to do at that age of sixteen or seventeen, that is about community service, that's about growing up, about being part of something bigger than yourself, that's about what it means to be a citizen, and crucially is about meeting and living and working with people from completely different backgrounds ... and it's a really good idea. What I did was, because I don't believe in top-down central control and would rather work with people than tell them what to do, I got the leaders of the voluntary sector and youth organizations together – including the Duke of Edinburgh's Awards and the Prince of Wales Trust – and told them my idea and asked them what they thought. And since then we've made huge progress. We've set up a charity to run some pilot schemes, we've hired some good people to advise us, and my hope is, by the time we get to the election, we'll be able to set out very clearly what the programme would look like, who would take part, how quickly we could roll it out, how much it would cost and all the rest of it. And we're quite a long way down that road already.

But how do you make it appealing to kids? It's a very grand idea, but it's not very sexy.
That was one of the challenges to the voluntary sector, because they know how to make these things interesting. These guys don't march these people up the Brecon Beacons at gunpoint; they go because they want to.

But they don't take very many. You're talking about the whole country …
They go in increasing numbers. They know what excites young people. This mustn't be some sort of dull, worthy enterprise about learning to be a British citizen, it's got to be inspiring, it's got to be challenging. And people like to be challenged, so part of the programme would be training with the army on Dartmoor or doing the Three Peaks Challenge or working with the social services in Hackney … but all in a way that would excite people. More and more people I explain it to get excited about joining in. Only recently I was talking to some people in Formula One about it, and they got very keen. And there's nothing sexier than Formula One. But it only works if people recognize their social responsibility, if businesses understand that they have to invest in the future of this country. And good businesses care about the future of the country, as they'd be mad not to.

But surely children of that age, it's the last thing they're thinking about …
If you look at the number of people who get involved in the Duke of Edinburgh's Award Scheme and what they get out of it, it's amazing. I'm not cynical in that way. It's not the same as serving in the Swiss army for two years, nor is it meant to be. But we need to try and find some more things for people to bring them together from different backgrounds,

and tell them they're part of something bigger, that they're part of the country, part of society, and that you have an obligation to each other.

You would implement this law?
Yes, it should be a universal experience that we all have at sixteen. It's going to be very difficult to get right because it's got to be both meaningful and robust on the one hand, and interesting, and on the other it's got to inspire and excite people.

Do you need to do this? After all, it's not a bloody holiday camp.
No, it's not a bloody holiday camp, but on the other hand if you think about the things that some young people are lucky enough to do when they're young, whether it's doing the Duke of Edinburgh's Award Scheme or joining the cadet force, or doing social services, helping elderly people …

But at sixteen you don't want to do that; at sixteen you want to drink beer and chase girls …
You can do both! It's not meant to be boot camp. But imagine doing the Three Peaks Challenge, or going out on exercises with the army on Salisbury Plain, or learning how to build a Formula One car, it should be exciting.

What ideas would you propose to keep children from loitering on the streets after school?
Tony Blair would have passed the 'children loitering on street corners after school' bill, but you have to ask yourself why they are on the street corners. It might be because their parents are hopeless and don't know where they are, and they should, and that's something we need to address. We need to reverse the tide of family breakdown. It might be because the youth club has closed down because we're rubbish at funding the voluntary sector in this country, and it could be because they're waiting for a bus and not doing anyone any harm. There's no single answer.

Street crime

We've probably got more CCTV cameras in this country than anywhere else in the world. Is this a good thing, or a potentially malevolent thing?

I'm a fan of CCTV. It's funny, really. French people don't understand why we're so uptight about identity cards and so relaxed about CCTV cameras, but the funny thing is, I think that's what we are. I profoundly object to someone giving me a piece of plastic and telling me, this is your life, here are your papers, but on the other hand I don't mind closed circuit television cameras. Is that entirely logical? Not really, but that's what I feel, and I think millions of my fellow countrymen feel the same way. I mean, no one wants closed circuit TV cameras on the streets where they live; what we want them for is the public spaces, the high streets, and in market towns like the ones I represent they've had a huge effect.

When were you last the victim of crime?

I've been burgled twice in the last eight years, I've had my car stolen and I was on my bike the other day and this white van had been following me, stopping and starting. This was very late at night, about midnight, I was coming back from some dinner. I got rather nervous about it so I turned down a road I don't normally go down and I slowed down and sort of pulled in behind a line of parked cars and as this van drove by this hand came out and just bashed me in the back with the aim of pushing me in front of the car. Luckily I managed to put the brakes on. Gave me a hell of a shock though … someone just taking the piss. But I've never been the victim of proper violent crime. In the years living in London, in the last ten years, I've witnessed a mugging, near where I live. I saw this guy lying on the floor after he'd been attacked. It's sort of all around you in London. I often see one of those yellow incident signs near where I live. A mugging. A robbery. A murder.

The revenge of white van man ... Do you ever feel nervous walking the streets in London? There are some terrible pockets around you ...

No, not particularly I don't. I do walk around when I can, but I don't want to get into this or else I'll sound like Jacqui Smith [in January 2008 the Home Secretary admitted she would feel unsafe walking the streets of London late at night].

Are the police still the friends of the middle classes? Do you believe that the police, in order to hit their targets, persecute the middle classes suspected of minor offences while ignoring crimes which are more serious but harder to clear up?

I think the police have lost a lot of the confidence of hard-working, law-abiding people, and that's for a number of reasons. One is the target culture that has been imposed upon the police by Labour, which means that they tend to go after easy cases rather than difficult cases, and that means obviously demonizing the middle classes to a certain extent and targeting people who are fundamentally law-abiding. I think the endless paperwork arising from political correctness is another one, and I think there is a growing sense among the police that unless a new law is passed for a specific offence then they can't do anything about it. I think this is very worrying and I think that has been partly caused by Labour's legislative obsession. The police have got themselves into this mindset of 'I cannot intervene because there isn't a specific law about it'.

DNA, ASBOs and ID cards

Should every person in Britain be put on the DNA database? Both Ipswich serial killer Steve Wright and Mark Dixie, who murdered Sally Anne Bowman, were on the database, making it easier for them to be caught.

I don't think that in itself is right. No, I think you should take DNA from suspects in the normal way, if they've been involved in a crime. I don't believe in taking everyone's DNA at birth.

Okay, but why shouldn't we have ID cards?
a) Because they're fantastically expensive, b) because they don't work, and c) because I think the only way they could work is if you make it compulsory to carry them, with the police having the power of arrest for anyone found not carrying one. And I don't want to live in that sort of society. I don't know why this government is lobbying so hard to have all these details when they're only going to go and lose them anyway. I think it's an interesting point, and if you'd asked people four or five years ago whether or not they wanted ID cards I would imagine that most people would have been in favour – and that has shifted completely, and I think it's shifted because this government is bringing together masses of data about us all and then losing it. Do you really want to give them some more? I don't, I know that. It's not a very persuasive argument from their point of view.

What about ASBOs? Should we hand out more?
I think they've got a place. The problem is that they've been scattered like confetti and then nothing happens when they're breached. I think that Blair was right in one regard that the processes of the criminal law were often too slow and clunky to be really effective to deal with these new problems. So you need new solutions. So having an order in which you say we're not going to have any public drinking in this area, and banning people from behaving in such a way, these things can work. But ASBOs have been massively overused, and then when they're breached, nothing happens.

Surely they've just become a badge of honour …
As you say, for some young people they've become a badge of honour and a bit of a joke. I keep coming back to this point that the law is not enough – you have to deal with the root of the problem. And this is where Blair failed. Having coined this wonderful sound bite 'Tough on Crime, Tough on the Causes of Crime', he rather gave up on the second part, the causes of crime. It is chaotic homes with absent fathers, people sitting on the dole and not working, it is schools where children run riot

where there is no discipline, it is the fact that the voluntary sector is not being encouraged to run youth clubs, so there's nothing for the young people to do; it is those things.

To what extent, realistically, could the charitable sector contribute to the welfare of the country?

Massively, hugely. I mean, look at what we saw today. Who runs those refuges for the victims of domestic violence or forced marriages and helps them put their lives back together again and give them hope? That's why I was asking them if they get more than one year's funding from the government. It's all very well funding the Home Office, but government needs to be more lateral in its thinking. We need to give the voluntary sector longer-term contracts, we need to trust them more, we need to be prepared to say we're going to give you larger bits of work, and we're going to give you the money to do it. And we're going to take some risks. If you fail in business it doesn't necessarily mean you can't start again and succeed. The idea may have been good, and so next time we attempt it we're going to do it in a different way. We should encourage people to take risks, and acknowledge that sometimes that might mean failure. In the public sector, or in crime prevention, or solving problems like drug abuse or whatever, we don't encourage entrepreneurialism, and we should.

Give me an example ...

If you take homelessness, for example, who has been brilliant at tackling homelessness? I would argue that it's the *Big Issue*. Now that was a very entrepreneurial idea. And it could easily have failed. Imagine if you were going along to the government, and saying I've got a good idea to help the homeless, I'm going to go to them and give them magazines to sell, and if they sell the magazines I'm going to give them some money ... the government would have kicked you out of the front door. But that's exactly the kind of innovation and creativity that there's so much of in the charitable sector – these days we call it social enterprise. And you've got to stop squashing that sort of innovation. We should trust the

147

community organizations, social enterprise groups and the voluntary sector a lot more than we do.

It is now almost impossible to park a car anywhere in Britain; is this a good thing?

Er, no, it isn't. This is an interesting one, because you have market towns that have always been about the people from the outlying villages and countryside coming in to shop and to meet and eat, but they can really suffer if you completely pedestrianize the centres of these places. There is no bus service in the world that can supply bus routes from every one of the eighty-five parishes in my constituency into Witney, and inevitably people rely on the car to take them into the market town, a market town where you can park and shop and drive into and out of. So I'm not anti-car and I think that some of our town centres have become stuffed full of so much clutter and furniture and pedestrianization that it's impossible to get around.

Oxford has to be the most anti-car town in the Western world …

Boris [Johnson] and I both became MPs in Oxfordshire around the same time and I remember at the first meeting of the county council, Boris turning up, as ever, about half an hour late and asking whether the city fathers in their wisdom had decided to make it impossible to drive anywhere in Oxford. I know exactly what he means. The thing that really irritates me is the people who park in disabled parking spaces. We have a blue badge because of Ivan, and there is something incredibly annoying about seeing someone bounding out of their car with the full use of their arms and legs when they've just parked in a disabled parking bay. You want to thump them.

Drug classification

We've talked a lot about crime and the disintegration of society tonight, but I'd like to end on a question about drugs, which I'm going to refer to when we next meet, and ask you some questions that you

probably won't want to answer. But there we are. You've had to talk about drugs rather a lot in your career, but what was your thinking behind your suggestion, as a member of the Home Affairs Select Committee, that ecstasy be downgraded from Class A to Class B? What would this have achieved, other than alienate core Tory voters as well as the media? You're now saying that cannabis should be reclassified as Class B rather than Class C.

Yes, I did look at this on the Home Affairs Select Committee and the conclusion we came to then was that the classifications weren't right. The trouble with cannabis is the sort of hydroponically grown skunk is so powerful, and so much more powerful than it used to be, that it needs looking at. There is so much evidence now that it is completely different from what was available twenty or thirty years ago. But I think the whole classification system is in need of a major overhaul because it seems to me that the ABC method doesn't really get it right …

Why not? It seems perfectly understandable to me, to most people, I would imagine …

Well, with cannabis, for instance, there's an enormous difference between hydroponically grown skunk and other forms of cannabis. I think we probably need to have a look at the whole thing … I mean where does alcohol fit into the picture?

But alcohol's not illegal.

And what about ketamine, crystal meth, all those things …? There was some ecstasy alternative in the papers the other day that wasn't illegal or classified at all. So I think we need to look at the whole picture. These evaluations are all based on the 1971 Misuse of Drugs Act, and a lot has changed since then. And I think without in any way weakening the illegality of any drugs that the classification system needs a major overhaul.

* * *

After our day in Bradford and evening in Manchester, I was to spend much of the next day with Cameron, in and around Manchester and in nearby Bury and Bolton, as he did media interviews, toured a market and visited a police station. The morning's itinerary read like this:

0745 Depart hotel for Channel M studios at Urbis, Cathedral Gardens, Manchester, M4 3BG (GCS Car)

0800 Breakfast slot with Channel M – covers MEN, Century FM, Smooth FM at Urbis

0825 Depart for Radio Manchester, New Broadcasting House, Oxford Road, Manchester M60 1SJ

0835 Arrive Radio Manchester for breakfast show

0855 Depart for Astley Bridge Police Station, Crompton Way, Astley Bridge, Bolton BL1 8UN (GCS Car)

0935 Arrive Astley Bridge Police Station. Meet with police officers and visit station and cells

1025 Depart Astley Bridge Police Station for Bury Town Hall, Knowsley Street, Bury, Lancashire BL9 OSW (GCS Car)

1040 Arrive Bury Town Hall to launch the local election campaign. Mingle with councillors and candidates and then do photograph on steps of town hall

1055 Depart Bury Town Hall for short walk to Bury Market. On foot. Tour the market, meeting stall owners and shoppers, with Cllr Bob Bibby, Leader of the Conservatives on Bury Council

1115 Depart Bury Market ...

On the morning that Justice Secretary Jack Straw made a desperate appeal to magistrates to send fewer people to jail as the prison population in England and Wales zoomed past 82,000 for the first time, David Cameron visited a suburban police station in Bolton. Earlier in the day he'd done the Channel M breakfast show, sharing the sofa with Paul

Horrocks, the editor of the *Manchester Evening News*, and impressively worked his way through casinos, congestion charges, crime, the NHS and the need for a mayor in Manchester. He was charm personified, in spite of the rottweiler in a skirt who was interviewing him.

And then it was on to Astley Bridge for a tour of the police station, and a debrief about local crime. The minute we walked in we could sense that this event had been more stage-managed than one would have imagined. And not by Cameron's team. As we were given a twenty-minute audio-visual presentation on the area's 'robust approach to offender management', and shown dozens of crudely executed graphs demonstrating the department's success at tackling vandalism, litter, drunkenness, drugs, abandoned and burned-out cars, bad behaviour, noisy neighbours and rowdy teenagers, it became apparent that all the officers really wanted to do was show off their ability to meet their targets. Some of it was very impressive – especially their success in the local areas of extreme social deprivation and crime, but when you deciphered the New Labour gobbledegook it became apparent that many of the PCs found the enforced bureaucracy burdensome in the extreme. 'Case building' seemed to be one of the most typical problems, as well as the backlog of those cases coming to court: one youth arrested for carrying and selling cannabis in January was not due to have his case heard by a magistrate until July at the earliest, and, as he was out on bail, the PCs who arrested him knew that he was still selling drugs on the streets of Bolton. We were taken through the paperwork required for taking down someone's details to put on file. Eight minutes seemed to be the minimum time needed to complete a form successfully (longer for stop and search), and when Cameron asked, 'Why don't you just write down their name and address and what they look like?' he was met with bewildered stares. Only one sergeant went off-message, telling us what he really thought of the internal bureaucracy at the station: 'These days there are forms for everything,' he said, 'and sometimes you just can't get out of the office. I spend 50 per cent of my time here completing arrest forms when I should be out on the street collaring people. But even collaring people these days is made difficult by the convoluted computer systems. They've been down for half an hour this morning and we're just waiting for them to come back up again. It's just as well you're here or else we would have nothing to do.'

Criticism of the arbitrary nature of government crime targets had recently become deafening, with allegations that serious crime was largely being ignored and minor misdemeanours being elevated just to reach targets. One police officer had been quoted in the *Daily Mail* as saying: 'We are bringing more and more people to justice, but they are the wrong people.' Constables used to take great pride in coming back after a night shift and reporting that nothing had happened, said the paper, whereas now they were being asked why no one was picked up or issued with a penalty notice.

As Cameron spoke to the station staff, a couple of PCSOs (personal community support officers) were preparing to go out on their rounds. They appeared to get on well with the people on their patch, but whenever 'Blunkett's Bobbies' had any problems they had to call in the real policemen, by which time the troublemakers were usually long gone.

We were led into the cells, although we were only shown a women's cell because the others were occupied by a number of prisoners on suicide watch. After talking to some of the officers for a while it transpired that most of the cells were used to house newly convicted prisoners on their way to jail. Every prison in the area being full to capacity, more and more local police stations were being used to house prisoners, sometimes for up to a week before they were moved on, sometimes to another local station.

As we said our goodbyes and started to leave, Cameron noticed a small electronic screen by the entrance of the station. 'What's this?' he asked, with genuine interest. It turned out to be a rotating photo parade of the men in the area that Astley Bridge police most wanted to find. But the staff sergeant asked Cameron's camera team to turn their equipment off (this was being filmed for Cameron's website), in case it caused 'complications'. Why? Would it affect their human rights? Would it add another tranche of paperwork to the arresting process? Cameron was dumbfounded, and when he asked why the photographs couldn't simply be put up in every off-licence and bus shelter in West Yorkshire, again the blank stares returned.

As we were bundled back to the car, Cameron said, 'Society seems to stop at our front gate these days and start again at work. Many people feel that even the police seem unable to control what is going on in our streets. Just look at these police officers in this station; they really want to get out there and fight crime. Ten years ago it was fashionable to say that the sight of policemen on the streets had no effect on the likelihood of crimes being committed, but it's proved that the opposite is true. Put police on the street and they act as a deterrent.'

Unlike a lot of politicians, David Cameron becomes easier to like the more time you spend with him. His performance in Bury market later that morning was a master class in electioneering. He was engaged, interested and sincere. One of the fatal mistakes that politicians make with the public is asking a question without really wanting a reply. But Cameron took in everything, using the responses either to confirm his suspicions, or – more impressively – alter or improve his attitude to whatever it was he had just been told. He was followed by a phalanx of eager and highly professional assistants, who steered him whenever he went walkabout, trying to make sure he stayed away from nutters, or didn't stand for photographs in front of huge 'Condoms' signs. 'But sometimes I go towards trouble just to see what the people with me will do,' said Cameron, smiling. 'You can talk to most people if you're measured, even if they aren't interested in listening to you. Just make sure you never answer a question about Rugby League ... because you'll get it wrong.'

In Bury market, people appeared genuinely to like him, wanted to touch the cloth, press the flesh. You could see a proper politician getting better and better at his job, and never once looking as though he didn't enjoy every second of it. Like William Hague on a previous visit a decade before, he stopped to buy a hot black pudding at Chadwick's ('Manufacturers and purveyors of the original Bury black pudding since 1954') before being accosted by another young girl, a shop assistant, who asked – politely, but firmly – if she could have her picture taken with the

Conservative leader. As she scuttled off, mission accomplished, she shouted over her shoulder, 'I love you, David Cameron!' and everyone in earshot (which, considering her scale of her bellowing, appeared to be everyone in the market) smiled.

Such was the well-oiled machine behind Cameron that the itinerary was constantly updated, and such was the slickness that you felt as though you were on the campaign trail with a presidential candidate. But the following morning the itinerary was tweaked by Cameron himself, who wanted to visit the Salford Lads Club to try and recreate the famous Smiths photograph that appeared on their 1986 album *The Queen Is Dead* (the original of which, taken by Stephen Wright, hung in the National Portrait Gallery in London). This was a pilgrimage of sorts, as Morrissey is something of a musical hero to him, and Cameron chose the Smiths song 'This Charming Man' on *Desert Island Discs* (Morrissey's appearance on *Top of the Pops* was 'an iconic moment for people of my age'). He had originally tried to have his picture taken a month earlier when he was meeting volunteers there, but local Labour Party members took part in a small demonstration outside the club, which prevented Cameron from posing for a photograph in front of the building. Salford Labour MP Hazel Blears said his visit would remind people of 'the dog days of Thatcherism'. The club, which opened in 1904, lists actor Albert Finney and Allan Clarke, lead singer of the sixties pop group the Hollies, among its former members, and has become something of a pop-culture icon. It has become a shrine for Smiths fans from all over the world, who frequently scrawl graffiti on its outside walls.

The pit stop at the Lads Club in February went according to last-minute plans, and Cameron finally got his picture. And that night, on the train back to Euston, I found myself humming 'This Charming Man'. For the charming man himself it was the opening of the North West Conservatives conference at the Reebok Stadium in Bolton, before rushing back to London for his daughter Nancy's postponed fourth birthday party ('I'll be there for the sugar rush,' he told Samantha on the phone). His speech was ten pages of double-spaced lines, carefully annotated in fountain pen … 'It's great to be here,' he said. 'It's my third time in the North West this year – and we haven't even got to the end of Feb. I came up straight after Prime Minister's Questions. We learned something this week, as apparently it's Bruce Forsyth's favourite programme. He says it reminds him of Frankie Howerd and Les Dawson, although I haven't yet worked out which one I am …'

SIX

'*I don't think the fact that there are lots of people going to different churches makes for a divided country*'

Single mothers, homosexuality, the Royal Family, multiculturalism, Sharia law, terrorism, the grammar school problem, God's own BlackBerry

Friday 29 February. 'Who wrote this rubbish?' said David Cameron rhetorically, flicking through his briefing notes as the silver Avis mini-van sped away up the M1 on its way to Birmingham. The Leader of the Opposition was not in an especially good mood. The morning had started badly, with former Tory grandee Norman Tebbit attacking him aimlessly in that day's *Spectator*, and as he finished his buttered toast and did up his brand new red tie ('We'll keep the red flag flying here,' he sang) in his North Kensington home, a stream of expletives left Cameron's lips.

But now, sitting in the van surrounded by the papers, and two of his pretty and redoubtable press aides, Cameron was ploughing through the black box full of the various briefing notes for the speeches he was giving later that day. 'Who's responsible for all the bloody typos?!' he said, to no one in particular, looking especially at one piece of paper. He then glanced quickly at the two-page itinerary for the day. 'It says here I have two lunches, which usually means I won't eat anything at all. Gabby, will there be sandwiches?' Even though he had only finished his breakfast forty-five minutes ago, here was a man acting as if his blood-sugar level was sinking fast. 'It's going to be one of those days,' he said, before reaching back and asking for a copy of *The Times*. 'I hate to be in such a bad mood but I really don't like the way these briefing notes are ordered. I don't like the type justified as it makes it incredibly difficult to read.' He scanned some more. 'Bloody hell, does anybody actually read this stuff before it's given to me?'

There was certainly a full day ahead. First there was a formal speech at the Conservative Councillors' Association in Kenilworth (on camera, for the Webcameron webcam), then a short speech at a fundraiser in Norton Curlieu, near Warwick (off camera), before driving to Wolverhampton to visit the local paper, the *Express & Star*, and to have tea and biscuits (that's what it said on the itinerary) with the editor, chief news editor and managing director. Then at 4.40 the Avis mini-van was due to take him on to Dudley, where DC would visit the Castle High School and Visual Arts College – where he would meet children and teachers involved in an anti-alcohol workshop – and then motor on to Birmingham, where he was speaking in front of 500 of the great and the good at a dinner to celebrate 150 years of the *Birmingham Post*.

As he sat in the van, scanning his notes and scrolling his BlackBerry for updates from Central Office, he displayed two very Cameron characteristics: a well-honed brusqueness mixed evenly with the ability to absorb and articulate frighteningly complex ideas and strategies, usually at the same time. There is an old joke about a man emerging from a London taxi outside the Houses of Parliament, having had the benefit of the driver's opinions on everything from the economy (bad) and the roads (worse) to world hunger ('Don't get me started on world hunger or else we'll be here all day …') and the Middle East ('Now, this is actually easy …'). And as he pays his fare, the passenger suddenly thinks that what MPs should really do is drive cabs while all the London cabbies run the country. But today there were no interruptions from the driver; it would have been difficult with Cameron spinning out thoughts, lines and ideas in his machine-gun style. (When Cameron meets people he tends to form his own opinions and make his own judgements quickly, clearly and without much help from anyone else. He uses his Cabinet to hone and fine-tune, but the central shifts always seem to come from him. If he thinks of an idea that needs to be worked up or could be fed to the press, he immediately gets onto the phone, explaining it to Steve Hilton or Andy Coulson.)

At Kenilworth, the week was beginning to catch up with him, and he was looking forward to a weekend at home ('Hi, Mum! Look, I think we've got a lunch on Sunday but we could see you on Saturday if you're free …'). As he paused backstage in the hotel, waiting to be introduced to his band of councillors, standing behind a decidedly rickety looking backboard that looked as though it might fall over at any minute, he said, 'I've made eight speeches this week, which is why I'm in such a bad mood. It's actually too many. I don't know if I'm Arthur or Martha.' And then he was onstage, blinding them with charm.

'A debate is raging in Westminster,' he began. 'Some say this is the worst government since Jim Callaghan. And some say, no, that's completely unfair. It's the worst government ever … Honestly, I think Nancy Cameron could do a better job as Chancellor.' Up on the stage, using phrases and sound bites he'd used dozens of times in the previous weeks (in the Kenilworth speech he used the expression 'top-down government' fourteen times), he nevertheless looked like a man who wanted to make a difference, a man who was prepared to suffer all the abuse, all the motorway logjams and all the stale sandwiches in order to get his mandate. The *Guardian*'s Jonathan Freedland identified the following as the principal ingredients of a Cameron speech: charm, confidence and loose, easy sincerity; in Kenilworth, the audience got lashings of it. But whereas in the past Cameron the bum-fluffed milksop tended to behave as if he were RADA's top graduate who had just landed the plum role in the end-of-term play, these days he looks positively senatorial. And Cameron had already collected a considerable collection of the sort of simple, clear phrases for which Blair had such a flair. 'Sharing the proceeds of growth', for instance, which, as Freedland had identified, was an elegant slice of fudge that at the very least had bought the leader some time to work out his tax policy. 'We're all in this together' was hardly poetry, but it had a sort of colloquial, grass-roots appeal, while one of his most successful sound bites was his oft-repeated rebuke to both the 'me-me-me individualism' of Margaret Thatcher and to the top-down government-knows-best rhetoric of Blair and now Brown's Labour Party: 'There is such a thing as society, it's just not the same thing as the state.'

Using Westminster's always changing calculus of success and failure, Cameron – 'DC', 'Dave', 'Britain's Next Prime Minister', he had been called all three by the press in the previous forty-eight hours – was on the up and up, and there was beginning to be a sense that David Cameron might be an idea whose time had come. This meant that all of a sudden the negative press surrounding the Tory leader began to sound a little out of sync. The naysayers in the nationals – Norman Tebbit, Peter Hitchens, Michael Portillo – were looking increasingly marginalized, all bellowing into an oncoming wind. The Tories' policy drive had resulted in a lot of noise, which was beginning to capture the public's imagination. Cameron's policies were starting to resonate not just because they were refreshing and offered the sort of change that non-Tories were beginning to find appealing, but – as commentators were starting to say with increasing regularity – also because Brown and his government seemed incapable of taking care of those things the electorate had previously taken for granted. And these weren't peripheral things, these were the biggies – crime, the NHS, immigration, schools, welfare, the economy, topics the Tories had opinions about, topics they could grasp. Like so many times before in his short career, Cameron was benefiting from Labour's ineptitude.

Even in cyberspace Cameron was getting good notices. The notoriously cynical political blogs, many of which celebrated an 'anti-politics' agenda – encouraging apathy and non-participation – were now wondering whether or not Cameron could do it after all. After Cameron's address at the Conservative Welsh Conference at the beginning of March, Guido Fawkes wrote, 'His speech accepts that voters are going to demand more openness, transparency, honesty and control … Most of all he blames the government's culture of spin, the three thousand press officers and the cynicism of politicians who promise what can never be delivered, with the single-minded pursuit of favourable headlines rather than real results in mind. All of which is in the DNA of New Labour … Cameron's new politics shows promise, his post-bureaucratic agenda is about limiting the state and the unlimiting of society.'

Brown, meanwhile, used Labour's poorly attended spring conference – held in Birmingham at the very end of February – to launch a deeply personal attack on Cameron, which immediately resulted in accusations in the press that the PM was returning to old-fashioned class warfare, moving his party – as predicted by many – to the left. Making a gauche assault on Cameron's upper-middle-class upbringing and Eton education, Brown said he wanted to build a Britain where it did not matter 'how high up you start', trying to spark a debate that one commentator felt went out with Neil Kinnock and the Ark.

And as if to compound this halting lurch to the left, Brown even allowed one of his front bench – Culture Minister Margaret Hodge – to attack the Proms, one of the great British cultural institutions, saying it was out of step with much of the modern-day public. Apparently, the world's greatest music festival had not managed to attract a sufficiently diverse audience. It was socially stultifying, she said, elitist. Brown had already become infamous for an orchestrated attack on the middle classes (uninterested in their 'economic paradigm'), but criticizing what the middle classes consumed was a totally new, and rather bizarre, assault. Hodge's outburst may not have deserved the 'pig ignorant' soubriquet bestowed on it by one particularly outraged columnist, but it was inverted snobbery of the worst kind.

The previous regime didn't think things were going too well either, with Blair refusing to endorse or even acknowledge the new order, while those lunching Alastair Campbell that March could only report that the former spinmeister thought Brown was making a complete hash of it all. 'He's staying up all night and worrying about everything in minute detail,' said one frequent visitor to Downing Street. 'And then he's up again at five wondering what the sketch writers and the lobby and the columnists are making of whatever it was he did under duress the day before. You can safely say he's not enjoying things. Since becoming PM he has become hypercritical of his advisors, the press, and anyone who dares criticise him. He's got the Cabinet behind him, but then he chose them for that very reason.'

Around this time Fraser Nelson in the *Spectator* related for the first time that in the very early days of the Brown premiership, when the newcomer had no home access to the Prime Minister's computer, Brown was forced to sneak downstairs to his office in the middle of the night. At five o'clock one morning security guards were called in to apprehend an intruder only to find the new Prime Minister trying to enter his own office, still in his pyjamas, cursing as he bashed in the security code. As a snapshot of an insomniac obsessive it was as good as they come.

After Kenilworth it was a short drive to a fundraiser, where Cameron was speaking on behalf of the Conservative parliamentary candidate for Warwick and Leamington, Chris White (where Labour had a majority of just 300). Standing beneath an enormous cluster of blue balloons, in his speech Cameron made several references to 'Calamity Clegg' (Nick Clegg had recently been appointed leader of the Lib Dems), made even more references to 'that strange man in Downing Street', and used three of the jokes he'd used in Kenilworth, although to no less applause.

When he jumped back into the van, he turned to Gabby Bertin and said, 'Okay, what's happened in the world? Have I had to resign?'

When he reached the *Express & Star* he was given a tour of the building – news desk, subs, features and pictures. In the picture department he was shown a photograph of himself visiting Wolverhampton ten years earlier. 'Look,' said Cameron. 'It's Alan B'Stard.' The *Express & Star* is the largest local newspaper in the country, a paper that continues to reflect the fluctuating fears of its readers. Which, in short, are crime, violence and drunkenness, in that order. The paper hadn't just lost the bulk of its classified advertising because of the advent of the web – it had also lost it because people no longer felt safe advertising a £10,000 car because they couldn't legislate for who came round to look at it. All anyone cared about in Wolverhampton was crime. 'Whenever we put some ASBO kid in the paper, and put up a poster in the newsagents with their face on the front, all you get is the kids taking pictures of themselves in front of it with their phones,' said the editor, Adrian Faber.

And then it was the long drive to Dudley, to the school, to sit with a counsellor explaining to a dozen rather dazed ten-year-olds why the likes of Paul Gascoigne, Paul Merson, George Best, Brian Clough, Tony Adams and other alcoholic footballers weren't role models. In another sports hall he joined another group of similarly aged boys playing football, taking a free kick over a wall of five cardboard defenders. Cameron narrowly missed. As he left he was presented with a Wolverhampton Wanderers football shirt, with 'Cameron' printed on the back. He gets given lots of stuff on the road, but he actually looked as if he would keep this one.

Cameron spent his time being whisked from rental car to photo op, from town hall lectern to local radio microphone. He was forever walking up to people to shake their hand, forever hopeful that it was the right person's hand he was shaking, and not the hand of some random bystander who had just come in from the cold to see what all the fuss was about. 'Sometimes my life is not what it should be,' he said, aware that he had a missed call from his wife and needed to ring her back. 'It sometimes feels like I have a thirty-four-hour day.' Usually, no sooner had he become embroiled in an intense discussion (Cameron never appears to have arguments) than he was tapped on the shoulder or given a finger signal by one of 'Dave's Babes'. Sometimes, if an interview was obviously not going well he would cut his losses, bounce up like Tigger and then find a seemingly perfectly plausible reason to forgive the idiot who had just told him the next Tory government was at least a generation away.

As the van drove past the tea shops, half-timbered houses and gentrified pubs of Warwickshire, Cameron told anecdotes about the mammoth operation behind Matthew Vaughn's party political broadcast which had just been aired, the script for which Cameron had made up on the spot. It was launched on the social networking site Facebook, and had caused enough of a stir to be considered worthwhile (at least internally). He also sang the praises of Paul Abbott's TV series *Shameless* ('It's the new *Coronation Street* …'), expressed his desire for a 'pint' and jokingly wondered if the Labour MPs staying in a nearby hotel would be up for a night of partying. Cameron looked wistful. 'I expect the answer's no, unfortunately, although it would make for some rather good headlines ...'

All the while the Leader of the Opposition ploughed through the briefing notes, learning the names of Wolverhampton Wanderers players from the 1960s, and reeling off sound bites for radio interviews done over the phone. He then spent twenty minutes moving paragraphs around in a piece he was writing for the *Mail on Sunday* on the Tories' plans to reinstate Britannia on the 50p coin.

By the time we reached Birmingham he was getting tired. 'I can do after-dinner speeches, and I'm good at them,' he said, 'but I'm really a morning person. You get a much better reception after dinner, but there we are. I'd much rather be in bed, and to be honest I prefer doing the morning shift.' But once he'd arrived at the *Birmingham Post*'s 150th anniversary dinner he spoke with passion and with humour. There were a *lot* of Tories in the room, true believers who may as well have been wearing button badges inscribed with 'Let's talks about my politics!' It was endearing and contagious. Former BBC newsreader Michael Buerk was our host for the evening, as ebullient and entertaining as ever, greeting Cameron as though he was already Prime Minister.

As I toured Birmingham with Cameron that day, I asked him a lot of questions, and we began by talking about his ideas on the family.

The family and marriage

We've visited a lot of areas where immigration has been responsible for some fairly extensive social reshaping. Do you at all believe that the white working class have become disenfranchized?
No, I don't, I don't think that's true at all. I think in politics there's always the temptation to play the grievance card, to play to grievances. You know, why are the English left out and why are the Scots running everything? Why does no one listen to the white working class ...? I just don't think that's true. Our system is imperfect. Sometimes people feel inadequately

represented or complain that their point of view is not being heard, but I don't think there is a bias against any particular group.

Okay, the family. Do you think the two-parent, man–woman married family should be encouraged? If so, why should you encourage this? Labour have been so inclusive that they've successfully ignored the family, something you appear keen to set right with tax breaks for married couples …

Look, this is not some view that springs from religion or morality, it's just common sense. The evidence suggests, everything we know tells us, that kids have a better chance when mum and dad are both there to bring them up, and I think saying that and backing it with policy does not mean that you are undermining one-parent families or attacking single mothers or belittling what they do. Single mothers do an incredibly difficult job in very difficult circumstances. But we are totally failing our country, our society, if actually we don't say, yes, of course they do a good job but let's try and arrange affairs so that we don't send out a signal that commitment doesn't matter, that couples don't matter, that marriage doesn't matter. These things do matter. The decisions individuals make have social consequences and we should be clear about that.

You're saying that marriage is the perfect model, then?

There are two different things that go together here, very clearly. At the moment the tax system doesn't recognize marriage. The benefits system recognizes any form of cohabitation or commitment and penalizes it. And we've said let's change both of those things. Let's change the benefits system so it actually encourages couples to come together and stay together, and let's change the tax system so it does specifically recognize marriage. The two things very much go together and I think they're both extremely important.

Is marriage not taken seriously enough these days?

My view is that marriage is simply a very good institution. It's not the only way that couples come together and stay together, but it helps people, the sense of commitment, the fact that you're standing there in front of friends and relatives and saying it's not just about me any more, it's about us, it's about us together, we have commitments to each other, I think it's a really important thing. I am unashamedly pro-marriage.

But there are many dangers in promoting this view …
Yes, there are. Some people will say, as they do, you're not being fair to single parents – I don't agree with that. I think I am. Some people will say, you'll sound a bit old-fashioned – I don't care. I think it's important. Anyway, I think I'm in a better position perhaps than some previous Conservative leaders to make this point, because when I made it, at a Conservative conference, in front of a Conservative audience, I said, by the way, I don't just back marriage but I also back civil partnerships. Commitment is a good thing, whether you are straight or gay. There was a bit of an intake of breath when I said that at the conference, but actually I think the Conservative Party responded to it very well. If you remember, they actually applauded it.

So what's the ideal family, then, what's the perfect family unit?
I don't think you can paint a picture of some sort of 1950s idyll. What I'm saying is that it's best for children if mum and dad come together and stay together and help bring up children together. That's what the evidence suggests and it's what I believe to be true. Not surprisingly, children with the very best outcomes are the adopted children of married parents. If you think about that logically, it means that those parents were so keen to have children that they went out and adopted them. They tend to have more success. That evidence is very powerful. The other way I put it in the conference speech is by saying that some people say you shouldn't back one form of family over another, or shouldn't back marriage or whatever, but I just ask myself, look, do I think we'd be a happier society if more people got married, if fewer got divorced and there was less family breakdown, then, yes, I do think that would be better.

One of the things you constantly talk about is the family, and in almost every session you've talked about some aspect of the family. But how, when encouraging marriage in a sort of settled sense of family, are you going to avoid a John Major back-to-basics fiasco if one of your ministers gets caught with his trousers down?

Whenever I've spoken about the family and about marriage I've said that politicians are human, and err occasionally, like everyone else. And we just have to be grown up when that happens. You've got a choice – you can either say that someone in my party at one stage might be found doing something inappropriate, therefore I will never talk about family issues, social issues, drug taking, alcohol abuse, domestic violence. The list would be so long, it would be ridiculous. You just have to be grown up about it, talk about the things that matter, and the family matters more to me than anything else. I'm not lecturing anyone. All I'm saying is that the choices people make have consequences for society.

Okay, but how do you propose getting single mothers to vote Tory?

This isn't about getting votes, it's about saying what's right. Look, the amount of people who actually go out wanting to be single parents is extremely low. We will help by explaining to them that we understand the pressures they're under, and the huge pressure of bringing up children on your own, and we want to help. And we will help. Helping with child care, helping with child benefit, helping people back into work when their children are old enough. It's all of those things. When I meet single parents I don't find that I'm cast as an uncaring 1950s man, because I think I understand the pressures they're under.

But how do you begin to encourage people to make better choices?

In the end, people are not going to get married for a tax break, and people are not going to suddenly stop separating because we change the benefits system. I'm not naive. But it seems to me that if we need a change in culture that is more pro-commitment, more pro-family, more pro-marriage, the very least the government can do is make sure the benefits and the tax systems are not going in the opposite direction. So I just think that the benefits and the tax systems are just one small part of a much bigger cultural shift that needs to take place. At the moment they are going in the wrong direction. There are hundreds of thousands of people in our country who pretend to live apart because of the benefits system, and how crazy are we to encourage that? It's mad. Other European countries recognize marriage and have more favourable treatment for couples than we do, and I think it's very sensible.

Do you think that fathers and husbands suffer disproportionately on divorce?
Not necessarily. I've followed the Fathers for Justice debate, and I think there are some legitimate points that either parent could make. There is a legitimate point that fathers who are denied access after a settlement can find it very difficult to get that access unless they get a court order. But I don't buy their argument outright. The fact is that many women suffer very badly from divorce.

Have you ever stopped to imagine what British society might look like in 100 years' time?
Economically it's an intriguing question because often people will say, look, does it really matter if the economy grows at 3.5 per cent rather than 3.2 per cent, and over a long period of time, yes, it really does. I had dinner with the Swedish Prime Minister this week and their economic record in the last century was incredible because they did have relatively rapid growth and they went from being one of the poorest countries in Europe to being one of the richest. I know socialists think otherwise, but I don't think we should ever take things for granted, which is what economists are always telling me.

You've spent so much time travelling around Britain, visiting youth clubs, police stations, newspaper offices, markets, prisons, schools, town councils. You must have built up a fairly good mental picture, built through personal experience, of what the country is like. What do we all have in common? With each other ...

Oh, I do think we have a fairly good system of shared values, of tolerance, reasonableness, good sense of humour, a kind of gritty common sense, we tend to support the underdog. The impact of history, institutions, weather, popular culture, does mould a certain set of common values. We have a lot of shared experiences over a very long period of time, and we've been formed by them. We're still being formed by them.

Homosexuality, and Royalty

Do you think the Tories are less open-minded about homosexuality than other parties?
I think we were, and I now don't think we are. It's one of the changes that needed to take place, and I think it's important. The civil partnership thing was quite an important moment because the fact is gay people can't get married, and so why should we have a situation where gay people who want to make a commitment to each other can't find a way of registering it? Which is why civil partnerships are absolutely right. That issue is almost laid to rest.

What about the Royal Family? How do you see their role in the near, mid- and long-term future?
Incredibly strong. I am a great believer in constitutional monarchy both in the individual and in the collective sense. The Queen has just been incredible; she's just a remarkable public servant. But I also believe in the institution. Some people question whether the Royal Family will last, but I believe it will. It's like any institution; it has to reform and evolve and it has to think very carefully about how it does that, but I think the concept of a constitutional monarchy is incredibly important. The Royal Family is one of the things that helps bring us together.

So you're a royalist then?
Well, the idea of replacing that with the elected President Kinnock or Blair or John Major, or anyone, is just awful. And I'm sure that in a hundred years' time we'll still have the monarchy.

Religion

Talking about constitutional foundations, why didn't you criticize the Archbishop of Canterbury when he said that it was only a matter of time before we lived under some sort of parallel Sharia law? I know you were away on holiday, but your silence was extraordinary.

I wouldn't accept that at all. I was absolutely focused on responding to what he said because I thought what he said was wrong. But I also believed it was vital, because of the nature of the subject, to handle this in a thoughtful and reasonable way. So the first thing I did was talk to Sayeeda Warsi and I sanctioned what she was going to say in reaction to the Archbishop's speech. I thought I would leave her to do that and then take the time to read, very carefully, not only what he said in the original speech, in the interview that actually kicked off the whole row, but also what he said in his speech partly retracting what he'd said a few days later. I was then able to make a much longer and more clearly reasoned intervention into the whole debate. Which I feel very strongly about. Because, in the end, I'm not a religious scholar, I can't criticize what he said on some sort of religious grounds, and I'm not a constitutional expert so I can't criticize it on constitutional or legal grounds ... But what I think I can legitimately criticize it for is on cultural grounds, because we need to build a more cohesive, integrated country in which everyone feels they're part of the future, and I really don't think we'll do that by having separate legal systems and by treating different minority groups differently.

Inclusiveness ...

Exactly. What we want is for people to be different but to be treated equally, rather than for people to be treated differently. But as I said in my speech, the introduction of Sharia law could only act to undermine society, particularly at a time when more not less integration is needed. The big questions facing the country today are: how do we end state multiculturalism, enhance cohesion, promote opportunity and build a stronger society?

So how do we all live together? How can people from different backgrounds, and who live by different cultural and religious codes, come together and live side by side? It's a problem that is becoming increasingly acute because of the incredibly varied mix of cultures we now have here.

Well, we need to make sure that the balance between Church and state, faith and politics, religious identity and political identity that has developed over centuries is maintained. That's why I've been saying for a long time that we've been handing a victory to our enemies – to those who want to divide and those who oppose liberal values – if we respect different cultures to the point of allowing them – or, worse still, encouraging them – to live separate lives, apart from each other and apart from the mainstream.

Can you give some examples of how this has manifested itself?

In the voluntary sector it's meant giving financial aid for artistic and other projects purely on account of ethnic background – with various groups, purporting to represent various minorities, competing for money against each other. In public services it's meant not just essential information, but all information endlessly translated into lots of different languages, so people can go about their daily lives without ever having to learn English. I suppose what I really mean is treating groups of people as monolithic blocks rather than individual citizens.

Fundamentally you believe that state multiculturalism is a wrong-headed doctrine that has had disastrous results, that it has fostered differences between communities, stopped us from strengthening our collective identity.

Absolutely. By concentrating on defining all these new cultures we have forgotten to define the most important one: our own. So we now have a situation where the children of first-generation immigrants – children born and raised here – feel more divorced from life in Britain than their parents. If you look at the difference with America it's really startling – something like half of American Muslims think of themselves as Muslim first, American second. In Britain, it's nearly twice that – with over 80 per cent of Muslims thinking of themselves as Muslim first and British second.

You don't think the Archbishop should have resigned?
No, I don't think that at all. I just think that on this subject he was wrong. The argument about how we end what I call state multiculturalism and how we have a stronger society I think is so important. What he said shouldn't stand, as it were.

Faith, race and more multiculturalism

How did we get to a state in this country where we are now more divided by faith than race?
Are we? There's a growth in religious belief, and religious attendance, partly because of the wide-scale immigration from Eastern Europe and Africa, which has strengthened the numbers of Catholics. And there are obviously more Muslims now than ever. But are we divided by faith? I don't feel that it's the faith that causes the division. I think the division has been caused more by a failure to integrate that has been made worse by a policy of state multiculturalism, and almost encouraging people not to integrate. I don't think the fact that there are lots of people going to different churches makes for a divided country.

We've already talked a bit about immigration, but what is your exact position? The recent MORI poll showed that nearly 70 per cent of British people thought we had let too many immigrants in. Surely the British people should be listened to. Let the doctors and the footballers in, keep a keener eye on things ... What have been, and are currently, the benefits and problems of immigration?
I think we recognized, rightly, that the British people were becoming concerned about this issue, but we didn't recognize the fact that while people might have agreed with some of the things we had to say, they questioned our motives in saying them. Which is why I took quite a long

time before entering this debate, because I wanted people to understand that I support the multiracial country that we have. I think Britain benefits from immigration, I think minority communities make an enormous contribution. I wanted to get all that groundwork clear so that people could see where I was coming from before going on to explain that, while immigration is a good thing, not any immigration and not all immigration. Now there's a very good case for an overall limit.

It would be easy to say that Gordon Brown used his years of prosperity to keep five million Britons on benefits and imported a workforce – which is why two in three jobs created by Labour since 1997 have been filled by migrants. You could also say that this is also why economic growth has not translated into true 'social justice' as it has passed millions by. But your big thing is that the levels of immigration we've seen have put too great a burden on public services. So how are we going to control it?

I think that the burden on public services is the most important thing. Trevor Phillips spoke up in support of my speech because he described it as 'deracializing' the debate. And I'm so pleased he said that because that was exactly what I was trying to do. I hope that what we've managed to do is get away from immigration being an issue about race and ethnicity. Because that's not where the British public are at all. Where the British public are is being concerned about the pressure on schools, and housing and hospitals. It's about population rather than anything else, and that's a very healthy development and means we can have a sensible, reasonable debate, and therefore we can have a proper limit on immigration, which means that those pressures can be better handled.

And how do you go about organizing that?

Well, the truth is, in terms of immigration from existing EU countries there's nothing we can do about it directly. What you can do is have transitional controls on future members, and I think we should do that. And of course you can do something about it indirectly, by reforming welfare to get more people into work. In terms of non-European immigration we do need to have a limit. And that I think is very important. When you look at the figures you can see there's been a very large increase. I'd love immigration not to be an issue in British politics, and it wasn't an issue when it was reasonably controlled. It is now an issue again because people feel the numbers and the pressure are too great.

How long do you think the threat to Britain from Islamic terrorism will last?

For years, decades; this is a long war, or at least a long struggle. The Cold War wasn't won in a few decisive encounters, it was a long cultural, ideological and political battle, and that's what we're engaged in. We need to stand up for our values and defeat what is a poisoned offshoot of a great religion. It can be done but it's not going to happen through military action alone; we have to win every single battle in terms of soft power and hard power, of democracy as well as everything else. It's going to be a very, very long battle.

Is the government engaging with British Muslims in the right way?

No, I don't think they are. To be fair to them, 9/11 was a huge wake-up call to lots of people and it's not surprising that not everything was put right straight away. But it was extraordinary that we were both in the vanguard of invading Iraq and Afghanistan and yet at the same time we were tolerating extremists back at home who were poisoning the minds of young British Muslims, and not really doing anything about it. I think now we have a more holistic approach in the UK, but we shouldn't be funding extremist groups, and we should be expelling and deporting preachers of hate, we should be working with the Muslim community to make sure that when imams come in they speak English. There is a whole menu of things that need to be done to try and help the Muslim community itself isolate and eliminate the extremist elements. And we have to give more thought and attention to that. And so far we haven't.

Shadow Cabinet members aside, when was the last time you had a Muslim round to your house for dinner?
I can't remember if that's ever happened, to be honest with you. That's exactly why last year I took a few days out to go and live with a Muslim family in Birmingham.

Immigration

How would you characterize what the government is now proposing for immigration, with this convoluted points system?
I think what they've done is borrowed part of our policy but then haven't understood its full consequences. The Australian-style points system, which is meant to ensure that non-EU immigration is beneficial to Britain, is sensible. But they have not accepted the limit that we have suggested. You have to have a limit. So I don't think they've done quite what needs to be done, but then they wouldn't.

To what extent do you think people should simply be prepared to accept any changes to the country that result from the arrival of lots of new people from abroad?
I think we should be, and I think generally we are, a tolerant country that has successfully integrated different waves of immigration over the years. You can go back to the Huguenots, or the Ugandan Asians or the Jews from Eastern Europe 100 years ago. The problem is that in the 1990s and early 2000s the scale of immigration was so great that the integration was more difficult to achieve and the pressure on public services became too much, so therefore there's been public disquiet about it. And politicians have a duty to respond to this, which hopefully is what I've done.

To what extent has debate about immigration been stifled, particularly by political correctness?
I think it was stifled by the Enoch Powell speech [exactly forty years ago]. The damage of that speech was not just that in using the language that he

did he stirred up racial hatred, but the longer-term damage was he stopped British politicians having a sensible debate about immigration for years. And we've sort of been living in his shadow, and that's been very damaging. Because we should be able to have this discussion, we should be able to say these things, to have a sensible, reasonable debate about immigration – about numbers, about pressure, about how we integrate, without people pointing fingers and screaming 'racist'. And Enoch Powell's speech made that much more difficult to happen. In a way it's easier for me to raise the debate because I was only one year old when he made the speech. And when one of our candidates [Halesowen and Rowley Regis candidate Nigel Hastilow] said that Powell was absolutely right he was asked to make a pretty swift retraction.

But do you accept that the Tory Party is more closely associated in the mind of the electorate with racism than the Labour Party?
I think historically there may have been that association, because Powell was a Conservative, and because, as I say, sometimes in the past people have questioned our motives when raising this issue, and what I've been keen to do is get us to a situation where we can raise it in a sensible and responsible way without having our motives questioned. And I think we are there. But it means all the time being very intolerant of racism and discrimination, which I believe the modern Conservative Party is.

How are your policies on immigration any different from traditional Tory policies on immigration?
I was so young when Enoch Powell made his Rivers of Blood speech, and I don't see the issue of immigration as one of race or colour or creed, I see it as one of numbers and pressure on public services and population. Likewise welfare. Yes, the mass unemployment of the 1980s was tragic and difficult and awful for some communities in our country, but actually the problem today is not that sort of mass unemployment, it's people out of work and on incapacity benefit, often generationally. And again, we can deal with this through the eyes of 2008, not looking at it through the eyes of 1983. The centre right have

still got some of the best arguments about how we change society, how we improve the economy, how we get people back to work, how we get better results from schools, and a modern generation of Conservatives can make those arguments free of the baggage of the past. This last year I've learned a lot of things, and I think this is the argument that I really want to develop between now and the next election.

The Human Rights Act

The human rights issue is complicated and emotionally charged, yet we continually read about people we have to feed and clothe because it would be an infringement of their human rights if we sent them home …
When the government introduced the Human Rights Act, it basically imported to British courts lock, stock and barrel the whole European Convention on Human Rights. I think a better solution would be for Britain to write its own Bill of Rights. It would in many ways be similar to the European Convention on Human Rights because Bills of Rights tend to be quite similar, but it could include a better explanation of rights and responsibilities, it could include clearer definitions, it could include some particularly British rights that we feel strongly about, like jury trial, and I think it would be better to have that in British courts.

But it's only ever going to work if it's autonomous and properly recognized, not if we're still subordinate to Strasbourg. Give me half a dozen examples of how that might change verdicts.
That is a very good question. I hope it would help on the issue of public safety, where under the ECHR and the cases brought under it, we've got to a position where the Home Secretary doesn't seem able to deport people who could put the country at risk, and I would hope we can get some slightly clearer definition on that. I hope it would be able to incorporate some elements of common sense to prevent some of the outcomes that have happened under the ECHR where, for instance, life prisoners are given access to hard-core pornography because it's their

human right. A lawyer will say to you that it's terribly difficult to write into a bill anything that will give you that sort of protection, but I think it is worth trying to have rights with common sense. Rights with national security, rather than throwing up your hands and saying it's not possible. So that's what we're looking at.

And presumably the country needs to be able to take effective action against incitement to terrorism …
Yes, the government must be able to expel unwanted and dangerous foreign nationals from our country, and proscribe groups and organizations that pose a threat to our security. But today, it is sometimes virtually impossible to deport foreign terror suspects from Britain. The European Convention on Human Rights, on which the Human Rights Act is based, has been extended by case law far beyond what the founders originally intended. Under the Chahal judgement of 1996, the Court in Strasbourg ruled that the British Home Secretary can't balance the human rights risk to individuals if they're deported against the security risk to the UK if they stay. And the Human Rights Act has made the problem worse. So our approach has got to change. If our security services believe that a foreign national is a dedicated terrorist and a danger to national security, then the Home Secretary should be able to balance the rights of the suspect with the rights of society as a whole, and go ahead with deportation.

Why should a British Muslim vote Conservative when they are demonized at every twist and turn? What would you do for them that Labour doesn't already?
I think our clarity about cohesion and integration, our plans for National Citizen Service, teaching English to new arrivals, I think they will appreciate that. I think if you emigrate to a country most people do want to integrate. I think they'll appreciate our candour. Some British Muslims have looked at the Conservative Party and thought, well, it's not really for me. And if we can get them over that, because we have Muslim councillors and candidates, they can see that we are open to all, then I

think we can unleash a great wave of support among British Muslims. Many of them are part of a culture that shares our belief in strong families, enterprise, self-reliance, and many of them when they do join the Conservative Party say it's actually a natural home for me.

More so than the Labour Party?
A lot more than the Labour Party.

How would you characterize the problem of Islamic extremism here in Britain?
The problem is that there is a perversion of Islam that argues in favour of violence and support for terrorism, and it's got to be confronted and defeated with all the means at our disposal. Through security, policing, and also through argument. In the broader Muslim community, while they don't support this view, there is too much tolerance of it. A while ago I went to the central mosque in Birmingham, and a good 10 per cent of the people I spoke to thought that 9/11 was a Jewish plot. Now, those people are not terrorists, and neither do they support terrorism, but their attitude is making life easier for those who are and do.

What about anti-Semitism, the great forgotten intolerance?
You beat it by being very intolerant of it. You can't tolerate anything that borders on anti-Semitism.

Do you think we're generally too tolerant as a country?
No, I think our tolerance is a good thing. I think we can be too tolerant of wrongdoing sometimes. I think we certainly became too tolerant of multiculturalism, and became too tolerant of things that are clearly wrong like forced marriage, because of misplaced cultural sensitivity.

Do you believe in God?
Yes, I do. I don't have a personal direct line, and he's not on my mobile or my BlackBerry.

So how do you characterize your belief? Or your religious views?
Well, I always find this very difficult. I'm a typical 'Church of Englander' and I believe that there is a power greater than us and the life and work of Jesus Christ is an important guide to morality and action.

But you don't believe that what is stated in the Bible is actually, literally, true …
No, I'm not a literalist. I'm a pretty classic Church of England 'racked with doubt and scepticism' believer.

When did you last go to church?
On Sunday. I actually took the crèche. We take it in turns to take the crèche and this weekend it was my stint. We have to do singing and you have to tell a story. There were about twenty kids between two and four and it was utter chaos … I did the Woman at the Well and it was chaos. Do you remember that one?

I do. My wife takes Sunday School and she did that one fairly recently.
Well, I had a bucket with water in and a cup and I was demonstrating how you got the water out of the well, and of course the children all left their seats, rushed up and peered into the bucket and I lost complete control of the classroom.

Not fit for purpose!
Not fit for purpose, indeed. So I go to church I suppose monthly rather than weekly. More than Christmas and Easter but not every week. I go a little bit in the constituency and a little bit in London.

What did you last pray for?
That is very private. I think I might take the Alastair Campbell 'We don't do God' line …

Should politicians 'not do God'?

I think it's up to you. I always think in politics you should answer questions you feel comfortable answering, and if people are upset that you haven't answered something then they can always not vote for you. I don't think there should be some sort of guide.

What do you make of what appears to be Tony Blair's religious journey?

Very personal. I think people's religious views are very personal. And that's the way I think it should stay.

Should we still be a Christian country?

Well, we are a Christian country, it is an important part of our make-up and I don't see any reason to change. Obviously there are people of many different faiths now in our country, but does that mean we should disestablish the Church? I don't think so. Of course you should root out discrimination and make sure you are fair and reasonable and all the rest of it, but there are a lot of things which could be classified under unnecessary fiddling with things that are there and work very well. In all my years of canvassing I've never come across anyone who wants the Church disestablished so I would leave things as they are!

Okay, what do you think about people taking a greater interest in religion in order to gain places for their children at faith schools?

I was once asked this question by someone from *The Times* and I think I made a bit of a hash of answering it, so let me have another go. I'm a supporter of faith schools, I think they are good schools, I think the Church brings a culture and an ethos into schools that is a helpful thing, and many people support that. Of course, no one should pretend to have a faith that they don't have, but I don't want to criticize parents who want to do the best for their children and struggle to get a place in a good school. The answer to all this is, more good schools! We have these arguments about faith schools, about grammar schools, about whether or not it's suitable to have selection, should we have lotteries for how we decide to send children to school. They're all symptoms of the same basic problem, which is that there are not enough good schools. And that is why people who are anti-Church schools are so wrong because these are good schools. Why? Well, partly because I think the involvement of the Church helps to bring something else to the school and helps to give it a focus and a culture and an ethos, which tends to be a good thing.

Education

So tell me about the grammar school problem … I'm at a loss to understand why you don't want them reintroduced.
Well, let's be clear. Grammar schools are good schools. There are 164 of them, and they have nothing to fear from a Conservative government. They have extremely good results and I have absolutely no plans to do anything that would undermine them in any way, shape or form. That's because I'm a Conservative, and in this party we totally, passionately, believe in opportunity, that everyone should have the chance to get on and make the most of their life. The question is, what's the best way of achieving that today? And the answer is, bring exactly those qualities that we admire in grammar schools – the discipline, the ethos, the focus on high standards – let's bring that to all those kids stuck in all those failing schools which happen to be concentrated in the poorest parts of our country. That's what I was trying to get across.

But why? People like grammar schools. The public like them, many of your MPs like them, and lots and lots of core Conservative voters like them. Children like going to them, children like aspiring to go to them and parents like them. They produce better students, because the education is better. You obviously don't believe this.
No, I'm just much more ambitious than that. The fact is, you won't get the change we need if the limit of your ambitions is a few more grammar schools here and there – which, by the way, isn't going to happen anyway, as no one has set any up, even during eighteen years of Conservative government. If you're serious about giving every child in our country the

opportunity they deserve, you've got to think way, way bigger than grammar schools. You've got to be prepared to completely transform our education system, so that you just don't allow those failing schools to continue. You've got to be as radical in school reform as Mrs Thatcher was, for example, in trade union reform.

You haven't exactly articulated this in the best way possible.
My only regret is that I may have sounded a bit short-tempered and intemperate about it, because I think you should never do that in politics. But I do feel quite strongly that we're not serving the people we represent if we waste our time with a long argument about whether or not we should bring back the 11+.

Are you sure you're not just being stubborn? You strike me as quite a stubborn person.
What I'm doing is focusing on my job, which is to speak up for all those parents whose kids are stuck in failing schools; for all those people who live in areas where the schools just aren't good enough, and develop a policy for radical school reform in this country, which is so desperately needed.

But it played very badly in the press. I think it definitely diluted support for the Conservatives at the time. The press were certainly out to get you.
I accept, and I've said many times since, that this is something we should have handled much better. But look past it all. What's really going on underneath all this? This is important. There are one or two important things I want to get straight in the Conservative Party, and one is, when it comes to the health service, we're about improving it for everybody. We're not about trying to find ways to help people opt out of the health service with tax breaks and private medical care. It's really important to get this across to people. The NHS should be for everyone. Ditto with education. The real challenge is how you improve opportunities and schools for everybody. Yes, there was a specific issue of two counties that

have wholly selective systems [Kent and Buckinghamshire], and what happens if the population in those two counties goes up, and do they have new schools built along the existing lines. But that doesn't change the bigger picture, that the modern Conservative Party stands for improving schools for everyone.

So you can confirm that there's not going to be a great grammar school renaissance.
Much, much better than that, there will be a total transformation of our school system so that we banish forever the idea that we can tolerate a situation where your chance to get on in life depends on where you live or how much money your parents have.

Should middle-class, pushy parents be curbed or encouraged? Should middle-class kids be sucked into poorly performing schools to improve them? The government seem obsessed with making it difficult for the middle classes to educate their children properly. It's like they're being demonized. Labour seem to be obsessed with making it difficult for middle-class families to send their kids to good schools, by introducing lottery systems and quotas and the like. This is social engineering of the worst kind.
What Labour are doing is struggling with the problem of not enough good school places, so instead of trying to get more good schools into the system, they're obsessed with admissions, looking at lotteries and trying to work out admissions that way, and it doesn't work. The point is at the moment it's a scandal that the way to get into a good school is buy a big house in the expensive area where the good school is. And why are people doing this? Why are we having this debate about selection? It's because there aren't enough good schools. And we'll go on having this argument until we actually get some new schools built. So yes, the government are involved in social engineering, and bussing schemes and all the rest of it, but that's because they're Labour, they believe in all that, and they've got a left-wing schools secretary who's pitching for left-wing votes in his party's leadership campaign. We'll

never get schools right with that kind of attitude; we need to look at the cause rather than the consequences, and not just this sterile focus on admissions.

Should there be more selection in schools?
Yes, we think the evidence shows that it's good for kids to be taught at the right level for their ability, and have streaming for better results, so that's definitely something we want to encourage. But we don't think selection between schools is the way forward. What you really need is parents choosing schools, not schools choosing pupils. If you look across the world, where school reform has worked best is in places like Sweden and the chartered schools in America. They've been very good at getting new schools into the state sector, new backing for schools, on a basis of being open to all rather than the basis of selection.

You want to initiate a supply side revolution in schools by adopting the Swedish system of allowing any group of teachers or parents to set up by themselves, so long as they meet certain minimum standards. Can you expand a bit on this?
It's had an enormous impact. Sweden didn't think it was going to see such an extraordinary change when it was first made.

When were you first made aware of it?
I'd read about it for years, and I suppose one of my formative influences was going to see the Tabernacle School in Notting Hill, which was a school set up by frustrated teachers and parents because they were so hacked off with low standards and poor discipline at state schools, particularly with young black boys. And they showed me what could be done if you set up a school from scratch by yourself. The tragedy is that the school had to be in the private sector. But why? Why couldn't it be in the state sector? I've always had a pretty straightforward view on education. The independent sector is extremely good in this country, and there are very good schools which are very competitive, very well funded and financed, with very good, very motivated teachers. Why

can't we have a bit more of that in the state sector? Why can't we take some of the lessons we've learned in the private sector and apply them to the state sector?

It's a good idea, a sensible idea, but rather a radical one for lots of people to understand. It's also not obviously a Conservative idea …
I think it's incredibly Conservative, but I agree that the scale of our ambition means we've got to do a lot more to explain it. But remember it's not an education policy on its own, because parents also want to know, rightly, what our views are on existing schools and how we're going to make them better. We have to set out very clearly our belief in a disciplined environment, getting the basics right, using traditional teaching methods. Testing, but not excessive testing. Independent exam boards, properly regulated, all of that stuff. Trying to get to grips with the amoeba of the educational establishment.

A few months ago I had lunch with a teacher who works in a north London comprehensive. He said that the schools in his area are completely dysfunctional. The pupils have the upper hand and know exactly how far they can push teachers before being reprimanded. Because they have been in trouble so often they have a greater knowledge of legislation in this area than most teachers or journalists. And they play the teachers to the hilt. He said that the pupils own the classroom, and there's little the 'classroom' can do about it. The thing that shocked me most was his admission that they – the class teachers – are regularly encouraged to disguise the race of the troublemakers in order to present a more 'balanced' (i.e. inaccurate and misleading) view of secondary school life. The troublemakers are always the same boys, yet the school executive doesn't want to know that. Because to admit 'that' would be tantamount to condoning institutional racism. When I asked him what he considered to be the one thing that would help kick-start long-term improvement – was it discipline, syllabus, class sizes, the ability to act independently? Was it simply money? – he said, 'Oh, that's simple. Two parents.'

That sounds like a counsel of despair. The Mossbourne Community Academy in Hackney has a very large number of children from single-parent households, a very high ratio of children on free school meals, and very high social deprivation, but it's a fantastic school because they recognize that because these children come from quite fractured backgrounds they need to have incredibly strong discipline, order, boundaries and barriers when they get to school. And so the uniform policy is very tight, the day is very structured, poor behaviour is not tolerated in any way. Almost the poorer the background and the less good parenting at home, the more the school has to be *in loco parentis*. And that's just logical. So I don't believe you can't do anything about this, I don't believe there are some children who are uneducable or predisposed to behaving so appallingly they're going to make life hell for everyone else. That shouldn't be the case. It might mean having smaller schools. I think what Mike Bloomberg has done in New York with smaller schools is really interesting. It certainly means very strong discipline.

Our children go to a state primary in Marylebone, probably the best state primary in London, and the discipline is ferocious. Everything comes from the head and she won't tolerate any hint of aggression or bad behaviour. She's a genius. The kids all want to do well for her and so consequently the school has great results. Like any company, everything comes from the top.

I had a conversation with a head teacher in my constituency the other day, a new one, and I said I'm going to be really frank with you as you're new – I said I think the schools in west Oxfordshire are great but there are two things that always bother me. One is that although we are quite a wealthy area our results are not nearly as good as they should be, and I think there's a bit of coasting. And part of that is a lack of competitive edge between the schools. And then she said I completely agree with you, which surprised me. And then I said the other thing that bothers me is that, while I think the comprehensive ideal is a noble thing, there's always been a sense that I won't discipline that child or exclude them because they'll just have to go to another school and then it will be their problem. And there's been this sort of tolerance of poor behaviour that has seeped into the culture and become very damaging. So I don't think it's just sink schools, and sometimes we focus only on sink schools, it's a problem that goes right across the social spectrum. It's a problem in the leafy suburbs and rural areas as well. It's what George Bush called 'the soft bigotry of low expectations'.

And you're obviously a fan of Blair's academies, aren't you?
Yes, they're mostly very good. But it's more than having some flash new Norman Foster building. That doesn't make a good school. As you say it's the leadership provided by the head teacher more than anything else. Although Blair was copying city technology colleges, which we introduced. So what he did was put boosters on a good idea. And what we need to do is put even bigger boosters on his idea. Part of that is not having to raise the two million quid to become an academy, and also the process is too slow. We need to make it easier to build them.

What about raising the leaving age to eighteen?
I think the idea of getting more people to stay on is good, I think the idea of offering people choices like education, training, apprenticeship up to age eighteen is good. What I don't get with the government's plan is to what extent there is compulsion, because I don't think you can compel people.

That's what they're proposing.
That is what it sounded like, what the spin was, anyway, although they appear to have come quite a long way off it. There was a moment when it looked as though if you didn't stay on until you were eighteen you were virtually going to go to prison. And that was clearly going to be ridiculous.

Will you educate your kids privately?
I want them to go through the state sector, but I'll always do what I think is right for them.

That's what politicians always say.
Maybe it's because it's the truth.

Do you care about that debate?
Yes, I do. You shouldn't have to pay to get a good education. After all, we've already paid once through our taxes. So there should be good local schools. And also I think there's great value in the social mix. But I'll do whatever is right for my children when the time comes.

How closely do you study the curriculum? Would you like to change the emphasis of what is taught in schools?
That's a very good question. I don't believe that the curriculum should be written by a minister at his desk. But I do have a very traditional view of education. I really feel you have to get the basics in place. And I'm a great believer in giving people a framework in which they can learn. Take the example of history, which is a subject I'm passionate about. The fact that I was taught narrative history means it's always much easier to fit into it wonderfully imaginative ideas about the past because you know where they fit. I'm very much a traditionalist when it comes to teaching methods – testing, examining.

Would you try to increase the number of state school pupils getting into Oxbridge?
Yes, of course; it's much lower than it should be. It matters because we want to have a mobile society where you can go from the very bottom to the very top. As I understand it the current numbers are disappointing because, while there are lots of people getting fantastic results at state schools, they're not even thinking about trying to get into the best universities in the country. That means they're missing out but we're missing out too because we're missing out on the talent. But as well as that we've got to completely rethink how we see higher education in this country. We've got to have a situation where it's the norm for pretty much everyone to have some kind of post-eighteen qualification, whether they do that in their early twenties, or thirties, or forties or later.

And it may not be three years in a university away from home but a year in a college round the corner … We've got to be much more open about it all. That's the only way we will have a country and an economy that does well and a country where people have the maximum chance to get on in life.

SEVEN

'Yes, I do bounce policy ideas off Samantha and because she doesn't think like another politician it's very refreshing'

The NHS, the problems of living with a profoundly disabled child, Cameron's kitchen cabinet, Samantha's rules

It was a bright, crisp day at the beginning of March, and the Cameron constituency home in Dean, near Chipping Norton in Oxfordshire, looked rather modest in the rain. Hardly a country pile, their house was relatively small, sitting in a tiny garden full of lawn chairs, a kids' wigwam and the detritus of family living. Inside – light was pouring into the kitchen – it was full of the same sort of stuff that clutters up many such homes, including a fashionable but fairly useless Dualit toaster, a flashy but probably soon to be discarded coffee machine, the same scrubbed wooden work surfaces and the same much-thumbed Jamie Oliver cookbooks.

There was a fancy Maytag fridge freezer, but then there was also the usual random assortment of cereal boxes – Cheerios, Weetabix, Shredded Wheat and all the rest. The Camerons' kitchen could be described as the most generic middle-class-by-numbers kitchen in Britain, a kitchen most people would instantly recognize, an open-plan area full of garlic-stained work surfaces, old wine bottles and yellowing butter on a breakfast table under a pale halogen wash. There was the white perforated kitchen roll, the John Lewis kettle, the Bodum cafetière, the Fairy Liquid, the sticky jars of Marmite, the Waitrose marmalade and the plastic jars of sea salt. There were also scuffed carpets and comfy sofas – furniture meant for sitting in, not staring at. His downstairs loo was adorned with framed covers of *Private Eye* and the *Spectator* (the ones featuring him), plus a cartoon from *Viz* in which he appeared (in his London home he had a framed *Sun* front cover, featuring Cameron standing in front of a gesticulating hoodie with the headline I SUPPOSE A HUG IS OUT OF THE QUESTION).

The porch was a typical mess of dirty Wellington boots, Barbour jackets, a Hackett raincoat, an old Dunhill jacket, children's jackets, children's coats and children's hats. Two Marks & Spencer scarves hung on a hook. There was kids' clutter simply everywhere, just like every family house, with Charlie and Lola books lying on a pile of women's magazines, odd socks drying on a radiator, newspapers stacked by the back door. There was the odd blue Smythson box, but mainly there were a lot of toys in primary-coloured plastic. On their side of their neighbour's pristine grass verge borders was Cameron's vegetable patch, which had recently been profiled in a Sunday newspaper. 'I love my vegetable garden,' he'd said, a few months earlier. 'It's a really nice place to go and sit and contemplate the world. I don't grow vegetables out of the kindness of my heart. I enjoy it, I like eating them, I'm greedy, I love cooking, and it's a good way to unwind.'

The living room looked like a bookshop, and there was an overspill on one of the window sills – mainly political biographies and popular novels. That day's *Daily Mail* was folded on top, bathed in sunlight. This was a home rather than simply a house, a home that looked refreshingly lived in, a home that looked strangely normal. Intriguingly, the house didn't look like the home of a politician, and – judging by the somewhat ordered domestic chaos and the cultural detritus – could just as easily have been the home of a doctor, a lawyer, a farmer or a vet.

Ever since becoming leader in 2005, Cameron had made the family one of the cornerstones of his vision. Under New Labour, he believed, the family had been denigrated, diminished and even demonized. But in Cameron's world the family would rule once more. 'If it comes to a collision between our wealth as a nation and the well-being of families – I choose families,' he once said. In his mind, his was the party of the family – and that, far from there being no such thing as society, it should be at the heart of everything politicians do. He has also said the first test of any future Conservative policy would be whether or not it helped families, saying: 'Let us have no more grandstanding about the exclusive importance of competitiveness in business. Nothing matters more than children.'

In his speech at the Conservatives' spring conference in Newcastle in March he would put the family at the centre of Conservative policy, as he set out his vision for solving Britain's social problems. In a highly personal speech he argued that the only way to reduce demands on the state was through 'social responsibility, not state control'. He said: 'My ambition is to make Britain more family-friendly. To make our country a better place to bring up children. Not just because it's the right thing to do; not just because my family is the most important thing in my life; but because families should be the most important thing in our country's life.'

And the family was at the centre of compassionate Conservatism, which was soon being seen as the backbone, the DNA, of Cameron's rebranded Tories. 'Compassionate Conservatism seeks social renewal through devolution of power and responsibility to people and local institutions,' said Jesse Norman, who wrote one of the first policy documents on the subject in 2006. 'Through greater personal freedom from bureaucracy and regulation, through breaking up state monopolies to improve public services, and through a renewed emphasis on the rights of the citizen and the rule of the law. Its diagnosis of the causes of social failure is increasingly accepted.'

The press were beginning to say that Cameron's ability to sell the idea of social responsibility and genuine family values was not only impressive, but that also he was managing to do it without appearing overly right wing or retrogressive. Even Brown's increasingly worried Cabinet began accepting that the 'family' could be a vote winner, but then obviously stopped short of admitting that stable families were better providers of social security, health care and education than the state.

'Blair's response to a problem [was] a summit in Downing Street, a new law,' said Cameron. 'He created three thousand new criminal offences! Mine is to ask what the family can do, what the voluntary sector can do, what the community can do.'

When I visited Cameron at his home in Dean, we began by talking about his son Ivan.

Coping with Ivan

I'd like to talk for a while about Ivan. He has cerebral palsy and severe epilepsy and needs twenty-four-hour care. Can you articulate how you and Samantha felt when you were told just how disabled he was when he was born?

Well, it took a long time to fully understand, because we knew something was wrong a couple of days after he was born and he was making these funny movements. We got more and more concerned, and then we went into hospital and had lots of tests … but we didn't know what to expect at all. Little babies are so little and it's very difficult to tell if something's wrong. He looked beautiful. And then obviously when you are told after these tests that he has a very severe disability, you're in shock. Doctors often use quite complicated words to explain things and you don't know what's going on. I remember saying, when you say severe learning disabilities do you mean not very good at maths or won't walk and talk. And then they say, well, actually he probably won't walk and talk, and you are in complete shock. It hits you like a freight train because suddenly all the expectations you have for your child change immediately. It's rather hard to remember now what a massive shock it was because you do get over it. And having got over it it's quite difficult to go back and remember exactly how you felt.

You've made absolutely no political capital out of Ivan's disabilities and apart from the ITN film you've been quite rightly circumspect about discussing him.

Some people don't say that, actually. To be fair I think I've been relatively open, and I have spoken about it. I don't mind people criticizing me because I think it's a very difficult balance: on the one hand having a disabled child changes your life and brings you into contact with all sorts of things that you might not otherwise see, it informs your view as a politician and it enables you to make quite good sense about the services families with disabled children have to face. I took a decision quite early on that I would talk about it, but that I would try and maintain a reasonable balance of what was public and what was private. But I'm the sort of person who's quite open. Some people have said, well you shouldn't have your picture taken with him, or talk about it too much or whatever. But oddly enough it doesn't upset me when people say that because I think there is a balance of judgement about how much you should talk about someone like Ivan, and how much to protect their privacy, and I try to get the balance right. It's a weird thing to say but I don't mind if people attack me for it.

Can you describe your day-to-day dealings with Ivan? Let's start in the morning.
We're very lucky because we have some excellent night care. She brings Ivan upstairs at 7.30. We've converted our house and he lives downstairs – he's got his own bedroom with a bathroom in it, with its own pulley and hoist system so he doesn't have to be lifted. Although actually we all do lift him because he's lovely to pick up and cuddle. So I normally take over at 7.30 and do what we call his oral routine. I do his face creams and teeth and hair and all that, get him dressed and put him in his wheelchair and get him ready for school. That's my contact with him in the morning. And then in the evening if I'm home to do some things with the kids I'll do something with him. I'll read him some stories or do some exercises.

It must be unbelievably hard work …
At the weekends, when we obviously have him all the time, it's very hard because with a seriously disabled child you have to work very hard to stimulate and entertain them. When children really can't walk or talk you just have to work an awful lot harder to find out which books they

like and what activities stimulate them, what exercises are good for them etc. … it takes a lot more effort. Samantha is brilliant. I go in bursts but she sort of has it all the time. I just love cuddling him and looking at him and there's such a sense of joy when he turns to look at you because you know you're getting through. It's great when you find something that stimulates him.

I would imagine that the situation becomes more difficult the older he gets.

He's about to be six and he's beginning to get quite heavy, and that's why we have the hoists and the pulleys, so it's obviously much easier being able to pick him up. I still have a bath with him, and I still lift him in and out of the bath … all those things that Health & Safety would have a heart attack over. So inevitably it will get more difficult. Also, all the illnesses and problems they have could get worse, too, but we've learned how to try and keep him reasonably healthy and stable and we'll just cross all those bridges when we come to them.

I know you've totally transformed your home in London in order to make it more suitable for Ivan, but what provisions have you made for him as an adult?

Right now, not very many. We haven't established some sort of trust or anything like that because we're both healthy and we both work and Samantha puts an enormous amount of her earnings into his carers, and we have a very supportive family. But at some stage we will have to work out what more needs to be done. At the moment his life is going to be lived through a loving and supportive family, but also the school.

How is school for Ivan? He goes to Jack Tizard in Hammersmith.

I think all parents of disabled children feel that if you get the school right then it makes everything else so much easier, because you know that while he's there he's getting the right stimulation, he's getting the right care, he's getting a lot of one-to-one attention, a lot of colours and sounds and shapes and stories … When you go to the schools that cater for disabled children, as a parent you think it's wonderful because they are obviously getting so much stimulation and attention. And it takes an enormous amount of energy from the teachers to do that. Most children at playtime, they run around and discover the world. Ivan can't do that, you have to help him discover it. And so you have to work very hard to stimulate him. His school is just round the corner from us in Hammersmith, but the reason we fought so hard to keep the Cheyne Centre open, where he was, was because it wasn't working for Ivan at Jack Tizard at all, because previously they put together children like Ivan – who is quadriplegic and very passive – with very active kids with autism. And the children in Ivan's group just weren't safe. And Ivan can't defend himself. But the new head teacher is wonderful, and he has Ivan in a class with five or six other children like him. Some are wheelchair-bound, most of them are tube-fed like Ivan, and they can do things together. And they have lots of one-on-one attention. The times that I've been I've been really encouraged by what I've seen.

It must be very hard to balance caring requirements within a family when one child is disabled – is that true in your experience?
It is, just because their needs are so much greater. What it means is that one person looking after them – whether that's me or Sam or the help we have – it's not enough. It's very difficult to look after all three. I sometimes take all three to the park, and it's really quite touch and go, because you've got to be with Ivan because he can have a spasm or a seizure at any moment. So if one of your children decides to strangle a cat in the corner of the playground – not that the Cameron children make a habit of it, I hasten to add – it's very difficult to stop them doing it. You do often need two people. Also, it does make you think that because having a disabled child leads to lots of marriages breaking down, I can't imagine how difficult it would be bringing up a disabled child and other children alone.

You must think about him all day long.
No, I don't. I love him dearly, but we've definitely managed to get to a situation where he has not taken over our lives. The parents of disabled

children are not necessarily angels. They didn't ask for this to happen. And you mustn't pretend to be an angel if you're not, because if you do I think you'll exhaust yourself or your marriage will break down or your other kids will suffer. You have to try and be who you are. I'm not an angel and neither is Samantha. We're good parents, and we do our best, but we need lots of help, we need lots of breaks and we need time with Ivan and we need time without Ivan. I think it's important to have that and to try and keep your life together.

How much therapy does he have, and have you totally given up hope of any sort of rehabilitation?
Rehabilitation in the sense that he will suddenly take to his feet and walk, no we haven't given up. But we decided not to torture ourselves by endlessly seeking out the best clinics in the world and seeing if there was some magical cure, because the advice we had from doctors was, look, this is a very severe disability, and he's not going to be able to walk. He's got very limited mobility. And so what we've focused on is quality of life. And that means trying to make sure he's fundamentally well. We made a big decision to have a gastrostomy so he is tube-fed. He was losing weight and not eating properly and was becoming very ill. He wasn't able to keep his medicine down, and so that was a big decision to do that. But the most important therapies I think are the ones that keep him healthy and those that give him some quality of life and some stimulation. So he loves swimming, for instance, and he likes bath time. He loves those extraordinary play centres they have at these schools where there is lots of light and stimulation. So we concentrate on those things. Plus the other important aspect is making things consistent, the regular diet, the regular feeding times, regular medicine times and sleep patterns etc. All of those things are terribly important, even if they seem so little.

Did your father's disability (living for most of his life with only one leg) equip you emotionally in any way in order to cope with Ivan's disability?
No, not really, because my father has never, in any way, considered himself to be disabled. Dad, even though he now has only one eye and no

legs, he is very robust. Even with his disability he was very active, and played tennis and swam and rode and did all the things he would have done if he'd have been 100 per cent.

The National Health Service

How have Ivan's disabilities affected the way you think about the health service in this country, both public and private?
It's brought me into very close and regular contact with the NHS, and I've spent a lot more time there than I otherwise would have done. I think generally I've had a good impression, especially of the people, who I think largely are incredibly devoted. It's given me some frustrations – we've been stuck on waiting lists, we've been in Accident and Emergency at night when you're surrounded by drunks and people who have been violent. I've seen the good side of the NHS and the bad side of it. You know the thing they say about hospitals in Britain is that they're very difficult to get into and they're very difficult to get out of, because you never get discharged … but they're great when you're there. There's an element of truth in that.

I thought you would be a fan of polyclinics, which have been touted as the future of the NHS. [Polyclinics house up to twenty GPs to provide extended opening hours, carry out minor surgery and order X-rays and tests from on-site services. They would also deal with most patients who would otherwise have gone to A&E.] But apparently not. After all, most people queue for reassurance, and on paper, at least, polyclinics should help more of us to be seen by a doctor, and perhaps allow hospitals to upgrade themselves.
The trouble with the NHS is that there's been a lot of change for change's sake, a lot of faddism. There have been endless, top-down, structural upheavals just wasting time and money and the goodwill of NHS staff. The polyclinic is the latest example. In some places they might be a good idea, but they shouldn't be imposed from above. Sometimes I think this Labour government is just run by management consultants. They

haven't got a clue about what really matters; they just think about what looks efficient on a PowerPoint chart. They just don't understand the social value of things. It's so short-sighted to close down small local hospitals and GP surgeries in places where they perform an incredibly important social function.

What are the pros and cons of a target-driven culture in the NHS? As in education, as in the police force, the introduction of targets seems to have made it far more difficult for professionals to do their jobs. Are targets the fundamental problem?

They're part of the fundamental problem, which is all the top-down centralization. I've seen at first hand a sort of target problem which there is with Ivan. Because if he has a very bad set of seizures, what you want to do is go to A&E and have a series of drugs to try and get the seizures down and then observe him. What you don't want is to be admitted, but because of the four-hour waiting target you can't be in A&E for four hours, so they tend to try and push you into a ward. Look, if you're running any organization like a hospital you need to have some ways to measure progress and to motivate your staff. I think what's wrong is the idea of targets handed down from Whitehall for the whole of the NHS without thinking about the clinical consequences, and targets which micro-manage professionals in terms of the processes they should follow. What we've said is that we need to measure the results, not the processes, and so we're going to get rid of the top-down process targets and instead focus on what really matters, which is, are people getting better, are they getting high-quality treatment?

You've said that keeping and improving the NHS is your top priority. But what scale of reform does the NHS need? And what form should this take?

What it doesn't need is more bureaucratic reorganization. What you don't want is another round of let's call primary care trusts health authorities or health authorities primary care trusts. What I think you need is a more fundamental change to decentralize and empower. Now,

I know that they are two words overused by politicians, but let me try and explain. The GP should become your sort of gatekeeper, to help you choose where you go, and, having chosen where you go, the hospital you've chosen is much more independent of the NHS and the state, so hospitals are basically free-standing organizations that are paid according to the operations they carry out or the people that they treat. And so the health service becomes more decentralized, more based on patient choice, more based on decentralized management, and then the Department of Health becomes more of a department for public health – not running the NHS day-to-day but working to improve the nation's health so we reduce demands on the NHS. So it's quite a fundamental change but it's not about bureaucratically reorganizing the structure.

Surely one way to save the NHS is to turn the whole thing into a trust. You would depoliticize the NHS in one fell swoop. If you did this it would take away one of the strongest reasons people have for voting Labour.
Yes, the NHS as a whole should be more independent from the government. It should have a board, an executive; it should be more independent rather than ministers fiddling in its every decision. And that's what we've said we'll do. I think that hospitals should all be independent trusts. So if you are St Mary's Hospital, Paddington, you manage your budget, you are paid by results, you determine your specialization, you have a sort of pride in the institution.

It's all very well saying that you can solve the NHS crisis, but whether we opt for polyclinics or more local hospitals, how can you save the service when the Labour Party have so very publicly failed? We have a much larger population than ever before. Health care costs more. People live longer. It's a poisoned chalice …
In one sense it will never be solved because in any developed country the demand for more health care will exceed the supply. As we get older and wealthier, and as drugs get more expensive and new treatments come on,

health demands will always go up. And so there's never going to be a day when people sit back and say, that's fantastic, that's it, project NHS completed. But I think we could do a lot better than we are today, and I think that would be the case if we made the NHS more independent from government, trust in professionals more, give the GPs greater power to choose with you where you want to go. If you take the best of what's happened in Spain and Sweden and elsewhere and apply it to the UK, we could make it a lot better. But the NHS will still be a political issue in all future elections. I just hope it can be less of a contentious issue because we can get to a place where it's more independent as these reforms bed in.

I must say that whenever I've come into contact with the NHS, I usually go away with a very positive feeling towards the staff, but absolute horror at the conditions under which they work, the hours they work, the disillusionment of the ancillary staff. In terms of specific policies, you've said that a Conservative government would aim to provide a dedicated maternity nurse for every new mother in her home for up to six hours a day for the first week after her baby's birth, and a huge expansion in the number of health visitors. But what about mixed-sex wards? Labour once pledged to end mixed-sex wards but then Health Minister Lord Darzi says it's impossible. Would you promise to end mixed-sex wards?

I understand the difficulties about this, because the health service is having to cope with increases in capacity, but in the modern day and age, mixed-sex wards are completely outdated. If you go round a hospital and ask them what they'd change if they had a magic wand, lots of them say more private rooms and fewer open wards. But, yes, this is something we should aim to do.

Samantha and family life

How hard did you think about the effect on Samantha and your family before going into politics?

I thought about it a lot. I remember I decided some time in the late 1980s and early 1990s that I wanted to be an MP. The more I worked at Central Office, the more I became an adviser, the more I felt I wanted to get out of the back room and become a Member of Parliament. And when I started going out with Samantha, which was when I was working for Norman Lamont, at that stage I really knew I was going to do it. Before we got married I remember talking to Samantha about it and saying that being an MP is what I really want to do, and if that's going to make you really miserable then we'd better talk about it. But I was always very frank with her about it because it does have an effect on your life.

You obviously discussed going for the leadership with Samantha. You must have discussed the toll it would take on your family life, and in particular on Ivan …
I talked to Samantha about it quite a lot, initially straight after the general election of 2005. My instinct was not to go for it, actually, but the more I thought about it and the more we talked about it, I thought actually I do have the right ideas to change the Conservative Party and get it back on track, and I do have a sense of what's wrong with the country and how we can fix it, so why wait and why not go for it?

Did she object in any way?
No, she was quite supportive. Her view was sort of, I think you've got the right ideas, I think you could do it and why not go for it. She once said, only half joking, that she was so bored being married to an MP in a party that's going nowhere, if you think you can sort it out then you'd better get on and do it. She didn't quite put it like that but that was the sentiment. It was a very practical, business-like approach.

Were there rules about what you could and couldn't do, about what she would and wouldn't allow?
Yes, there were. If you don't have some rules in a very demanding job like this it just runs away with you.

So what are the rules?

That we have plenty of time together, plenty of time with the children. And for two nights a week, I come home early enough to be with Sam: one I should be back for suppertime and the other I should be back to do bath time with the children. And on the whole I stick to that. On a Wednesday and Thursday I always try and get back at a reasonable time. I do masses of constituency stuff on a Friday but I try and keep Saturday nights and Sundays free. You can do it, but it just needs very strict diary control and means me saying no to a lot of things. But I think Sam has been absolutely right by saying, let's try and make this work, because what looked like a couple of years as Leader of the Opposition now looks more like four, and that's quite a long period of your life, especially when the children are growing up. And so it's good to have some rules. And, actually, because I've got a good team around me, I know that if I'm not at the morning meeting it's chaired by William Hague, and if William Hague's not there it's chaired by David Davis. I also have a very strong private office. If you get exhausted you make bad decisions. If you're away from your family all the time you get fractious, and that's not good. You've got to try and keep your character and personality together and not let the job change you too much. Because if it does, then all the things you thought you were going to bring to it aren't there any more.

Although Cherie Blair came to be seen as something of a liability, Samantha is regarded as a glamorous asset, both inside and outside the party.

She's an incredible woman. To be as successful as she is in business is great, and I'm really proud of what she's achieved. From a standing start, to design handbags and then sell them in such vast numbers around the world is a huge achievement. I've never achieved anything like that. She's very, very good in business, she's a brilliant mum … I mean, some people say she's not interested in politics but she is; she likes to know what I'm up to, and we talk about policy stuff, but she has a distance from it, which I think is very healthy. And as a result, instead of always being on your shoulder, saying what about this, what about that, every now and again she'll take me to task over something and that is very helpful. She'll say, can you explain to me why you're voting this way or why you're doing that or why the hell can't the Tories sort out this ...? And that's more powerful because it's from the perspective of a businesswoman and a mother rather than another politician.

You've said she got you into recycling.
Yes, she was green a long time before other people. She supported Greenpeace or Friends of the Earth right back when we first started going out with each other. She was an early green. Also, recycling is one of those things where you have to change your behaviour at home in terms of what you do with packaging and food waste and dustbins, and men are terrible at all that. We always put the empty carton of milk back in the fridge.

So you need a bit of prompting.
I need a bit of prompting. She is very organized, and that I do need, because if you live a busy life, like we do, to get three kids off to school and get to work and get everything done, you need quite a lot of routine, including in your own life.

Did you cry at your wedding? Why?
I did actually. This lovely Oxfordshire girl sang a beautiful piece of music, and we were right up in the nave, sitting down, and it was just a very beautiful moment and I felt very emotional. I was overcome with such very happy emotions. There I was, marrying Samantha, this wonderful, beautiful girl who I'd fallen in love with, and there were all my family, all my friends, this lovely church, and this beautiful singing. I tend to cry when I'm happy, and I did then. And then Samantha started crying, and she's very cleverly arranged the pictures of the wedding in our bathroom to make them look as though she started crying first!

When did you realize Samantha was the one for you?

Quite early on. We went on this holiday that my parents had organized to celebrate their wedding anniversary. And their children were allowed to take a couple of friends, and my sister Clare took Samantha. That was in 1992 and that's when it all started. Because there was quite a big age gap, I don't know, I just began being more and more certain about it. I can't pinpoint the exact moment when I thought, that's it, it just became the right thing to do. I fell in love with her.

What do you and Samantha row about?

We sometimes row about politics, but I'd say the most common thing we row about is arrangements. Why have you organized this? Well, because it's time we did that. Well, you didn't ask me etc. The normal sort of stuff that married couples row about. Normally we row over the things that need to get done. Why haven't you fixed the car? Why haven't you done this or that? And that could be me saying that to her, or the other way round. It's very even.

What are the main similarities between you?

We're not that similar, in fact we're quite different in many respects. She is very artistic, and we have different outlooks in some ways. The age gap (five years) becomes less important as you get older, but when we first started going out she was one of my sister's friends, who were a lot differ-ent and a lot younger than mine, but those sorts of differences fall away as you start having friends who are both your friends. We now have many more things we like doing together.

Do you bounce policy ideas off Samantha?

Yes, I do bounce policy ideas off Samantha and because she doesn't think like another politician it's very refreshing. She'll say, why do you want to do that, or what's the point of that? And also she doesn't read all the newspapers so she's not part of the Westminster bubble. She's very good at saying, it's all very well saying this but then what about this that's happening right on your doorstep?

How often do you tell Samantha you love her?
Quite often, actually. We have a very intimate banter with each other. I tell her I love her when we go to bed at night, when we're happy, which, fortunately for us, is quite a lot.

What did you last cook?
I last cooked an excellent slow-roast belly of pork. I'm so greedy I got up at six in the morning on Sunday in order to put this pig in the bottom of the oven so it would cook for six hours. I'd stuffed it with fennel and garlic and it was fabulous. After six hours it just fell apart like Peking duck. It was really good, even though I do say so myself.

What do you watch regularly on television?
Samantha started watching *Shameless*, so I started watching it with her. It's on quite late and she started watching it in bed, and it is quite addictive, because it is so awful. We have very mainstream tastes, and we're big on murder, mystery and suspense. *Trial and Retribution, Midsomer Murders, He Kills Coppers* ...

What did you think of *Lewis*?
I like it because I loved *Morse* and I adore Oxford. They're always stepping in and out of Brasenose and that always takes me down memory lane. And I quite liked *Lewis* and, funnily enough, I think his assistant, what's he called, Fox? ... is actually rather good, too. But I don't think the story lines are as good as *Morse*, and sometimes you get to the end and think, hang on, he murdered her, but she wasn't in the first half of the programme ... But it's beautifully done.

What radio station do you listen to? Radio 4?
I think you can have too much of the *Today* programme, so I've started switching it off. If you listen to it too much you want to call the Samaritans. So sometimes I switch to Radio 5 Live or even Radio 1. I've got a digital radio and they're incredibly easy to turn to stations and get wonderful reception. And in the car I listen to quite a lot of

Virgin, and, whisper it, Tragic … [Magic FM]. But only for short bursts!

Do you, or will you, limit the amount of time your kids spend on computers or watch TV?
Yes, definitely. We try and be quite strict even now with DVDs because the kids love watching them and we try and make sure that maybe it's a little bit before bedtime, or a little bit after lunch, but only for twenty minutes or half an hour. We try never to have the television on in the morning. If we're in the constituency, or in London, the morning should be about going out for a walk, or to the park. But I'm sure my parents were probably stricter about how much TV we watched. In those days there really wasn't much television until *Jackanory* at five o'clock or whatever. I think it is important not to let your children endlessly fester in front of the box, and I think the same goes for the computer, but we're not at that stage yet. And sometimes, I admit, when you're knackered and the kids are playing up a bit, it is very tempting to get out Makka Pakka and just slip it on and have five minutes' peace and quiet. We've all done that. But it's like all these things; you've got to work at it.

What would you do if, after their eighteenth birthday, one of your children planned to vote Labour?
I'd try and talk them out of it, obviously. My mother used to take my sister to the polling station and threaten to go in the booth with her. I wouldn't go that far. That's the great thing about voting; you can vote for whoever you like. That's what I say when I go to schools – I don't mind who you vote for but please go and vote for somebody. I just encourage people to take part and get involved and to try and get interested.

What's the most useful thing you have learned about raising children? And what mistakes have you made?
I've made loads of mistakes. I expect I've made all of them. Like when you say, you're a naughty boy rather than say that's a naughty thing that you've done. I make that one all the time. Inconsistency. You're told you

must be a consistent parent and you should praise as often as you should blame and I totally get that one wrong. Not getting them overexcited just before they're going to bed, that's another one I'm bad at. I get that wrong virtually every night of the week. Ivan teaches you a lot more because it's such a specialist skill, feeding someone who is tube-fed, dealing with medicines, dealing with seizures, that's just a totally different set of skills that I suppose I have picked up. But I'm quite interested in the whole parenting thing. Samantha's read a few books about it because she's really interested in it, but the main thing you do is talk with friends, comparing and contrasting. I think that the problem lots of parents have is they don't have people to talk to. They don't have their parents to help them or the wider social networks, people who could say, you know that chocolate you're giving them at ten o'clock, well, it might not be the best idea in the world.

Going around the country you must see a lot of this.
I saw in a shopping centre the other day a mum pouring Coca-Cola into her child's milk bottle, and I thought, she must be completely loopy. You'll probably find out he's diabetic and that's totally the wrong thing to say, but you know what I mean.

Because you're such a keen advocate of good parenting, do you think this plays well with the Worcester woman?
I don't tend to worry about it in that way. I don't think that success in politics is about totting up support from different groups and ages and classes and ranges, it's much more about getting it right, about getting your policies right. If your policies appeal you will win, and if they don't you won't. And I think the sort of Ken Livingstone version of politics, forming some kind of rainbow alliance, is in the end always wrong. I don't think Mrs Thatcher thought, aha, I need the votes of C2s in towns outside the M25, therefore I shall sell council houses. I think she thought people should be able to stand on their own two feet and so I'm going to sell council houses, and the consequence was lots of people inside the M25 bought council houses. It's that way round. Have the ideas, have the

inspiration and then see how to explain it to people. I think family life, parental responsibility, these things are just incredibly important for our society.

The drugs question

Was there a point at which you started behaving more carefully in order to protect a future political career?
Yes. Look, as I moved out of the world of business and of being an adviser and thought I wanted to be an MP, you do start to be more careful about remembering to indicate before you turn left. And other things.

Are there any other indiscretions you wish to tell voters about now?
No, I think they've heard quite a lot about my indiscretions. I didn't go through the whole of my life thinking I wanted to be a politician, so I had teenage years full of the sorts of things that teenagers do. As I've always said, you're entitled to a private past. Since being a Member of Parliament, people have a pretty good view of my life. I've made mistakes, I don't always obey every traffic law. But I don't think there's some hideous truth that you need to know.

Barack Obama has been honest about his drug past and it has not affected his ability to appeal to a huge number of people. Why have you been so coy about your drug past?
Because I think you have to find a reasonable dividing line between a past that was private because you weren't thinking about going into public life, and a current life which is public and which people are entitled to know. That's the dividing line I choose to draw and I think it's a perfectly reasonable one. Some people don't agree and think it's a completely unreasonable one, but I think they're wrong. So I try and combine that with the relative openness about my life. In the end in politics all you can do is make your own decision about that. And let other people judge you.

You could say that your reticence is our fault, the public's, because of our hypocrisy – wanting politicians who are in touch with the real world while simultaneously expecting them to have lived monkish lives before they take public office.

You might say that. The point is you want to try and find a dividing line, and that's what I've chosen to do. And I think if you find some rather unstable resting place you just get asked endless further questions and that takes over everything rather than people paying attention to what you're trying to do for the future.

I know what you're going to say, but I have to ask it anyway. Have you ever taken Class A drugs?

I've answered this question in the way that I choose to, which is to say that I believe all politicians have the right to a private past.

To what extent have you had personal experience of the damage that drugs can do?

Lots, through friends, but I don't want to go in any detail as otherwise newspapers will find them and splash them all over their pages. But enough to really understand the damage that drugs can do, enough to understand particularly the damage that Class A drugs can do, and enough to be very interested in and be quite passionate about the importance of rehabilitation, particularly residential rehab where you really rebuild people's lives. And I've seen that at quite close hand both in the constituency context and also with people close to me and my friends.

In relation to previous experiences with people you know, and relations, are you not worried about things coming out in the press when you become even more prominent?

Of course people will go on asking questions and digging and delving, but I think what I've said about this is the right place to be. In terms of friends or relations I don't want to say any more because I don't want those people to be identified. So far the press has been pretty reasonable about that. I think the rules are that it's perfectly acceptable to push and prod and probe me, but it's not fair to do that with friends and others …

If it had emerged that Gordon Brown or Nick Clegg had taken drugs as a young man, what would you give as the Tory line?
That it was a personal matter. Unless, of course, there's some sort of hideous hypocrisy.

Et cetera, et cetera

What has been your best moment in politics so far?
Best moment was giving my conference speech in 2007, because I was incredibly nervous beforehand but as soon as I started I knew I was going to be okay. There was a wave of relief.

What's been your worst moment in politics so far?
The grammar school row was concerning because things weren't going the way I believed they should, but it was frustration more than anything else.

Have you finally given up smoking?
Yes, but I have to admit there are relapses.

When did you last smoke a cigarette?
I'm not going to answer that question, but I am clean!

How much do you drink in an average week?
Moderately, but probably more than I'm meant to. The unit count is sometimes quite challenging. I like having a couple of glasses of wine in the evening with dinner. Most nights I'll have a couple of glasses of wine.

Have you ever been arrested? Have you ever been charged?
I have never been arrested. And I've never been charged to my knowledge, although I have had motoring offences on my driving licence. I

think most of them are disappearing. But there have been speeding offences.

Margaret Thatcher bought her underwear at M&S – do you buy your own, and if so where?
I'm a big Marks & Spencer fan and I do own Marks & Spencer underwear. I don't have a Jeremy Paxman issue with them.

How often do you go to White's Club? How would you characterize it?
I go about once a year, with my dad. It's a typical St James's club where people have lunch and talk to each other. I really ought to have resigned because I never go there enough to justify the cost of membership.

Where, at this moment, is your Bullingdon tailcoat?
I never owned one. It was borrowed.

Why do you often swim in cold rivers, lakes and seas?
I really do like swimming in very cold water. I find it very exhilarating.

When did you last go hunting?
About three years ago.

If you become Prime Minister, will you still ride your bike?
The security people who came to see me the other day told me I couldn't. But I think I would. They said I can't unless it's unexpected. So I would.

How many hours' sleep do you need?
I need about six or seven.

When you were asked in 2006 why you appeared to be aping Blair, you replied, 'He has won three elections, you know.' Do you regret remarking that you are the 'heir to Blair'?
That came from a private dinner. If I literally said, 'I want to be the heir to Blair', it's not what I meant. What I meant is that Tony Blair, having

spent most of his time in office without a clue about how to bring about change in schools, the NHS and other public services, finally realized, just before he was booted out, that the way to do it was what we'd been saying all along. You need really radical reform – to get rid of all the top-down bureaucracy and centralization – to devolve power to the local people and to bring in much more choice and competition. He realized that far too late and then, when he tried to do it, he was blocked by Gordon Brown and the Labour Party. Because we in the Conservative Party completely believe in these things, we'll be able to finish what Blair, very tentatively and half-heartedly, started. The other aspect of it is that to become Prime Minister I think you have to understand, and the country wants you to understand, what's changed over the preceding period. Both good and bad. And in many ways Blair was the heir to Thatcher because he understood what Thatcher had done, and he wanted to keep the good bits. He certainly didn't understand everything and he's not her heir at all, but he realized what needed to be done. What I was trying to say was I wanted to be the person who understood what Blair had changed in Britain, and keep the good and get rid of the bad. Rather than wind the clock back. And that was a good point, although sometimes words fall out of our mouths in a way that we don't mean them to.

EIGHT

'Every day there is another murder, another assault, another rape, another front-page horror story'

Penal reform, Jack Straw's sleeping habits, social responsibility, bureaucratic bravery, the strange case of the Notting Hill mutterer

Wandsworth Prison, 9.30, a fresh spring Monday morning, and David Cameron almost vaulted up the gatehouse steps, hand in black suit pocket, face beaming, fresh from the silver pool car parked on the edge of Wandsworth Common. The day shift prison officers had arrived three hours earlier, ready to manage the 1475 inmates in a prison already full to capacity. With 700 guards, the prisoner to officer ratio was better than most hotels, but Wandsworth Prison is no hotel. Built in 1851 to house London's unruly mobs, by 2006 it had become the largest jail in Britain, and one of the biggest in Europe. Every day, around thirty prisoners are transported to court, and, as Wandsworth is an 'allocation prison' (category B – the second highest of the four levels of security), many of the prisoners here are either awaiting trial or, having been sentenced, waiting to start their sentence somewhere else. For some, though, it is simply a housing pen. Former inmates include Oscar Wilde, William Joyce (Lord Haw-Haw), Ronnie Kray and Ronnie Biggs, the Great Train Robber, who successfully escaped from the prison in 1965 before fleeing the country, and Pete Doherty – incarcerated for burgling fellow Libertine Carl Barât's flat.

The prison Cameron was visiting was no longer the 'hate factory' it was in the 1980s and 1990s, and conditions and attitudes since then had improved quantifiably. Its last damning report was in 2004, when it rated dreadfully on all four of the Prison Inspectorate's 'healthy prison' tests (safety, respect, purposeful activity and resettlement). During 2003 and 2004 the prison had 'failed to meet basic standards of decency and activity for most of its 1460 prisoners'. Another report from the same period said the 'Wandsworth Way' was imposed through a pervasive culture of fear. Conditions in the segregation unit were described as appalling: inspectors discovered cockroaches in two cells and dead rats in the exercise yard. 'Never have I had to write about anything so inhuman and reprehensible as the way that prisoners, some of them seeking protection and some of them mentally disordered, were treated in the filthy and untidy segregation unit,' said one of the authors of the report, dispiritingly.

But in the four years since, it had been institutionally spring-cleaned, even though four men found it necessary to kill themselves here in 2007. And Cameron knew all about it. As a researcher at the Home Office under Michael Howard, in the early 1990s he would often spend much of his working day digesting the prison system and all its many foibles. Prisons were in his blood. 'I've done prisons and I know prisons,' he said, walking towards the governor's office in the main wing. 'Prisons I know about. They're not nice places, but it's important to see them to get a measure of how we're rehabilitating those people who we exclude from society.'

What he also knew was that while the prison might have been hitting its targets again – internal targets set by the government – the penal system still had no way of gauging the number of re-offenders finding their way back in, making a mockery of the process.

On this bright, sunny day Wandsworth was not quite as grim as it can be. The former Surrey House of Correction is one of Britain's most infamous Victorian jails, and it's an intentionally imposing edifice. But once past the automated sliding glass doors, the heavy metal grilles of the gatehouse and the high outer walls, wooden flower boxes juxtapose with the harsh Victorian brick and the walls painted municipal green. But as you approach the resident wing you start to see the detritus created by 1500 men living together in close proximity. Old yoghurt pots, plastic sandwich containers, squashed cigarette packets, soiled tissue paper, yellowing sweet wrappers and rusty fizzy drinks cans lie trapped between the grilles on the cell windows facing the courtyard, as eerily benign reggae blasts out from behind them.

Seventy per cent of the inmates are either in for drug-related crime or have drug-related problems, making them far more docile than their female counterparts. Visit Holloway and the atmosphere is far more vicious, far more hysterical than it is in Wandsworth. Here there was a strange calmness about the place, one that Cameron appeared to take in his stride, even when poking his nose into some of the cells. As he cruised the length of C Wing, a short, bearded, animated chap clutching a copy of *The Times* kept step with him, muttering 'Notting Hill, Notting Hill, Notting Hill …' under his breath. Not knowing what the man was going to do next, Cameron stopped and said hello – a big smile, displaying Cameron's crow's feet – to which the man responded with 'I'll vote for you, Dave! I'm a Notting Hill man myself. Be out soon. I'll vote for you!' It transpired he lived in Powis Square, not far from the Cameron home-stead, and thought his neighbour was definitely getting the better of the Prime Minister. 'Keep at it, Dave, keep at it. Keep bashing Brown! I'll vote for you!'

Prisoners are locked up, two to a cell, for their meals, and at night. At other times, they can wander around, gossip, trade, call their families on the payphones, and play cards, table football or pool. There is mental illness, diabetes and HIV, while 60 per cent of the inmates have numer-acy and literacy problems. Many are monosyllabic. Wandsworth used to be full of Jamaicans, but no longer. About 40 per cent of prisoners in Wandsworth are foreign nationals, with an increasingly heavy emphasis on Eastern Europeans. Although twelve different languages are spoken here (meaning more work for local translators), a quarter of the inmates are now Muslim, and the weekly prayers, at 12.30 on a Friday afternoon, had proved to be so popular that the governor was considering introduc-ing a second service in the afternoon.

Two years ago the Press Association reported that the Independent Monitoring Board said there was a schism among Muslim prisoners in Wandsworth over the prison's newly appointed imam. The board's annual report said there was evidence suggesting that some Muslim inmates were applying pressure on fellow inmates to adopt more militant lifestyles and belief systems. 'There is a difference of views between the Asian Muslims and the North African and Afro-Caribbean Muslims.' There were also worrying implications of the rocketing use of illegal mobile phones. The document reflected press reports that attendance at religious services had increased simply because inmates were using them as venues for drug dealing and trading in illegal mobile phones.

All the inmates appeared to smoke, and there were cigarette papers and tobacco boxes everywhere in the 10ft by 7ft cells – concrete boxes smaller than most family tents; like every other prison everywhere else in the world, cigarettes and drugs are the currency in Wandsworth. 'You have to accept that drugs are a way of life,' said one of the governors to Cameron, as they sat in a twelve-step RAPT (Rehabilitation for Addicted Prisoners Trust) programme meeting in the drug treatment centre deep in the prison, listening to three inmates describing their combined thirty-six-year addiction to crack. 'And there is very little we can do about it. We try, but if they're determined to get them, then they will. The visiting process would have to be seriously altered if we wanted to try and get rid of them completely.'

And because of their various addictions, nurses are on hand to administer medication (methadone and another heroin substitute, Subutex). On average it costs £50,000 a year to keep a prisoner here, drugs or no drugs.

At any one time the prison has about 320 vulnerable prisoners, the majority of whom are sex offenders. 'There are a couple of hundred very horrible people in here,' said one officer. Years of experience means the officers can tell who will give them trouble the second they walk through the gates. 'You can absolutely tell what they're like as soon as you see them,' said one. 'You know the types.' But the guards soon become accustomed to their charges, and, according to one assistant governor, overfamiliar. 'What I'd really like is the money to buy more guards, so they could become more peripatetic,' said one. 'After a while everyone gets to know each other, which makes discipline extremely difficult.'

A handful of prisoners in the 'DIY' wing were plastering walls, all watched by trained builders or prisoners who had done the course and wanted to help others. As Cameron walked through the wing, and then onto one of the residential wings, you could see prisoners with metal cups, biros, tools, and you thought how easy it would be for one of them to inflict serious damage on him, or indeed on anyone with him. One might have expected all the officers to be towering men of steel, but many looked as though they would collapse at the slightest provocation.

'The biggest problem we have is with re-offenders,' said another officer. 'They just don't know how to adapt to the outside world, and many are back in here within weeks, sometimes days. They go back to the same estates, to the same pubs, and in five minutes they're on drugs again, and stealing to pay for their habit. It's habitual and incredibly soul-destroying, because there's no one to help them, or steer them. You've got criminals in there whose fathers were criminals, and whose grandfathers were criminals. They're not suddenly going to change. I mean, why would you? Why would they? We take care of them in here and there's nothing out there. So there's no incentive for them. To them, the outside world is just a nuisance, a complication.'

The day that Cameron chose to visit Wandsworth, on a day he was launching a new policy paper on the criminal justice system, an internal Ministry of Justice report claimed that a growing number of terrorist prisoners were forging connections with the existing gangs inside many of Britain's high-security jails. The Tories' messages were simple. With Britain's prisons suffering from overcrowding, Cameron was promising to build 5000 additional prison places, taking capacity to over 100,000. Among the other suggestions in the 'Prisons with a Purpose' Green Paper were minimum and maximum sentence periods, with no parole until the minimum term has been served; an end to automatic release for all determinate sentences; the decentralization of public sector prisons; and offenders needing to compensate their victims through a Victims' Fund. Cameron stressed that what Britain needed was 'a new principle of honesty in sentencing, a new generation of prisons and a new model of prison management'. Surprisingly, these ideas were not trashed by the usual liberal commentators, while the *New Statesman* even reported the fact that Juliet Lyon of the Prison Reform Trust had welcomed the new emphasis on rehabilitation, asking Brown's party to rise to the challenge and do something about it.

The same week, Justice Secretary Jack Straw played down the fact that the prison population in England and Wales had just hit a record figure of 82,180. 'Am I exercised about the prison population? I am. Am I losing sleep over it? No. Lying awake at night is completely useless, so I don't do it.'

As Cameron and I drove away from the prison, we started talking about what we'd seen.

Penal reform

So what have you learned today, David? Having spent a considerable period working for the Home Office I wouldn't imagine that seeing the inside of another prison changes the way you already think. Does it?
Well, it reconfirms the fact that prisons are still ridiculously over-crowded, and that this prison in particular is full to bursting. The second thing is that there are obviously some good things going on in prisons, and the training schemes in Wandsworth are especially good, and in particular the various drug rehabilitation schemes they have. In this country the difference between the best prison and the worst prison is huge, and the best ones are doing training and purposeful activities and contributing to the re-education of prisoners. And the worst ones are, as the governor just told me, keeping prisoners banged up in their cells for twenty-three hours a day, unable to leave because of neglect and over-crowding. And it's getting worse.

Worse? Some might say that Britain is turning into one big open prison.
This government just doesn't understand how best to cope with the prison population, and in fact has a problem with prisons, full stop. In

Gordon Brown's eyes they are somewhere to keep people incarcerated without a glimmer of hope. There is no joined-up thinking going on here, and you only have to spend a short while in a prison like Wandsworth to see that. It's just outrageous that they've had eleven years and done so little.

What was the most significant conversation you had today? You talked to a lot of prisoners, and a lot came up to talk to you. They were, dare I say, friendly.
Unfortunately the most significant conversation I had was with one of the governors, and when I asked her what the re-offending rate is, she simply didn't know. And that's not really her fault, in fact it's not her fault at all: they actually run a very good prison with the resources they have. It's because the system is completely wrongly set up. If you think about it, what do we pay our prisons to do? We pay them to take people off the streets who've made our lives a misery, to take them away from society. But we also pay them to try and turn those people's lives around and reform them and rehabilitate them so there's some chance they might go straight when we eventually let them back into society. And if the various prison bodies are not actually measuring that then they're not doing their job in the way that they should. What I find on these visits is that you always discover something of benefit, you always learn something. You pick up impressions, but in the answers from prisoners you sometimes discover a deeper problem you might not have been aware of. The most important thing I discovered this morning from the prisoners' point of view, which is not exactly surprising, is that the prison is full, there is no more room.

There appears to be no more room – and no more rooms – in any prison in Britain.
When you walk into one of the cells, and see how cramped they are, with a toilet open for the rest of the wing to see, full of clutter and rubbish and stuff, it's no wonder we find it difficult to rehabilitate people. We need to lock people up and try and rehabilitate them to a standard where they

can be safely reintroduced into society. There needs to be a certain amount of hope. A lot of the prisoners I met this morning look like they could easily be rehabilitated, but they won't be if we just treat prisons like people factories.

But you weren't surprised by what you saw this morning, were you? While overcrowding in prisons has been one of the Labour government's great failures.

No, no, I wasn't surprised. The thing that always comes home to you when you visit prisons is that the people you talk to either have a drug problem or are functionally illiterate or were at young offender institutes, and this is not the first time they've been in prison, or fell out of school very early on and then fell into a world of drugs and disorder and then crime. Or sometimes a combination of all of these things. Prison is always picking up the pieces of failures that have happened elsewhere, and I always think you come home with that quite strong impression. I must say I was mightily encouraged by the long-term drug users we met, the ones in the middle of the twelve-step programme. They will obviously keep some of the more difficult cases away from visitors, but you could see that the scheme was working. To be frank, one of the things I was surprised by was the fact that no one gobbed on me. In these places you always tend to come out with a fair bit of spit on your shoulders!

Your 'payment by results' scheme is quite radical, and certainly one that the Victorians wouldn't recognize. Their policy was 'lock them up and forget about them …'

Yes, we have radical plans, but we need to be radical to deal with the problem. So we want to turn prisons into self-governing bodies that will win cash rewards, including bonuses for governors, if they cut re-offending rates. Prisons that prevent former inmates from re-offending for two years after release would get paid the amount the state spends on processing an offender through the criminal justice system. Sixty-five per cent of offenders are reconvicted within two years of being released, which is a ridiculous figure. We need to get all the institutions in the system, the prisons, the probation service, public, private and voluntary agencies, working together with one clear incentive: to stop criminals re-offending once they've left prison. And we'll also bring in honesty in sentencing, a new generation of prisons and make sure prisoners make restitution to society for their crimes and leave prison with prospects. So, while in jail, convicts would be encouraged to do paid work, with 60 per cent of their earnings going into a fund to pay compensation to victims.

Your prisons policy, in fact your whole criminal justice policy, is about joined-up thinking ...
As I said in one of my first speeches on this topic, the criminal justice system is like a chain and every link in that chain – the police, the Crown Prosecution Service, the courts, the prisons and the probation service – matters.

The government has done a lot of work in this area, but they appear to have reached a dead end.
Yes, but only a quarter of recorded crimes are brought to justice, and conviction rates, including those for the most serious crimes, like rape and assault, are massively down. It can take so long for cases to wind their way through the justice system. The number of prisoners re-offending is going up. That's just unacceptable. How are we ever going to cut crime if we don't deal with this properly? The number of prisoners committing further offences within two years of release is rising, while more than nine out of ten juvenile offenders on the intensive supervision and surveillance programme have been reconvicted of a crime. We need a more effective approach with people when we lock them up, and when they're released.

You've been very clear about your prison-building programme. If you were in charge right now, how much business would you put into the private sector in terms of building prisons?
We're going to sell these thirty run-down inner-city prisons and build thirty new ones, and, while they wouldn't all be private-sector prisons,

the private sector would have a very big opportunity to build and operate them. And I'm completely unembarrassed about that because I think the evidence is that the private-sector prisons have worked incredibly well. What's interesting is that lots of people who objected to them on ideological grounds – i.e. like the entire Labour Party – as soon as they got into power realized that actually there's nothing wrong with a private-sector prison as long as it is properly regulated and managed and overseen and all the rest of it. Because in the end what you want are relatively independent organizations that are judged and paid on their results. And that's what we've got to get to. We'd provide a 'diversity of provision' by ensuring that private and voluntary groups are given a chance to work with prisoners.

Do you think this visit today would have been any different if you had been the Prime Minister instead of the Leader of the Opposition?
No. I don't think he'd find out more; in fact he might find out less because he'd have more security around him. I mean, I was able to wander into rooms I wasn't meant to [go into]. And while lots of people think that the only smell that fills the nostrils of politicians is fresh paint, actually I'm still capable of visiting somewhere and finding out new information and barging off and talking deliberately to people they didn't want me to meet. Which is what I did.

I'm actually surprised by the lack of security.
Well, we both got out alive!

Somewhere like Wandsworth obviously differs enormously from high-security prisons like Wakefield or Parkhurst, as the prisoners are more docile and a lot less dangerous.
Obviously those places are slightly scarier because you know you're with the baddest of the bad. There were some lifers we saw in Wandsworth today, and they didn't let us in the sex offenders' wing. You saw what I saw: prisons are not nice places, and they shouldn't be. But they need to work properly, they need to be part of the process of rebuilding our

society, and at the moment they're just holding pens. We lock you up, we keep you in the dark, and then we release you sooner than we ought to because we have no prison places left. Wandsworth has the same problems all prisons face – loads of drugs, loads of foreign prisoners – and there were more white faces than the last time I visited, so there are obviously more Eastern Europeans here. The racial balance has definitely changed, which is a reflection of how low- and high-level crime in this country has changed, principally because of immigration. But as you walk in through the gates of Wandsworth you do expect someone to say, 'Norman Stanley Fletcher, you have pleaded guilty to the charges brought by this court, and it is now my duty to pass sentence.'

The criminal justice system

At present, the criminal justice system in Britain teaches young criminals a single lesson: you can get away with theft, burglary, robbery, even violent offences including sexual assaults, without incurring any punishment at all beyond a mild reprimand. Youngsters typically commit scores of offences before the police finally decide they have no choice but to arrest them. Then they commit dozens more before they appear in court. And then they usually go on to commit yet more crimes before they are given any form of custodial sentence. Violent crime has doubled in the last ten years. What would you do about it? The government seems determined to do everything they can not to build more prisons, and flood our streets with what they judge to be 'low-level' repeat offenders. Surely there must be new legislation and new guidelines covering sentencing.

In the last decade what we've had is an approach based on law rather than on broader law and order. We've had all these criminal justice bills and thousands of new laws, and I think what we need to recognize is that fighting crime is actually about more than passing new laws. Of course you need to have the tough penalties on gun and knife crime and burglary and the rest of it, but unless you reform the police and get them out from behind their desks, unless you get rid of the culture of paperwork and political correctness, unless you deal with the issue of drugs on our streets, unless you have a broader response to crime, addressing the underlying causes, like family breakdown, unless you start saying no to things – to people falling down drunk in the streets, to shops selling booze to people underage, unless you change all that then nothing will change. Changing the law is not enough.

The Youth Justice Board's record of successfully reforming young thugs is so poor that it would be a joke, were it not that innocent people die when these louts are allowed to roam our streets seemingly with impunity.
It's appalling, unbelievably bad. If you came down from Mars and looked at our prisons and our young offender institutes – well, you don't even have to come down from Mars – their record is truly atrocious. That's not to blame them – they are often dealing with very difficult and disturbed young people, sometimes hardened criminals who have been in and out of prison on a regular basis, but we haven't got a proper penal system that is designed properly to rehabilitate people. There needs to be a fundamental change. At the moment our prisons are like warehouses of criminals; the government just looks at banging people up, three to a cell, in a cell that can only take two, often locked up for twenty-three hours a day, and then they let them out early because they need the cells for someone else because they haven't built enough prisons. It's not just the fact that we need more prisons, we need to change totally the way that prison works.

We also need more custodial sentences, too, surely. And we need to be tougher with bail …
At the moment people are sentenced but then are released halfway through, so that completely undermines the system. They haven't got enough prisons so they let people out before the end of their sentence. And while they're in prison they do almost nothing to reform or rehabilitate them because the prisons are overcrowded so there's no room to do anything. We want to scrap the early release scheme, and have proper

minimum sentences. One half of all crime is committed by ex-prisoners, so whatever we're doing we're doing badly.

Why didn't you criticize Labour for only giving the police a 1.9 per cent pay increase? When he was asked the same question on *Question Time*, Liam Fox avoided it.

We think the government made a complete mess of this, but what we can't do now is say to the police, look you've been short-changed by the government, when we get into power in two years' time or whatever, we will pay you back the money they owe you. You just can't make deals with specific groups, not even the police. It was an uncomfortable situation but it was right. Politics isn't about wandering about and promising everyone everything.

How do you make it less attractive to be in jail?

I've been to a number of prisons – Parkhurst, Camps Hill, Wandsworth, Feltham Young Offenders' Institute – and they're not nice places, they're places you would not want to return to. You send people to prison as a punishment, but prison conditions should be decent and humane. They should not be luxurious and you shouldn't have things you can get in the outside world. Of course stories about prisoners lounging around watching wide-screen televisions will drive people insane, and quite rightly. But prisons don't need to be harsher for the majority of prisoners; they need to be more effective. When I was visiting Wandsworth, 70 per cent of the people inside couldn't read, so how do we expect them to leave and make their way in the world if they don't have the tools to do it? I've seen volunteer groups encouraging prisoners to teach other prisoners how to read, and it's quite something to see it all come together.

What surprised you the most about them when you first visited? Were the conditions better or worse than you thought they'd be? Was the racial mix the same as you'd assumed? It's certainly changed now …

Having worked in the Home Office I've always known how large an Afro-Caribbean population there is in our prisons, but it always does strike you how large it is when you visit one. But a lot of the people in prison are from broken homes, who have been in care, who have been abused, had wretched educational opportunities, got into drugs, crime, and who have been on a conveyor belt that ends in the criminal justice system. We seem to be bad at catching them, punishing them or turning them around, and actually we need to improve all three of those things. Of course there are some prisoners who are just plain bad, in some cases evil, and for them it's obviously not about rehabilitation but about keeping them locked away for a long time.

Sentencing

What offences would you consider upping the sentences for?
I think we need very simple minimum sentences for things like gun and knife crime, because this is an area where a clear law needs to be part of the culture change. It must become unacceptable for someone to think that it's okay to carry a knife or a gun. And we need a tough minimum sentence for that. Burglary, or breaking and entering, I think is a violent crime and should be treated as such. There are so many first-time burglars who are not being sent to prison it's outrageous. That's just wrong. Crossing someone's threshold is the threshold you should not cross. It should be really clear that this isn't a minor offence. Okay, you've burgled someone, oh well okay. Burglary is wrong. Breaking into someone's house and stealing their goods shouldn't be decriminalized. We should send out a very clear, very loud message, one that can't be ignored. The state needs to control the streets or else the streets will control society. Under our 'min max' sentence, prisoners would be released after a minimum term which would kick in only if they had behaved. Otherwise they would serve the full term. We would also toughen community sentences by making offenders wear special uniforms and docking benefits payments if they don't turn up for work. We have to show the community we're taking action.

Would your Conservative Party ever entertain the death penalty?
No, not at all. Obviously this is a very emotive subject and if someone murdered one of my children then emotionally, obviously, I would want to kill them. How could you not? But there have been too many cases of things going wrong, of the wrong people being executed, of evidence coming to light after the execution, and sometimes there is just too much of an element of doubt. And I just don't honestly think that in a civilized society like ours that you can have the death penalty any more. What you have to do is to make sure that the punishment fits the crime, and make sure the really bad, really evil people never ever leave prison.

You intend toughening up stop and search, and making it much easier for the police to stop people on the street without filling out a foot-long form, don't you?
We have to look at the world as it is today and stop thinking about the past. Stop and search should be really effective, it should be quick and you shouldn't have to fill out this long form every time you talk to someone. If you're going to be dealing with young people carrying guns and knives you can't really do it without a reasonable level of stop and search. The police have become glorified form fillers rather than crime fighters. So what we've proposed is getting rid of the stop form altogether and basically changing the rules on stop and search to make it easier. And as is the case in so many of these areas, the government seems to have followed suit!

What does seeing the inside of a prison tell you about British society?
If you're in Parkhurst it tells you that there are some very evil people in the world that need to be locked away for a very, very long time ... but if you're in a less severe prison it tells you that there are people who have committed crimes and done terrible things but their lives took a wrong turn somewhere. And one of our duties as a society is to try and turn those lives around, which is something the current government just don't seem to have any clue about. The prison service has been one of the

disasters of the so-called New Labour era and the current Home Office ought to be ashamed of themselves.

One of the messages that chimed so well with the public last autumn was the broken society line, something you have been extremely vocal about since. This seems to be the true interpretation of Labour's tough on crime, tough on the causes of crime. It's a torch you seem more than willing to carry.

The interesting thing is that Labour don't want to admit that there is anything broken about our society at all, even after twenty-seven children were killed in London last year, even after the appalling death of responsible citizens on their doorsteps and in their front gardens, people who have only been trying to protect themselves, their children or their property. Every day there is another murder, another assault, another rape, another front-page horror story.

Homeland security

Ever since the 7 July bombings we have, as a nation, been living in a constant state of anticipation. We assume there will be more terrorist attacks, and that as long as we have an aggressive military presence in Iraq the UK will be seen as fair game by extremist Muslims. It has been suggested that we could set up our own Homeland Security Department – represented by a minister of Cabinet rank – which would have responsibility for ensuring proper protection of our borders and joined-up liaison between the various bodies responsible for intelligence and security issues. What do you think of that idea, and, in broader terms, how are we going to cope with British Muslim terrorists who are born and bred here?

Obviously fighting terrorism is the top concern of government today. I know that if we win the next election, the moment I walk through the front door of Number Ten I will have this huge responsibility of protecting the British public from terrorism. But anyone who thinks they've got a simple answer to terrorism just hasn't understood the question. We're dealing with people who are prepared to do literally anything, to kill as many innocent people as they can and to do it in suicide attacks. Plus there's no list of demands we can accept and no group of terrorists we could negotiate with, even if we wanted to. So it's a completely different kind of terrorist problem from the ones of the past – whether Baader-Meinhof in Germany, the Red Brigade in Italy, ETA in Spain or the IRA, as was, here at home.

Which you obviously don't think the Labour Party have …
Look, when it comes to national security, I've no doubt the Prime Minister's basic motives are honourable. We share much of the same analysis of the threat. But I just think they're going about it in the wrong way – as we've put it, a kind of ineffective authoritarianism instead of the hard-nosed defence of freedom that we need. It is the duty of a responsible opposition to look at all government policy in a forensic and clear-sighted way, and to suggest changes where we think they're necessary. This matters even more when it comes to our national security. So my approach to this issue is that we should offer cooperation where possible and constructive criticism where necessary. Which is exactly what we're doing.

But why could you do it any better than the government?
Because we've got a better, more thought-through plan. At the moment, counter-terrorism policy is in the hands of the Home Secretary, who also has to deal on a daily basis with vital issues like crime, immigration and antisocial behaviour – as well as national security. The threat we face demands much more focus than this. That's why we've said we'll have a dedicated Security Minister, working in the Home Office but as a full member of the Cabinet. Just as the Treasury has a Chief Secretary sitting in Cabinet with a single-minded focus on controlling public spending, so the Home Office should have a Security Minister with a single-minded focus on protecting Britain from terrorist attack. And in Pauline Neville-Jones we've got a tough, experienced, superbly qualified person to do that job.

The environment

It was once said of Richard Nixon that he would cut down a redwood tree and then mount the stump to make a speech for conservation, but I'm of the belief that you are a lot less cynical in your green beliefs – even if you were caught having your briefcase delivered by car as you cycled to work. You have made environmental issues a cornerstone of the new Conservative Party. At what point did you think this was the right thing to embrace? Can you remember the moment when you thought, a) this is important, and b) we must make this part of our manifesto?

My awakening to all this came with the great Thatcher speech of '88, or was it '89, and it was a sort of second-order subject until then. It was something everyone was becoming more conscious of, at the end of that decade when the economy had grown and people felt better off and there was a concern about a kind of throwaway society and the impact on the environment and the ozone layer. That speech for me actually suddenly showed that what was a niche issue was going to become more and more important. And once I became leader of the Conservative Party I had the opportunity to say that I think it's important, too, and I think it should have a billing up there with the economy and with the health service and so on.

What needs to change on transport policy in order to help the environment?

Just about everything. It has to be far more integrated. But there's a bigger picture here. John McCain said to me, and I completely agree with him, that we've got to get the argument about the environment exactly right. We've got to tell people it's not about wearing a jersey and sitting in the dark with the lights off shivering. And he's absolutely right. This has got to be an issue where we still click into people's aspirations and hopes about getting round the country in an easy way and travel not being such a hassle. It needs high-speed rail to replace short-haul flights, it means integrating much better with trains and planes and automobiles, as it were. Us humble cyclists – especially now that we obey the law! – take our life into our hands every time we get onto our bikes. There aren't proper provisions for cyclists and there ought to be. A lot of things have to change but it doesn't mean we'll have to sit in a traffic jam and go nowhere. And it's worth saying that stationary traffic is more polluting than moving traffic. So bypasses and road-widening are not necessarily unenvironmental.

That's interesting what McCain says, but surely the US is one of the major stumbling blocks to meaningful climate action.
Yes, Bush has been a disaster on the environment. The good thing is that whoever wins in America the environment is going to get a higher billing and climate change will move further up the ladder of importance and hopefully we'll see some sort of global deal. And that's definitely the case with McCain.

Will you enact legislation to change our carbon habits?
Well, we are doing that through the climate change bill, which was our suggestion and the government's taken it up. And that will lead to quite big changes because it will start to put a price for carbon into the economy.

Nuclear power: where do you stand on that?
I don't think governments should pick technologies. I don't think we should sit there saying we want this many coal-fired stations, that many gas stations and that many nuclear stations. That to me is not the role of the government. Government should set the rules for security of supply, make sure the market is open, make sure the planning system works, make sure that safety is guaranteed, make sure the environmental rules are there, and then allow the energy providers to provide. And so in terms of nuclear we need to clear away the obstacles – Sizewell took over twelve years – we need to change the planning system, we need to have a proper price for carbon and if nuclear can cross those hurdles and be part of the picture then fine. We should not give it some giant subsidy.

My history on this is as someone who learned about nuclear power in the 1980s. I thought, this is very exciting because it is cheap and clean – but then we learned the enormous costs of cleaning up nuclear power. So that was a big blow to people who were instinctively pro-nuclear. I do not want to be the Prime Minister who suddenly writes out some vast cheque on behalf of the taxpayer to subsidize nuclear power stations that can't otherwise pay for themselves. So they have to pay.

You've said that while you want to help families with their carbon footprint, you want to penalize aviation.
We do need to have smart taxation rather than dim taxation and that means taxing flights rather than passengers.

This must make things slightly tricky when you're speaking to the likes of British Airways …
Well, I think they understand that if we're going to control climate change then everybody has to make their contribution, and that's the transport sector as well as the housing sector as well as the business sector, and you can't just ignore aviation. But neither should you demonize it. Currently aviation is just a few per cent of our emissions, but if we don't do anything about it it will become a very large part of our emissions. It needs to come into the carbon trading system and we do need to look at the taxation regime. It's not about saying to people you can't fly or you can't go on holiday, it's about saying that as a society we need to pay the full cost of our pollution.

You're a big fan of decentralized energy, aren't you – solar panels, wind turbines, combined heat-and-energy boilers, selling electricity back to the National Grid, that sort of thing?
Yes, and we've put forward a really serious reform plan to encourage decentralized energy in this country. It's a massive change from where we are today. Once you've understood the potential of decentralized energy it really is very exciting. If you think of it as a few solar panels and a few windmills on roofs it means nothing. But what it really means is a funda-

mental change from a system where at the moment we take our energy off a national grid with big power stations being built in different parts of the country. We have to change that mentality towards something where, as well as taking energy off the grid, you have the opportunity to sell it back to the grid. Now why is that exciting? Because what it means is that new factories that are built think to themselves, well, what bit of my energy can I generate myself and sell back? New housing estates will go ahead with community boilers. Farmers will be producing straw which they can use to produce their own energy, which they can sell back to the grid. It will mean that new schools will think, let's put on the solar panels because that will reduce our energy bills and give us a revenue stream. So once you start thinking about a decentralized energy world, it is a very big change. It's like going from analogue to digital television. It's that sort of scale of change. The problem with the government is that they haven't got it yet.

How central is Zac Goldsmith now to your environmental policies? You haven't distanced yourself from him?

He's been a really helpful adviser. He's now a candidate. But we have a lot of people on the environmental team and he's one of many. He doesn't overpromote himself but I think sometimes people attach an enormous amount to him because of his name and all the rest of it. He's an extremely persuasive environmentalist, I think he's a very good candidate, I think he'd make a great MP. He's one of the good guys.

Culture

What did you read as a boy, what books? You're a big Ian Fleming fan ...

Funnily enough I didn't read him first time around. When my grandmother died I got a lot of Ian Fleming novels from her and started reading them and loved them.

And when you were younger?
I remember loving being read [H. E. Marshall's] *Our Island Story*. I read lots of adventure stuff. When I was little I read lots of Hal and Roger books, Rider Haggard, quite sort of traditional adventure stuff. Then I went through a manic Graham Greene phase and read every single novel. In fact I'm quite looking forward one day to reading them all again because I've forgotten them all. I just think he is wonderful, brilliant.

What was the last novel you read (not a children's book)?
Engleby by Sebastian Faulks. It's brilliantly written and an incredibly disturbing portrait of a murderer. I don't read every night because I go to bed and I'm knackered. But I do tend to read more non-fiction than fiction. The last non-fiction book I read was *Shame* by Jasvinder Sanghera, about a British Asian woman whose parents forced her into a marriage. That was brilliant. I finished that. Although I can usually never remember novels ...

What is your favourite novel?
My favourite book is *Goodbye to All That* by Robert Graves, because it's a brilliant memoir of the First World War and it's such a great book. My favourite novel would have to be by Graham Greene, *Our Man in Havana* or *The End of the Affair*.

Favourite film?
Lawrence of Arabia.

Favourite soap opera?
I once went through a period of watching *EastEnders* but I haven't watched it for ages. Oh, and *Neighbours* 1986, the Kylie period.

Favourite sitcom?
Porridge.

Favourite work of art?
Guernica by Picasso. I went to see it in situ in Madrid.

Favourite building?
The Radcliffe Camera, Oxford.

AC/DC or Led Zeppelin?
AC/DC.

Wrong answer.
Samantha would not understand that at all. She is a massive Led Zep fan.
I don't think I ever went to an AC/DC concert but I did have two AC/DC
albums, including *Back In Black*.

Snooker or pool?
Snooker.

Bitter or lager?
Bitter.

Alan Partridge **or** *Little Britain***?**
Little Britain; it's funnier.

I'm A Celebrity **or** *Big Brother***?**
Oh, if I have to choose it's *I'm A Celebrity*. One of the weirdest conversations I've ever had was explaining *I'm A Celebrity* to Margaret Thatcher.
I said, You don't understand, Lady T, your daughter is on this
programme and she is about to win a million pounds! It's on the third
channel, it's on the third button at nine o'clock. Set the video. She got
quite excited, actually. I think I was the first person to really explain to
her what was going on.

**I thought you acquitted yourself very well on Jonathan Ross, but you
were criticized for doing the show …**

I decided to do it because I think one of the challenges is to get through to people who don't watch political programmes or the news, and that was a chance to communicate with them. It was a bit of a risk because he is a wild card. And having been on the show I know he's even more of a wild card because you don't see the bits of the show that aren't broadcast. He does the audience warm-up himself, and it's a tremendous night, Samantha was in the audience and said afterwards that she'd like to do that every Thursday night. It's a risk because you don't know what he's going to say next; I suspect that he doesn't know what he's going to say next. But I thought it was fine. In the end they decided to broadcast the question that got the papers so excited [about whether Cameron ever masturbated over photographs of Margaret Thatcher], and perhaps they shouldn't have done. But if you watch the programme it was amusing and light-hearted. It was a risk and I'm glad I took it.

Lily Allen or Amy Winehouse?
Both. I bought both albums last summer, but I think I prefer Lily Allen because the lyrics make me laugh.

You support Aston Villa don't you? Why?
Vaguely, yes, because it was the first football match I ever went to.

Have you ever eaten a Pot Noodle?
Yes, lots; didn't really like them.

Who is your favourite *Simpsons* character?
I like Homer, because he's a useless, bumbling dad. There's a bit of Homer Simpson in all of us.

Are you middle class or upper class?
I don't really buy these labels.

Come on, gun to your head.
Gun to my head, I suppose I'd describe myself as well off. I don't buy these class things because they're all going. What do these labels mean any more?

What is your favourite Smiths song and why?
Probably 'This Charming Man'. I always think if you say 'Cemetery Gates' it sounds as if you have a death wish, if you say 'There Is A Light That Never Goes Out' it means you believe in double suicide. You can't win, really, can you? So I think 'This Charming Man' is safest.

What was Madonna like?
I thought she was very friendly, very driven.

Get away. That's a real shocker.
I got the impression that she just works incredibly hard all the time. After meeting Madonna I felt positively lacking in ambition and drive.

Who else have you enjoyed meeting?
Obviously Mandela. You just can't grasp the magnetism of this man, and the total lack of any bitterness over all that he experienced. You get that out of reading his book, but when you meet him it is so palpable that it's extraordinary. That was a huge honour. I've also been enormously impressed with some of the soldiers I've met in Afghanistan. We politicians sit there with bits of paper and say yes or no to this policy or that policy, but to meet the people on the front line is always a huge honour.

What's your favourite political joke?
Nick Clegg at the moment.

Come on, what's the joke you use most in your speeches, or the one that you find yourself returning to most because it works?
The one that I use far too much because it is so often appropriate is, As someone once said, Having heard myself introduced I can't wait to hear

myself speak. Which is actually a very good and disarming line. Most of my jokes are cribbed off other people, although I do try and do my own every now and then. I get wonderful letters now. Every week I get a set of letters – those for, those against, the issues of the week. And there's a section at the back called And Finally, and some of those are wonderful. One the other day suggested I should have a civil partnership with Gordon Brown along the lines of Elton John and David Furnish.

NINE

'Gordon Brown better watch out today, as I'm wearing my Blue Peter badge'

PMQs, the EU treaty, Boris Johnson's Che Guevara watch, acting out *The Godfather*, the implosion of a Prime Minister, Jeremy Clarkson

On the morning of Wednesday 5 March 2008, David Cameron was in his office in Portcullis House, opposite the Houses of Parliament, at 8.30, having cycled to work in the bright spring sunshine. He was dressed in a dark blue fleece, a grey sweatshirt full of holes, blue sweatpants and a pair of not exactly box-fresh trainers. Today was Prime Minister's Questions, and Cameron always arrived early, to plan exactly how he was going to skewer his adversary across the dispatch box. Today was the Commons vote on the Lisbon EU treaty – which would see a tranche of powers signed away to Brussels – and Cameron fully expected the Conservatives to lose. 'We're toast, frankly,' he said, leaning back in his chair before putting his feet on the long wooden table. 'The big issue today should be the Liberal Democrats, because Calamity Clegg has ordered them all to abstain. Because of this we will lose the vote.'

Cameron's casual dress contrasted sharply with the austere surroundings, his crumpled fleece looking decidedly odd juxtaposed with the framed line drawings of Harold Macmillan, and the photographs of DC with the likes of Margaret Thatcher and Nelson Mandela. As he quickly munched his way through a banana and then an apple, pondering the day ahead and gazing out over the Thames towards the London Eye, the traffic thundered down the Embankment, making his office seem even more like an Edwardian oasis of calm. His desk was covered with bottles of spirits, waiting to be signed by him and then given as auction prizes. 'Judging by the amount of booze on my desk you'd think that all the Leader of the Opposition does all day is sign bottles of whisky ...' He smiled, glancing up at his suit, shirt and tie hanging on his wardrobe. 'Prime Minister's Questions is always a big day, but today is even bigger because of the EU vote, and although I'm fairly resigned to losing it I need to make Brown's day as difficult as possible.' He sipped his coffee, took a couple of calls on his mobile, worked his way through the papers and carried on talking as though he were planning a family picnic. 'It's also good to get in early before everyone else arrives, as this morning can usually get quite feisty.'

The first person to arrive was Desmond Swayne MP, Cameron's Parliamentary Private Secretary, who careered in carrying a huge bunch of papers, some cappuccinos, bottled water and the obligatory copy of that day's *Private Eye* (a Prince Harry souvenir issue, complete with the cover line, 'War is Hello!'). Then Michael Gove hove into view, rushing into the room full of stories about Hillary Clinton's narrow win that morning in the Texas primary. 'It just prolongs the agony!' Gove is something of an intellectual powerhouse, and is considered by many in the lobby to be the brightest member of the Shadow Cabinet. One of the great late-night debates in Westminster restaurants is whether he could ever be leader. Some say yes, but others claim he has a deal with his wife not to do so, and that his constitution is not up to it. There is also the not inconsiderable problem of his nationality: he's Scottish.

Then Oliver Letwin walked in, then Andy Coulson, and, a few minutes later, Boris Johnson, carrying his copy of *Private Eye* (already well thumbed). This was going to be Boris's final appearance at these meetings, although he had never been a regular. The discussion turned to various national newspaper editors before reverting back to the London mayoral race, and whether they could think of a question that would force Brown to defend Ken Livingstone. 'Brown hates Livingstone and will hate being drawn on him,' someone said. 'You should look at the quotes Brown's given over the years about Livingstone. They're epic. Brown simply cannot stand the man. He dislikes Livingstone almost as much as he hates Blair.'

George Osborne walked in next, and immediately started discussing Nick Clegg's dismantling by Jeremy Paxman on *Newsnight* the previous evening. Like their leader, they all called him 'Calamity Clegg', hoping the tag might stick. I had just asked Piers Morgan to interview Clegg for *GQ*, and as the conversation turned to the Lib Dem leader I volunteered some of the more salacious parts of the interview (principally moral ambiguity over Iraq, cross-dressing, and the number of women Clegg claimed to have slept with). As the conversation veered away from Clegg, and the London mayoral race, Osborne began recounting a meeting between Boris and George W. Bush a few years previously. Bush was very intrigued to meet Boris, and appeared to be enjoying himself; until, that is, he spied Johnson's wrist. 'Are you wearing a Che Guevara watch,' asked the President, with a confused look on his face. 'It's actually my sister's,' blushed Boris. 'I don't care about that,' smiled Bush. 'In Texas we execute people for wearing Che Guevara watches …'

The meeting, like all meetings in Cameron's office before PMQs, was to work out various lines of attack for Cameron to use at the midday, midweek question and answer session in the chamber of the House of Commons. Traditionally, this is where the incumbent PM gets to defend himself on whatever travesty he's perpetrated that week. And while it occasionally comes across as old-fashioned and childish, this is where an MP can prove that he is worth his salt; this is where a leader can prove that he is worthy of his job, and where a Prime Minister can demonstrate that he has the mettle for whatever the world decides to throw at him.

Cameron wanted five or six questions he could ask (the Leader of the Opposition is allowed up to six questions – which he will normally use as two groups of three – and the leader of the third largest party, currently the Liberal Democrats, has two), based around two topics: the failure – yet again – of the government to offer the public a referendum on the EU treaty, and Ken Livingstone's refusal to disassociate himself from an employee who had been accused of abusing public funds. Not for the first time as leader, Cameron had woken up in the middle of the night and decided to change the questions he was going to ask the following morning. So his team had to work harder than ever to come up with the points he wanted to make to the PM. A key purpose of PMQs was to embarrass the Prime Minister, to force him to address topics he didn't want addressed, to force him to acknowledge things he didn't want to acknowledge, and generally to kick up some dust. It was also the one time in the week when Cameron had the opportunity to bring the Prime Minister to account.

For fifty years PMQs has been one of the most entertaining regular events in the Commons, at times almost a barbaric ritual. When John Major and Neil Kinnock began facing each other across the dispatch box they made a gentleman's agreement to attempt to do it in a dignified fashion, although, as both their teams enjoyed the spectator sport of the adversarial knockabout, it soon returned to its traditional battle of attrition. It didn't get any better when John Smith became Labour leader, either – John Major: 'As one of my predecessors might have said, we've had a little local difficulty. We shall get over it. I am going on with the work in hand.' John Smith: 'Doesn't the Prime Minister understand that when he announced business as usual this morning he caused apprehension throughout the land?' Since the televising of Parliament, PMQs has formed an important part of British political culture. William Hague may have failed to get elected, but he won respect for his performances in PMQs, and he often succeeded in making Tony Blair look a fool. So when Blair found himself answering Prime Minister's Questions instead of asking them, he moved the twice-weekly fifteen-minute sessions on Tuesdays and Thursdays to one thirty-minute session on Wednesday. While this meant that Blair only had to prepare for one interrogative bout, it had the added effect of making PMQs appear even more gladiatorial. (Blair understood the importance of this televisual duel: towards the end of his leadership he even started wearing make-up for his weekly battle.)

To be an effective speaker in the chamber you need to be fast and furious, not ponderous and verbose. Poor old Paddy Ashdown, the former Liberal Democrat leader, never understood this, and whenever he stood to speak he would be drowned in hoots of derision. And then everyone would get up to leave; whenever Ashdown spoke in the House you could guarantee he wouldn't sit down for at least ten minutes, causing MPs from all parties to head for home, or, more usually, the bar. And Ashdown hated it. 'As soon as I was called by the Speaker they all started shouting,' he wrote in his diary. 'The anti-Europeans wanted to vent their wrath on somebody and I was the obvious target. I hardly said a word before Dennis Skinner [the Beast of Bolsover] shouted, "Make way for Captain Mainwaring". This caused everybody to fall about in mock mirth. God, I hate this place. It is puerile, pathetic and utterly useless and I long for the day (if it ever comes) when we have the power to change it completely. I left incandescent with rage but trying not to show it.' Poor old Menzies Campbell hated it, too, when he briefly led the Lib Dems: 'It's theatre, not debate,' he said. 'I'm uncomfortable with that kind of politics.' So uncomfortable that he needed notes to ask the Prime Minister a couple of questions each Wednesday. Cameron, on the other hand, relished it.

Like Hague with Blair, Cameron regularly ran rings around Brown in the chamber, regardless of how he was doing in the real world outside. He still got nervous before the Wednesday lunchtime onslaught – 'I just try not to show it' – but it's a part of the job he has always enjoyed. And he enjoyed it even more with Brown than he did with Blair; you could tell that from his very first bout with Brown, just after he became Prime Minister, in July 2007. After Cameron's call for the hard-line Islamist group Hizb-ut-Tahrir to be outlawed, Brown said: 'I think he forgets I have only been in this job for five days.' He hadn't; he'd been in the job for a whole week. The Tories laughed, Cameron looked incredulous and the press were merciless.

As another round of coffees was brought into Cameron's office, Boris Johnson suggested a particular line of attack but then Cameron batted it back, leaning back in his chair so he was almost parallel with the floor. Cameron then suggested a few more questions, with Gove pretending to be Brown (it is acknowledged in the room that Gove actually does

Brown better than Brown himself), getting all gruff and grumpy and banging on the table. This was like writing a play by committee, with Cameron always having the final say; like composing rhyming couplets, with everyone at the table pitching in ideas about what to ask Brown, and then anticipating his response. Bosh! This was Punch and Judy. Verbal chess. Shadow boxing. The team tried to consider every possibility, working out just how far they could push a line before having to draw back. 'That's very similar to what Michael Corleone says to Luca Brasi,' said Gove at one point, bringing up a plot point in *The Godfather*.

(A few weeks previously, Cameron had made a short video of his preparations for PMQs, and while this showed he was more than comfortable in his own skin, one critic rather unkindly imagined what Brown's version would be like: 'The word is he spends hour after hour practising, with Geoff Hoon playing the part of Cameron. The resulting film would be longer than *The Godfather*, Parts *I*, *II* and *III*, with nearly as much shouting.')

And on and on it went, with Cameron, Osborne, Gove, Letwin, Johnson, Coulson and Swayne building up the arguments, fine-tuning the questions, and making sure the whole performance wouldn't be too theatrical, or give Brown any opportunity for amusing responses (unlikely); all the while DC keeping it as light-hearted as possible. Cameron was definitely the energy in the room. After two and half hours, it was all over, with Cameron having the five questions he needed. As the team all knew, getting the mix right here was all important, and the last thing the Conservative leader needed was a series of questions that focussed too much on one subject, just in case he fell at the first hurdle. Given his track record, it was unlikely that Brown would trip Cameron up in the chamber, but one could never be too careful. Not in this heady environment, anyway.

Rehearsal over, his Cabinet members left, with Cameron offering a typical bouncy adieu: 'Gordon Brown better watch out today, as I'm wearing my Blue Peter badge (he had been given one when he appeared on the show a few weeks before).' He sat down at his desk, and for the next twenty minutes went over and over his questions, analysing every one in detail. Having finalised them, he threw the briefing notes away, and then got changed.

Coulson retired next door, to a communications office full of 'Bottler Brown ale' and 'Bottler Brown beer mats' and a huge framed photograph of Margaret and Mark Thatcher reading a copy of the *News of the World* on a park bench, which Coulson had brought over from his Wapping office when he left the Murdoch empire. On his pin board was a sheet of A4 paper listing all the nationwide political polls undertaken since Brown had come into office. It showed that since 25 November 2007 the Tories had never been less than 2 per cent ahead in the polls, with the average being ten percentage points. Since then they had never achieved anything below a 40 per cent popularity rating. Not enough maybe, but certainly good enough for now.

Portcullis House, often compared to an inverted cow's udder by those who work there, is linked to the Palace of Westminster by a bomb-proof underground passageway that cuts under the northern end of Westminster Bridge, and it was through this tunnel that Cameron walked at 11.30. Twenty-five minutes later, the House of Commons chamber was full. Cameron sat on the front bench, staring straight ahead, flanked by William Hague, George Osborne, Theresa May and David Davis, and watched impassively as Brown made his way to the green leather benches opposite. Brown came into the chamber carrying his six-inch-high pile of papers covered in highlighter pen and Post-it notes. These briefing notes are usually the only thing standing between the Prime Minister and calamity, although any psychologist will tell you that a pile that high says two things: the person carrying them desperately wants to be seen to be busy, and that they couldn't make a decision if their very life depended upon it. But all the leaders have had them: Blair loved his folder of tabbed-up facts, while Margaret Thatcher called it the 'plastic fantastic'.

(Soon after Brown became PM, MPs reserving their places in the Commons chamber before business on a Thursday had begun noticing a member of staff scrubbing the dispatch box with increasing regularity.

The reason was that during PMQs, Brown insisted on using a black felt tip pen to scribble notes, and whenever he got angry – i.e. all the time – he ended up waving his hands in the air and getting ink on the dispatch box, so someone had to come in and clean it first thing on a Thursday morning.)

Sitting in the chamber, from the press gallery you very quickly get the sense that the house is split in two, and not along party lines. Essentially this cavernous wooden chamber contains two very different types of people – those of an age where will and dreams have evaporated, and those of an age where change and ambition are the two salient driving forces in their lives; men and women who feel their life is before them, not behind them. Sit on the front bench and you could reasonably say you have a career in politics. Some might say, sit anywhere else and you are simply a politician. In that respect it's not that much different from the geographical hierarchy of a catwalk show: if you're not on the front bench you're invisible.

Today, all the action was down the front. 'All three main parties in this House made a promise to our constituents for a vote on the EU constitution,' said Cameron, staring Brown fiercely in the face. 'When we turn around and say, "You can't have it any more", it is no wonder people feel cheated and cynical because promises are being made and broken.' And then Brown leaped up, looking over Cameron's shoulder, almost shouting: 'If his party had truly changed and moved to the centre, he would be standing up to his backbenchers; he would be leading them instead of following them. He would be moving to the centre of Europe instead of being left at the margins of Europe.' If the Tory front bench looked confused it was because Brown's outburst didn't really mean anything. It wasn't clever, wasn't funny, and in reality was almost childishly aggressive.

Brown looked genuinely angry, not just because Cameron tends to get under the PM's skin whenever they are together at PMQs, but also because there is something about Brown's demeanour that suggests he thinks he shouldn't have to explain himself to Cameron. He simply hates having to take Cameron seriously. Brown's front bench looked angry, too

– perhaps out of sympathy – and as one sketch writer put it the next day, they were all nodding like members of Stalin's politburo standing on the frozen rivers of Leningrad, with Jack Straw aimlessly pointing away at the Shadow front bench. Thankfully, for once, Brown didn't employ 'the smile'. Ironically, Brown's smile – or at least the one he was told to employ ever since failing to convince the public that he hadn't lied about his reasons for not holding an election – had become one of his defining characteristics. Previously – i.e. before the infamous Andrew Marr performance, back in October 2007 – Brown would arrive at and leave Downing Street with gravitas; although I have the weight of the world on my shoulders, he seemed to imply, my shoulders are so broad and so sturdy and so Presbyterian that none of you have anything to worry about. Everything was fine, he seemed to say, everything was A-okay (not that the Big Clunking Fist would ever say anything resembling A-okay). The smile came into effect for every televised interview, and actually became more intense and rictus-like the more portentous he became. He also appeared unable to smile without muttering the phrase 'ensuring prudent economic stability and prosperity going forward'.

But this manoeuvre made everyone extremely worried, not least members of his Cabinet. In fact, it made many people very worried indeed, because if he was smiling this much, then things were obviously much worse than they originally thought they were. And guess what? They were.

Consequently everyone had an opinion about it. George Osborne thought it made him look deranged, while the Radio 2 presenters Mark Radcliffe and Stuart Maconie thought it made him look like the Child Catcher from *Chitty Chitty Bang Bang* – the one with the long nose, the lollipops and the Russell Brand outfit. As for myself, it reminded me of the nervous smile he employed while watching Toby Young's cataclysmic (if hilarious) best-man speech at Sean Macaulay's wedding in Washington some years ago. Primarily because it was the same smile we were all employing.

The smile (which would later be described by the novelist Gordon Burn as an 'anxiety-shrouded, tortured grin') made it into the cartoons, too. The political cartoon is the calendar by which we remember it all. The feuds. The back-stabbings. The hubris. As well as the previously unnoticed facial tics and the crudely drawn ears, noses and five o'clock shadows. Who will ever be able to forget John Major's underpants ('Super Useless Man' as drawn by the irrepressible Steve Bell) or Mad Maggie's nose (a beak that could pierce tins of Carnation Milk, as imagined by the one and only Trog)? That such simple techniques as crude caricature and the juxtaposition of two unrelated news items should still be so powerful in the twenty-first century underscores the fact that cartoonists have never been more important to the livelihood or the good health of their newspapers. As electronic news delivery becomes ever more popular, and ever more diverse, so the iconic scribblings of a few bug-eyed obsessives continue to give their papers a warmth and personality (and, indeed, an astringency) you don't get on a TV screen or a website. Or a telephone, in fact. The PM must have realized that the smile wasn't going to do him any good (and that he should revert to the Stalinesque solemnity he did so well) when a cartoon appeared in the *Spectator* at Christmas. A woman is shown holding a camera up to her sombre-looking husband. 'Give me a smile, dear. Not the one that makes you look insane.'

It was the Lib Deb MP Vince Cable who really got the measure of Brown. In the Commons at the end of November 2007, the acting leader of the Liberal Democrats said, somewhat indelibly, to judge by the number of times it was used in the press afterwards, 'The house has noticed the Prime Minister's remarkable transformation in the past few weeks – from Stalin to Mr Bean.' The phrase began pinballing its way around Westminster and instantly became enshrined in political folklore. 'A great howl of laughter seemed to fall from the very ceiling,' wrote the *Guardian*'s Simon Hoggart the day after. 'Even Labour members desperately tried to hide their amusement from the whips … This one is going to hurt.' Later, Cable said he didn't want to overdo his Stalin joke, but then compounded the crime by capturing the pathos of Brown's decline thus: from ruthless to rudderless; bully to bumbler; from Brezhnev to Blackadder.

The real issue, of course, was one of competence, and whether the PM had much more in his arsenal. Indeed, was there anything in his tool kit at all? The Brown we all saw speak at Prime Minister's Questions in the chamber of the Commons on the day of the crunch vote on the future of the EU didn't look like he had anything in his tool bag at all. All there appeared to be was his formidable and repetitious droning. And it was this repetition that made many political editors think the tank may have been dry. Iain Martin in the *Daily Telegraph* said of a Brown speech on the NHS around the same time, 'The content is very much downtown Havana and the presentation style also has Cuban echoes, like one of those speeches by Castro it goes on, and on and on.'

There is no place at PMQs for the overdramatic pauses and studied rhetorical flourishes so common in most political speeches; here it's all cut and thrust, point and jab. Which Brown rarely managed very well. Today, already flustered by Cameron's refusal to accept his explanation, he shot back with a recitation – in his distinctive booming voice – of semantic reasons why the British public weren't going to be allowed a referendum. Brown waffled with weak rebuttals, some of which Cameron's team had correctly identified earlier.

In the end, however, it wasn't the great battle between Cameron and Brown that would be remembered that day – even though every one of Cameron's questions was plain and pointed like a spear – but the implosion of Nick Clegg. Perhaps in homage to Paddy Ashdown, when Clegg started to speak he made the mistake of adjusting his trousers, generating a great gale of derision from the backbenches. 'The Prime Minister once said …' he began, and then made the fatal mistake of pausing, a pause which was filled by an unidentified heckler shouting, '… he'd have a referendum!' At which point the House collapsed and there was nowhere left for him to go, other than back to his seat.

According to Iain Dale, the Conservative Party activist behind Iain Dale's Diary, one of the most influential political blogs, 'It was a fairly boisterous House today. In terms of body language and style I thought this was Brown's strongest performance so far, but he was sadly lacking in argument and content. He even said that Ireland wasn't having a referendum at one point, which was clearly wrong. David Cameron linked the EU question rather well with public dissatisfaction about politicians who break their promises. He seems to be saying to the public: "I know you think politicians are shysters. I feel your pain." Nick Clegg had a torrid time and just wasn't at the races. He's become a political masochist version of Britney Spears, as if he is subliminally saying: "Hit me baby one more time." I'll score Brown 6, Cameron 6 and Clegg 2.'

That night, Gordon Brown killed off hopes of any referendum on the EU constitution for good, breaking Labour's 2005 general election pledge as he ordered his troops to reject the idea. Even though twenty-nine of Brown's MPs rebelled, and three senior Lib Dems resigned their positions, the referendum was sunk. The real loser, apart from the British people – 80 per cent of whom wanted a referendum – was Clegg, as thirteen of his MPs ignored party orders to abstain. This row eclipsed any problems that the Conservatives or Labour might have been having, and caused Clegg to have a mini-crisis of his own, his first since becoming party leader in December.

After PMQs, Cameron and I spoke about taking on Brown over the dispatch box, and then about Europe and foreign policy.

PMQs

In terms of your own personal stress levels, I would imagine Prime Minister's Questions is as tough as it gets. It's like watching a good men's singles final, like watching two lions.
Prime Minister's Questions is theatre, and you are judged very quickly; you can tell in the mood of the House of Commons if you've had a hit or a miss, and you are judged instantly after it. But I really enjoy it, look forward to it. It's one of the highlights of the week and I actually don't think you can do this job unless you have an ease with it. You obviously get nervous before a session but with me it's the sort of nervousness I like. I thrive on it. You can't not look forward to something like that. You often have no idea what's going to be thrown at you, even though obvi-

ously you come as fully prepared as possible. The sort of thing like Budgets – when you have no idea what's in the bloody thing – and the debates on the Queen's Speech and the big parliamentary occasions, that is when the stress levels go up.

You're very powerful when you are speaking in the House, and, as I've said before, people respond to that very positively. They like the fact that you're being ballsy, being tough. But are you ever wary of coming across too strong because you don't want to look as though you're just browbeating Brown, but then with Brown it seems to work.

During PMQs you do need to be quite strong and aggressive, you can't make it an interesting fireside discussion; it is not that at all. It is two teams facing each other across quite a hostile House of Commons and the false setting is rather macho and aggressive. It's a bear pit, I don't like being macho, but I have learned how to get my point across in the right way and it does mean being quite aggressive at times because it's that sort of theatre.

He hates it when you rile him, obviously hates it when you force him to lose his temper or go off track. He's no mean speaker himself, but you can see steam coming out of his ears when anyone dares to disagree with him.

The main thing is being comfortable with what you're doing. Brown just isn't like that. Blair was brilliant at being very aggressive. He could be political, consensual, statesman-like, but you always felt like he was relatively comfortable with what he was doing. Brown, I feel, is more two-speed.

You're right. When people criticize Blair for being insincere they ignore the fact that he actually had multi personalities, and could chop and change according to whom he was with. He was – is – actually rather brilliant at that, whereas Brown only seems to have a volume control, so you either get quiet Gordon or loud Gordon. Now,

obviously a certain part of your education would have prepared you for this sort of gladiatorial debating.

Not really. I never did the debating society at school and I never did the Oxford Union at Oxford University, I just didn't do debating.

Why? That seems extremely odd ...

I don't know, I just wasn't interested in it at that time. I just didn't think I would like it, so I'm not a sort of classic Oxford debater. But I have always liked argument, discussion and debate so I have found it quite natural.

Do you ever freeze? When you have to comment upon something and you just don't have the figures and you just don't know what to say. It must be terrible to be in a situation like PMQs and find yourself failing ...

Yes, that has happened. In a live interview, you just have to find some way through it, but sometimes you're asked a question and you can say, sorry can I just stop the tape, because, actually, it's ridiculous to expect someone to have an opinion on absolutely everything.

That's the gig. That's why they pay you the big bucks.

Yes, that is the gig, but sometimes the best thing to do is just say, I'm sorry. Someone once asked me to comment on a Douglas Hurd speech, and I said I'm sorry I haven't read it – I think that honesty is the best policy in that situation. Sometimes when you're making a speech and you lose your train of thought and you don't know where you're going, if you take quite a long pause – always thinking to yourself, where the hell am I going with this – actually people just think you're taking quite a long pause.

What about appearing on television? What about *Question Time*? I remember Jeremy Clarkson once telling me that although he's flown upside down in jet fighters and driven a million miles an hour in drag racing, driven 200mph speedboats, nothing is as frightening as David Dimbleby saying 'Jeremy Clarkson'.

I don't do it any more because you don't do it as leader of the party, but I did it a few times when I was in the Shadow Cabinet and I enjoyed it. The drugs one was quite a famous one [on the edition of the programme broadcast on 13 October 2005, Cameron defended his right to a private life 'before politics' and refused to say whether or not he had ever tried hard drugs. Asked whether he had taken Class A drugs, he said: 'I have said all I want to say about this.' He said everybody was allowed to 'err and stray' in their past. And he told the audience he would not bow to a 'media-driven agenda' to 'dig into politicians' private lives'], I always quite liked those, I like the process of communicating, I love doing questions and answers, and after every speech I normally do a very long question and answer session. I love that, it's about engagement. I like the process, it's the best bit of the job.

Europe

Is the EU good for business?
The single market is good for business, but the regulation that surrounds it can be terrible. Some regulation is inevitable in creating a single market, but it's far too prescriptive as it is now. But there are also signs of hope, actually. If you listen to President Barroso, the current head of the European Commission, he's making all the right noises and actually abolishing some regulations.

You've succeeded in almost totally removing Europe as an issue in the Conservatives, whereas fifteen years ago it was tearing you apart …
Fifteen years ago? More like five years ago. Of course it's an important issue, but it shouldn't be the issue that dominates our party to the exclusion of everything else.

Do you feel instinctively that European integration should be put on hold or reversed?
I think it's gone too far, and gone too far in the wrong direction. We need a European Union that works as a looser and more flexible, open

organization. The hopeful signs are that now that countries from Eastern and Central Europe have come in, having just rediscovered their national identity, they are less likely to want to subsume it into a European nation state. But we need a British government that's there arguing for that rather than endlessly caving in to the latest demand that comes out of Brussels.

Iraq

Blair always maintained that he'd go to war with Iraq all over again. And you've said you would too. Why?

Well, I wouldn't quite put it like that. What I've said is, looking back, it was a very difficult decision that I agonized about, thought about, and, even though one of the planks of it which was the weapons of mass destruction, if I look back at the reasons I made the decision, it was about getting rid of Saddam, it was about enforcing the will of the United Nations. The alternative was to hand him an enormous propaganda victory, and so I still think it was the right thing to do. But I think huge mistakes were made subsequently.

Up until the most recent Iraq War, people on British soil had rarely been targeted by Islamic extremists, even though historically we've had a strong presence in the Middle East. We were also instrumental in setting up the state of Israel etc. If you were PM, how would you plan to win over the hearts and minds of the Arab states and destroy the motivation that leads to war in the first place?

I think it is a twin-track approach. You need to integrate better, and work with and take into account moderate Islamic opinion and Muslims who want to be part of a successful Britain. But at the same time you have to isolate and defeat the voices of extremism, throwing out preachers of hate who don't have a right to be here. You need to take those tough steps while at the same time implementing a less multiculturalist approach and more of an integrationist approach. Also, you need to think through very carefully everything you do in foreign policy in terms of domestic policy. The two should be brought together.

The Middle East

Can you please, in fairly broad brushstrokes, explain your Middle East policy? Do we need a much less aggressive interventionist foreign policy? Tell me what your solution is to the Israel/Palestine problem. Which roadmap would you use?

We have to be both tough with the Palestinians and sometimes quite tough with the Israelis in order to try and push them towards making a deal. You've got to be tough on the Palestinians because you can't have a situation where Hamas won't even recognize the state of Israel, while wanting still to be involved in negotiations about the future of the Middle East in general. But then we've got to be tough on the Israelis because we cannot have a situation where the settlements keep going up in the occupied territories because that will eventually make a two-state solution impossible. I had quite a vigorous exchange with the Israeli Foreign Minister on this point when I visited Israel last year. Seeing the situation at first hand really brings home to you how directly this tragic conflict impinges on people's everyday lives. The sense of encirclement as you walk the streets of the Old City of Jerusalem, the day-to-day impact of road blocks and checkpoints, the security challenges that face Israel, from the Lebanese border or Gaza, to the ever-present danger of suicide bombing. I have had several meetings with both Prime Minister Olmert and President Abbas, and I understand the pressures they face. But the twin elements of the solution – a viable Palestinian state and real security for Israel living in peace alongside it – are clear. I met Blair recently about this, and there's no particular split between us and the government. It's a common-sense solution that just needs an extraordinary amount of work and the will of the people involved to reach agreement.

What would be, say, the six or seven principal aims of your government in terms of bringing more security to that area?

In terms of basic principles, Conservatives believe in strong defence, and our membership of NATO is absolutely key to that, we believe in using the overlapping institutions that we're members of, like the EU, the UN, the Commonwealth, to make sure we punch above our weight in the world. Regarding the Middle East specifically, I think what is missing is an emphasis on the economic, social and cultural aspects as well as the security aspects. For example we're looking at something called a partnership for open societies: an organization a bit like the organization for security and cooperation in Europe, that was so successful in helping to end the Cold War by binding countries into progressive democratic values. We need that same sort of organization. We don't have to say to those countries you have to adopt democracy tomorrow, but let's form an organization that isn't led by the West, that is led by you but involves countries like India and China and Japan and others, that believes in the steady progress of the rule of law, human rights, and more open societies. That would be a good way of engaging some of the moderate states of the Middle East.

That sounds rather ambitious …
Some people say it's not ambitious enough. A neo-con would say, to hell with that, let's just drop the democracy in from the back of a plane at 40,000 feet. This is a more realistic proposition. Democracy is a delicate plant. And democracy without the rule of law and without human rights and without a strong civil society doesn't really work. The problem in Zimbabwe is not that they don't have elections; it's that all the other bits of civil society have been destroyed. Like the courts … Democracy on its own is sometimes not enough, so our vision is that you work from the bottom up.

The government has recently told us that our troops could be in Afghanistan for decades. What's your position on this?
Obviously the faster we can help secure a stable and successful Afghanistan the faster we can start to bring the troops home, but actually it's right that our troops will be there for some time to come, indeed for quite a long time. It's a very complex and difficult country and there is no easy solution. If you look at some of the original intentions in

Afghanistan, getting rid of the Taliban was obviously the right thing to do. With the Northern Alliance and the Americans, effectively invading and decapitating the regime, this was absolutely the right thing to do, no question.

Correct.
Our troops are doing a great job in Helmand. But there's a real need for better coordination of the international effort in Afghanistan. That was the overriding impression I've got from both my visits there, and which I've discussed with President Karzai. I strongly supported Paddy Ashdown's nomination to fill that role – he would have been very well suited to do that job, and I'm sorry it didn't work out. The world is a lot safer now that the country is not run by the Taliban. But, if you look at some of the original thought on what we were going to do with and for that country, they were hopelessly naive and unrealistic.

Just like they were, and continue to be, in Iraq. Destabilizing the country, demotivating the security forces, the drip-feed effect of too few troops, and then the worst war of attrition in living memory.
In Afghanistan I'm told the expectations were unrealistic, and even now one country is building police stations with crèches in them, even though the idea of women police officers in Afghanistan is still, if I can put it like this, some years away. A more gritty, hard-headed and practical approach is what's required. One that puts security first. You're right; in Iraq it's the same situation. You can't drop democracy out of an aeroplane. You've got to think through the fact that order comes before law, still. Stability comes before democracy. And security comes before everything. And then you can begin to help develop the delicate flower of democracy.

Is Iran unfairly demonized?
The leadership of Iran is not unfairly demonized because they have said some fairly demonic things, but we shouldn't demonize the people of Iran.

Britain and the USA

Has Britain's closeness to America damaged our own interests?
No, I don't think so. I think the Atlantic relationship is incredibly important, I think that link between Britain and America and Canada that
helps keep the Atlantic community involved in Europe is vital. Sometimes mistakes have been made, and that's undoubtedly true over the
post-war situation in Iraq. But it doesn't mean that our relationship with
America is wrong, it just means we have to work together to make the
right decisions, as British governments have had to do, from Churchill to
Thatcher to today.

Is there any way for Bush to salvage his reputation?
George Bush has done a number of good things. The trouble is they
tend to get overlooked by the more controversial aspects of his record. I
think if you look at what he's done in terms of AIDS in Africa it is truly
remarkable. Bob Geldof has had the courage to come out and praise
Bush on this basis, and that's made some people sit up and listen. I saw
it myself in South Africa. I remember going to an AIDS clinic where
every last drug had been paid for by the US because of Bush's initiative.
I'm not saying that people will completely reassess every part of the
Bush presidency, of course they won't, but in the context of history
people will appreciate what he did in Africa. It will be seen as a very big
step by a very rich country and it made a lot of difference to people's
lives.

**The prospect of a Democrat administration in America would have
sent a very clear message globally, especially to the Islamic world, of a
change of attitudes towards America's visibility in Iraq, and their
interventionist tendencies under Bush. I think it's fair to expect that's
less likely to happen under a Republican president. Would you be
happier with a Republican in the White House? John McCain has
already committed to staying in Iraq for generations to come if that's
what it takes. Both Obama and Clinton have advocated speedy with-**

drawal. Sarkozy advocates a withdrawal 'horizon'. Is the McCain way the Cameron way?

That's a very good question. I'm a huge fan of John McCain and think he would make a great President, and I've said that. But I don't think that Obama or Clinton would click their fingers and withdraw troops as quickly as they said they would, as it's almost impossible. And once you've become the commander-in-chief of the American military your responsibility for stability and security is such that you would not be able to do things precipitately. It's very difficult.

This is an ideological battle as well as a physical one, and apart from the fact that it would be unconscionable for us and the Americans to abandon the Iraqi people, surely we need to leave the area with Iraq and her neighbours thinking better of us than they do now.

However, it cannot be a long-term success if American troops are required to be in Iraq in very large numbers for a long period of time. That can't be a successful formula. You need something in between.

But a Democrat government would have sent out a different message to the world, wouldn't it, in terms of the Anglo-Arab conflict?

I'm not sure that's the case. I don't want to get involved in the presidential race; it's up to the Americans to choose who they want as their President. They've got some fine candidates; I know McCain better than the others, and I think he'd make a great President. But I think actually with John McCain you've got someone who has rather an impeccable record against torture, who's got an impeccable record on thoughtful and progressive foreign policy, and I think that he'd have the sort of impact that you hinted at in the question. Every candidate represents a change, and I think that's the interesting thing. Whether it's Clinton or Obama or McCain, they all represent quite a change, not just in terms of American politics but also in the eyes of the world.

McCain less so, I think. What did you make of the Obama speech, where he went out of his way not to distance himself from Reverend

Wright? His speech was certainly impressive, but although it was aimed principally at the delegates rather than the voting public, it's scared a lot of Americans.

Well, I thought it was a fantastic speech, but I suppose he probably didn't do enough, with respect to the pastor, to distance himself. It was a brilliant speech but it got clouded by that, which is a terrible pity, I think.

Also, previously, i.e. before that speech, he had been standing as a breath of fresh air, this sea-change candidate, the new JFK, without many of his supporters actually knowing what he stands for. But it also alerted a lot of people to the fact that he is mixed race, whereas before that he had gone out of his way not to address race.

I think one of the great things about watching Obama is that he's not just a black candidate, he's an incredibly powerful candidate, and as you say he's run as a Democrat and not as a black Democrat. The second thing is I think there is a lot more substance and a lot more depth in what he says, in the answers he gives to questions, than perhaps the media give him credit for. You simply can't get through enormous leadership campaigns and primaries and all the rest of it, by giving flip answers to flip questions. He's had to deal with a lot of tough stuff.

You have been compared frequently to Obama, having the rare talent to wear your ambition lightly, and to allow toughness to be taken for granted. Do you see any resemblance yourself?

I think it's very different. If anything, American politics and British politics have grown apart. I think he's an inspiring orator and he has a wonderful way with phrases and I love listening to him. I wish I had that sometimes. But in American politics they do make much more flowery, grandiose speeches. If we made some of the speeches they make there would be howls of laughter. You know – that's great all that brotherhood of man stuff, but now tell us what you're going to do. He's trying to break a hegemony of another party, so I suppose there's a similarity there, but I don't see serious similarities.

What do you make of Bush?
He's very charming. There are two extra parts of his character that you just don't see from watching television. One is the charm and the fact that he's very personable, and the second is the intelligent conviction. He has thought about some of the most important issues of our time and has a very intelligent and conviction-driven view of them. You just never see that.

What do you think of John McCain?
Very good sense of humour. You have all these preconceptions about people, and you think, here is a person who has been through a prisoner-of-war camp, for five years, he is a certain age, but he has a terrific sense of fun. I like a lot of things about him. I like his plain-speaking style, his very strong convictions, but he's a maverick because you can't put him in a box. He's not a mainstream Republican. He's got lots of different views on different things that come out of his character and his experience, and I think he's enormously attractive like that.

Global policy

On a broader level, do we need to be more interventionist, or less?
I think we just need to learn the lessons of the last few years. I think there was an excessive reliance on hard power rather than soft power and a sort of intervene anywhere and everywhere view of the world that wasn't sufficiently practical, grounded or realistic. I've always described myself as a liberal Conservative: liberal, because we do support the spread of human rights, and democracy around the world, but Conservative because before intervening I think you have to demonstrate a practicality and a scepticism and ask all the difficult questions about the consequences of your involvement. And I think the problem with Blair was that he was a humanitarian interventionist without putting any kind of practical brake on these impulses. I think you do need that sceptical, enquiring sense when it comes to foreign policy, so you think through the consequences of your actions, and Blair was just too eager to jump in anywhere.

Was there a naivety to the Blair approach?
I think you could say that. He was certainly too eager to get involved.

Should we be in Zimbabwe, or have gone in, with an armed presence?
No, I think there's a real problem here, in that we feel this enormous tie to Zimbabwe and we care deeply about what happens and we all want to reach for the toughest possible stick to beat Mugabe with because he is a dreadful dictator, but the problem we had is the more that we in Britain were seen to be leading the charge, the more it played into Mugabe's hands, allowing him to say: here comes the old colonial oppressor. And that's why it's been frustrating. There is a lot to be done with South Africa, with the African Union, to explain our passion for the issue, rather than just wave our big stick around.

But it's a human tragedy and no one in the West is doing anything about it.
Well, we should be absolutely specific about what we deplore and we should do all we can to apply international pressure to enable the will of the people of Zimbabwe to prevail. When I see Mbeki and Mugabe hand in hand, and Mbeki says there is no crisis in Zimbabwe, we should be utterly clear about our condemnation of that. South Africa has an enormous influence on Zimbabwe and it could have an influence for the good. African leaders who cosset people like Mugabe are making a huge mistake for themselves, for their continent and for the people of the countries concerned.

What are the most worrying flashpoints across Eastern Europe at the moment?
I think there are certain areas where there are difficult decisions to be made, over Georgia and Ukraine and whether or not they should be full members of NATO. I think it would be better if we were clear and straightforward and said yes. Those countries that want to look West, that want to be democracies, that want to be part of the democratic family of nations, ought to be allowed into NATO if they want to join it.

That is one set of difficult decisions where I have a very definite point of view.

Where else, to your mind?
Obviously there is still a set of problems in the Balkans, with Serbia very unhappy about the greater independence of Kosovo. Again, I think we have to be absolutely clear: Kosovo could not simply remain part of Serbia in the light of everything that has happened – that was just not possible. The people of Kosovo are entitled to independence, but that must not mean borders elsewhere in the Balkans are reopened.

Should Turkey be allowed into the EU?
I'm fully in favour of it. If Turkey wants to be a Western-facing, secular democracy that's part of NATO, then they should be allowed to join the European Union. It's simple.

How soon would you like to see that happen?
In my view, as soon as possible. As long as Turkey meets the necessary standards. I think we've been pushing back and pushing back Turkey in a very unhelpful way because it's basically saying to the Turks, look, however much you reform, however much you maintain your position as a secular democracy, we don't really want you. And that strengthens the hand of the Islamic extremists and those that want to take Turkey in a different direction.

What do you see as the major challenges emerging globally, aside from terror and global warming?
I think energy security is a huge challenge, in terms of oil reaching an incredibly high price, the fact that the supply won't last forever, that North Sea oil is running down, that we're going to be more reliant on gas from unstable parts of the world. I think that energy security needs to sit alongside foreign policy and we should take a much more strategic view about our relationships with countries that could help to give us greater energy security in the future. More time needs to be put into that,

especially with the former Soviet republic and the Scandinavian countries, because there are all sorts of opportunities there.

Is population growth still an issue, in your opinion?
Globally, yes it is. I'm not some sort of neo-Malthusian, but there are countries where there's a sort of battle going on about whether you can get the economy to grow faster than the population in order to lift them out of poverty, and you see this very clearly in places like parts of Southern Africa, where growth rates are improving but population growth rates are actually still so high that you're not going to lift people out of poverty, and therefore the country as a whole is not going to get richer per capita.

What do you think of South Africa today? I think it's a tinderbox, as, apart from the appalling divisive nature of the poverty there, the race issue still hasn't been successfully resolved to anyone's satisfaction. I've a feeling it's going to start moving backwards.
I really feel it could still have a great future ahead of it. It's a regional superpower, it's got great natural resources, it's got good national infrastructure, a good growth rate, but there's so much entrenched poverty in the townships and so much pent-up anger left over from apartheid that the government is in a race against time to try and grow the economy and lift people out of poverty, and if the combination of excessive population growth and also the AIDS pandemic, which is taking so many people out of the economy, stops that from happening, it will be a tragedy.

My brother is an officer in the Royal Air Force. He has some questions for you. The size of the military is not big enough to continue to fight two theatres of operations concurrently, so are you going to invest seriously in the military? Do you want more people in the armed forces, and if so would there be a serious recruitment drive?
There is a very strong case for a bigger army, and this will sound like a fudge but it isn't meant to be: what we need is a defence review based on

our national security, not on Treasury guidelines, and that will tell us either that we need to reduce the commitments we have or we need to increase the spending. But let's have that review first. I think that will also make pointers about how much bigger an army we need, and what is the right configuration of the air force and the navy.

Doesn't closer involvement with China mean tacitly endorsing their poor human rights record?
No, it doesn't. I think you need a relationship with China which recognizes the fact that it's a great power, that we have common interests, we should be trading, we should be cooperating, but at the same time having a very frank dialogue about human rights. When I went to Beijing, I raised not just human rights in my meetings with Chinese leaders, but also the role that China plays in places like Zimbabwe and Darfur. I went to Chongqing – modern-day China's Chicago – to make a speech at their university, and said some quite candid things about democracy. I focused in particular on the role that the Leader of the Opposition plays in our own constitutional set-up. There was some polite shuffling of feet when I said my role was to hold the PM and the government to account, but I think the students welcomed an open and frank exchange. It's important that all visiting Western politicians in China make those points, because China's role in the world is going to be increasingly important. China is changing fast, and the more its star rises in the world, the more it will have a direct stake in the stability of our world. If we want positive things to happen in Darfur and Zimbabwe, the Chinese have an enormous role to play.

There's increasing speculation that the Union may break up, and if we assume that you don't want this to happen, what steps would you take to stop this happening?
What I've said is that I am a believer in the Union, in the United Kingdom, and I wouldn't do anything to undermine it or put it at risk. I don't want anyone to think that if I were elected Prime Minister and the Conservatives didn't do very well in Scotland, that we would just wave

goodbye to it or do some sort of hideous deal. I don't want to be Prime Minister of England, I want to be Prime Minister of the United Kingdom, so we won't do anything that puts the Union at risk. In recent weeks it's transpired that it's the Labour Party that is prepared to play games with the Union, but we wouldn't do that.

What sort of relationship do you have with Berlusconi, and what do you make of him as a politician?
None at all, and I've never met him.

How are your relations with Angela Merkel at the moment?
Very good. We've had several meetings recently, and it's exciting that there are strong, centre right leaders across Europe now – Sarkozy, Merkel – who are making the running on things like the environment and economic growth and some of the social policy areas we've talked about. We have our disagreements, but my approach is always to be as frank as possible, and not try and cover anything up, and I think as a result of that the relationship's quite good. And we have set up some working groups between our parties on climate change, counter terrorism and competitiveness, which will help strengthen the relationship further.

Is Sarkozy someone you can work with?
Yes, he's enormously likeable and enormously energetic. I saw him make his speech in the Houses of Parliament and he was gesticulating and purposeful and full of energy. He's a remarkable figure.

And policy-wise?
I think there are lots of good things about him. To have a French president who wants to integrate into NATO, who's pro-American, who thinks that Iran is a problem rather than a country to do business with regardless, these are huge breakthroughs. But at the same time you have always got to respect the fact that there really are some genuine differences over our attitude towards European defence, over our attitude

towards the reform of the common agricultural policy. It's great that he's saying and doing some things that we can really agree with, but there are still going to be areas of disagreement. And the proof of the pudding, as ever, will be in the final consumption.

He's great company, isn't he?
He certainly is. A human dynamo, a source of constant and irrepressible energy. It's sometimes a challenge to get a word in edgeways. But we've had a few meetings now and get on very well – he's just a huge pleasure to deal with. A huge pleasure …

* * *

A week later, on 12 March, the House of Commons chamber was treated to Alistair Darling's first Budget, a lacklustre offering that was widely interpreted as a thinly veiled attack on the middle classes (with Darling's rhetorical style being compared to a suburban building society's answering machine). Brown's new technique for showing disdain towards Cameron was to mutter to whoever happened to be sitting next to him. On Budget Day it was Darling, and Brown kept up his muttering throughout Cameron's blistering response, making him look unusually childish, and just a teeny bit petulant. But Cameron tore into Darling, accusing him of having the 'most disastrous start' of any Chancellor in modern British history. 'Let's be in no doubt as to the real source of the government's problems,' he added. 'Ask any question about this Budget and the answer comes back to one man: the Prime Minister. Why is the Chancellor hitting the low paid with higher tax? Because that's what the Prime Minister did in his last Budget. Why is the Chancellor left with the biggest budget deficit in Western Europe? Because the Prime Minister's spent all the money over the last eleven Budgets. Why is the Chancellor imposing £1 billion of tax changes on capital gains tax and family businesses? Because the Prime Minister got himself in a panic trying to copy our proposals on inheritance tax. The Chancellor was put in a hole by the Prime Minister – and they've both kept digging.' And on it went, as the PM visibly squirmed. 'In the years of plenty they put nothing aside and now the lean years are coming, the cupboard is bare. They didn't fix the roof when the sun was shining.' He didn't stop there, either: 'What we needed in this Budget was real leadership and a serious plan to get this country out of the mess they made. Five months ago, the Chancellor stood at the dispatch box. He proposed changes to capital gains tax. That lot cheered [referring to the Labour benches] – and the policy fell apart. Five months ago, he announced plans on non-doms. That lot cheered – and the policy fell apart. Month after month, they said they didn't want to nationalize Northern Rock and they did. They cancelled an election, which – unbelievably – they planned to fight on competence and then promptly lost half the country's personal data in the post. The City may be having a credit crunch but the government has a credibility crunch.'

As Cameron sat down, to a crescendo of applause from his own benches, all the PM could do was seethe. He also turned on the Children's Secretary Ed Balls, who made the mistake of interrupting Cameron in full flow. Cameron looked witheringly at Balls and said, 'I know he's Minister for Children, but he doesn't have to behave like one.' He added: 'I know he wants to be Chancellor so badly it hurts. I have to tell him: another Budget like the one we've heard and he won't have to wait too long.' (A week later, at the Conservative spring conference, a mobile phone went off in the middle of William Hague's speech. Whenever this happened during the 2001 election campaign, Hague would say: 'If that's Tony Blair ringing, tell him it's too late to call off the election.' This time the gag had been changed to: 'If that's Alistair Darling, tell him, "No, we haven't figured out what's in his Budget."')

This wasn't much of a Budget for the Tories to get their teeth into, but even the partisan *Guardian* grudgingly admitted that Cameron got the better of the Labour front bench. And that was an understatement.

'In many ways the Budget is the most difficult thing I do all year,' said Cameron the next day, 'because the first you know about it is when the Chancellor gets up to speak. So you have to listen very carefully, and take notes and digest everything as you're hearing it.' Neither the Leader of the Opposition nor the Shadow Chancellor is given prior notice of the contents of the Budget and the first they hear of it is when the Chancellor begins reading it. Cameron had composed most of his speech cycling to Portcullis House that morning, as increasingly this was becoming one of the few times of the day he was actually alone. It allowed him time to think, time to clear his head. 'After going for Darling I was going to go for Brown a lot more but in the end I thought it wasn't worth it. I used to mock him and Blair by saying that Budget Day was the only time in the year they spoke, but there is even less chemistry between him and Darling.'

The following day, ITN screened a film of the Cameron family having breakfast at home ('Shreddies or Cheerios?' Cameron asked his kids), not only the first time he had allowed news cameras into his London home, but also the first time he had allowed cameras to film his disabled son Ivan, as well as his other children, Elwen and Nancy. 'I'm asking people a very big thing, which is to elect me as their Prime Minister. And I think people have a right to know a bit more about you, your life and your family, what makes you tick, and what informs your thinking. And to me, nothing informs my thinking more than family because I think it's the most important thing there is in our society. So that's why I did what I did.'

The same day, the Tories called for more flexibility to allow parents to share the duty of bringing up children. Speaking ahead of the Conservatives' spring forum in Gateshead, Cameron said a Conservative government would allow parents to take up to twenty-six weeks' leave together if they wished, and that flexible parental leave would help make Britain more family friendly. 'The world is changing,' he said. 'Men want to be more involved in bringing up their children. That's why flexibility is a really good thing. It's not just when the baby arrives that can be exhausting, it's after about three or four months when the mother is tired and the baby's not sleeping through the night. That's when families may need more flexibility and choice. Labour believe that the state should dictate from the top, but we believe that it is the mums who are doing the really heavy lifting in terms of bringing up our children and so we should give them the right support.'

They also announced new plans guaranteeing new mothers regular home visits for the first five years of their child's life. Suggesting the number of health visitors be increased by 4200, Cameron proposed allowing new mothers to be visited every fortnight until their child was six months old, and then twice a year up to the age of five. 'I want to make this country more family friendly,' said Cameron, 'not just because it's the right thing to do, not just because my family is the most important thing in my life, but because families should be the most important thing in our country's life.'

George Pascoe-Watson, the political editor of the *Sun*, probably reflected the mood of the nation when he said: 'David Cameron's decision to open the doors of his family life to voters was a big gamble. It revealed a side of him few have ever seen – and some will accuse him of exploiting his son. Yet they'd be wrong. The Tory leader wanted to highlight his party's family credentials.'

Cameron's popularity certainly had an effect on the polls, as by the end of March support for Labour had hit a twenty-five-year low, the lowest since Michael Foot was leader back in 1983. Voters essentially delivered a withering verdict on Labour's Budget, with Gordon Brown's party slipping to 27 per cent – sixteen points behind the Conservatives – amid escalating concern about the government's ability to successfully manage the economy. More importantly, if the results of the YouGov survey had been repeated in a general election, the Conservative majority would have been 120 – a landslide. At the time, the Tory lead was also the largest in any survey for twenty-one years, just after Margaret Thatcher's third and final election victory. And, perhaps unsurprisingly, Brown's approval rate was minus twenty-six, his worst since being in the job. His unpopularity became even more apparent later that month when he reneged on his promise to cut the number of British troops in Iraq by 1000 by the end of the year. Tory MP Patrick Mercer, himself a former soldier, warned that the military did not have the manpower 'to carry on war on two fronts at this level'. He said: 'This is not only a broken promise but directly impinges on our ability to fight in Afghanistan.' As Alan Milburn, the former Health Secretary, accused Brown of administering self-inflicted wounds, many backbench Labour MPs began to realize just why Blair had tried to keep Brown on a tight leash for all those years: rather extraordinarily, the man seemed as though he just couldn't cut it by himself.

There were rumours that Brown had begun to think the same thing, and those close to Number Ten could talk of little else than Gordon's black moods, and his corrosive depressions. During March, he had started to articulate his feelings of frustration with his own inability to do the job, and – almost unbelievably, considering how much he had wanted to be Prime Minister – was questioning not only his decision to run for PM, but also his ability to function properly in the job. 'He's started to intimate that he might not last the full term,' hinted one close adviser. 'He's not sure he wants to do this for much longer. He hates it, and wonders why he wanted the job in the first place.'

By mid-April 2008 Brown could simply do nothing right. One evening towards the end of the month I went to a party given by John Kampfner, the former editor of the *New Statesman*, at his home in Bloomsbury. Even though many of John's friends lean to the left, they are often highly critical about what happens in Number Ten. But even I wasn't prepared for the barrage of abuse Brown got that night. The words on everyone's lips that evening were 'inept', 'implosion' and 'inertia', while almost everyone felt that serious disharmony was just around the corner. Tellingly, Brown was even starting to be blamed for things beyond his control, notably the shambolic opening of Heathrow's Terminal 5.

TEN

'Social responsibility is the essence of liberal conservatism. This is the Britain we want to build'

Carla Bruni, another YouGov poll, SNAFU, income tax, Northern Rock, non-doms, corruption, Nick Clegg, it's the economy, stupid

By the beginning of May 2008, David Cameron's popularity was at its highest point since becoming Leader of the Opposition in 2005. He was certainly doing better than his opposite number. Over in Downing Street, it was all going wrong, and even a visit to London in March by French President Nicolas Sarkozy and his sexy new wife Carla Bruni had failed to lift either the Prime Minister's spirits or his standing in the polls. While the Labour Party were beginning to look tired, David Cameron's Conservatives were starting to resemble a party with a certain sense of destiny, a party the public were beginning to acknowledge as New Labour's most likely successors.

More and more people were starting to think, you know what? Maybe Cameron can do it.

At the end of March, a YouGov poll for the *Daily Telegraph* suggested that the feel-good factor – which monitored voters' confidence in the future of the economy – stood at minus 52 per cent following the sharp rises in mortgage, food and energy bills; this was its lowest level since measurements began back in 1981. Remarkably, in the space of six months the Tories had established themselves as the party most trusted to safeguard the economy; while the paper reported that 'Essex man' – the kind of typical family voter that tended to decide elections – was, in particular, deserting Labour.

Alistair Darling's Budget – which had affected motorists, drinkers and small-business owners with inflation-busting tax rises – had spurred on the dissatisfaction with the government, which by now seemed seriously beleaguered. Labour were now trailing the Conservatives by a whopping fourteen points, with 43 per cent of people planning to vote Tory and only 29 planning to vote Labour.

Not surprisingly, things were now extremely tense within the Labour Party, and the whispers of discontent were getting louder and louder. And where previously Cabinet members, ministers and backbenchers had been either too scared or sufficiently impressed to hold their tongues, they were now starting to wag. Soon after the YouGov poll, Ivan Lewis, a health minister, said 'The government is losing touch with what fairness means to the mainstream majority who work hard.' He said the Prime Minister's challenge was to persuade the country that 'we are truly the servants of the people', warning Brown's party that they were in danger of losing the next election unless it quickly got to grips with these issues.

Top of the list was the 10p tax rate: the thing that no one could really fathom was why a Labour government would want to abandon it anyway. Not only was it unfair, but it also smacked of incompetence. Could Brown really have calculated that deleting the 10p band was what anyone, at all, wanted? Labour MPs stood up to Brown at a meeting of the Parliamentary Labour Party, ministers started to question his decisions and the commentariat brutally drew attention to his shortcomings. At one point Brown was even compared to Chamberlain, one of the cruellest barbs of all for a British Prime Minister. The *Sunday Times* said, 'The collapse is the most dramatic of any modern-day prime minister, worse even than Neville Chamberlain, who in 1940 dropped from plus 21 to minus 27 after Hitler's invasion of Norway.'

This internal disharmony exacerbated Gordon Brown's earlier decision to shake up his private office in Downing Street, drafting in the chief executive of Alan Parker's powerful Brunswick PR company, Stephen

Carter, a former Goldman Sachs bigwig called Jennifer Moses and David Muir from the advertising group WPP. Their arrival not only saw the immediate departure of Brown's senior political advisor, Spencer Livermore, but the appointments contributed to an increasingly sulphurous atmosphere within his inner circle. The old lot hated the new lot, the new lot didn't know whom to trust (the correct answer would have been: 'no one'), and the internal power structures were beginning to look decidedly shaky. One started to get the impression that, like any administration in decline, relationships in Downing Street were becoming extremely strained.

During the Northern Rock debacle, where the Prime Minister and the Chancellor were (according to one insider) 'marooned on sandbank after sandbank', the British press and public alike very quickly became accustomed to living with a broken government, and by May the situation hadn't improved. To those of a certain age it conjured up an old armed forces acronym, SNAFU (Situation Normal All Fucked Up). And as senior police officers said publicly for the first time that the huge rise in the number of teenagers being killed on the streets of London was the country's biggest threat after terrorism, so both the press and the public began paying more attention to the salvos on crime coming out of David Cameron's office.

And the press were merciless in their condemnation of Brown. The *Sun*'s Trevor Kavanagh wrote a full-page editorial criticizing Brown's 'sinking ship', the *Financial Times* called the Prime Minister's management of the country 'a mess', and the *Sunday Times* devoted two pages to the various Cabinet members who might conceivably succeed Brown (including Harriet Harman, James Purnell, David Miliband, Jack Straw and the seemingly ubiquitous Ed Balls). Some said that this was in part due to the 'fifteen-year rule', in which any politician who had been a fixture on the nation's television screens for that length of time was bound to begin grating with the public. Although why the likes of Purnell, Miliband or Balls would want to succeed Brown was another matter entirely. If Labour were about to enter a period in the political wilderness, who on earth would want the job of marshalling them while they were there? A whisper slid through the commentariat like an electric eel: even if Brown did decide to step down, who would be mad enough to take the job? This was a party in decline, a party on the ropes, a party that was beginning to give off a very bad smell.

I spoke to many politicians, newspaper editors and political journalists throughout April, and most of then tended to say the same thing: anyone who had anything to do with the Labour Party – be they adviser, analyst, researcher, policy wonk or flag-waver – was starting to look outside the party for work. The tide was turning, they knew they wouldn't be employed in two years' time and they were all looking for jobs. There was a feeling in the air, a stench more like, and the only way to get rid of it was by walking away from it.

The barbs in the press weren't limited to the UK, either, and during April even the *Los Angeles Times* reported on a piece of juicy gossip that had electrified Westminster – a rhyme, penned by a mysterious parliamentary poet who, it was rumoured, was quite possibly a Cabinet member, was on everyone's lips: 'At Downing Street upon the stair, I met a man who wasn't Blair; he wasn't Blair again today; oh how I wish he'd go away.' There was even unease about Brown in Washington, and when he visited the American capital in April – itself a PR disaster as he arrived twenty-four hours after an historic first visit to the United States by Pope Benedict XVI – the press mainly focused on Britain's unfolding disengagement in Iraq.

And when Cameron started publicly to accuse Brown of being a 'ditherer', not appearing to know which way to turn on everything from his attendance at the opening ceremony of the Beijing Olympics (after some serious faffing about he'd decided to attend only the closing ceremony) to what solution to impose upon Northern Rock (there seemed to be a different answer every day), all Brown could do was fume. This wasn't just the story of a descendancy, but one of ascendancy, too, because as Brown tripped up, so Cameron gathered pace, looking sleeker and sturdier than ever.

While being careful not to gloat publicly, Cameron took all of this in his stride. It's been said that the self-confidence required of a politician is the enemy of self-knowledge, but, to his credit, Cameron's self-awareness was far more acute than was strictly necessary, principally because what he was saying was beginning to chime so well with what the country appeared to want to hear.

He, unlike Brown, understood that perhaps people had now had enough of big government. One of Cameron's fundamental principles – one of the legs of his political table, if you like – is the idea of independence, that government should be willing to hand over governing to the best people for the job – which, sometimes, might not be the government. 'The welfare state brought the state into everyone's lives, but the consequence has been that it turned ministers from lawmakers to managers,' said Jeremy Paxman shortly after Tony Blair's re-election in 2001. As Paxman pointed out, echoing Cameron's own concerns, where once governments impinged very little upon people's lives, there was now scarcely an area of human behaviour that was not touched by the law.

Cameron seemed to understand this instinctively, and this was one of the reasons he had based so many of his policies on the principle of radical change to the role government plays in people's lives.

As for the perennial question regarding any potential future PM – were they fit for purpose? – David Cameron had proved that not only could he unite his party, not only could he haul himself back from political oblivion, and not only could he present a viable alternative to a government that was looking more moribund each day, but he also showed he had the will, the steel, and perhaps the resolve to make it all work. The prerequisite for any Member of Parliament is not just their ability to convince the public that they are fit to represent them in Parliament, but also their ability to show that they can operate the levers of the organization that runs the country. Cameron had proved on more than one occasion that he could do both extremely well.

More importantly, over the previous twelve months he had also proved that he had the thing a politician needs much more than ideological commitment: he had proved he had character.

At the end of April, Cameron and I spoke on the train from Paddington to Didcot Parkway, as he travelled to his constituency.

Taxation

Oliver Letwin once dismissed tax cuts as a 'bribe' but then George Osborne says he's a Conservative who believes in lower taxes. And now we hear that there aren't going to be any tax cuts in your first term! What do you say? The Tories have promoted so many different variations of the tax solution, it's difficult to know where you stand. So are you saying you won't cut taxes in your first term if you win an election?
No, that's not right.

Well, that's what your party has said, so presumably you've endorsed it ...
What I and George Osborne have been saying is, we're low tax Conservatives, we're believers in a low-tax economy. It's good for the economy, it's good for all of us. We believe in it for economic reasons, for moral reasons; we think it's good to leave people with more of their own money to spend as they choose. But – and this is an important but – if you look at the state of the country's finances it would not be responsible to go into an election promising upfront, unfunded tax cuts.

Why not? You've done it before, so why not do it again?
Look, we've been very strict with ourselves and with the party, and saying of course we want to cut taxes over time, but we've got to be clear that there isn't some magic pot of money we can dip into to pay for tax cuts. We can't make promises like that. But as things improve, as the economy grows, as money comes into the Treasury, we will share the proceeds of that growth between the public spending we need and the tax cuts we would like to see. So we may well be able to reduce taxes in the first term of a Conservative government; but be in no doubt, we won't make irresponsible promises. Rest assured, we want to reduce taxes as soon as we can.

Why hedge your bets? You have the wit and the maths to make this work. A lot of people will be disappointed that you can't just come out and promise cuts ...

A lot of people will be disappointed, I know, because they would love a big promise up there in lights. But in fact neither do I think that's right economically, and nor do I think it's good politics. I think it's irresponsible to say you're going to make tax cuts when you can't say where the money's coming from.

But I refuse to believe you're not clever enough to balance the books in order to offer a modicum of tax relief. And whenever you do, you surge ahead in the polls ...

No, I don't actually agree with that.

Okay, just look at inheritance tax!

Look, if you take the last couple of elections, we've gone into them with incredibly complicated schemes to reduce waste and cut this bit of spending, and fund that bit of tax reduction, and I think it's both confused people and I think they found it lacking in credibility. I think it's better to say, look, this is the state of the economy. Frankly, after Labour's economic incompetence we're going to have to make some pretty tough decisions to get the public finances sorted. And as and when we can, we will reduce taxes. I think that's fairer. The tax reduction, that as you say we offered via inheritance tax, that was a fully funded tax reduction. We said inheritance tax will come down, and another tax, the tax on non-domiciled residents, will go up to pay for it. And because it was credible, I would argue, that's why it was so attractive. What I'm pleased about is we've set out a clear and credible strategy for controlling public spending so we can get taxes down and keep them down for the long term. So we've said we need a bit of good housekeeping, and we need to start to live within our means. And we've got a clear plan for doing it, not just cutting government waste and inefficiency – that's just the start – you've also got to tackle the things that increase demand on the state, and you've got to reform the way public services are delivered.

That all adds up to a proper long-term plan for, as I've said repeatedly, sharing the proceeds of growth, so that over time the economy grows faster than the state and we can bring taxes and borrowing down.

But the non-dom tax was a total disaster. Luckily you haven't had to bear the brunt of it because the idea was stolen, albeit in a cack-handed fashion, by the Labour Party. But it was still a PR disaster ... The Treasury has already admitted that at least 3000 non-doms will probably leave Britain because of the new charges – 3000 non-doms who contribute around £12 billion to the economy. Even though Labour have tinkered with their proposals, this is something you yourself endorsed.

The way the government have introduced it has been very cack-handed, because they didn't follow our procedure. Our policy was very simple: £25,000, a straight charge, paid by everyone, in return for which there's no looking at your overseas income, no change in the rules of trusts, no fiddling with people bringing capital onshore. Instead, the government has set the charge higher and opened up this whole Pandora's box of starting to look at people's overseas earnings and delving into their tax affairs. Our point was, almost make the non-dom charge a kind of safe harbour. Pay that, and you can stay in Britain and maintain that status. But the government have opened up a box, and once it's been opened it's very difficult to put the lid back down again.

Okay, under what circumstances would you cut income tax?

When it would be responsible to do so. Under the circumstances in which the economy is growing and the public finances are sound and you're able to say to people, look, I know who earns the money in this economy, it's you, the taxpayer, the business, and I can give some back to you ...

So why can't you do that now?

Look, every time we go into a Budget, we're going to be thinking, how can we reduce taxes, is it possible, is it prudent to do so? We won't be doing what this government has been doing, which is going into every Budget trying to think how they can get away with actually putting taxes up.

Regarding Northern Rock, many people say that the government should have simply accepted the Lloyds TSB offer, agreed to their interest rate on the borrowing and then moved on. In hindsight, what would you have done?

I hope I would have done exactly that. The real lesson from this is, whatever you're going to do, do it quickly, because the longer a situation drags on, the worse it will get. The worse the damage to the reputation of Britain and the more difficult it gets to resolve. They should have taken the offer.

The Northern Rock fiasco didn't fracture the government as much as one might have thought, and the Cabinet is still largely in one piece because there is no dissent in the ranks. Brown has got rid of most of the bad apples. But have you ever considered that you won't be fighting him at the next election?

Yes, I have thought about it, but I don't think it's particularly likely because I don't think he's the kind of guy to just throw it up in the air and let someone else have a go, but of course things could go wrong. There was one moment a few months ago when there was a bit of talk about whether there was going to be a Labour leadership challenge, but that soon went away.

Which of Gordon Brown's stealth taxes would you abolish? There are so many of them, many people feel they're being attacked at every corner. What are you going to do to make them feel better about being taxed?

I think the one we'd like to make immediate progress on is stamp duty, because I think stamp duty used to be something that was not paid by the least well off, and was not paid on a standard house purchase, and now it is a massive stealth tax. Nine out of ten first-time buyers would come out of stamp duty altogether.

What about capital gains tax? This is a bugbear for many. What are you going to do about it?

Well, again, Labour have rather botched their reform of capital gains tax. Because they had the 10p taper relief rate that was obviously very beneficial to entrepreneurs, and, as my wife never stopped telling me, this was something that entrepreneurs really valued. And they scrapped that, inexplicably, and that has probably done more to damage their reputation in the business community than any other single thing they've done. I can't tell you now what we're going to do with capital gains tax because I don't quite know where it's going to rest. By the time of the next election we will have been able to see what reform they have put in place, and then have worked out how we're going to improve it.

Nick Clegg has hinted that he's going to make tax cuts part of his manifesto ...

Look, I don't set policy according to what other party leaders are doing, or say they're going to do. We have to do what we think is best for the British economy, and right now the right thing is to be stable, cautious and responsible first and to be a tax-reducing government when you can be. If you look at what the Liberal Democrats are proposing it tends to be one tax goes up while another comes down.

Do you agree that the middle classes must be given back some of their money? We've paid a lot over the last decade or so, and been penalized for our aspirations ...

I think a lot of people on middle incomes are really feeling the pain at the moment, in terms of higher prices, higher petrol prices, higher mortgage costs, but I don't see this in a sort of class-based way. I just see there are a lot of people who work very hard, and who try and do the right thing, try and put money aside, and try not to be reliant on the state. They are finding it really tough at the moment. I don't know whether you want to call them middle class or working class or coping class, or whatever. But those people who are working hard, and who try to do their best, they are the ones who are struggling and it's those people who I would like to try and help.

The economy

There's been such a huge gap that has opened up between the very rich and the rest of us. How would you seek to close it? What can you do about that? There really is a huge earnings chasm ...
Obviously income inequality does matter, and I'm a Conservative who says that very clearly and maybe in the past we haven't said that clearly enough ... But I think the gap that matters most is the gap between the bottom and the middle. I think that when it comes to inequality our priority in Britain should be focusing on people who are stuck in multiple traps of deprivation and poverty, because they are losing connection with the mainstream of society. And it's that gap, between the bottom and the middle, that worries me the most. And it's actually getting worse. There are over 400,000 more people in extreme poverty than there were ten years ago.

Is it ever possible to have too much money?
I certainly think it's possible to have more money than you need. And I think there is what an economist would call a diminishing return as you get wealthier. In a global economy very rich people will obviously get even richer, but they pay taxes and make a great contribution to the economy and we should do more to encourage philanthropy. It's very important that we don't create a sort of class of Davos man or woman who is completely cut off from the rest of society. You could say, in this age we should just tax rich people more, but I don't think that's the right answer. They're very mobile, and if we taxed them they would just move away. You'd just reduce their incentives. Much better, I think, to encourage philanthropy – endowing universities like they do in America – let's have the same sort of private philanthropic giving on the scale that you have in other countries. The fascinating thing about this, as I discovered recently, is that philanthropy is not determined by income, it is determined by how

connected you feel to your community or your society. One of the ways you get the very rich to invest money is by encouraging their sense of community, of society. Of course there are lots of other ways, but I think that's one of the most important.

All right, but bringing it back to the tax-paying voter, the men and women on the street ... you talk a lot about welfare reform, you talk a lot about social responsibility, about long-term policies to look after the underclass ...
It's not looking after them, it's trying to get them out of the cycle they're in ...

You know what I mean. But how are you going to persuade them in the short term, i.e. before the next election, in the next eighteen months, that you aren't the enemy, that you are in fact the answer to their problems?
I think the attitude we have is, without stating the obvious, although it needs to be said, that while the consequence of poverty is a lack of money, the causes of poverty are much more deep and complex. And what we're saying to people who are stuck in an underclass – although I don't really like that term – those people who are increasingly cut off from society and caught in these traps of multiple deprivation and poverty, is that we ought to get to grips with the causes of that – with the family breakdown, the debt, the drug abuse, alcohol abuse, poor schooling, poor housing, the fact that you've been stuck on benefits for three years and lost all contact with the world of work. It's those causes of poverty that you've got to get stuck into. And I think people are beginning to recognize that the Conservative Party has a convincing set of arguments on tackling poverty in a way that it hasn't had in the past. When I say today that I see our party as the true champions of progressive ideas, I really mean it. And I think people are starting to see that.

Compassionate Conservatism ...

Well, yes. Today's poverty is much less about lack of money and far more about these traps that people find themselves in. So in a whole range of areas we're the ones really thinking about how to solve these problems. Of course in the past you could deal with poverty and in fact make a real impact on it through the mechanisms of the left – through income redistribution and big state programmes – but it's quite obvious that those approaches have had their day. They're not working any more. That's why I think we have a responsibility on this side of the political fence to show that we can do better. And that's exactly what we've been doing. So when you say compassionate Conservatism, yes, that definitely captures the values that lie behind all this for me, but actually I think the slogan or sound bite, or whatever is most relevant here, is the phrase we've been using about a 'post-bureaucratic age'. I know some people say that's a terrible slogan, it's not very catchy and all the rest of it, but it's not supposed to be a slogan – it's actually an extremely precise description of the approach we'd take in government to solving some of these really intractable social problems. The days of the big bureaucracy, working it out from on high, are over. We'll only solve the problems if we decentralize power, give people more control over their lives and entrust them with more responsibility. And of course it's now possible to do that in a way and on a scale never before contemplated because of the information revolution. That's what we mean when we talk about a post-bureaucratic age.

Okay, I can see that. Going back to the middle classes, they – we! – feel that the state services are unreliable and under Brown private services have become unaffordable. How are you going to tackle this disaffection? How would you seek to capitalize on this?

Well, here we are on a [First] Great Western train, whose service is so bad that some people in my constituency recently went on strike and refused to use it. I actually had a public meeting at Charlbury, where we're going to get off, where the manager of Great Western nicely came along to hear our complaints, and described his service as 'crap'.

Gerald Ratner all over again!

It didn't quite have the Gerald Ratner effect, but it was at least an admission of failure. Generally, I think there is a real sense in Britain that the public services have had a lot of money but don't provide value for money and that life is very expensive. But you can't say I'm going to come in and cut the cost of living for you with the stroke of a pen. The first thing we have to do is stop making things worse. We've got to stop taxes going up, we've got to stop the council tax going up, stop hitting people so badly. And then, progressively, trying to reduce the burdens on ordinary people by giving them back some of the hard-earned money they've lost.

Do you think an emphasis on wealth creation has made Britain a shallow place?

No, I don't think so. I think we need to make sure that a richer economy leads to a richer society, and the two don't necessarily go together. I think the Conservative Party at one stage became too focused on economics, and I think I've tried to emphasize the long history that the Conservative Party has had in relation to social policy and strengthening society and tackling poverty. Life is not just about money or balancing the books. I think towards the end of the 1980s we did become too much the economics party. And I think we needed to rebalance. Because a stronger economy doesn't have to lead to a richer society but it does if you make the right decisions. That's why I've spoken about the need for us to think about improving people's well-being, as I put it. We need to think about not just GDP, but GWB, or General Well-Being.

The ageing population

How would you address the growing imbalance between the retired population and the working population?

That is a very good question, and it's going to get worse. The baby boomers have had free university education, and have got great pensions, and they're going to retire relatively well off. Whereas the generation below them, well, below you and me as well, actually, are paying for their university education, getting into debt, finding it very difficult to get onto the property ladder, and actually now face a pension system that is going to be far worse. It's a generational problem, rather than just the difference between working people and retired people. There is no easy answer. We have got to encourage lifetime saving in a way that people trust. In Australia at the moment they've cut taxes massively on pension contributions and it's had an incredibly potent effect. Not just with pensions, but with all types of savings. Maybe it's old-fashioned to think that savings should all be about your pension. Actually, maybe we should be thinking about a simple, lifetime saving scheme, where you actually encourage a savings culture. Today, in Britain, if you're rich, and you're saving for your pension you get 40p tax relief; if you're poor, every bit of saving you do is actually killing you because it means you won't get the pension credit when you retire, you won't get the free residential care. The incentives for relatively poor people not to save are massive. And that needs a big change. That's one of the things we've got to do next.

Have you targeted the old enough? Have you told them what the rest of their lives would be like under a Conservative government? With the changing demographic, is the victorious party simply going to be that which appeals most to old people?
The silver surfers? They're probably even reading *GQ*!

I certainly hope so.
Saga [*Magazine*] will soon probably overtake your readership. It probably has already.

Quite considerably, in fact. But what are you doing to woo them? You haven't addressed the senior citizen at all, have you, not seriously?
Well, there are a number of things we've done. If you go back over the last few years, we've repeatedly argued that you shouldn't have to purchase an annuity, you should be able to keep your savings; they're

your savings and you should be able to use the money as you see fit. We've repeatedly looked at ways to exempt pensioners from tax. In fact the government took up our proposals to uprate the pension in line with earnings rather than prices. I'm very keen that we come forward with a plan to show everyone that if you put aside money when you're earning you can protect your home and put this against long-term care. But if you are looking for the real generational fairness argument, then there's a strong argument for saying, actually it's the next generation of retired people who we need to do more for now, because they're really going to miss out.

The City

Let's talk about business. Do you believe the City is behind you? If so, why? And what kind of compromises will the City have to make in the light of your policies?
I think the worlds of finance and business and industry are behind us. There was a tension in the early days of my leadership because, to be frank, I would say to business audiences, look, I took over a shop where people weren't even coming to the store, let alone buying the goods. Our problem was not that we were insufficiently pro-business or pro-free market or pro-City; our problem was no one knew what we thought about the health service, or the environment or society. So I don't apologize for emphasizing that side of things before then going on to talk about the things we are going to do to put business back on track and the economy back on track. I think business understands that, because businessmen and women are also mums and dads. I think now that actually the link between business and the Conservative Party is really coming back, in a very positive way. Not in a way that says we just cross out the logo on a CBI press release and put the Conservative Party at the top. I've been vocal in saying, yes we back business, but we also expect business to behave responsibly. And more than that, I've made it clear that I see business playing a big role in helping to tackle some of our biggest social and environmental problems, because I believe passionately that we are all in

this together and that everyone, including businesses, should play their part in making this a better country to live in.

And how will you police this?

I've been happy to praise companies that are making that kind of positive contribution, but also I think it's my job to criticize companies when they get it wrong. Now, I know that may have come as a bit of a shock in the early days of my leadership, but I think now that the City and business generally understand and respect my position, and that a Conservative government would be good for business as well as good for society.

But can a Tory Prime Minister ever really be a meaningful critic of the banking sector?

I think a Conservative Prime Minister can and should be a friend of business, where you praise and reward good business practice and then feel absolutely free to criticize bad business practice. If you believe, as I do, that the answer to every problem is not regulation and legislation, part of the role of a politician is to give a lead and to spark these debates and to say that business needs to fulfil its responsibilities to families, or to the environment or whatever. And I don't think progressive business leaders mind that, in fact I think they welcome it. Because most of them are actually quite proud of what they do.

What kind of businessman is your kind of businessman?

There are lots I admire. I think Sir John Rose at Rolls-Royce has a commitment to the manufacturing base, and I think he's done a great job. I think Stuart Rose has done a great job at M&S. They don't all have to be called Rose, but I think anyone who has turned around a great British company deserves praise.

Stuart has taken something of a kicking recently.

Yes, but there's someone who has turned around a great British business, turned around a brand that was fading, and re-energized it. And at the same time has shown enormous commitment, not just to the environment, but look what Marks & Spencer does to employ people with mental illness, it's fantastic. Good business and good ethics can go together.

But can big business really be good for the environment?
It can be.

Rarely …
No, look at what Marks & Spencer and Tesco and others have done. Their targets for reducing carbon emissions are actually more aggressive than the government's.

Granted. But is anything more important than the continued prosperity of the City?
A strong economy is the foundation of everything we do, that's right. Without a successful economy, none of the other things politicians dream of are possible. And within the economy the City of London is incredibly important. It is a deeply innovative, impressive place made up of all sorts of different firms doing all sorts of different things, the vast majority of which are extremely healthy for the world's financial systems. My father was a fourth- or fifth-generation stockbroker so maybe this was inculcated from an early age, but I do believe it. We mustn't overestimate what the City is, but innovative financial services are going to be important industries of the future and we should be very proud that we've got so many of them here in London.

Modernising the party

You could say that one of your greatest achievements since becoming leader is modernizing the party. At the very least you have totally changed the way the Conservatives appear to people. In what exact ways had the Tory brand become toxic before you revitalized it?
Well, I'm not sure I like the word toxic. I think what had happened was a series of things. I think there were ways in which we had lost touch with

the country, and so we didn't look like the country we were trying to govern. You know, the shortage of women candidates, the under-representation of ethnic minorities, the fact that we were representing mainly rural seats, many in the south of England. We needed to change the Conservative Party, literally to be more reflective of the country we wanted to govern. That was one part of modernization. I think another was thinking more deeply. For too long the party had got rather intellec-tually idle, and so if asked the question about education it was Bring Back Grammar Schools! If asked the question about health it was Bring Back Matron! If asked about policing it was Bring Back the Bobby on the Beat! It was all a bit formulaic, and I think we needed to think more deeply and more widely about problems and I hope we have done that. Also I think there were some consequences of the changes of the 1980s. Britain had become a more open, more tolerant society over issues like race and sexu-ality and I think the Conservative Party needed to modernize and catch up there as well. And there was also a more literal kind of modernization, with a properly run Central Office and press office and better organiza-tion all round. I think it was all of those things, some of which we've made good progress on, and some of which we've still got some way to go ...

What word best sums up the Conservative Party in 2008?

It's a mixture of visionary and practical. I think we've got a new dynamism in the Conservative Party, people are excited, we're setting the agenda, we're the ones coming up with the ideas, we're the ones having those ideas stolen and diluted by the Labour Party. I say I'm going to meet the Dalai Lama, a week later the Prime Minister says the same thing. I say we're going to cut inheritance tax, three days later he says the same thing. There's a dynamism about the party, but I also think there's a practicality, a down-to-earthness. When the Conservative Party has been at its best it's always been a sort of common-sense party. Not too driven by ideology, but practical, down-to-earth, deeply understanding the history and institutions and instincts of the British people. And I hope we've still got that as I think it's a really important part of what the Conservative Party has always been about.

Due to its funding arrangements, is the Tory Party still in thrall to the rich? In that way it doesn't really differ from the way the Labour Party is funded – you're both in the pockets of benefactors, even though they are very different benefactors ...

Less than it was. The worry I had was that we had become overly reliant on some very wealthy individuals. Good people they are, because some of them funded the Conservative Party during its very darkest hours and without them we would have faced some very difficult times. But I think it's not healthy to be overreliant on a small number of wealthy individuals, so we're now more reliant on a larger number of often quite wealthy individuals! We now have over a hundred people giving £50,000 a year, which is a lot of money. And they are all, by definition, extremely wealthy people. But actually, by broadening the base of finance, you are less reliant on any one benefactor.

Do you feel now that you have properly unified the party? What's the Lyndon Johnson maxim? Better to have them inside the tent pissing out than outside pissing in ...

It's a mixture of unification and modernization. They are two twin challenges that are never fully met. I think there's a high degree of unity now. I think people can look back now and look at what we've done and agree that it's working. There's certainly more unity in the party than there was two years ago, although there's always the potential for disunity, and it's something you have to work on.

Churchill used to advise against confusing the opposition with the enemy. He said the opposition are the Members of Parliament sitting on the benches facing you. The enemy are the Members of Parliament sitting on the benches behind you.

Well, I think Gordon Brown has that problem right now. With the Conservative Party it was a cultural change more than anything. You can't just change an organization by slapping on some paint, you have to take everyone with you. And I think a lot more needs to be done on that. Modernization is something that doesn't really stop, because a country's always changing and a political party needs to keep in touch with the country it's trying to govern and also modernize its own structures and organizations. I mean on the Internet we've got masses to do ...

Maybe, but to be fair you've done a lot more than other parties ...
But if you look at what's happening in other countries regarding politics on the Internet then we are way behind. We've put a lot of effort in but we have to do more. Look at what Obama did with fundraising on the Internet, I mean that was just amazing.

That was a zeitgeist moment in politics because it had never been done that way before.
Maybe that would never work in Britain but no one's really tried yet.

Corruption

One thing that the public admired you for in the wake of the Peter Hain and Derek Conway scandals – the misuse of party funds on both sides of the House – was the swiftness with which you dealt with irregularities on your side, and also the decisive way in which you did it. When people irritate you they're gone, aren't they? But in hindsight do you think you acted swiftly enough?
Well, some people say I didn't. I slept on it. I didn't withdraw the whip immediately, I issued a reprimand, and then went to bed, thought about it, and got up in the morning and thought, no, this isn't good enough; he had to go. I think it's very important to have a sense of natural justice about things. You have to demonstrate what you won't put up with, and be clear and decisive. When there have been problems with councillors distributing poems or whatever, you know I always want to get to the truth and get to the bottom of it. I don't do these things on a whim. With all these things I got to the bottom of what was said or done and I took action. But I hope I'm never petulant.

It was meant to be a compliment!
Well, good. But when people have served the Conservative Party all their life you have to think very carefully before removing the whip.

UKIP, the Liberal Democrats and a hung parliament

Would you like to destroy UKIP?
Look, there will always be some that would like to pull out of the European Union altogether; there will always be some sort of fringe party like the BNP or UKIP that wants to do that. If there are people who feel so strongly about that issue that it overrides all their other political views then I feel very sorry for them. It's the wrong approach. There are many people who think we should pull out of the European Union, but they understand that it's not the most important thing in politics so they're very happy to vote Conservative or Labour or whatever.

There is still the possibility of achieving a hung parliament at the next election, and while both you and Gordon Brown have made overtures to Nick Clegg, right now he doesn't appear to be that interested in any sort of alliance. Do you think he will change his mind the closer you get to an election?
I don't read it quite like that. I think the Liberal Democrats spend every waking hour dreaming of a hung parliament and their moment of power when they can finally foist themselves on a grateful nation. I actually think it's perfectly possible to win the election outright, and that's what I'm aiming to do. I think you should always try and have a decent enough and cordial relationship with the leader of the Liberal Democrats, and to work with them when we agree on policies. Because Clegg's leadership election was so inconclusive, I think it's more difficult for him to reach out and work with either the Labour Party or the Conservative Party before the election because he's got to keep his eye on his own party. You can't have a whole bunch of your supposed front bench not doing as you ask them to do, or vote in a way that you don't want them to.

He probably had the worst first week of any Lib Deb leader.
It was a shambles. He told his party how to vote on the EU treaty referendum, and his views were ignored by some not insignificant Members
of Parliament. You can't have that; it just makes you look like a fool.

Do you find Clegg impressive?
I think some of the early decisions he made were dreadful. The vote on
Europe was just a disaster. How to get yourself, from having a very clear
position on Europe, to looking divided, weak, indecisive and fence-
sitting all at the same time was really quite an achievement. Normally it's
either 'Labour Splits' or 'Tory Splits', but to blast them out of the way
with a giant 'LIBERAL DEMOCRAT SPLITS' was remarkable. Sacking
people all over the place, it was just shambolic.

In that respect he did both of you an enormous favour ...
Well, he didn't because actually, if he'd have stuck to his guns and stuck
to his word and voted for a referendum, we'd have had a good chance of
beating Labour.

ELEVEN

'I'm going to be as radical a social reformer as Mrs Thatcher was an economic reformer'

Boris Johnson, Mayor Bloomberg, Gordon Brown's leadership challenge, the *Spectator*, the Olympics, success in Crewe, the coming election

The fifteenth of May 2008. 'What's occurring?' asked David Cameron as he climbed into the back of the black VW people carrier parked outside the Crisis Centre in Commercial Street in London's East End. The night before he had watched the last episode of the first series of the BBC3 hit comedy *Gavin and Stacey*, and had not only fallen in love with it, but had started talking to people in the strong Welsh accent used by one of the show's main characters, Ruth Jones's Nessa, the rather statuesque, tattooed ex-roadie. He'd also fallen for Bryn, the sexually ambiguous character played with great finesse by Rob Brydon. He even said he wanted to install sat-nav in his car, just so he could pronounce it the way Bryn did in the series. 'Sat-nav,' Cameron repeated to himself, with great amusement.

'I just love Smithy, he's great,' he continued, eulogizing another character, played by comedy star James Corden. 'And Stacey is very attractive. At first you don't think she is but she just becomes more beautiful the more you watch the show. As she'd put it, she's tidy and lush. I've been to Barry [where the show is set] three times and now desperately want to go back. From now on, whenever we have any success in Wales, I'm going to congratulate my Welsh MPs on a tidy result.'

That morning Cameron had been to launch a Conservative initiative, the Homelessness Foundation, along with John Bird, the rather strident founder of the *Big Issue*, Adam Sampson, the chief executive of Shelter, Jenny Edwards, the chief executive of Homeless Link, and Leslie Morphy, the chief executive of Crisis itself. The Foundation was set up to act as some sort of link between the voluntary sector and those with proper political influence to help with policy solutions. As Cameron said in his speech that day, even twelve months before it would have been unthinkable for the Conservatives to be at the forefront of a charity for the homeless, but now it seemed perfectly natural. 'We're not trying to take the "We're brilliant and Labour are rubbish" view here,' he said. 'We've just got to embrace the problem.'

It had been a good couple of weeks for the Tories. Just two weeks previously, Boris Johnson had – against the initial odds – trounced Ken Livingstone in the London mayoral election, while Labour lost an astonishing 331 council seats in other local elections – the party's worst performance at the polls for forty years – perhaps indicating that the country was finally ready for a change in administration. And just a few weeks before the anniversary of his first year in office, Gordon Brown was taking another massive hammering in the polls. On Friday 9 May, a YouGov poll showed that Labour had slumped to its lowest levels of support since records began back in the 1930s, putting the Tories on a massive 49 per cent with Labour trailing on 23 per cent – a gap of twenty-six points. Two days earlier, another poll showed that more than half of Labour supporters believed that Brown should step down to make way for a more electable alternative. As a Westminster insider said to me the day before we went to Crewe, 'There's a feeling in the House now that he ought to just close the door of Number Ten and put the keys through the letterbox. There is nothing that Gordon can do to make people like him. It almost feels as though he is an ex-Prime Minister.'

Back in the people carrier, Cameron was on the phone to his private office, asking questions about that day's itinerary. Cameron and his team – Steve Hilton, enigmatic architect of the modern Conservative dream, and Liz Sugg, Head of Operations – were on their way to Crewe, to lend support to the Tory candidate Edward Timpson, the son of a shoe-repair magnate, who was standing in the Crewe and Nantwich by-election. 'I want to visit shops, I want to meet some real people,' DC said in the back of the car. This was Cameron's third visit to Crewe to drum up support for Timpson, and he would also come up again two days before the election. As the West Coast mainline Virgin train had been cancelled that very morning, there was no option but to drive the three long hours to Crewe on the M6.

Cameron had told his entire front bench that they had to visit the area at least three times or else they were fired ... 'And I wasn't joking,' he said, laughing.

The day had started with John Humphrys laying into Gordon Brown on the *Today* programme. Brown had been doing the rounds of TV sofas and radio studios for what internally the Labour Party were calling 'the big fight back'. Ironically, Brown's projected bounce–back was launched on the same day the Governor of the Bank of England delivered a fairly withering assessment of the economy. And so that morning Humphrys faced an exhausted PM, a man so beleaguered that both Westminster and Fleet Street were alive with gossip about succession, most of it centred around Foreign Secretary David Miliband and the thirty-eight-year-old Work and Pensions Secretary, James Purnell. In the political cartoons in the papers, Brown was pictured falling into manholes, walking under ladders and even, in one especially unpleasant depiction, standing neck deep in faeces. A photograph of a laughing Tony Blair in *Private Eye* had a speech bubble escaping from his mouth, advising his successor to invade Iran.

Those close to the Labour Party began saying that internally the talk was not about 'if' Gordon left, but 'when'. The perceived wisdom was simple: if Brown stepped down in early 2009, then the party had the opportunity to elect someone like David Miliband (few people appeared to like the idea of the other main contender, Ed Balls, particularly those in his own party), thus making their defeat at a general election less cataclysmic and making Cameron's first term less effective because of his reduced majority. This was the exit strategy being discussed within the Cabinet: call an election for May 2009 with Miliband and prepare for a bad but not awful loss, or call it a year later in May 2010 with Brown and get ready for an election disaster, perhaps the worst in Labour's history. But the decision was Brown's to make: did he want to go early, leave with dignity and begin building a respectful and potentially lucrative post-office career, or did he want to cling to power until 2010, delivering a disastrous result for Labour, and ruining his chances of redemption in the process?

It was difficult to find anyone in the party who thought that Gordon would do anything but cling on for dear life, screaming to anyone who would listen that, no, actually, the ship wasn't sinking, so why didn't they scurry back to their offices and start building that long-term economic security he was always talking about. According to the Prime Minister, the economy wasn't faltering, it was just pining for the fjords.

Things couldn't have been much worse. Towards the end of the month Brown was vilified for trying to abolish the 10p tax band, and then was forced to abandon the move. 'I'll be honest about it, we made two mistakes,' Brown said. 'We didn't cover as well as we should have that group of low-paid workers and low-income people who don't get the working tax credit; and we weren't able to help the sixty to sixty-four-year-olds who don't get pensioners' tax allowance.'

In a desperate bid to salvage his reputation, and perhaps to avoid a similar mauling at the Crewe and Nantwich by-election, on 13 May the Chancellor Alistair Darling proudly announced he was going to borrow £2.7 billion to give those on low and middle incomes an extra £120 for one year. Unsurprisingly, financial analysts weren't impressed, while the press just thought it cynical.

As cracks in the Brown project opened up, so stories began emerging of the very real war of attrition between Brown and Blair when the latter was still in office, when Brown was still Chancellor. In the space of two weeks in early May, Lord Levy, John Prescott and Cherie Blair all published autobiographies, and all were – in their own ways – highly critical of the new PM (with Levy even suggesting that Blair had said that Brown could never win against Cameron in a general election). Other unflattering gossip started to filter through, too: there was a bizarre and wicked rumour that in the spring of 2007, when Blair was still very much in office, he suggested to those around Cameron (via a News International editor) that if he needed help with Rupert Murdoch then all he had to do was ask – no doubt a New Labour in-joke. Likewise, soon after Brown became Prime Minister, at a dinner at the home of Roland Rudd (the founder of communications agency Finsbury), Peter Mandelson teasingly asked the *Spectator*'s Matthew d'Ancona why his magazine was being so tough on Cameron. Gordon Brown appeared to have more enemies than a new Prime Minister really deserved.

But there were many who thought he deserved it, and by acting so childishly had brought it all on himself. A few years ago the editor of one of the country's most influential Sunday newspapers had been called into Brown's Downing Street office for a meeting. After it had ended, he was kept talking unnecessarily by Brown and two of his aides for another ten minutes or so. They were only allowed to go as Tony Blair's car pulled up outside. The editor believed he had been kept waiting just long enough for Blair to see him leave.

Childish? Only completely.

Another editor said that during Blair's third term, Brown's personal press office seemed to do nothing all day except brief against the Prime Minister, and that they appeared to be employed not to further Brown's cause, but to aggressively undermine Blair's. Surely not?

If true, was it any wonder the press had turned against Brown?

In Westminster, and in the newsrooms of TV stations and newspapers all over the country, the underlying feeling was that, mirroring the end of the Major years, Labour had not only become arrogant and complacent, they had also run out of ideas. More importantly, perhaps, there was beginning to be a sense that the public had started to turn away from Labour, and had begun to collectively think, 'Enough is enough.' Crucially, many of those who rarely gave politics a second thought had begun thinking that it might be time for a change.

And while Brown was determined at least to try and ingratiate himself with celebrities and power-mongers and newspaper editors at Chequers, his weekend lunches would prove disappointing for his guests. He would scoot into the dining room having spent fifteen minutes doing the 'Brown mingle' (which essentially involved a lot of shaking of hands and polite inquisition), and then vanish after just over an hour, without giving any indication that he wasn't coming back. But coming back he wasn't. It appeared he had the ability to confuse his guests as much as he could confuse the electorate.

As for Cameron, his ideas were beginning seriously to resonate with the metropolitan commentariat, and all those columnists who had taken great delight in rubbishing his ideas of social responsibility were starting to appreciate that his commitment was genuine. As Brown's Labour Party began retreating to 1970s-style hobnail top-down management, Cameron's ideology – an ideology that was fundamentally sociological – was beginning to excite those whose opinions mattered: the press and the public. 'The great challenge of the 1970s and 1980s was economic reform,' said the Tory leader. 'The great challenge in this decade and the next is social reform – schools, welfare, family and responsibility.'

The Crewe and Nantwich by-election

Tell me about Crewe. What does this by-election mean to you? It's a long way from Ealing …
Well, all elections are important because there are Conservatives standing and I want to support them. I think Crewe is an interesting by-election because it's a Labour town in the middle of England that hasn't been Conservative for decades and it's a real challenge for us and we're going to put everything into it. It's a very big ask, but obviously it's been given further weight because the government is in so much trouble, having come up with this enormous £2.7 billion budget U-turn, and relaunching itself in the Queen's Speech, the government has almost hyped up the Crewe by-election by trying to throw all these things at it in an attempt to try and win it. And maybe they will; who knows? I just

believe that if there's an opportunity to get a Conservative elected then the leader of their party belongs by their side, giving them all the help they can.

If you win it, what will it mean for the fortunes of the party?
I'm always very straight about these things: if we win it's good news and if we lose it's bad news. It's as simple as that. I won't be calling the Samaritans and throwing myself out of a window if we lose, but it would be much better if we won. Whatever the outcome, it should be seen alongside a set of local elections and the mayoral election in London where some very important things happened. The Conservative Party got 44 per cent of the vote, which is the sort of breakthrough people have been asking why we haven't made. Well, now we have. The swing to us in the north of England was the same as in the south and we won in places like Sunderland and Salford and all points north. And then, of course, London, one of the most diverse, multiracial, progressive, cosmopolitan, metropolitan cities in the entire world is now run by a Conservative. Those things are remarkable and give a good basis for building for the future. But – and it's a big but – now we have to work even harder to prove that we deserved to win, not start patting ourselves on the back and telling each other how brilliant we are. I don't want us to try and glide to victory on the back of a failing government, I want us to deserve to win on the basis of the plans that we've put forward to change people's lives and our country.

So what are your objectives today in Crewe?
To battle through Britain's crumbling motorway infrastructure and to make it to Crewe!

And back again …
Yes, I think that would be a reasonable ambition for the day. Look, I've been twice already, and what I like to do is spend time with the candidate, hear how he's getting on, and do what I can to get out and meet people with him. We'll visit some businesses, we'll do a bit of a

walkabout, we'll do some media interviews and hear from the team. We've got a huge team of people up there and I ring some of them each day to thank them for their support and to find out what's going on. They're all quite knackered because they've been campaigning solidly, all through the local elections, through the London elections, and now this, and I want to try and give them a bit of a boost.

The Labour Party is trying to drum up some old-fashioned class warfare, aren't they?
Yes, they are. And because of that [with Labour activists parading around in top hats and tails] I shall probably be the worst dressed man in Crewe today! I think it's both pathetic and politically completely misguided. Just ask yourself the question, would Tony Blair ever have done this? He believed, rightly, in trying to build one nation, a nation of aspiration, not backward looking and class war and all the rest of it. And Labour are throwing all that away, and I don't think it's going to work and I think it's a great mistake. If ministers are actually confronted with the leaflets they're putting out, I hope they'll be embarrassed, because they're pretty unpleasant.

A poll in *The Times* today suggests that his U-turn on the 10p tax has made absolutely no difference to the voters in Crewe anyway …
Well, time will tell. My instinct is that voters are clever, and this guy [Brown] keeps taking them for fools. They know that this is being rushed out before a by-election to try and buy votes, and they will be incredibly suspicious of that, and rightly so. And also the payout is only for one year. I think the motives are so naked that people will see through it.

As the government flounders, does that affect how you try and get your messages across?
I have this sense of frustration at the moment because there are lots of things I want us to do, policies I want to launch and reports I want to publish, but there have been a couple of weeks where you didn't know

what mess the government was going to make next or what U-turn they were going to execute next, so you just have to stand back and let it happen, because no one's in the slightest bit interested in what the Conservative Party has to say while that is all going on.

You mentioned Boris and his extraordinary win, and you've said that he acts independently of you, but what instructions or suggestions have you given him?
Genuinely, devolution to mayors and first ministers in Wales, and first ministers in Scotland, will only work if they are absolutely free to draw up their policies, their appointments and their plans in response to what they perceive as the needs of their communities. I talk regularly with Boris, we exchange ideas, but I don't instruct or order him about. If he does something that I don't agree with then so be it. That's the nature of devolved administration.

If that's the case, then how do you keep him on a tight leash, how do you control him?
I'm not going to keep him on any sort of leash. I think Boris is unleashable anyway. But mayors shouldn't be leashed. They should be unleashed. If you're mayor of London you've got to be able to stand up and speak for the people of London without fear or favour, and if that conflicts with something the Conservative Party has said, to hell with it. You've got to stand up for your job and your position. That's the only way to do it. Look at what happened when Tony Blair tried to glove-puppet Frank Dobson into the job of London mayor: it was a disaster.

I asked you this a year ago, but do you still think you'll be fighting Gordon Brown and not David Miliband or Ed Balls or Jack Straw at the next election?
I think so, and I probably gave you the same flip answer a year ago, which is that it's hard enough running your own political party without trying to work out who's going to run all the other ones. But there's a genuine truth in that, which is one of the things I hope I've brought to the leadership of

the Conservative Party, which is to end this obsession with what the other side are doing, and to say, never mind whether Labour are going left or right or triangulating, or playing a game of Twister, let's not worry about them. Think about our own stuff. Think about what's wrong with the country, what we need to change and what we'd like to do ... discover, if you like, your inner Tory. And sort that out and explain what you're about. If the government suddenly announces they're going to cut tax by 2p, don't say you're going to cut it by 4p; just do what you were going to do in the first place. This whole concept of clear blue water, they're over here, so we must be over there, is completely wrong. So don't worry about who's going to lead the Labour Party as they're going to sort that out for themselves.

You could be Prime Minister when we have the Olympics in London. How are you going to make them the success that we need them to be?
This is something that you do need to work on very closely with the mayor of London and with the Olympic organizing committees and organizations, and that's why I set up an advisory team to advise me – not to be an alternative to Seb Coe and his office, but to advise me on questions we should be asking and the things that we should be pushing for, and to make sure we are as well informed as we need to be.

The Cameron manifesto

We've talked endlessly about what you stand for, and people hear phrases like 'social responsibility' and 'the post-bureaucratic age' etc., and many of them probably don't understand what it's all about, so what are you ultimately trying to achieve? Not just for the party but for the country – what's the big picture?
The big picture is explaining to people that real change is not delivered by government on its own, it's delivered by everyone playing their part in a responsible society. So individuals, families, businesses, everyone playing their part in dealing with the problems we have. And the big thing we want to change, just as Margaret Thatcher mended the broken economy in the 1980s, so we want to mend Britain's broken society in

the early decades of the twenty-first century. In many ways that's more difficult and complicated to do, but it's no less an ambition, it's no less a task, and at its heart it's dealing with the issues of family breakdown, welfare dependency, failing schools, crime, and the problems that we see in too many of our communities.

Do you accept that this is still a bit of a work in progress?
Look, of course all politics is a work in progress because all the time you're developing the ideas that flow from your philosophy, but I think the philosophical underpinnings of modern Conservatism are incredibly clear. We're saying that Labour got it wrong because they thought change was about spending money and top-down lever pulling from Whitehall, whereas real change is about social responsibility, it's about a responsible society in which everyone plays their part. So it's recognizing the limitations of government. You can trace very clearly the line between the Thatcher Conservative Party that was about transforming our economy and recognizing the limitations of government in regard to the economy and what I'm saying, which is that we need a similar scale of transformation in terms of our society.

Have you been surprised by the limitations of government since you've been doing your job?
Yes, all the time, particularly under this government, because they've tried to do so much from the centre, that you keep coming across examples of where their policies have had completely unintended consequences. Perhaps the best example is tackling poverty, where on a national scale you can see that, yes, they've taken some people out of poverty and pushed them above the poverty line. But actually more people are in deeper poverty than before. And you see it in a very human level in your constituency surgery when people come to you with their eyes filled with tears and their tax credits forms, saying, look at the bureaucratic red tape I'm caught up in, and if I try and work harder they are just going to take my money away from me and what a terrible mess my life has become! Both at a national and a personal level

I think we can see that the big top-down state-controlled model isn't working.

You seem highly focused on the daily political battle, how your message is coming across in the media. Do you accept that when some people describe you as the ultimate professional politician, that they're not wrong?

I think they are wrong because politics to me is about changing things and changing the country for the better, and none of this means anything if you're not elected. Politics is not an end in itself, and I make no apology for the fact that if you want to put your ideas into practice you've got to win an election. And if you want to win an election, what I have found, very clearly, is that you've got to win the day-to-day battle of the media and getting your message across and explaining what you're about. If you don't win that battle then you're history. The second thing, which is much more important, is the big strategic picture about your priorities in government. I believe that the Conservative Party under my leadership is doing both things. We're not just some bunch of great salesmen selling a clever message day after day, and beating Brown and his bunch of salesmen; we actually have done the fundamental thinking about how we're going to change this country for the better. And I would say we've done it much more than New Labour ever did, because Tony Blair was a great campaigner, he was a great party leader, but he didn't really know what he wanted to change in health, in education, in crime, in policing, when he first came in. By the end he was beginning to get an idea, but when he first came in I don't think he had a clue.

Do you think your message is now getting through?

I think it is. There are a lot of people who, when they say, 'Where's the substance?' mean, where are the old right-wing policies I knew about? And there are others who say, 'Where's the substance?' who mean, can I have your budget for 2011, please? But as the government is still rewriting the budget for 2007 let alone 2008, I think that's a bit rich. I think an increasing number of people, often on the left of politics, are beginning to say, hold on, I get this, the Conservatives are saying we're always at our best when we're being progressive, just as Robert Peel was, just as Disraeli was, who spoke about the elevation of the condition of the people, here is a progressive Conservative Party that is focusing with laser-like intensity on the problems of society and the underlying causes of those problems and it wants to do something about it. And I often think the left commentators understand more than those on the right, that there is a clear link with the Conservatives of the past, and that we have some clearly thought-through ideas about driving down power to the local level, about giving people more control over their own lives, but it's a progressive agenda and I think it's one whose time has come. As I was arguing this morning at the Homelessness Foundation, the idea that you pursue a progressive agenda just by spending more money and pulling a few levers from the centre has run its course.

How consistent do you think your message has been since you started your campaign three years ago?

If you go back and you read the speeches in my leadership campaign you will see all of the main ideas there. You will see that I wanted the Conservative Party to be focused on the problems of society, I wanted the Conservative Party to be more family friendly, I wanted us to give the environment a higher profile, I talked then about social responsibility, and how you don't change society just by state action but by all of us playing our role … I took social responsibility quite far by saying that I think all young people should take part in a school-leaver programme, the National Citizen Service. I talked about tax advantages for marriage, an end to state multiculturalism, more emphasis on the family, community programmes for sixteen-year-olds … all of those things were set out in my leadership campaign. I always maintain that I won that leadership campaign because I had the clearest idea about what needed to change in the party and what needed to change in the country. I don't think people thought I was some bright face who might be able to brush up the

Conservative Party with a new coat of paint. I think people thought I had some interesting ideas.

How has the noble vision changed since then?
Obviously circumstances have meant that I've had to spend more time addressing economic issues and the credit crunch and the cost of living. But the Conservative Party's problem wasn't that we were insufficiently pro-business or pro-markets, our problem was people didn't think we had a good vision of society, of what constituted good public services, of how you actually improve the quality of life and well-being. It's quite clear that sorting out the economic mess we inherit from Labour will be a major undertaking. But equally we have made clear that social policy will be the focus of our reforms. The focus on those social aspects of modern Conservatism was right and they'll be a very big part of my premiership if I get elected. Social responsibility is the essence of liberal conservatism. This is the Britain we want to build.

In one sentence, what do you stand for?
Giving people more power and control over their lives, and strengthening families and making society more responsible.

Does the Conservative Party yet look like the Conservative Party you envisaged three years ago?
Yes. Change in a political party is constant, and a party that stops changing and stops understanding the society it's trying to represent would be finished. The Conservative Party's brilliance over centuries has been to change to reflect society. Disraeli understood the conservatism of the suburbs, Peel understood that there was a growing urban population and we had to repeal the corn laws, Salisbury understood the importance of patriotism, Churchill understood the importance of home ownership, Mrs Thatcher understood the importance of giving trade unions back to their members. It's always been about change. But has the party changed enough? No, of course not. There are more changes I'd like, but we've come a long way. If you go to a Conservative conference now or a

Conservative dinner or a fundraiser, you will find a wider group of people in terms of their age, their outlook, their sex, their sexuality, their ethnic origin … I'm now sometimes surprised that a nineteen-year-old Asian woman bounds up to me in St Albans high street and says she's standing for the Conservatives. And I think, yes, that's great.

What does the road to the election look like?
Long and bumpy!

But maybe not as bumpy as it once seemed …
Possibly not, but there's no straight line between here and the general election. There will be ups and downs. There will be difficult periods. And also you don't even know how long the road is going to be. Most people are now assuming that there's not going to be an election until 2010, but anything could happen, and we have to be in a state of permanent readiness. We have to be in a continual state of readiness but also continually developing our ideas …

If you're elected PM, how soon would the country begin to notice the difference?
I hope some things you'd notice very quickly. Just as when Boris was elected mayor of London, there are some things you can change quite quickly that make a difference. But the really big fundamental changes, like education reform, and generations of new schools in the state sector, welfare reform that gets some of the five million people on out-of-work benefits into work, strengthening families through all sorts of measures, these things will take time. Because real change is not passing a law, real change is not issuing a directive, real change is a big social and cultural undertaking that goes on for a very long time. I would argue that the changes Mrs Thatcher made to the economy, we're still reaping some of the fruit of it. There's a greater spirit of enterprise in Britain because of what happened in the 1980s, and that has a very long tail. And I hope the more responsible society that we can build will be here for a very long time. The consequences will flow far down the line.

You said we'd notice some things immediately. Like what?

Let's just take one area, education. There are some things that you could do quite quickly, you could stop the closure of the special schools, you could do more to give heads more control over discipline in their schools, you could abolish the appeals panels: some things you could do really quickly. What matters is that the things you do in the short term don't undermine what you have planned for the long term. And I think that was Blair's great failing.

Even you must have been surprised by how quickly the government has imploded?

Yes, and I think just as 'Brown is a genius colossus bestriding the world stage' was overdone last year, I suspect that 'He's completely useless, couldn't erect a garden shed even with twelve assistants' is overdone this year. That's what politics is like.

You claim that increasingly Brown is stealing your policies, but it doesn't appear to be doing him much good, does it?

Well, the problem is, if you just take a few individual policies and don't put them together into a coherent vision and theme, then they don't mean anything. As [Hitchin and Harpenden MP] Peter Lilley put it the other day, there's no point having an elected Police Commissioner to make the police accountable to someone local if at the same time you're endlessly nationally telling them what to do. So it's no good stealing policies magpie-like, stealing some of the jewels, unless you can put them together into the overall framework on the basis of a real understanding of them. That's the trouble with Brown, and Labour generally – they have no real understanding of the modern world, of what I call the post-bureaucratic age. They just don't get it. They literally cannot understand how to bring about change except through top-down state control.

So why should we vote for you, David Cameron?

Because I'm going to be as radical a social reformer as Mrs Thatcher was an economic reformer, and radical social reform is what this country needs right now.

* * *

It had taken me half an hour to ask the above questions, but we still hadn't made it out of London. As we pulled up to some traffic lights as we headed north, the Indian driver of a white mini-van rolled down his window, forcing Cameron to do the same. 'Nice to meet the next President, I mean the next Prime Minister,' said the driver, beaming.

Half an hour later, as we hurtled up the motorway, working our way through a paper bag full of crisps and sandwiches, I told Cameron about a conversation I'd had with New York's Mayor Bloomberg the previous Friday, in which he'd said that Boris Johnson should take the tube rather than cycle, as cycling has the unfortunate perception of being white, elitist and middle class. But Cameron was having none of it. 'Look, the only way that Boris's image will change is if he's a good mayor or a bad mayor. Taking the tube won't change it. I cycle to work because it makes me feel happy and it's a pleasant experience.'

The sky was overcast, yet the mood in the car was quietly upbeat. Remarkably, the polls were saying that this was a by-election the Tories might actually win. 'Where is my Samantha?' said Cameron, as he tried to reach his wife on his mobile. 'Aha, it's you! It's easier to get hold of the Pope,' he said when he eventually got through. 'I'm beginning to think you must be having an affair.'

Discussions about the itinerary, the polls and what bloggers, TV crews journalists were going to meet them in Crewe, were interspersed with gossip and general Westminster chit-chat – including whether or not Bruce Forsyth, who had been watching PMQs from the public gallery the previous day, was 'on message'. (At one point I thought about initiating a game of 'I Spy' – 'I spy something beginning with L.' 'A Labour voter!' – but thought better of it.) 'You can't worry about the competition, you've just got to throw yourself into it,' Cameron said, almost absent-mindedly.

In Nantwich, the more upmarket part of the constituency, there appeared to be Tories – and Tory voters – everywhere. This was where the Battle of Nantwich was fought in 1644. As one commentator noted, the weapons of choice for the Battle of Nantwich 2008 weren't swords and muskets, but campaign balloons. The Labour candidate, Tamsin Dunwoody, kept saying that her mother, Gwyneth, whose death had brought about the by-election, would have wanted her to fight for the seat. But perhaps not in the way her party had decided she should fight it: in the weeks leading up to the election, Labour canvassers had been parading around town dressed in top hat and tails, resurrecting old-school class-war symbolism. It was the type of Labour campaigning that Tony Blair had tried to banish, and now Brown – who liked to think of himself as something of a class warrior – had brought it all back again. 'I think it's pathetic,' said Cameron, as he greeted the press in Crewe. 'I don't think people want to judge you on your background or where you went to school. They want to know if you're any good at your job. It's very divisive. This lot, they don't. They like looking back, they like class division, they like class war.' Labour's Frank Dobson (who famously lost the London mayoral election to Ken Livingstone in 2000) was also canvassing in Nantwich's town centre, unsuccessfully trying to paint Edward Timpson as some sort of aristocratic posh boy.

Cameron himself was in feisty walkabout form, leaping into the cabin of a Class 66 Freightliner diesel locomotive with Timpson for a photo op. 'I feel an orange jacket coming on!!' he said.

'How does it feel to be at the controls?' cried the photographers. 'Good!' said Cameron, beaming. What else was he going to say? 'I just wanted to press the horn but they wouldn't let me,' he continued, clearly enjoying himself. A photograph of him in *The Times* the next day was accompanied by the headline, 'Walking On Air?' As he climbed down from the train, he said, 'This is trainspotter heaven. You could come here with your cagoule and your sandwiches and stay here forever.' As for his own attire, the orange jacket was fine, although he was becoming wary of donning hard hats. 'William Hague once said to me, "Being leader of the Conservative Party and wearing a hat are incompatible." And he should know, because he wore a baseball cap to the Notting Hill Carnival.'

Twenty minutes beforehand he had done a tour of the nearby Freightliner offices, which were housed in a sort of extended prefab that appeared to contain more photocopiers than people. And while he asked questions that sometimes began, 'What happens down this end of the office, then?' or 'Look, I know this is a really dim question but ...' most of the time, regarding transport policy at least, he seemed to know what he was talking about. 'So if you were Transport Secretary for the day, what would you do,' he asked one trainee driver, who scrabbled for an answer before blushing. Elsewhere, the responses varied from rapidly improving Network Rail's restructuring programme to altering signalling and scheduling patterns. Cameron appeared to be welcomed everywhere he went.

And on Thursday 22 May, Cameron received a full and triumphant vindication of his leadership as the Conservatives achieved their first by-election gain in twenty-six years, taking Crewe and Nantwich from Labour in a landslide victory. It looked like it could be an historic turning point. Edward Timpson won 7860 more votes than his Labour rival, Tamsin Dunwoody, overturning a 7000 Labour majority at the general election – an enormous 17.6 per cent swing. Speaking the next day, Cameron said it was 'encouraging that thousands of people who have never voted Conservative before have come across and put their trust in the Conservative Party'. Although he said he was aiming to show the voters, and the country at large, that the party would not let them down, his most memorable quote referred to Labour's ill-judged campaign: 'It was backward looking, it was divisive, it was in many ways the end of New Labour.'

Labour's deputy leader Harriet Harman told the BBC: 'It was a bad result for Labour last night. But I think we have to understand what lies behind it and what lies behind it is people's sense of their own prospects and the fact people are feeling the pinch.' She said people wanted 'their immediate concerns addressed, that food's going up, fuel prices are going up and they want the government to very strongly focus on what we can do to back them up'. What Harman didn't acknowledge was that the by-election result was simply a heartfelt rejection of Gordon Brown's leadership. Not only was this defeat an indictment of Brown's ham-fisted government, it begged the questions: what now, what next? And when?

For Brown, it wasn't going to be easy. House prices were falling, food and fuel bills were going up, and every day it seemed the papers were full of yet another gang-related teenage death. It wasn't exactly the perfect platform for a convincing fightback – and Brown was hardly the sort of politician to take defeat lightly; he was far more likely to brood and ponder late into the night, wondering where it had all gone wrong.

The thing was, you didn't meet many civilians (i.e. those not in the media, or in some way involved with the political arena) who were anything but surprised and disappointed by Brown's behaviour – and his performance – since becoming PM; there had certainly been enough goodwill towards him, he had over a decade of accrued credit with the public, and it wasn't as though he hadn't been given a chance. But the public, the polls and the press all agreed: it wasn't working.

Writing in the *Daily Telegraph* a few weeks later, arch Tory Charles Moore – a man whose opinions regarding the Conservatives' future tended to be taken more seriously than other members of the 'old guard' – admitted that Cameron's interpretation of what had gone wrong with British society recently was bang on, adding that Labour had failed to understand that these days people really did expect more control over their lives. 'After more than ten years of Labour, people inhabit two worlds. They live in an unprecedentedly connected universe, in which they can choose a holiday, complete with car hire, maps, flights, hotels, in half an hour on the Internet. But they might not be able to choose the right school for their child.'

And as the country spiralled into something approaching economic chaos, there began to be a general feeling that far from being a party of emancipation – Blair's bottom-line New Labour pledge – Brown's

Labour Party was all about authoritarianism. Ironically, however, while Brown's government was eager to interfere in so many areas of our lives, in the areas that mattered most to voters – violent crime (and in particular youth crime) and escalating food and fuel prices – they were chronically toothless.

While Cameron was still being criticized – albeit these days with a lot less venom – for being soft on policy, it was proving impossible to discern exactly what Brown stood for at all. What formed the vertebrae of Brown's policies? What were his big ideas? After all those years plotting and brooding, where was everything? Where had he put it all?

Whatever there was, it didn't appear that Brown was able to articulate it, and when he intimated in the third week of June that he wouldn't be seeking more than one term in office, and would step down some time after winning a general election, there were many on his side of the House who thought Brown had begun to understand this (although by now the idea of him winning an election seemed fanciful in the extreme: Brown was on the rack, as demonstrated by the 22 June poll on a Labour members website, in which 64 per cent of those polled said they wanted him to step down before the next election).

According to one Downing Street regular, the Prime Minister was beginning to display the same characteristics as John Major when the Tories started unravelling in the mid-nineties, when he was caught in a vortex of 'sleaze' and the war of attrition between various Conservative Europhobes and Europhiles – as former British ambassador to Washington Christopher Meyer said of Major towards the end of 1993: 'He was tense, irritable and tired.'

Brown's celebrations acknowledging his first twelve months as PM were muted. You would have had to have been living in a cave for the previous year to think that Gordon Brown had had anything but a disastrous year in office. What we appeared to have was a government that was rapidly coming to the end of its usefulness. Much like the end of the Major government, we had an administration that had not just run out of ideas, but was becoming increasingly arrogant about its ability to run the country. Talk to Brown in private and he would reason that the UK's economic woes were simply in line with what was happening elsewhere in the world, and that all we could do was batten down the hatches and wait until it was all over (he didn't say we should just shut our eyes and cross our fingers, but it certainly felt like it). On 22 June, Alistair Darling even had the gall to suggest publicly that employers should try and counteract inflation by capping salary increases. 'Where in the past inflationary pressures were home-grown,' said Darling, 'in common with every other country in the world, they are coming from international pressures.' As 'wage restraint' became a Downing Street mantra, so public sector strikes started to become a real possibility.

Brown wasn't despised by the electorate – far from it: many were actually beginning to feel sorry for him – but he appeared to have the reverse Midas touch, and there was a strong feeling in Westminster that if he persisted in staying beyond the following spring, he would lead his party into the wilderness.

Publicly, while Rupert Murdoch was keeping his feelings about Brown's capabilities largely to himself, for some months it had been assumed within the higher echelons of News International that, come election time, his papers would come out for Cameron. Murdoch might still have a decent personal relationship with Brown, but he wasn't about to endorse a loser. The mood was shifting elsewhere in Fleet Street, as David Cameron continued to look like the only viable alternative. In fact, there was a sense that this was becoming a foregone conclusion.

As for myself, the downfall of the Brown government had been a sideshow, the background noise during my twelve-month journey with the Conservative leader. Cameron had, in that time, grown into not just an extremely formidable politician, but he had done so surely, steadily, and without any great fanfare. For some I think there was still a worrying sense that he was becoming the default option for the electorate – quite literally the only alternative – but if my year with David Cameron had taught me anything, it had taught me that he not only had genuine political principles – and policies – but also that, when he needed to, he had the ability to articulate them, too. Social reform, social responsibility, and the breaking-up of top-down government – these were the things I was taking away with me, these were the big-tent ideas that were going to carry him forward over the next twelve months or so.

I started this project in the summer of 2007, not really knowing where it would take either of us, not really knowing if I was shadowing a chancer, a maverick or a true visionary. David Cameron is not without faults, although it soon became obvious to me that he has a very clear idea of what he can do for Britain, and how he can start to produce change. Not everyone warmed to him – and there was still an element of inverted snobbery running through the country that hadn't been eradicated by a decade of New Labour – but, more importantly, people were now saying that whatever their reservations, they were prepared to give him a chance.

Towards the end of June 2008, almost a year since I'd started my journey with David Cameron, I was having lunch with the editor of a national newspaper. The topic of conversation – as was becoming the norm – was the government, and in particular Brown's ability to cling on, and Cameron's chances of becoming PM.

'You know what, no matter what you say about Cameron, he's got it,' said my guest. 'I remember when I first met him, just before the 2005 [Tory] conference, just after he'd been made leader.' There was a pause, a sip of wine and a nibble on a piece of bread. 'You could tell he was bright, you knew that he was charming, but there was something else about him. He looked like a winner. And the last thing that Brown looks like now is a winner.'

For Gordon Brown, at least, it seemed like it was going to be a long, hot uncomfortable summer. A summer during which he had to show convincingly that he didn't really have the reverse Midas touch at all.

And for David Cameron there was still a huge amount of work to do, work he looked as though he was looking forward to. Standing outside his home the morning after the pivotal Crewe by-election, clutching a bunch of briefing papers and newspapers, and looking like a man with destiny ahead of him, he said, 'I want to build over the coming months, over the coming years, the biggest coalition for change in our country so we really can remove this government and give Britain a better chance.'

And there were few betting against him doing exactly that.

TWELVE

'The age of irresponsibility is giving way to the age of austerity ... Unless we deal with this debt crisis, we risk becoming once again the sick man of Europe'

The collapse of Lehman Brothers, 'Yachtgate', Davos, Gordon Brown's YouTube moment, the worsening economy, success in the polls ... and the death of Ivan

On 15 September 2008, Lehman Brothers filed for Chapter 11 protection, the largest bankruptcy filing in US history, with Lehman holding over $600 billion in assets. The decision by US Treasury Secretary Hank Paulson, a former chief executive of Goldman Sachs, unleashed mayhem in the financial markets. Investors were left reeling as the abrupt demise of the investment bank caused the largest shake-up on Wall Street in decades, while fears of a fundamental global financial meltdown grew, as markets plunged and share prices fell all over the world, and banks unveiled urgent measures amid concerns that the world economy was entering a treacherous new phase.

As the 5000 Lehman staff in Britain were told to clear their desks, so the Bank of England injected £5 billion of emergency lending into the money markets, following the £50 billion they had provided in August, and the £125 billion already spent since March (which would be followed, a few days later, by another injection of £20 billion). More than £50 billion was wiped off London's bluechip shares as the FTSE 100 index tumbled by 212.5 points, nearly 5 per cent.

Just when the markets thought that the crisis couldn't get any worse, the Lehmans crash turned a crisis into a full-blown drama. Recession had arrived, and with it, the threat of a Depression. The demise of Bear Stearns earlier in the year had caused panic throughout Wall Street, but the collapse of Lehmans, coupled with the sale, on the same day, of Merrill Lynch to Bank of America, fuelled a vicious spiral, forcing banks to refuse to lend.

Then, only a few weeks later, an entire country went bust. In October, the Icelandic Parliament passed emergency legislation to minimize the impact of the financial crisis by taking over the domestic operations of the country's three largest banks. In the space of just a month Iceland's economy effectively ceased to exist. Built on mountain upon mountain of cheap debt borrowed when times were good, the country's financial sector imploded as the collapse of the financial markets made the cost of refinancing the debt impossible.

On 8 October, Gordon Brown and Alistair Darling wrote a cheque for £500 billion to try and ensure that Britain avoided its own, Icelandic-style collapse, and they pumped taxpayers' money into Lloyds TSB, HBOS, Royal Bank of Scotland and more, trying to restore confidence in the domestic banking sector and break the logjam in credit markets. The package included £50 billion of taxpayer funds for a partial nationaliza-tion of stricken banks, with the Bank of England pumping at least £200 billion into the money markets, and the government making a further £250 billion available for banks to guarantee medium-term debt to help restore confidence and get banks lending to each other again. Brown and Darling acted decisively, promising that billions of pounds' worth of guarantees would be given and new loans underwritten. The bailout was copied all over the world, and made Brown look statesmanlike for the first time in months. Suddenly the government had the initiative, although David Cameron interrupted his own party conference to fully endorse the recap, giving a speech in which he made clear the impor-tance of showing support at a time of crisis. Brown's euphoria was short-lived anyway, as markets continued to crumble. Brown was becoming so risk-addicted, borrowing money right, left and centre, that he started to embody a famous Italian saying – '*Politici sono delle persone che, quando vedono la luce alla fine del tunnel, ordina più tunnel.*' Or, for those of you who don't know the Italian for dénouement, 'Politicians are people who, when they see the light at the end of the tunnel, order more tunnel.' (My favourite is even more apposite: '*I governi sono come la biancheria intima. Devono essere spesso cambiato e per la stessa ragione.*' Or, more simply put: 'Governments are like underwear. They need to be changed often and for the same reason.')

For many this new crisis could be summed up by a sketch by John Bird and John Fortune: 'Imagine, if you can, an unemployed black man sitting on a crumbling porch somewhere in Alabama in his string vest and a chap comes along and says, "Would you like to buy this house before it falls down and why don't you let me lend you the money?" … Then this mortgage is bought by a bank and packaged together on Wall Street with a lot of other similar debts … Somehow this package of dodgy debts stops being a package of dodgy debts and starts being what we call a structured investment vehicle … I buy it and then I will ring up somebody in Tokyo and say, "Look, I've got this package, do you want to buy it?" And they say, "What's in it?" and I say, "I haven't got the faintest idea," and they say "How much do you want for it?" and I say, "A hundred million dollars," and then they say "Fine" and that's it. That's the market.'

October also saw the return, yet again, of Peter Mandelson, who was appointed to the Cabinet for the third time in his career, this time as Business Secretary – and, it would soon transpire, de facto deputy Prime Minister. Brown's relationship with Mandelson had always been difficult – well, at least since Mandelson backed Tony Blair over Brown after John Smith died in 1994 – but bringing him back in this way showed that not only was the PM prepared to bury the hatchets (and there was a closet full) in order to save his own political career, but also that if he were prepared to do this – recall one of his greatest political foes – what wouldn't he do? It showed daring, it showed gall, yet it also showed a certain amount of desperation.

In his pre-Budget report a month later in November Alistair Darling announced that VAT would be lowered to 15 per cent for 13 months, 'as part of a fiscal stimulus package designed to reinvigorate the economy'. But not only did this go down badly with retailers – all that accounting!

– but the public weren't much interested either. As every high-street shop was going on sale – dropping prices by anything up to 50 per cent – a two and a half per cent cut in VAT wasn't exactly blowing wind up anyone's skirt. Soon after, Simon Wolfson, the chief executive of Next, said the cut had had 'no effect whatsoever' on retail sales. Darling also introduced a new 45 per cent tax rate, and, rather more importantly, announced that borrowing would soon hit £118 billion.

As the *Daily Telegraph* would say a few months later, 'Mr Darling is a man in desperate need of ideas.' Having said that, as the year drew to a close, the Conservatives were still struggling to articulate a strong message about the recession, and while they were still considerably ahead of Labour in the polls, they had suffered badly from the government's accusation that Cameron's party were the 'do nothing party'. The Tory leader had his own problems, because later that month police raided the home and Commons office of Conservative MP Damian Green after a long-running investigation into unauthorized disclosure of confidential material from within the Home Office. It immediately transpired that not only did they have no warrant to enter Parliament, but Home Secretary Jacqui Smith claimed to have no prior knowledge of the arrest. As the 'confidential material' related to failures over immigration, the arrest appeared highly suspicious.

Towards the end of the summer, the Conservatives had held the safe Home Counties seat of Henley after it had been vacated by Boris Johnson, with Labour humiliatingly getting fewer votes than the BNP. Just a few weeks later the SNP trounced Labour in Glasgow East, after which Foreign Secretary David Miliband tried to kick up some dust by writing a piece for the *Guardian* which was construed as a leadership challenge to the Prime Minister. And having slapped young Miliband back into his place, towards the end of the summer Brown was handed a PR lifeline when George Osborne made the mistake of getting on a yacht with Peter Mandelson. The future Business Secretary claimed that, while partying on a large yacht in the Mediterranean, Osborne had solicited donations from a Russian oligarch. Osborne refuted the allegations, but the sand stuck, causing huge waves within the Tory Party, and in the press. This was one big wobble, and there were calls in the press for Osborne to resign. Remarkably – some thought – he managed to hold on to his job, although his behaviour only added fuel to the fire being stoked by those in the lobby, and by those in the Labour Party who wanted him gelded.

Elsewhere in Westminster, the talk was still of succession, and Brown's increasingly bad moods. There were leadership whispers about Yvette Cooper, Alan Johnson, Ed Miliband, Ed Balls ('Although no one is going to vote for someone called Balls,' appeared to be the consensus), even David Miliband. But there was no appetite for a fight, and while intellectually the Cabinet knew that Brown was going to lose them the election, they found it impossible to work together to oust him. 'These are exceptional days,' said a former Labour apparatchik to me at the time. 'Our government has run out of ideas and political courage. There really is the most bizarre atmosphere here in the Commons right now.'

Throughout the autumn, hordes of Fleet Street editors and political journalists were summoned to Brown's rooms in Downing Street, there to listen to the Prime Minister's bewilderment that the press and public alike just couldn't understand what he was attempting to do. 'What did I do wrong?' he would ask, 'What more could I have done?' After several hours of this, followed by some light brooding, which the poor journalist would have to sit and witness, the red mist would come down, and Brown would start shouting about the injustices of the press, and – as if by rote – how much he hated this new batch of Tories. One visitor, who had to endure three hours of this, one evening after that day's PMQs, recalls how he eventually extricated himself, only to have Brown accompany him to the top of the stairs, moaning at every step. As he passed one of his children's bedrooms he spied a football, lashing out at it in anger. He missed the ball completely and kicked the wall instead. To his credit, even he could see the metaphor. One didn't have to have much of an imagination to conjure up an image of Peter Mandelson, just a few hundred yards away, sitting in a leather armchair, legs crossed, and stroking a large white cat ... a cat with a face suspiciously like Gordon Brown's.

By December the Conservatives had increased their poll lead over Labour to seven points – the party's first increase in the ratings since the collapse of Lehman Brothers. A similar poll in January 2009, giving the Tories the same seven-point lead, meant that if there had been an election there and then, there would have been a hung parliament, with the minority government led by Cameron (leaving him 36 seats shy of a majority). But even though the Brown Bounce was officially over, Cameron's personal standing in the polls was still flat.

Egos are often so distended that talent is often best viewed from afar. Although in Cameron's case, such is his innate charm that being around him rarely sets people on edge. As *Time* said about him in 2008, in a review of the first edition of this book, he has an 'ability to hide in full view'. Perhaps unsurprisingly it's this charm that still puts a lot of people off, and during Brown's accelerated demise in the spring of 2009, Cameron's attitude irritated many of those who had already decided to vote for him. There was a sense that even though it was assumed by many – including many in his own party, although they were obviously, almost pathologically obsessed with denying this – that Cameron was going to win the next general election, his victory would be a little hollow. Because anybody could beat Gordon. Standing just six feet away from Cameron at a West London party a week before Christmas in 2008, one industry titan said to me, 'Because Brown is so fucked he could be beaten by a monkey on a stick.'

What many wanted to see was more of the man they saw on Prime Minister's Questions, the articulate bully who hurled brickbats at the PM as though it was second nature. They wanted to see Cameron make a move.

There was certainly movement within the party, as they banked everything on the debt argument, reframing the 'credit crisis' as 'Labour's debt crisis'. As the polls tightened, so talk of a possible spring election began again and the CCHQ election plans were pulled back out of the cupboard and dusted down. The teams around Cameron and Osborne gathered for a series of strategy meetings. At one – held at David's constituency home – a series of posters was laid out on the sitting-room floor. There was one simple but stand-out idea … a picture of a newborn baby with the caption 'Dad's Nose, Mum's Eyes and Gordon Brown's Debt'. The vote (including Sam's) was unanimous – debt would be the focus of the New Year campaign and this poster would carry the argument. It combined a hard-headed message on the economy with an emotive idea in line with Cameron's 'it's all about the family' vision. The poster launch was a huge success and the Conservatives' debt argument took hold. The effect on the polls was dramatic and by the end of January the idea of an early election was back on the agenda.

That month Cameron also created a media flurry when he publicly anointed William Hague as deputy Conservative leader, declaring the Shadow Foreign Secretary as 'my deputy in all but name'. Cameron said, 'I have been in this job for three years. William did it for four. He has seen the pitfalls and is a very wise counsel. It's a good relationship. It has worked extremely well.' The appointment played well, particularly with those that mattered in the media, like George Pascoe-Watson, then political editor of the *Sun*, who called it a 'masterstroke … He gives the measured advice to his leader and puts the fear of God into Labour's front benches. The Blues Brothers are in business. And Labour will be worried.'

The same day, 13 January, Labour declared war on the middle classes – those affected most by the recession – by announcing plans to make public bodies discriminate against Middle Britain: as the *Daily Mail* so gleefully reported, existing laws under which policies have to consider race, gender, age, sexuality and disability now had to be extended to include social background. Designed to remind voters that the Tory echelons were still the product of an elitist education and social system, it had the effect of alienating even more potential voters from Labour.

Then, on 19 January, the day that Cameron again stunned his party by welcoming back Ken Clarke to front-line politics, making him Shadow Business Secretary, the Royal Bank of Scotland was driven to the brink of nationalization, unveiling the worst loss in British corporate history, some £28 billion. Brown said he was 'angry' with RBS over their risky acquisition strategy, although this was rather like shutting the stable door after the horses have bolted.

At the tail end of January there was the annual World Economic Forum in Davos, although this year no one was expecting any great salvation, or indeed any definitive answers come to that. There are usually so many celebrities and world leaders arriving at the private airport in Altenrhein, the nearest airport to Davos, that the car park is full of star-spotters clutching autograph books and ballpoints, and amateur paparazzi brandishing digital cameras and mobiles. Was that George Clooney climbing down from his jet? Isn't that Will Smith pulling on his North Face? And isn't that a hole in Gordon Brown's purse?

As soon as you reach Davos itself you see the television camera crews too, hoping to catch a keffiyeh-clad protester land a snowball on the back of Tony Blair's head. Davos is the Glastonbury of world politics, the Cannes of world politics, the playground of the rich, the famous, and – in 2009, at least – the profoundly worried.

But the celebrities were thin on the icy ground this year, principally because they were asked not to come, lest the world media think the assembled economists weren't taking their work seriously enough. Spend any time in Davos and you begin to feel as though the whole thing is being directed by Fellini. There are financiers here, politicians there, and pretty girls with clipboards everywhere. There are photo ops, glittery panel discussions, parties, private dinners, public flayings, the lot. At the 2009 summit there were 43 world leaders, double the usual amount, all there to try and find the one economist with the spade to dig us all out of the economic hole. And while there were plenty of seminars about charitable and philanthropic projects, mostly what concerned the 2500 delegates this year was: what the hell were we going to do?

There were so many politicians and media moguls here that after a while you felt as though you were walking through a newspaper. I went to the MCC (Malaria Capital Campaign) Donor Reception at the Belvedere Hotel hosted by Bill and Melinda Gates and there were nearly as many famous people in the audience as there were on stage, including

Rupert Murdoch, *Wall Street Journal* editor Robert Thomson and advertising guru Martin Sorrell as well as Gordon Brown himself. So star-studded was the audience that the panel discussion – 'Galvanizing the private sector', 'Supply chain management issues' etc – soon became something of a sideshow. There was a similarly stellar crowd at the James Murdoch dinner later the same night, which, at various points in the evening boasted Murdoch senior, Boris Johnson, George Osborne, David Cameron, Andy Coulson, *The Times*'s James Harding, Fred Krupp – the president of the Environmental Defense Fund – and a dozen other environmental bigwigs.

Unsurprisingly Davos had a more sombre feel than usual, with everyone walking round with faces so long their chins touched their ski boots. But while people were looking at their shoes rather than looking up at the slopes, there weren't that many people skiing this year anyway: all British politicians were ordered by their leaders not to, just in case they were photographed by the paparazzi.

In the panel discussions there were lots of jokes made at the expense of bankers, although everyone was careful not to appear too smug. And what did I see as I wandered from panel discussion to cocktail party to placement dinner? Embarrassment, that's what. Written in invisible ink on the foreheads of the great and the good, standing there naked without a decent policy between them. Chinese premier Wen Jiabao attacked Western financial institutions' 'blind pursuit of profit' and their 'lack of self-discipline' with absolutely no hint of irony, although the least welcome quote of the week came from James Schiro, the chief executive of Zurich Insurance, who suggested that all members of the financial services industry should apologize for the crisis. He didn't, however, say whether or not he expected them all to do it individually.

As I flew out of Altenrhein it occurred to me that Davos is a lot like Hollywood in another respect too: nobody knows anything.

As he flew back from Davos on 1 February, Gordon Brown was greeted by a damning column by Matthew d'Ancona in the *Sunday Telegraph*, proclaiming that this was the week that Labour finally lost the next election. Brown was fully aware of what d'Ancona was referring to.

'Last week's opinion polls have shocked even the Tories in the uniformity of their hostility to the Government.' In the ComRes poll in Monday's *Independent*, Labour fell below 30 points for the first time since September. In the *Guardian*, an ICM survey had the Tories on 44, up six points since last month, with Labour trailing on 32. The YouGov poll in Friday's *Telegraph* indicated a similar lead for the Conservatives (43 versus Labour's 32) and – no less important – a seven-point advantage for David Cameron on perceived economic competence. Brown had something of a bounce after he announced his first bank rescue package, but it was wiped out by the first week in February, when his approval rating dropped again, slipping five percentage points to 28 per cent. This perceived economic competence was largely the result of George Osborne's opposition to Brown's decision to pile up more debt and try to spend his way out of recession. Osborne called it, 'A monumental mistake, both for today and for the future. It is the road to economic ruin for our country.' He also continued to attack Brown for – in his opinion – abandoning fiscal prudence. Cameron also started mentioning the sort of cuts in public spending that would be necessary for any incoming government, cuts which Gordon Brown or Alistair Darling had so far refused to accept were needed.

And how would Brown's Chancellor be remembered? It was easy to imagine Darling as Piglet, in a scenario already imagined by David Benedictus, the man responsible for *Return to the Hundred Acre Wood*: 'Pooh and Piglet, Christopher Robin and Eeyore, were last seen in the forest, though can it really be 80 years ago? But dreams have a logic of their own and it is as if the 80 years have passed in a day. Looking over my shoulder, Pooh says, "80 is a good number, really, but it could just as well be 80 weeks or days or minutes as years." And I said "Let's call it 80 seconds and then it will be as though no time has passed at all!" Piglet says: "I tried to count to 80 once but when I got to 37 the numbers started jumping out of me and turned into cart wheels, especially the sixes and nines." "They do that when you're least expecting it," says Pooh.'

* * *

David Cameron's standing in the polls was beginning to look unassailable, but then in the early hours of 25 February, something so terrible happened it made his political fortunes appear immaterial. After a series of dramatic seizures, Cameron's son Ivan passed away. Cameron left the office slightly earlier that day, going home for one of his designated 'family nights'. But Ivan had a terrible night, suffering monstrous fits, and so the Tory leader and Samantha went to their local hospital, St Mary's in Paddington, at 5.45 the following morning. The medical staff tried for 45 minutes to revive him but at 6.30 a.m. conceded defeat.

Living with their son Ivan was never easy, not that you'd ever hear David or Samantha Cameron say so. Why would they? He was their son, their beautiful blue-eyed, oh-so-cherished son. Born in 2002, with cerebral palsy and one of the most severe forms of epilepsy, Ivan had needed round-the-clock care almost from the moment he was born. He was unable to walk or talk, and – tragedy upon tragedies – rarely smiled. For several years he didn't smile at all, but when his medication was altered in 2006, his moods altered too, fundamentally changing the mood in the Cameron household as a whole.

Our youngest daughter was born with considerable physical problems, and we spent the first two years of her life in and out of hospitals, not knowing if she would ever walk properly, so I can begin to empathize with what they may have initially felt, but only fractionally. Marginally. Simple physical disabilities often seem so much more tangible.

Ivan's Ohtahara syndrome left him with severe problems with movement, sight, speech, hearing and breathing. The condition also causes seizures that progressively worsen as the sufferer ages. It was these sudden and seemingly random seizures that caused so much disruption in the Cameron household.

One of the first things you notice about parents with profoundly disabled children is the way in which their disability is hardly ever mentioned. Their differences, their distinctions, and the joys and the difficulties that come with them, are treated as normal. As they should be. Their disabilities become a gift of sorts, one to be embraced wholeheartedly.

And so it was with David and Samantha Cameron and their six-year-old son Ivan. In all the time we spent together for this book, whenever we met, and whenever Ivan was mentioned, David behaved like any other decent father – with frustration, with pride, and with love. An awful lot of love.

While I wouldn't want to imagine what it is like to lose a child – if it hasn't happened to you, how on earth could you possibly know, other than to know that there can be nothing worse? – neither would I know what it's like to bring up a profoundly disabled child like the Camerons did. But it informed everything they did. When they ate. When they slept (or rather, when they didn't). When they went out. Who they invited into their house, who they invited into their lives. How they treated their other two children, Nancy and Elwen. What they told their other children about Ivan. Where they went on holiday with the children (the south coast, northern France at a push). How David and Samantha treated each other.

But it was unbelievably hard work. Ivan needed over 20 different drugs daily, delivered, like his liquid food, through a gastronomy tube that was inserted into a huge hole in his stomach. Whenever Cameron discussed Ivan, he almost always smiled, although only a fool would be unable to see the pain behind it. David Cameron has all the surface smarts you expect from any successful politician, but he can never disguise what he feels about Ivan. At least I've never seen him disguise it.

I spent a lot of time talking with Cameron about Ivan, but those conversations were usually kick-started by me. And when Cameron spoke, he was never maudlin, or overly dramatic. In fact he was almost dispassionate, treating his son's disabilities as a practical problem rather than something to wallow in. And whenever we talked about Ivan, I found myself unable to think of David Cameron as anything else but a profoundly decent person whose base instincts about human nature were sound and proper. No, caring about your disabled son doesn't make you a good politician, and no it doesn't necessarily make you a good person either, but the way you talk about your disabled child certainly makes it easier to understand your motivations, your strengths, your weaknesses, and even perhaps the nuances of your compassion. And anyone who says that Cameron can't understand the problems of every-day people, who accuses him of social elitism, only needs to stop and think of the mental anguish, the emotional conflicts, and the constant nightmare of having a decidedly disabled child before they do so again. Some say that having Ivan took some of the gloss off Cameron, made him less cocky, more humble. But what it really did was give him some-thing in his life that was more important than politics. It also gave him purpose and ambition.

Priorities, that was the salient point, the priorities that marked him out as a family man first and foremost, and a driven, political creature second.

What I found impressive about Cameron was his practical approach and the pragmatism with which he talked about Ivan. It is a practicality and pragmatism (and a resilience) that in part has shaped his personal-ity and his political philosophy. 'Compassionate Conservatism' is espoused by many in the party, but its roots stem from Cameron's own experience, which has manifested itself in the sort of One Nation Toryism that actually means something in an expectant, safety-net-free world. Ivan's disabilities have brought him into very close and regular contact with the NHS, and he has spent a lot more time in hospitals than he otherwise would have done (especially at Great Ormond Street, the children's hospital that justly has one of the best reputations in the world). In one six-month period, Ivan had 16 overnight stays in London hospitals. Ivan's seizures could come at any moment, putting even more pressure on his parents, and often disrupting working days that had to be finely calibrated in order for David and Samantha to juggle their hectic working lives.

Unsurprisingly, they were always by Ivan's side when he was rushed to hospital because they feared he might not return, often sleeping on the hospital floor throughout the night. The Camerons relied on the NHS as a vital source of support from the moment Ivan's condition was diagnosed, and because they have had so much first-hand experience with specialist clinics, have encountered the best and worst aspects of the system.

Because he grew to have regular contact with an array of different carers, in the NHS, in social services, with social workers and community nurses, specialist teachers, speech therapists, and all sorts of ancillary helpers, Cameron's understanding of care delivery became acute, changing the way he felt politically, and making him painfully aware of not only the problems the NHS faces, but of the measures needed to overcome them.

Cameron has been criticized for being willing to be photographed and filmed with his family ('Cameron does not hesitate to feature his wife, his children and his home in public relations material, and there has been some disquiet about this approach,' wrote mealy-mouthed Deborah Orr in the *Independent* just a few days after Ivan's death). But if you analyse his behaviour since becoming Tory leader in 2005, you'll see that he has been almost impeccable in this respect. He famously allowed ITN cameras into his home for breakfast, and there was last year's rather magnificent Christmas card, but other than that Cameron has actually been quite circumspect about exposing Ivan to the press.

Ivan's life gave more to David and Samantha than his death can ever take away from them, and I would imagine that, in many ways, he will live with them for ever. His memory should also ensure that his father's compassion and steely resolve will continue to make him a better politician.

* * *

By March, the tide was turning so far in the Conservatives' direction that Cameron's resolve was not always necessary. Gordon Brown was beginning to crumble. As he flew 30,000 feet over the Atlantic, en route to a series of meetings with President Obama, Brown exploded at various journalists on board: 'You want me to go on television and apologize, but I am not going to do it. I have nothing to apologize for. It is not my fault. Get in the real world. You guys just don't get it, do you?'

Hosting the G20 in London the following month, Brown drew good notices on the aid package he had secured (even though much of it was old news), giving him something of a bounce in the polls. When I asked a banker friend in Hong Kong what he thought of this, he emailed back immediately: 'Won't last. Hot air. Amazing spin.' This was a view shared by many, not least those affected by the announcement, in the Budget on 22 April, that the government would increase its top rate of income tax to a higher than expected 50 per cent in 2010. The tax band had originally been due to rise to 45 per cent from 40 per cent in April 2011, but Alistair Darling's new hike would come into effect sooner and apply to any income above £150,000.

As if this hadn't made Brown unpopular enough, in early April Brown's retired spin doctor Derek Draper and Damian McBride, one of the Prime Minister's closest advisers, were caught sending emails to each other, in which they suggested various smears that could be spread about the Tories. McBride boasted that the sleaze campaign 'will put the fear of God' into the Tories. The Conservative leader was understandably furious: 'It's no good him [Brown] saying he didn't write the emails. This happened in his office in Downing Street, he's the leader, he's the head of the culture, so you have to say sorry.' Draper has always been fiercely partisan, and the last time we met gave a good impression of someone who these days exists solely to hate David Cameron. We were introduced at an awards ceremony in London a few months before the scandal broke, and he immediately slammed into me, criticizing me for being too 'on-message'. We spent five minutes arguing before he wandered off in search of another victim. But in the words of Vic Reeves and Bob Mortimer, he wouldn't let it lie. And later, as I was walking by his table on my way out, Draper shouted at the top of his voice, causing his companions to collectively flinch with apparent embarrassment, 'Cameron will let you down in the end you know.'

On 21 April Gordon Brown appeared on YouTube, ostensibly to announce swingeing cuts in MPs' allowances. But what was most interesting wasn't the content of his statement, but rather his brand-new smile. As Simon Hoggart wrote in the *Guardian* the next day, this was a smile that had 'clearly been worked on for some time, possibly by a professional smile consultant.' ("Now, Gordon, darling, lift the corners of your mouth. Let's see those incisors! No dribbling, mind!")' Watching

Brown grimace on YouTube was like watching a man dancing to his own grave, an instant, modern-day attempt at a makeover. Harold Wilson spent his entire career ingratiating himself with the electorate by smoking a pipe in public even though he liked to smoke cigars in private; Brown's preposterous YouTube appearance was a misguided attempt to put a sticking plaster on a bomb crater, a crudely calibrated stab at image management that didn't fool anyone.

'It cannot have been tried on a focus group, since it is quite terrifying,' wrote Hoggart. 'Think of the Joker in the Batman films. Then again it is the kind of smile you might deploy on a first date with someone you'd found in the small ads. ("Hmm. She says 'GSOH essential'. Maybe if I smile a lot she'll think I have one.") It's the smile a 50-year-old man might use on the parents of the 23-year-old woman he is dating, in a doomed attempt to reassure them. It's a doctor saying: "Now this is going to hurt a teeny bit, but if you're a brave little soldier, Mummy might give you a biscuit."'

On 24 April a YouGov poll for the *Daily Telegraph* gave the Conservatives an 18-point lead over Labour, giving Cameron a 150-seat majority if the result were repeated at a general election. Perhaps the public had cottoned on to the fact that not only had Brown spent a lot of money, he'd then borrowed another huge sum, and then asked his fellow G20 leaders to lend him some more. It was perhaps not the most orthodox response to the banking crisis, but one Brown appeared committed to. Trust in the Labour Government had fallen to its lowest level since records began, and many party supporters were worried that Brown's leadership had taken it on a course even more circuitous, even more hazardous than the one taken by John Major in the mid-nineties. Some wondered if, when the probable post-defeat leadership race was over, Labour in opposition might be even less electable than it was under Brown.

Many thought the work Cameron was doing was OK, even abroad. He was certainly getting better notices in the US papers. A pollster I had lunch with in Santa Monica in early May was predictably disparaging about Gordon Brown and his chances of survival, but largely full of praise for Cameron. 'He is a good leader, but he needs to step up to the plate, although not in the way most people think. He needs to stop being so political, and stop rushing around the place trying to make headlines. You journalists kill them for it but the Tories have got to resist giving too much detail. Policy will kill them. Be big, be statesmanlike, but step back.'

By May 2009, with the polls suggesting that Brown had successfully become one of the least popular Prime Ministers of the last 50 years, one might have thought his rules of engagement might have been doctored a little, and that his original and much-heralded obsession with openness, full disclosure and – New Labour buzzword coming up – transparency, might have actually manifested itself into something tangible. But the gatekeepers of Number 10 decreed that the only acceptable position was one of retrenchment, and keeping their Supreme Leader's head down. And with dissent beginning to stir in the ranks, one began sensing that it might not be the economy that might ultimately undermine the government, nor the sleaze, but the disharmony.

However, no MP had anticipated what the *Daily Telegraph* were going to unleash on them on 8 May, when they started publishing their extraordinary revelations about MPs' expenses. 'Swinegate' not only helped hand Gordon Brown his P45, it was a plague on all the houses, causing mass revulsion from Fleet Street to Sauchiehall Street. And the Conservatives were implicated as deeply as Labour. 'Yet at almost every turn,' as the *Wall Street Journal* pointed out, 'Mr Cameron seemed to be a step ahead of Mr Brown in reacting to public outcry.' Emerging from his home on the morning the paper broke the story, Cameron addressed the cameras, making no attempt to hide his anger: 'I am angry about what has happened. It is out of order, some of this is an abuse of taxpayers' money and I'm going to deal with it.' He later jokingly compared himself to a sheriff in a Western heading for a showdown, John Wayne-style. He then spent the rest of that morning confronting the party members with the worst expenses claims, and telling members of the Shadow Cabinet they would have to pay back money for any questionable claims. He told them, 'This is a hell of a mess for everyone, it is crucially important that we don't wait.' The room burst into applause, and, as one who was there said afterwards, 'He didn't ask, he told.' Not that Cameron himself was entirely blameless, having to pay back £680 charged for repairs to his constituency home, including the removal of some wisteria and ivy from a chimney. He tried to redeem himself and his party by reopening the Tory candidates' list to people who perhaps shared the party's values but who had no previous associations with the Conservatives. Because he had been forced to persuade so many of his MPs to stand down, the party suddenly needed a raft of new MPs to fill the recently vacated (mostly) safe seats. In all, 4000 hopefuls came forward.

Then in June came another half-hearted leadership challenge, with Work and Pensions Secretary James Purnell quitting the Cabinet in response to the party's appalling European election results, and calling on Gordon Brown to stand down in order to give Labour 'a fighting chance' of winning the next election. But although the rebels said that 75 MPs had supported an email calling for a new leader, none was brave enough to support Purnell. However, even though this was a sign of Brown's strength, he showed his weakness by being unable to replace Alistair Darling with Ed Balls. Towards the end of the month, I received the following email from a former member of Brown's inner circle, a Blairite for sure, but one who had finally had enough of the Brown administration: 'Though McBride was the evil goblin in the Brown bunker, the YouTube farce and the Gurkha fiasco shows that where one nasty bastard has been forced out, the incompetents remain. I have to say having worked around Labour circles in the past and knowing most of the principal actors in this farce, even I am shocked by just how utterly useless, spineless, isolated and self-seeking both the Cabinet and PLP are. As one equally disillusioned ex-Blairite said to me yesterday, "I don't just want to dance on Brown's grave, I want to piss all over him and help the weeds grow."'

May also saw the Conservatives extending their poll leads over Labour into double digits, and the gossiping over Gordon Brown's future began to be audible.

Six weeks later, in early July, as Westminster was girding itself for the summer recess, the *Guardian* tried to create a little glory for itself by trying to drag Andy Coulson back into the limelight, by revealing 'fresh' details about phone-hacking by the *News of the World*, the tabloid paper that the spin doctor used to edit. Cameron not only defended Coulson – 'I believe in giving people a second chance. As director of communications for the Conservatives he does an excellent job in a proper, upright way at all times' – but stood by him. On 21 July, Coulson faced the culture committee and denied any knowledge of the phone-hacking scandal, saying 'my instructions to the staff were clear - we did not use subterfuge of any kind unless there was a clear public interest in doing so. They were to work within the PCC code at all times.'

Like all national newspapers, including those who were offered the story and decided to pass, the *Guardian* was seething that the *Daily Telegraph* got to spill the beans about MPs' expenses. It was a perfect *Guardian* story, and they didn't get it. Not only were they reduced to buying the *Telegraph* every morning to see what was actually going on (oh how that must have hurt), but also the sales of their rival during that period outshone their own by an even more profound amount than usual. And so the *Guardian* was thrilled that they had succeeded in creating their own little scandal with their story – one that has been seized on with particularly unsavoury relish by the equally partisan BBC. Coincidentally, and rather ironically, the day the story broke, Nick Robinson used his BBC blog to break ranks. His take on the story? 'Politically inspired protests designed to damage the Conservatives.'

On 23 July, I spoke with Cameron at the Buxton Festival, in the cultural capital of the Peak District. We had seen each other many times since the publication of our book, but this was the first time we'd officially spoken at length for over a year.

So, David, it's been a year since we last officially spoke for the book, and in that time Britain has become a very different place. How has the current economic crisis derailed the Conservative plan for the economy?

Well, I hope it hasn't derailed, but it is certainly a very big challenge – and obviously it's a much bigger challenge than I thought I was facing four years ago, when I became party leader. We've seen this extraordinary whirlwind across financial markets around the world, and the deepest recession in Britain that we've had for 40 years … and although I think we are now starting to look as if we can come out of that recession, the real headache is the massive budget deficit. And that is going to be the biggest test for a Conservative government if we win the election. I'm not sure it's fully understood by everyone, though; in 1976, when the country nearly went bust, with Denis Healey in charge, as Chancellor, we were borrowing 7 per cent of our GDP. Next year we are forecast to borrow 14 per cent, so it's twice as bad. And that I think is going to be the big test for all of us.

A senior Conservative said recently that if the Tories do get in they will be the most unpopular government in memory by the end of the first six months in power. Just how difficult will it be and what hard decisions are you going to have to make?
If we win the election we'll have to forget about short-term popularity. I think if you level with the country and you say to people, 'Look, we're going to have to cut public spending, but we are going to try and do this in a way that brings the country with us.' So for instance the government is going to do its bit – let's have a smaller House of Commons, let's have fewer ministers, let's cut the cost of politics, let's close the MPs' final salary pension scheme, do things like that to show that everyone is going to play their part and do your best to protect the front-line services. I think the country will respond by saying, 'Yes, we know we're living beyond our means, we know this needs to be dealt with.' So I don't know how unpopular you would be having to take those decisions but what I do know is that you can't expect the country to come with you unless you tell them how difficult it's going to be. I wouldn't pretend we've done that completely but as a party we've said we're going to have to cut public spending, and I don't think any opposition has ever said that. And I think we have started to identify some things we will not do: national identity cards, regional assemblies … We've now got to go on and say, 'Right, here are some things that would be quite nice to do if we could,

but actually we really can't afford them.' That's going to be tough and testing but I think people expect that before elections.

You announced recently that if the Conservatives win you would abolish the Financial Services Authority and hand regulation of all Britain's major banks to the Bank of England. This generated a largely positive press, but a) why did it take you nearly a year to announce this, and b) isn't this just the Conservatives sidestepping responsibility?

One of the things we've got to recognize is that the system in Britain has failed, and failed very badly. Of course banks were collapsing all over the world, and there was a financial crisis and a credit crunch but we were particularly badly affected. It seems to me we've got to learn the three big lessons of what went wrong in Britain. The first was the government was borrowing too much, even before we went into the recession, so we've got to have a more fiscally responsible approach, and that is exactly what we will do. The second thing that went wrong is that we had borrowed more as a country than almost any other country in the world and here I mean not just the government but all of us: individuals and businesses. I think the problem was in what Brown had set up, this tripartite arrangement with the Treasury, the Financial Services Authority and the Bank of England, there was no one who could actually call time on debt in the economy and say, 'Right, the party has gone on too long, we're all borrowing too much, these 125 per cent mortgages have got to go.' There was no one to do that, so we say the way to correct this is to give that power to the Bank of England, make them the referee who can be on the pitch who can actually blow the whistle and say, 'This has gone too far.' The third thing I think that went wrong is that clearly some banks made irresponsible decisions. The current system failed to stop them, so we're asking the Bank of England to call time on that sort of behaviour. And I think in the end a good regulation is not just about having the right rules, it's about having strong institutions that know when to step in. So it's not sidestepping, I think it's quite a big bold move. We took our time over it because we wanted to talk to the experts; we wanted to hear their views, to try and take people with us.

Gordon Brown has obviously cast the next election as the choice between Labour investment and Tory cuts. Would you cut public spending by 10 per cent?

I would cut public spending; I'm going to have to. For months the Conservatives have said that we're going to have to cut public spending because we simply don't have the money. As a country we've borrowed too much money, we can't just put up taxes, and spending has got to be subject to that, it's part of the burden. You've heard from the Prime Minister time and time again, this endless repetition, that Labour is going to go on investing. But what we're beginning to see is that even on the figures that Brown has announced he's actually planning cuts. Whoever wins the election will have to make cuts. Of course I want to ring fence the NHS, and treat that in a particular way, but there will have to be cuts elsewhere. So let's start with being honest – we are saying we're going to have to make cuts, and Brown needs to do the same. Because frankly, whoever wins the election has got to be straight with people and say, 'This is going to be a difficult and tough period, we will come through it, we're a very strong country, we have brilliant businesses, great entrepreneurs, fabulous universities, incredibly talented people, we'll get through it.' If we don't do that, it won't just break the government it will actually break the country.

What about tax? Would it be possible for you to reduce the top-rated tax, the 50 per cent tax rate?

Well, I don't think the 50p tax rate is a good idea because it waves a flag that says, 'Entrepreneurs and enterprising people not welcome here.' But I can't make a promise now that we're going to be able to do that straight away, because as I say, the country is borrowing too much money. We've got to get that borrowing down so the 50p tax rate has got to join the queue of all the tax raises that I don't like, and would like to get rid of. But I can't make a promise that we're going to do that straight away, I can't I'm afraid.

What about defence? I mean you said there was going to be a budget review, but you've not committed yourself to any increases in expenses. How do we know that you are going to take the military any more seriously than the current government?

This country today is at war, we are fighting a war in Afghanistan and we need the Ministry of Defence, and we need the government to be on a war footing. This is about commitment and focus. We need to be successful in Afghanistan, while over time being able to build up the Afghan national army and an Afghan police force and therefore to be able to leave the country. Because no one wants troops there for any length of time, we don't want it, the Afghans don't want it. That's what we should be focused on. And my criticism of the government is simply their lack of focus. I want the mission to be very tightly defined. It's all about security, it's not about building the perfect democracy. We're not going to achieve that, it's about stability and security and denying that country to the terrorists. If we can do that, then we can bring our troops home. And that's a priority. Yes, it would cost money, but it's the focus more than the money that's the issue.

But surely the escalation of fatalities in Afghanistan must have changed the way you feel about the way the military is funded?

Yes, it means that we've got to get the money on the front line. Just take this recent row about helicopters. Our forces have got around 500 helicopters. The number in Afghanistan is less than 30. I just think that's not good enough. We should have spent more of the last three years getting the resources out to the front line. One small example: there are eight Chinook helicopters, the big troop carrying helicopters that we bought in 2001 for a princely sum of £250 million. They've been sitting in this air-conditioned hangar in Hampshire since 2001, for eight years, because of problems with software and problems with equipment. Now, if you want to do something, if you want to sort something out, don't tell me it takes eight years to do it. If there had been a real focus, a real effort to get this right, more of those helicopters could be where we need them, which is in Helmand province.

You announced the 'Tickets for Troops' initiative, where returning soldiers will be getting free or discounted tickets for sports events, music events etc. This echoes many things you've said before about social responsibility, and the fact that you don't necessarily need massive legislation. In your mind there's a lot of little things that amount to quite a lot.

I think a lot of things have changed since 9/11. We've obviously increased our funding of the security services, and we have tougher laws against terrorism, but have we really as a country recognized enough the enormous amount that we're asking our armed forces to do? I remember my friends who joined the army as they left universities or as they left school and the experience that they had might have involved some very difficult and tough things, but the experience then and probably the experience now, where young people are joining up and almost instantly being thrown into a real war-fighting environment in Afghanistan, or previously in Iraq, is completely different. And I want to say that I think we need to catch up as a country and recognize that we need to do just way, way more for our armed forces. Now the government's got to do its bit and I've said, for instance, the leave of an army soldier should start the moment they get back home, not the moment they leave Helmand because often it takes three days to get back. For instance, if you are married to someone in the army and you're posted around the country, and you need a hip operation today and you go to the bottom of the queue. I think you should go to the top of the queue. So the government should do its bit, but what I'm saying is actually we should be asking everyone in society, 'What more can we afford?' And actually, football clubs, for instance, have responded to this call by saying they'll set aside tickets for matches. And the same goes for boxing matches, the O2 Arena in London have said they'll set aside tickets for our troops. So that actually we as a country recognize that we need to do more for these people because of what they're doing for us.

It's assumed that the general election will probably take place on 6 May 2010, but what sort of country do you think we'll be living in then?

By then I think we will be slowly coming out of the recession, but although confidence is growing, things will still be very tough. The problem we're going to face is this overhang of debt, and living beyond our means. I think that is going to get worse and I think it will feel worse next year. I think all the time we put off acting on this problem we build up greater problems for our future. And also I think it will start to sap the confidence of the consumer, of the businessman or woman because while they know this debt isn't being dealt with properly, it actually makes them feel less confident about the state of our economy. I worry that the next few months is just going to be a time of great drift. Because when you're eleven months away from an election, even if Labour were a brilliant government, it's very difficult to take long-term decisions. Because they're thinking, 'How do we get to the position where we might win an election?' So they keep making more and more short-term decisions and I think that's what we've got now. All opposition leaders always ask for a general election. I get out of bed in the morning, kiss my wife and then I call for a general election. Well, last night I was in Norwich [for the by-election] so actually there was no one to kiss. But I do think the case for an election now is very strong, on a couple of grounds. One is the expenses scandal, which I think has shown that no matter what a parliament does to sort itself out, the people have a right to get involved. But I think we've got long-term problems too: namely the massive budget deficit, making sure we get the strategy in Afghanistan right; dealing with the broken society; we've got these big long-term questions and we've got to start addressing them now. So my worry is that the next eleven months are going to be wasted. And that's why I get out of bed and do those things every day.

Today's by-election in Norwich North is the first chance that voters have for voicing their anger since the expenses scandal, and you're obviously expecting victory.

I never make predictions! I've been to Norwich six times in the last month, and what I've found is that the British public, rightly in my view, are very sceptical, very apathetic and also quite pissed off with all the major political parties. They're angry with us. And they want us to prove that we are worth voting for. One of the reasons I keep going back and why my team have worked very hard is that people want to see the politicians on their doorsteps, explaining themselves, answering questions, showing that actually they do care, that they do want to change things and that politics mean something. And I think that's a good thing actually. We should be working harder because we've got to make up for the mess of the expenses scandal.

How do you re-engage with people, how do you get people enthused in politics again? The expenses scandal has angered people far more than any politician or indeed any newspaper thought it would …

I think the answer is 'local engagement'. Some ask what we're going to do about the BNP. It's appalling that in our country, a tolerant liberal open friendly democracy, in the European elections we elected two dreadful fascists to the European parliament. I feel ashamed about it, but just attacking them and slagging them off isn't going to solve the problem. You beat the BNP and the extremists by getting onto the doorsteps of the people who are thinking of voting for them and saying, 'Don't opt for this. You know the problems that you're concerned about – whether it is the shortage of affordable houses, whether it's the need to get a job, whether it's the school you're worried about your kids going to. We, the mainstream politicians, are on your doorsteps, holding public meetings, engaging all the local issues you care about and not just floating around in Westminster.' I do a lot of public meetings, and what I do is hold a meeting with the local Conservatives beforehand to stop them coming to the public meeting. I do this because I want the public meeting to be actually those people who either vote for a different party or don't vote at all or hate all of us. Because those are the people you need to convince and I think old-fashioned public meetings is a good way of doing it. Even though they get a bit rough sometimes …

Even though you're obviously saying that you are taking nothing for granted, as you are quite right to, even if you think otherwise, what plans are you making for Downing Street … how will you approach the role of Prime Minister?

Well, I've not made any plans for the curtains or fixtures or anything like that. The way I approach it is simple. You have to look at the very big challenges the country faces, and we've talked about some of them. I approach it as teamwork. I don't think the Prime Minister of the country can be the Chairman, Chief Executive, Chief Financial Officer and the Chief Operating Officer. You've got to have a good team. And you've got to be able to stand back as a Chairman that appoints and runs your team and give your people responsibility and allow them to get it right or get it wrong. When I became leader, one of the first things I did was bring back William Hague. It took some persuading but I'm really glad and I think he will be a brilliant Foreign Secretary; he's an absolutely first class politician and a very capable man. At the beginning of this year, when the economy was in great difficulties, George Osborne and I spent a lot of time persuading Ken Clarke to slip those Hush Puppies back on and come back into the Shadow Cabinet. He was the last Chancellor of the Exchequer to lead the country out of the recession and into recovery. He loves to point out that he was elected to Parliament in the year George Osborne was born. You need a strong team that combines youth and experience that works as a team, and actually trusting them is one of the most important ways of approaching this job. It's certainly the way I act in opposition.

You're going off like everyone else to your summer break soon; what will you be thinking about, what plans will you be making for the autumn as we go into the conference season?

I've mainly been thinking about how to get my children to sleep between 8 o'clock in the evening and about 7 o'clock in the morning because there's quite a lot of bed-hopping that takes place in my house and that's not good for the rest that I need. So the first thing is just to have a lovely family holiday and switch off. I think you need to do that in a high-pressure job. You need to spend some time with your family and rediscover who you are. And you think about other things than work. One of the keys to making good decisions is making sure you bring to those decisions your character and your judgement and hopefully some poise and detachment. And if you work so hard that you get completely fried in the head, and totally ragged, you start making bad decisions and bad judgements. So holidays are very important to me, to relax a bit, and then get the batteries charged up for what lies ahead.

Here is a quote from Rupert Murdoch: 'David Cameron is a very charming man. He's a family man. I like him. But what does he really feel in his stomach?' He still doesn't know what you stand for ...
What do I feel in my stomach? Hungry! I think if people look back over the last four years, I would hope they would get a sense of what I bring to the Conservative Party and hopefully what I as the leader of the Conservative Party can bring to the country. The first thing that I wanted to do was to modernize the party. I'm a Conservative and I believe in the core principles of strong families and free enterprise and a deep sense of patriotism, but I thought we needed to modernize and adapt and apply our principles to the modern world. And we needed to make some changes, so I hope people see me as a modern Conservative. The family is the most important thing in my life, in fact I think the most important thing in any successful society is to strengthen families and to recognize that, as I put it, 'they are the best welfare state there is'. I'm a great optimist about human nature, and I think politics ought to be more about trust – instead of government trying to do everything itself, it should pass power outwards and downwards and trust people and communities to do more for themselves. I think we need that more than ever in Britain, as I think we've become a very centralized, bossy, interfering, overbearing government state in Britain and we need to get rid of that bureaucracy and political correctness and nonsense and rely on people

to do more themselves. I was very keen to modernize some parts of the party – for instance to get us to have more women candidates, which desperately needs to happen. I'm proud of the fact that if we win the election we will go from having a pathetically few 17 women MPs on the Conservative side to over 55 ... hopefully even 60. That's still not enough but you know, in the modern age, if your party doesn't reflect the country, then I think you've got a problem. I think some people sort of thought, 'Well what's this all about, what's the point of all this?' I think they just didn't necessarily immediately get the importance of it, but I don't regret any of those things, I think they are vitally important.

Nightmare scenario: Tony Blair is fed up. Obama is getting all the glory in the Middle East. He's spending far too much time at home with Cherie. He's made all the money he needs from his lectures and so he decides to stand again. Hey folks, Tony's back! He's not a sitting MP but I'm sure that's a technicality that could be easily solved. You would be petrified of going up against Blair, wouldn't you?

No, no. I'm on my second Labour Prime Minister, I'm on my fourth leader of the Liberal Democrats. I'm actually the longest-standing leader of a major British political party. I'm the old man. I became leader in December '05, Blair didn't go until, when did he go, '07? So I had a good couple of years of being up against him. I seem to remember we were doing all right then. In the end it's not the personal stuff that matters, it's the record of this government that matters – and they've simply been in power for too long. I think everyone can sense we need to change. And the key is whether the Conservative Party is ready and capable of delivering that change. And I don't think it would make that much difference if you suddenly swapped Brown for Blair or Alan Johnson or anyone else. All you can do in politics is focus on your job. And if I'm doing my job properly it doesn't matter who we're up against, we'd still have a fair chance at the general election. So, Tony, come on back, bring it on!

We seem to be having a rather tough time in terms of public and private surveillance and there are an increasing number of ways in which individuals can become criminals in this country. What would your party do, as a priority, to roll back the legislation that caused this?

I agree with you that the surveillance state has become too powerful, and we do have some very concrete plans for changing that. The last time I was asked a question like this I replied in a German accent and I got into a bit of trouble over it. I actually received emails from Germans saying it was a perfectly acceptable joke but I'm not going to do that again. But personally, what I think we should do is scrap the national identity card scheme in its entirety, not just the cards but also the identity register that is being drawn up. I also think there are too many public officials who are now allowed to enter your home or to spy on you in your neighbourhood. I think it's gotten completely out of control and we will hack that right back. Of course the police need to have the power of 'stop and search' in certain circumstances but the way they've been able to use terrorist legislation to actually stop and search people for offences that have nothing to do with terrorism I think is wrong as well. So we'd change that. Speed cameras? Don't get me started, but they should be about safety, not about just raising money. I'd like people to have a sense at the end of this process that they are living in a freer and fairer country.

It seems that taxes are the price we pay for civilization. If we are a civilized society, in which we care for the elderly, the disabled and invest in our children and in the services we have around us, then surely we need to think about increasing taxes. Is this something that the future Conservative government will do? What would your government do?

I'd like to avoid further tax increases. I haven't ruled them out because we are in such a critical financial situation it wouldn't be responsible to do that. But then you look at the last ten years, we've had a lot of increased taxes; just take one, the tax we probably all hate the most which is Council Tax. For almost everyone Council Tax has doubled over the last ten years. You probably all pay now £1500/1600 compared with £800 in 1997. So it's doubled. But can any of us actually say that the services are twice as good now as what we had before? We've got to get more value for money out of that public spending. Now of course, some public spending reduction will be painful and will be difficult and will involve making tough choices.

I'm working on the assumption that you'd love the opportunity to display your intellectual gravitas and wondered if you could imagine if a student who is interested in political philosophy came to you, say on the verge of university, and said, 'Could you give me three books that I should read?', what three books you would suggest ...

About political philosophy? I think I would suggest some John Stuart Mill. I think the great British tradition of liberty is so entrenched in his work and I think that would get the brain whirring and it would be a very good start. I think I would argue that a sceptical disposition is always important in politics. There are many politicians who've got fantastic dreams to remake the world, to change everything, to have some great utopia that they are going to deliver. And I think in politics you need to have a healthy dose of scepticism so I think some David Hume or John Locke, two of the great British sceptical philosophers, would probably be a good idea. And then I suppose when they got through the Hume, the Locke and the Mill, and they need a bit of light relief and that's the moment to reach for Immanuel Kant! I think if you think about the action you're about to take, what lies behind should be a moral rule for others to follow. I think that's a very good piece of moral philosophy to try and think about in politics. And I think it's one of the great philosophical battles we all have to face in politics, between Mill's concept of saying, 'Let's always pursue the greatest happiness of the greatest number,' which can lead sometimes to trampling on individual liberties ... The conflict between that and Kant's universal rule for all. It's a good battle to have, I think ...

What do you currently think of the state of the education system in this country?

The state of the education system in this country I think I would describe as mixed. I don't have any concern about the private sector, because people choose to pay if they want to and have the means, and I think we should frankly stop trying to meddle with it all and just let it get on with itself. My concern is about the state sector, and there the picture is mixed. There are some very good state schools but there are some that are still failing generation after generation of children. There are still parts of the country where a lot less than 50 per cent of young people are getting five good GCSEs and that's just not good enough. And so I think what we need to do is to open up. We need to do two things. The first is standards. I think we should have a real push for very stringent standards and discipline. I think we've got to end this concept of dumbing-down, and this idea that the system must be designed so everyone can win a prize. I think we've got to end this idea that indiscipline is OK. I want to have a really tough and rigorous and dare I say, almost quite old-fashioned approach to standards and discipline – teaching maths in the proper way, teaching reading in a traditional way, not accepting indiscipline, giving teachers the right control in the classroom, giving head teachers the ability to exclude people who behave badly, and not having a situation where they get overruled by an appeals panel and get completely undermined. So I want a real crusade for rigour and discipline in the classroom. Plus obviously I want to open up state education and have greater competition and diversity. One of the good things Tony Blair did was launch the Academy programme, encouraging the private sector to get involved in the state sector, offering a free and high-quality education. If there is so much innovation and competition in the private sector, why can't we have that in the state sector? In some of our cities it really is still very difficult to find good secondary education, which is quite frankly disgraceful and one of the ways of dealing with it is to open up the provision of secondary school education and allow other organizations to come in where there is currently failure.

Would it not be a small way of helping the elderly for the state pension to be taken out of the tax equation?

It's an interesting idea but would bring a huge cost with it. I think there is something simpler that we can do, that we actually recommended in this year's Budget. This year's Budget was basically going to put up public spending by another £30 billion and we said instead of doing that, save £5 billion of the increase and use it to abolish income tax on people's savings if they pay tax at the basic rate. It would have been good in the short term because it would have helped people who are getting very little money from their savings because interest rates are so low, but it also would have been good in the long term because it would have encouraged savings. I still think we've got to look at next year's Budget and see if we can find a way of paying for it again. But it's something I'm actively considering because I think it's an extremely good idea.

Do you think that the traditional terms left wing and right wing still have any real relevance in modern society? And if not, how would you yourself define the current political parameters?

They mean a lot less than when I first got interested in politics in the eighties, but they're still there. Back then the Labour Party was committed to state ownership, and the Conservative Party was – as always – very pro-enterprise. But those on the left still tend to look to larger state solutions and those on the right look at more societal or individual solutions, so I think it does still mean something. But I suspect we need to think about politics on a range of different axes – there's the old authoritarian versus libertarian battle ... I mean we've had a centre left government for ten years and we've actually had quite an authoritarian government for ten years. I see a bit of a connection between the two. I also think in the post-Cold War world of politics we should be more relaxed about saying sometimes that our parents did get some things right and that some of those old values worked. However I think the Labour Party got some things right; I think the minimum wage works and I'd keep it. I think giving the Bank of England independence was a good thing. I think it's refreshing if politicians can recognize the good that other politicians do.

Would the next Conservative government be prepared to support the hospices, not the other way round?

I think that's a bit unfair on Labour because there are certainly hospices that get no state money at all. The one that we used for Ivan, when he had some respite out in Oxford, never gets a penny of state money and actually they quite like having their independence. The government has given some money to some hospices but I think, as I said, money is going to be extremely short. I think what we need to do with the health service is try and have a bit more choice and independence. So that when people choose particular services the money follows them. I think that's the way to do it rather than a sort of blanket commitment that every hospice should get a certain amount of money. Having said that, a hospice is a classic example of how brilliant our voluntary and charitable sector is. You know these organizations are always superbly supported by local people. It sometimes drives me mad that the government condescendingly calls the voluntary sector 'the third sector'. Think about the things that the voluntary sector does; it's normally the first sector because it often gets there first. And I think we should give the first sector a lot more long-term contracts, a lot more independence and a lot more respect than they currently get from the government.

Will the Conservatives ever address the Scottish problem? Many English people feel that it's unfair that they get extra out of the cash pot. Have you ever thought about giving the English back their nationality?

I passionately believe in the United Kingdom. I think that Scotland, Ireland, Northern Ireland, Wales and England are stronger together. You know, we've achieved amazing things together, we're like a family and I don't want the family to break up. And what do families argue about? Well they argue about lots of things. But families can argue about money. And yes, let's have a sensible conversation about this issue of money but let's not pretend that there's some perfect answer that's going to make everybody happy and let's not fall out over it. What I don't want to do is say to an audience in the middle of England like this that somehow there is an enormous pot of gold; if only we could stop those greedy Scots taking all our money then we could have all that money instead. That's not the case. I think we should recognize that the different parts of the United Kingdom do want to have a say in how they are governed. Now in Scotland they've decided to have free university access and they've decided to put more money into long-term residential care; that's their decision and we in England, we need to make our own decisions about those things. I don't want us to set up an English Parliament, I think the last thing we'd need right now is another parliament with another lot of politicians with another lot of pension schemes, expenses and all the rest of it. You know I think it would probably be easier to be Prime Minister of England, but I don't want to be Prime Minister of England, I want to be Prime Minister of the United Kingdom. And I'm very keen on keeping it together.

If you become Prime Minister will you do away with the postcode lottery for medical treatment?
I don't think it's possible to say that we will wipe out the postcode lottery, once and for all, everywhere, but I think we can make some serious changes that will make a big difference. To give you one example: if we said to the drug companies, you think you've got this brilliant drug that is going to help cancer sufferers, then why not share the risk? You're never going to get completely identical services in all parts of the country, and find the same school, the same hospice, the same care worker, the same social worker, we're never going to have all of it but I think what we could do is give those carers the same and a much clearer idea of what their rights are and what they are entitled to. When you arrive at these centres you have no idea of what journey you are going on.

You are in Buxton next to the Peak District National Park, one of the most precious parts of the country. How do you see national parks helping in delivering your green agenda?

Unsurprisingly I feel it's fantastically important. I think that we're on the brink of a really exciting opportunity because we've now got an American administration that really does believe that these climate changes are really happening and that the problems are man-made and that we can do something about it. One of the ways we will have to try and make it meaningful to people is to bring it right back down to the local level, and I think national parks do have a role in affecting and enhancing our environment. The restrictions they put upon planning and on building sometimes can be irksome and difficult for people but actually it is wonderful that we have protected areas of the country where you can only build in the local materials and you have to be thinking of being in keeping with the local environment because we are protecting the great natural treasures that our children will benefit from, whether it's the Cotswolds or the Peak District. I think it's a really exciting agenda but we'll never tackle climate change if we leave it all to the government – it's got to be a big challenge for businesses, for individuals, for families, for schools. One of the most exciting plans we've got is to say to people that you can do a deal to spend £6500 on environmentally proofing your house to cut your electricity bill, and you share the benefits of the lower bill. Most people don't have the time, the inclination or the capital to insulate their home better. But if you do you save yourself a huge amount of money and in the Cameron household the central heating doesn't usually go on until December – that's not because I'm fantastically mean, it's because we've put the time into insulating our house properly, and the difference which it makes in terms of our quality of life and the profitability leave me absolutely speechless.

THIRTEEN

'I don't talk about Broken Britain but I do talk about the Broken Society and the parts of our society that are broken. I don't believe I overstate my case at all'

The expenses scandal, 'no drama Obama', public sector cuts, *The Wire*, the conference speech, the election campaign … and being stuck in a lift with Carla Bruni

Portcullis House – the ugly upside down cow's udder opposite the Commons – was designed by Michael Hopkins, although it looks as though he did this in the dark, possibly using Plasticine and some peat briquettes. This is the building through which those in David Cameron's inner circle march every day to get to their offices. After a while you can start to think of its lobby as a current affairs version of the bar in *Star Wars*, the one peopled by a galaxy of freaks. It is also something of a research assistant catwalk, and there are enough Tamzins, Tabithas and Tamaras here to put a serious spring in your John Lobbs. You never get the hordes of tourists you see at the Reichstag, but they wouldn't be disappointed if they pitched up here instead of across the road. If you spend enough time there it starts to feel like one of those places where, if you stood there long enough, you'd bump into everyone you'd ever met, everyone you'd ever read about. Whenever I visited I'd see Frederick Forsyth scuttling about, or Charles Clarke looking as though he was running from something large and forbidding. Steve Hilton would be rushing around looking like a backpacker in his T-shirt and baggy shorts without shoes or socks. He often looked so mad I thought he must be testing the parameters of decorum, seeing if he could get thrown out or not. Sometimes I thought he simply forgot to get dressed in the morning, as though presentation were something he shouldn't really concern himself with. Odd, really, when presentation is such an important part of his job.

On the morning of 18 September, 2009, a short walk away in Broadway House in Tothill Street, the Chairman of the Conservative Party, Eric Pickles, was parading some – mainly Asian – Liberal Democrats who had recently defected to the Tories in front of the press. Pickles was sporting a yellow Tintin tie in honour of his guests – 'It's the only yellow one I had!' he told Cameron when he arrived. The Conservative leader was due in Frome, Somerset, that day, to visit a marginal seat, and meet the local county councillors. But he popped in to a meeting with the defectors before they were thrown before the assembled hacks. The discussion revolved around the Lib-Dems' prime policy concerns – the environment, education, health, family, community. 'We've had such a lack of leadership, as has the country,' said one defector, 'and we like the fact you've extended your "hand of friendship" as you call it.'

'We're leaving the Lib-Dems because there is no team,' said another. 'Vince [Cable] is the team. There's Nick Clegg of course, but there's really only Vince.'

Cameron sat and listened to them for a while before butting in. With a smattering of small flecks of grey in his thatch, he suddenly looked about five years older than he had a few weeks previously; not that this was an issue for him, seeing that he had always looked younger than he ought to have done.

Anyway, his head was swelling with all the praise. 'You need to promise change, and we need someone who is innately an optimist,' said another defector. 'And you are.' 'I think the good looks and the sex appeal help!' said another (male this time). The feelings appeared to be mutual, because later Cameron would describe this new batch of defectors as 'mostly extremely beautiful, one of whom used to be a belly dancer'.

We took the Underground from Westminster to Paddington, along with Andy Coulson and Cameron's trusted aide, Liz Sugg, and mostly discussed *The Wire*, David Simon's much-acclaimed police series set in Baltimore – 'I'm on series three but Samantha's only on series one so there's a bit of disconnect in our house right now' – and *The Thick of It*, the Westminster spoof – 'The closest person to Tucker in our team is Gabby!' As Coulson fed him news stories from his BlackBerry we chatted about the use of virals during the upcoming election campaign, the possibility of a Labour leadership challenge ('Unlikely, although Ed Balls is keeping up his ridiculous profile') and Labour's farcical 'safeguarding' suggestions announced earlier in the week (making it necessary to fill out a form if you drive your neighbour's child to school).

The day before he had been speaking at the Woodstock literary festival along with the *Independent*'s Editor-in-Chief, Simon Kelner, although Cameron was rather coy about mentioning that two days previously they had both been performing karaoke at Blur's Alex James's birthday party. 'My previous line on karaoke was that it was perfectly acceptable if I was abroad, but at least I don't think there were any cameras in the room. I hope!' His chosen song that night had been 'A Hard Day's Night', 'because I find it's better to sing something old, something familiar and something fairly easy to sing. Even I couldn't muck up a song like that.'

On the train to Frome he was constantly interrupted by Coulson, who was sitting halfway down the carriage, and who kept receiving news of more spinning by Labour's press office about the Tories' spending cuts. 'Jesus, I love the way they spend so much time decoding our spending plans when they can't even work out their own,' said Cameron, laughing. 'If you can't believe what the government says about its own spending plans then why should you believe what they say about ours?'

He then asked me who Piers Morgan was interviewing for the next issue of *GQ*, and nearly spluttered into his tea when I said it was Gordon Brown.

'If we could get Piers to vote for the Conservatives then we really will have a chance!' he said.

'I think he may be the last skittle to fall,' I said.

The phone rang. It was Samantha. 'It's your turn to put dinner on the table, because I did it last night,' said Cameron, before haggling about how they were going to spend the weekend. Turning to me he said, 'At the last conference Samantha said, "You force me to come to conference, you keep me cooped up in a hotel room while you write your speech and get increasingly irritable and then I go out and say the wrong thing and then it's time to go home." Which is fair enough, I suppose!'

As the train hurtled down to Somerset, we spoke …

And why are we going to Frome?
Why am I doing these meetings? Because politics has become a bit boring – we visit a school, do a TV interview, and I want to shake it up a bit. I'm having an old-school, old-fashioned public meeting. And I'll be honest about it, this is a marginal constituency and the people in these rooms could decide the election.

What sort of election campaign are you planning to run?
Basically a positive one. We are asking people to change their government after 12, 13 years and we'll be giving people positive reasons about the things that we will do to make the country a better place.

This campaign is going to be very different from the campaign you thought you'd be running a year ago.
Yes, I think that, I mean the economy is always an absolutely key issue at any election but I think the scale of the challenge in rebuilding the nation's finance system is so enormous. Look, if you put it in perspective, in 1976 when Denis Healey took the country to the brink of bankruptcy, we were only borrowing 7 per cent of our GDP, but according to the OECD [Organisation for Economic Co-operation and Development], it's twice as bad, and we're going to have to borrow 14 per cent. So even if we wipe out the deficit we'll still be back to where Denis Healey got us. So the challenge is that big. That's why I spend a long time talking and explaining about it because I want people to understand how difficult this is.

And the only alternative to increasing debt is to reduce public spending?

Yes, that's why I've been saying very clearly for the last few months, if you elect the Conservative government we're going to have to reduce public spending. But you've got to tell the public that in advance of the election. And up until yesterday Gordon Brown was completely refusing to do that. Over and over in the House of Commons saying, 'We are the party of investments and the Tories are the party of cuts.' He called me 'Mister 10 per cent' because according to him I was going to cut 10 per cent of public services, and actually this week we revealed that the Treasury itself is planning cuts of 9.3 per cent. I mean we've got to be straight with people about this. It does require leadership and it will mean difficult decisions and it will mean some difficult discussions with the trade unions. The public sector trade unions are very powerful, they have a lot of members and I don't think at the moment they are being remotely realistic about the problem the country faces. But they've got to be, because we cannot go on as we are. If you go on borrowing huge amounts of money, then a) You increase the pressure on interest rates, b) It's going to mean much higher taxes, and c) We are going to add to our national debt in a way that our children would be rightly furious with us about. So we've got to deal with it. How do we do it? You've got to start with yourself. And that's why I said if we win the election, ministers' pay will be cut and then frozen, and the House of Commons will be 10 per cent smaller. We will get rid of all those subsidies that drive people mad, reduce the number of ministers having chauffeur-driven cars, subsidized meals and house loans and the rest of it, and we'll get rid of the regional assemblies. The whole of Whitehall is going to have to take a very big haircut. The next step is to get rid of the things we don't want to do, like the ID cards and the big databases.

Are you an optimist?

Yes, I really do believe in my heart that I am, that's why I'm a Conservative, because I do believe if you do give people more power and control over their lives they will make the right decisions about their own life.

Conservatives may not believe in Utopia but we do believe that a good society is one with empowered citizens making choices for themselves. If that's what you believe then you have to be an optimist.

Are you too much of an optimist?

No, I don't think so. I think if you take the issue of the deficit and the scale of it and you take what we were saying over the last year, that other countries, if they can afford to, should have a fiscal stimulus, but Britain couldn't because we couldn't afford to, that was a very realistic message, a very tough message. We attacked the VAT cut for the same reason. Look, it's lovely to cut people's prices in the shops, but we thought it was wrong and we said so. I think there's a hardheaded realism in the heart of my sort of Conservatism. It's not starry-eyed but I do believe there is genuine light at the end of the tunnel which is that if you get your national finances under control, you give people more control over their lives and you strengthen your society, then you have a more responsible and better country and we'd all feel better and happier for it.

What do you think are your greatest weaknesses?

I wouldn't describe it as a weakness, maybe as a challenge but clearly if you've been out of power for 13 years then clearly the challenge is that you've got to explain to people that you've got the right team, you've got the right experience, got the right ideas, you're asking people to take quite a big leap, because you're saying, 'Give up this government that you've had for 13 years and come to us!'

And you're obviously assuming they're going to make that step …

I'm not assuming, I believe that they should. I'm working to try and convince them that it's the right thing to do. We've had this conversation before about complacency and I was looking at a presentation only yesterday and it pointed out you have to win 117 seats to have a majority of one. Margaret Thatcher, Tony Blair, they didn't have to win anything like this many. This is a challenge of historic proportions. The Conservative Party has not gained this many seats in an election at any time since

1931! So there's a very good reason for not being complacent because it's an accurate reflection of the scale of the mountain in front of us.

What do you think Peter Mandelson is planning for the election?
I expect a very negative campaign, very personally hostile, that's the sort of thing that gets him out of bed in the morning.

He is extremely hostile towards you, personally hostile.
Yes, I expect so, and then if you look at the sort of campaigns they've run in prior elections you know, whether it's the Crewe by-election, dressing everyone up in top hats, whether it's pictures of me as a chameleon or this nonsense about Labour being the party of investment and pictures of me as Mr 10 per cent, you know they've been very personal, very negative. They try to frighten people by saying we will take away old people's free television licences, which is simply not true. So I expect a very negative campaign. I don't think they've got anything positive to say because they are negative. But I think people are just beyond that and they will see through it.

You must sometimes wish he worked for you.
No I don't, I wouldn't have anyone like that working for me, although I do sometimes think he is working for me!

You're continually telling the electorate that we live in a Banana Republic, and do you think the message is finally getting through?
Oh, I hope I don't overstate my case in any way but I think, the warning about the scale of the deficit, the scale of the borrowing, I think is right. I have been criticized on occasion for speaking in very frank terms about the risks that we run in terms of not being able to pay our debts, in terms of undermining the financial stability and Britain's good name and all the rest of it, but I think it's justified. I think everybody knows that the financial situation in the country is perilous. I think everybody knows about the situation in our society. I don't talk about Broken Britain but I do talk about the Broken Society and the parts of our society that are

broken, I don't believe I overstate my case at all. And like I said I don't have to because we have real problems with real people.

Obviously everyone is expecting cuts after the election, but what sector should expect them first?
To state the obvious, these are public spending reductions so obviously the private sector, and many companies and many businesses within it have had to go through what the public sector now needs to go through in terms of cutting costs, finding efficiencies and getting costs under control. But no other area – other than International Development – should be entirely exempt. The health service can expect overall real-term spending increases because the NHS is special and the cost pressures on it are so great, but otherwise no area should be exempt. But no area should be particularly singled out. And I've also said, I do understand you can't make progress unless you take a look at the big issues like public sector pay.

Aren't you going too far by ring-fencing the NHS from cuts? It's the third largest employer in the world, GPs earn a fortune, and yet, in order to make people think you're not the nasty party, you're going to completely spare it. Isn't this unfair on everyone else, both other public sector workers and taxpayers generally?
I don't think so, because it's right. If you look at the cost pressure from the drugs budget or the cost pressures from new treatments for the ageing population I think it would be unrealistic to expect a real-terms cut for the NHS. Clearly they're going to have real-terms increases, but every budget is going to be restricted and so these will be small real-terms increases and the NHS itself is going to have to find a lot of efficiencies because otherwise it won't be able to pay for the treatments and the drugs and the health care of the elderly. There's an awful lot of waste within the NHS that we can address and we will.

Well, like what?

Well just have a look at the bureaucracy. I mean we increase the number of bureaucrats faster than the number of nurses at the moment. Why? Well if you have a slew of top-down targets set by government you are going to have to have an army of bureaucrats measuring whether you're meeting them and then reporting back to you. The whole thing is generating an enormous industry. I was speaking to a psychiatrist in my local constituency a few weeks ago who said that ten years ago he used to feel that the management in the hospital was working to help the doctors do their job, and now he feels as though he's working for the managers to help them do their job. And I thought that was beautifully put. And I know exactly what he means because the target-led culture has replaced the patient-led culture and we need to have a patient-led culture.

OK, what about the police? You've said you're going to get rid of the paperwork but you're also going to cut their budget. That doesn't work. Chris Grayling said a few months ago that, if elected, the Conservatives would stop the practice of warning youths involved in assaults, and to make sure they are prosecuted. I think we'd all like this, but this would involve a huge amount of extra police time, at a time when you'll have to start cutting public services. How will this work?

The police budgets are a very good example of where there is an enormous amount of waste and inefficiency. I was at a police station the other day, and pointed out to the police force that they had five different types of car. They said that they have different cars for different areas, and that for highway use they'd just bought an £83,000 Lexus. Clearly there's a huge amount you can do to get police forces to cooperate and to procure equipment on a joint basis and to drive down costs, I mean this is just one example. And also if you get rid of the paperwork – and even Alan Johnson is now talking about this – you can get police officers onto the street.

Everyone knows the next parliament is going to be tricky – a sick economy is going to demand, along with sensitivity, some extremely tough measures. Are you concerned that you've alienated too much of your core support in the party – inside and outside Westminster – to be able to count on enough backing to enact tough measures? You might win the election, but will you really have enough support inside your own party to govern effectively at such a difficult time?

I don't think that's a problem. I think the Conservative Party is in a very good frame of mind because everyone in the party can see that we're winning again. We won the Norwich by-election, we're winning in local government where we took control of Lancashire county council, and I'm on my way down to Somerset where we beat the Liberals – again, somewhere we haven't held for over 20 years. So I think the mood of the party is good and I think the people involved in this party know that difficult decisions have to be made, and they remember, especially some of the older supporters, that government isn't easy. And it's a huge battle to get what needs to be done through and to take the country with you. I think much harder will be getting the nation's finances under control in a way where you can take the country with you and I think that's a real challenge. You need all the courage and determination of a Margaret Thatcher, you also need a way of trying to bring the greatest number of people with us on what will be a difficult journey but nevertheless one that once completed will then give the country the chance to succeed.

Here's a big elephant in the room: public sector pensions. It's plain they are unsustainable at current levels – what are you going to do?

Well, they do need to be reformed. We obviously wouldn't take away people's accrued rights, that would be wrong. But we have to start by closing the MPs' final salary pension scheme, which is one of the more generous schemes. And having done that we can then turn around and have a reasonable conversation with the public sector about pension provision which is rapidly becoming unaffordable.

Will you have to pay 45-year-old public sector workers less than they expect when they finally retire? Or will you stop giving 25-year-olds entering the public sector the same pension rights? I'm guessing that the latter is easier – but isn't it unfair that young people, when jobs are scarce, are effectively paying for a level of comfort in retirement that they themselves won't receive?

I think what it means is that people currently working in the public sector should know what they've accrued up to now, that's theirs by right, but looking ahead we won't be able to continue being so generous.

But the terms of the 25-year-old are going to be very different from the terms of the 45-year-old.

We will treat people fairly, we know that pension provision is a very important part of why people go into the public sector, we want a strong pension system, we believe in savings, we are pro-pensions but we have to make sure it's affordable and reasonable. And also the greatest costs are at the highest end. People who retire on generous final salary schemes who are earning well over 100K at the end of their career.

This is not necessarily money then that they deserve?

I want GPs to be well paid. I want consultants to be well paid, I want head teachers to be well paid but we have to make sure we have a pension system that is fair and affordable.

Given you'll be a leader giving the country some tough medicine, are you concerned about some sort of events like the poll tax riots, or some sort of insurrection like that?

Well, you try and take the country with you, that's why I think it's very important to say these things before an election, not suddenly afterwards: 'Oh my gosh, we didn't tell you we were going to cut public spending!' It's not exactly usual practice for the opposition leader to say we're going to have to cut public spending. That is a very big change from traditional politics. What needs to be done has to be done and we can't let anyone stand in the way of that. But as I say, one of the most important jobs of the government will be to explain and try and take people through what inevitably will be a difficult period.

Will unemployment lead to increased racial tension?
Well, clearly that's been suggested by others. We want a country with low unemployment and a country where people can feel that they are rewarded for their efforts, a country that is fair …

That's not going to happen though, is it?
Well you've got to demonstrate as you reduce public spending and get the deficit under control, you've got to demonstrate that what you're doing is fair. That the better-off in society are paying their share and that the powerful in society are paying their share. That's why I gave the speech last week saying we are going to cut the costs of Westminster, cut the size of the House of Commons and cut ministers' pay. Of course that raises a pinprick of money but is a demonstration of leadership. With this difficult national thing that we're doing the rich and the powerful must play their part.

How will you seek to ease fears of growing racial tension?
I don't see why getting the public spending under control, getting the deficit under control should cause problems in terms of racial tension.

If the economy suffers, unemployment will get worse and things could naturally lead to that. And the immigration make-up in this country is very different to what it was in 1981. We have far more potential racial tension these days, not least because of the number of Muslims in the country.
If you go back to 1981 then you go back to the riots where race was a factor; it was partly because those people felt excluded from society and felt they weren't treated fairly by the police. The country has changed immeasurably since then, the police has changed, we have to keep on demonstrating that you can rise as high as you like in this country according to your talent, and that the colour of your skin or the god that

you worship or where you're brought up is no barrier. As long as we can demonstrate that, then there shouldn't be any problems of race.

How worried should we be about the rise of the BNP? Because they're not going away ...
I think we should be worried because they are a very unpleasant group of people. I think that we'll have to take our responsibility for what we should do to cut them off. I try and make sure that wherever they stand there's a Conservative standing against them. I think the lesson that we've learnt is that you don't beat the BNP by running after them and shouting about their issues and waving a flag. You actually beat the BNP by getting on people's doorstep, by listening to people, by showing them politics that make a difference, particularly at a local level. And you can get things done in terms of housing, health care and education. The BNP go into a vacuum and they go into a vacuum often where Labour has failed so that's why the vacuum can exist. So all of us have to do our bit to show that they aren't going to improve our lives one jot. Because they won't.

Would you say that they are less a threat than five years ago, or more?
More of a threat than five years ago. Their growth is not quite as big as the press make out sometimes. The reason they got a seat at the European election is because the turnout for everyone else was so low. So, as I say, part of it is our responsibility, getting out there, getting our supporters out there, explaining to people that they won't get you anything apart from a divided and unhappy country.

Some in your own party, some would say many in your party, see you as aloof and cliquey. Does this worry you?
Well I don't think it's true, but any worries people have about you, you've got to try and address them. I think if you actually look at the sources of my advice and the breadth of my team and Shadow Cabinet, I don't think that's fair. I persuaded William Hague to come back, persuaded Ken Clarke to come back, the first leader to get George Young to come

back. I regularly meet with all the former chancellors – Lawson, Howe, Lamont, Clarke. Inevitably if you're going to lead a party you've got to get on and make decisions, you can't consult every last person when you make decisions. On the expenses issue I had to make up my mind about what I thought needed to be done and get on and do it. But I don't accept the criticism that I'm just surrounded by a bunch of young folks. That's not right. If you look at the people I've appointed, who did I make party chairman? Eric Pickles – someone who has quite a different life story to my own, and who's an extremely important person in the party. Who did I make Chief Whip? Patrick McLoughlin, an ex-miner and a brilliant example of why the Conservative Party is the real party of social mobility.

You're going to have to be much less green in government than you were when you first became party leader, aren't you?
No, the difference in government is you actually do something whereas in opposition you can only talk about it.

So what exactly are you going to do?
The low carbon economy plans are really exciting – the idea that every household could get up to £6500 spent on their house, cutting the cost of the electricity bill and sharing that benefit with the company that does it. This is a transformational idea. I think our plan for an interactive energy grid where you can generate your own electricity and sell back the surplus … I think the potential of the green technologies with a government that understands them and gets behind them is actually really exciting. I mean these are big things, these are quite transformational things and of course in a four-, five-year government you'd see quite a lot of changes. I think the scale of the ambition and the detail of our plan is pretty transformational and exciting.

What sort of discussions have you had with your wife about her role should you become Prime Minister?
None, really …

Oh, come on, I simply don't believe that!
No, no really because we're busy people and we are quite superstitious people and so there's probably an element of that idea that if you talk about things they won't happen.

I can't believe you haven't discussed it at some level and at some length, because your life will change immeasurably, for both of you. Come on David!
But of course, people said that when I became Leader of the Opposition. Samantha is a working mother, she enjoys working, she likes her job, she's a brilliant designer and me being leader of the Conservative Party didn't change that. And you know, she has a job, a life, a family and of course politics changes your life and I'm sure if we win the election that would make changes to our lives and our family life but I think we'd try to keep the core of it going. If I can put it that way.

In some respects she must be quite fearful of what might happen because you seem to have a pretty good balance at the moment.
Before we were married, when I said I wanted to be an MP, I think she was very nervous, because neither of us knew what was going to be involved. But the more time we've spent together, the longer-lasting your marriage is, you stop worrying too much about what the future holds and know that you are just going to manage it as you come to it.

Fair enough, but there's a real, palpable sense of the inevitable.
There is not! I just don't accept that at all, there is nothing inevitable in life and there is nothing inevitable in politics. And as I said, we have to wait. We haven't won an election from this position outright for 70 years, and this is an enormous challenge. So it isn't just superstition, it is that I know how much effort has to go into the battle ahead.

You will have already planned what's going to happen if you move into office, you must already have an extremely detailed outline of what your first 100 days are going to look like. You must have done this ad nauseam. There must be a plan!

I know what I want to do if we win the election and of course a lot of work is going into how you implement the policies that we have. I have a separate person in the Shadow Cabinet, Francis Maude, and there's a team with him who are going through all of our policies and plans, whether it's education reforms or welfare reforms … he's actually working out what bills we'd need to introduce, what legislation needs to change, what people need to be appointed, what bits of government won't work properly. That is good planning and that is right. And that is where you should put your effort but I think you shouldn't spend time thinking too much about the personal and the domestic, because that's just not the way I work.

Among your inner circle of policy-makers and aides – such as Michael Gove and Andy Coulson – what have the greatest disagreements been about in the past year?

We have good arguments I must say, they don't tend to be fundamental arguments about the direction of the Conservative Party, but the Shadow Cabinet has been incredibly united about the need to modernize and to change. The arguments tend to be more about issues of timing and priority, and of course the economy and how we deal with what is a massive challenge. There was a brilliant article by Hamish McRae in the *Independent* the other day about just what a transformational challenge the next government is going to be for every party. We argue all the time, but in a good way. I'm sure some people think that everyone is terribly deferential, but believe me, that doesn't happen in our office, as you've seen. It is argumentative. That's my style. I like a good argument to get to what the answer is. You test out arguments by having a debate about them. There's no point having a cosy consensus around a table with everyone agreeing with whatever my latest idea might be.

Why weren't you more concerned about the furore that saw Andy Coulson in front of a parliamentary select committee earlier this year?
Well, I was well aware of the circumstances of how he left the *News of the World* and I offered him the job and I said at the time I believe in giving someone a second chance. And all I can say is that in all my dealings with him he has behaved in a thoroughly professional, straightforward and upright way and I would challenge anyone to prove otherwise.

Were you surprised the story disappeared quite quickly?
No, not particularly, no.

Why?
Because, it seems to me, they were having a go at him for the same reason why he'd had to leave the *News of the World* and I don't think you should be punished for the same mistake twice. And the other point was that Andy had done the right thing. Something went wrong on his watch, he took the responsibility, he resigned. Which is not something that always happens in politics.

I know you have answered these couple of questions before but I think it would be good to ask them again …
To see if the answer's changed!

Exactly … To what extent has the City had too much of a free ride in the last ten years?
I think it's been badly regulated and I think politicians have been too willing to think that we can have an unbalanced economy. And I think we've had an absolute wake-up call on both fronts. The regulatory system failed, and we have been clear in saying how we are going to change that. You know, scrapping the tripartite system and suggesting we put the Bank of England back in charge is quite a bold move for an opposition. Normally these complex questions of financial regulation are things you discuss in government.

You benefited personally from the system of parliamentary expenses, some might say 'lavish parliamentary expenses', yet you've castigated certain Tory MPs who have benefited, some to a lesser extent. Do you think you've been guilty of double standards?

No, I don't believe so because I always said, I said this to my party long before the expenses scandal broke, that it was very important to recognize two rules. One is the rules that are in the Green Book but also the rule for what is reasonable. Can you explain to a reasonable person in a reasonable way what you are claiming and would they accept that? And that is why I personally didn't claim for gardeners or cleaners or food. And I claimed for things that were part and parcel of having a second home, like mortgage interest and basic bills. I've never claimed that everything I did was absolutely perfect, indeed one of the bills, famously the 'wisteria bill', which was a proper maintenance bill in the house but I thought because this is open to question I shall pay it back. And I said to all my MPs, look, because the public is angry and because we allowed the system to operate it's no good just saying 'I obeyed the rules', we should make payments back, the things that are open to question, to demonstrate that we understand that people are very angry with the system. And I think that was the right thing to do. As a result Conservative MPs paid back over £250,000.

And then you said you weren't perfect.

Yes, absolutely! I was very straight with my MPs about what needed to be done, about what had gone wrong. I think in terms of how the party has handled this issue, if you go back you can see that I was the first to whip my party on a vote in the House of Commons on the basis of ending the John Lewis list, ending claims for furniture, food and all the things that have caused so much unease. I was the one who suggested that MPs no longer vote on their pay. We've got a very strong track record of understanding that the pay and expenses issue needed to be dealt with and gripped. As for my own expenses, I've always been very happy to explain them, have public meetings about them, publish them all. I think they are a very reasonable set of expenses for a second home, but I can't claim they're perfect as I did pay back that one bill which was absolutely within the rules but I think, as I demonstrated, within the rules is not enough, if there's something you think the public might be unhappy about, pay it back!

Haven't you just been using the expenses scandal as a way of getting rid of older, less compliant Tory MPs who you don't like?
I don't think that's fair. Look, I wanted to make sure that I did my bit, and the Conservative Party did its bit to deal with what has been a massive national scandal and a massive national problem. Yes, there have been some retirements, and I think that's right. I don't accept either that I've been unfair and singled people out. In fact one of the people who's had to resign and retire is Andrew Mackay, who was one of my inner team. I've tried to deal fairly with the issue, and that's not easy like I said because many people were technically within the rules but didn't stand up to the full scrutiny as it were. It's not been easy to get that right, but I would argue that we've had a reasonable approach at the Conservative Party – we had a scrutiny panel go through people's expenses and a proper process was followed. Nothing in life can be perfectly fair but I think this was a better attempt than any other party made to be systematic about it.

We've talked about this before, but if you do become Prime Minister, will you definitely reduce the pay of cabinet ministers given the economic difficulties we're all facing?
We will cut ministerial pay by 5 per cent and we will freeze it for the Parliament. Now while it doesn't raise much money, because we're going to be asking people in the public sector to show restraint, I think it's important that we show a lead that everyone is going to have to tighten their belt.

And your ambition is to cut 10 per cent of MPs, is that right?
Cut the size of the House of Commons by 10 per cent, I think that is manageable. I think you can do it through a boundary review process

that will be not too disruptive. And I'd rather make a promise that is deliverable and do-able than make some pledge to cut Parliament where people will go, 'Hold on a second, will you really be able to get your new MPs to vote for you?' I think this is absolutely deliverable and do-able.

Would you introduce fixed terms for government?
I keep looking at the argument for fixed-term parliaments, and there are some merits but I think there are some demerits as well. I mean you could have a situation where a weak government had to continue, and I think one of the strengths of our system is that it has over time tended to produce relatively strong governments. So for that reason I'm not yet persuaded of fixed-term parliaments. But I think we've got a pretty radical set of changes to politics. Making all public spending available on the internet, to see where the money is going, giving local people the chance to sign up for an issue they want to have a local referendum on, making sure there is a referendum if your council wants to put up the council tax by more than a certain amount, having these open primaries to select candidates. These are big changes. The way we selected Boris in London, the way we selected the candidate down in Totnes, the first ever all-postal primary where we sent a ballot paper to every single person on the electoral register. We sent them the three CVs of the candidates, I think this is quite an important revolution in how we get people involved in politics, how we try and rebuild some faith in the political system.

You spent this morning with a bunch of Lib-Dems who have decided to leave their party and join yours. Would there ever be room for Nick Clegg in your government?
Well, I want to form a Conservative government and that means that there'll be Conservatives in it! I think clearly there are people who are leaving the Lib-Dems and joining the Conservatives as you saw this morning.

Are you remotely interested? Would you welcome him with open arms?
If he wanted to join the Conservative Party he can apply along with everyone else!

That's not exactly a ringing endorsement!
I get on with him fine, we work together over issues like the Gurkhas and over the reform of Parliament, where the government was about to take some rather crazy steps, and we jointly defeated them. I think we have to build the broadest possible coalition to replace the government and give the country another chance so I'm interested in doing that. But as I say I want to win a mandate for Conservative government.

OK, let's discuss the mandate. Polls show that people will vote for you because you're not Brown. The polls don't indicate the kind of positive support that Tony Blair had in 1997. Given that you look likely to be elected as a 'default' Prime Minister, won't it be difficult governing with such a lukewarm mandate?
Of course some people are turning to the Conservatives because they are fed up with Labour, of course that's true. But I don't accept that there isn't positive enthusiasm for what the Conservative Party is offering. If there wasn't, it would be the Lib-Dems that would be winning in Crewe or in Norwich. The fact that we're winning in counties like Lancashire, we're now the largest party in Cornwall, we won in Derbyshire, in Nottinghamshire, in Staffordshire, there is positive enthusiasm for the Conservatives. Would I like there to be more? Yes, but I don't accept the argument that the Conservatives are only doing well because Labour is doing badly. There were plenty of times in the past where Labour didn't do well and it didn't turn into Conservative support. This time it is because the party is changed, refreshed, modernized, it's one strong team. You do see people with an enthusiasm for what we're talking about. And it's a positive enthusiasm for us not just a rejection of Labour.

Does Britain really have the resources to be a global policeman? Aren't those days gone?

We have the ability because of our armed forces and their brilliance, we have the networks of relationships because of NATO, EU, the Commonwealth and our special relationship, but we can't do everything.

But we don't have the resources!

No, I don't accept that, what we have to do is to have a proper defence review so we can see how we match those resources to meet our goals. And the truth is, you know, I think future generations will look back and say, 'Hang on, 9/11 happened and you didn't have a defence review for a decade? What were you guys doing?' You know, we've been fighting a war in Afghanistan, a war in Iraq, Sierra Leone, Bosnia. What the military call 'Wars amongst the people' are going to be more common and yet we are still configured to put lots of tanks in the sort of Cold War-style battle. So I think we need to think seriously how to make sure that we are still a force for good in the world. We can do that, we have the resources and the relationships, but we need the strategies as well.

Let's talk about Trident. It's due to be replaced by 2025, and a decision about it needs to be taken around now. However, given that cuts will have to take place elsewhere, isn't it just wrong to spend billions on a defence system that is unlikely ever to be used? If you renew Trident, aren't you effectively spending all that money simply to maintain Britain's position at the top table of world powers? How will you justify that to people who are being laid off? Do you sacrifice public sector pensions in order for Britain to have a say in what goes on globally?

Well, I'm in favour of us having an independent nuclear deterrent. That's the big question for Britain – do we want one or not? My answer is yes. But then of course you should subject it to a value-for-money test and think how best to do this. But I think Britain remaining a member of the nuclear club with our own independent deterrent is right because it's the ultimate insurance policy for safety in an uncertain world. I mean it's clear the defence challenges we face now are all about having well-equipped, mobile troops that can fight effectively in the deserts and hills in Southern Afghanistan. We've got to think 30, 40, 50 years ahead and think, 'Well, how unsafe could the world be then?' Now clearly we don't face a Soviet Union armed to the teeth as we did in the eighties, but do we really know what will happen in the future? Do we know whether Iran will get hold of nuclear weapons? Can we be certain about other forces that may emerge in the world? And I think that the ultimate insurance policy of having your own independent nuclear deterrent has been right in the past and I think it's right for the future. Should we subject it to a value-for-money test and see if we can reduce the overall cost of it? Of course we should. But should we maintain independent military arms as an insurance policy against nuclear blackmail and against insecurities of the future? Yes, I think we should.

What circumstances will have to exist before you pull British troops out of Afghanistan?
The main circumstance would be there are Afghan troops to hand over to. And we should be working to accelerate that process, to build up the Afghan capacity to keep the peace in their own country. Clearly no one wants foreign soldiers in Afghanistan for any longer than they have to be there; British public opinion doesn't want it, Afghan public opinion doesn't want it either. If you left right now, you'd just leave a vacuum into which the Taliban and potentially terrorist training camps would go. So the circumstances are all about the capacity of the Afghans to do what we're doing themselves.

What's your end date? Is there a point you can't possibly see us being there beyond?
I don't want to say a date, but we can't be there for another decade. I think the tragedy is we have wasted some of the time between 2001 and now and so the pace needs to quicken.

Few people believe Gordon Brown's assertion that keeping troops in Afghanistan reduces the chances of terrorist attacks in the UK. Do you?

I have some sympathy with the Prime Minister here, in that if you look at where the 9/11 bombers came from and if you look at the history of those involved in terrorist plots in the UK – and remember lots of British people died in 9/11 – those terrorists, almost all of them were trained in Afghan training camps. So where the Prime Minister is right is if we pull the troops out now and the Taliban take over again there will be a risk of terrorist training camps setting up again in what would become a failed state. The problem is that there are terrorist training camps still in Pakistan so you have to look at Afghanistan and Pakistan together.

You took a firm line over the conflict between Russia and Georgia last year. People don't believe you will be able to be so firm on similar issues when you're Prime Minister – is there really support for the idea of sending troops to defend countries like Georgia? What do you say to such people?

I think the government was just a bit slow off the mark on that one. Their position is that Georgia should be allowed to join NATO, and that's my position too, but to me it was very important to stand up and be counted straight away when the Russians stormed into Georgia. It was Russia engaging in a bit of brinkmanship in an area of influence, this was one sovereign state invading another and we should be clear about that.

How much sway do you think we have with Obama really, how much notice do you think he really takes of Britain?

I think a reasonable amount. If you look at what's happening in Afghanistan, the British and the Americans work incredibly closely together. I'm not sure if people fully understand how much that's the case and how much the Americans like working with us and we all like working with them. There are particular British officers that the Americans hire and want to work with and we're pretty much embedded in their teams. That's at the sort of micro level. At the macro level I've met

Obama twice, I think he has a very outward-looking view of the world, about America's responsibilities. I think when he comes for instance to Afghanistan, his recognition involves Pakistan, Britain's historic relationship with Pakistan, and how much we need to work together with them to try and make that country more secure. I think there is an understanding that Britain has a role to play and that we are a valuable ally. We shouldn't overstate it, but we should make the most of it.

You've obviously enjoyed meeting him.
Yeah, we got on very well. And the 'no drama Obama' label is definitely right. The last time I met him our meeting was sandwiched between the Chinese President and the Russian President where anyone else would have squeezed the meeting with the virtually unheard-of Leader of the Opposition, but Obama was very calm and just likes to kind of do things in the way he wants to do them, and I admire him greatly.

What surprised you about him?
I think the calmness. He is every bit as calm in private as he appears to be in public. The balance, the equilibrium, the judgement, the reasonableness, are very much there. But he also has a huge grasp of the strategic challenges and the difficulties that lie ahead.

But then I would imagine you probably expected that.
Well yes, but he's very frank in explaining what he's up to. Lots of people, when you say, 'OK, how are you going to handle X?' will give you five reasons why they've got the perfect answer to X. But the President will go straight to the thing he's worried about, and say, 'How are we going to deal with this?' He's very frank, candid, open but intelligent.

And Michelle? You didn't spend much time with her …
Didn't really have a chance to talk to her, Samantha had a meeting with her, she seemed charming and they got along just fine! I didn't because I was with Obama and Hillary Clinton, so I didn't get much of a chance to say hello to them. But she is a formidable First Lady.

Setting the practicalities aside for the moment, would you like to see Robert Mugabe removed by force? Should that involve British force?

I'd like to see Mugabe exit the scene, that is what I would like to see happen. We have a different situation now, where we've got this power sharing. I met Morgan Tsvangirai when he was in London recently and we all desperately want this to work – by which I mean we want Zimbabwe to go in a completely different direction, to address the starvation of the population, to get its economy under control, to stamp out inflation, to be a democracy, to have civil rights. Though can these things happen while Mugabe is still there? Well, I find it extremely hard to believe that. But we're in a different situation where we should do what we can to try and bolster Morgan Tsvangirai and give Zimbabwe a good future. But the faster Mugabe can be encouraged to stand aside, the better everything will be.

To what extent is the focus of the world moving away from Britain? To what extent could this decline be stopped?

The focus of the world is going East and South, and what is happening now in the Pacific is clearly far more important than it ever was. And the rise of China, India, the relationship between China and America, these are centrifugal forces in the world. We shouldn't try to fight that, what we should do is work out how Britain can maximize its influence in this new world. Which is why I've put a lot of stress on the relationship with India. I think we have a shared history and a strong relationship, great exchanges and advantages. We are both democracies, we have some similar challenges, I think this is very important and kind of a new special relationship. We also have to work harder with the relationship with China. But we still have things to bring to the world. We have the English language, we have brilliant universities, we have fantastic armed forces, we have this network of relationships, for instance the Commonwealth, which I think sometimes we don't make the most of. We should be thinking of how we maximize our relationships with this modern world rather than decrying the fact that it's not all about Europe any more.

Do you accept the need for an EU President?
Not as the Lisbon Treaty sees it, no, I don't. I think that if you give an organization a president it will become less like an association of states and more like a country and that's one of the reasons I don't like the Lisbon Treaty.

But you've publicly backed Blair for the role, haven't you?
No, I have not. I don't know where that bizarre article came from. I do not want a European President and I do not want Tony Blair to be the European President. End of story.

The Tories would be powerless to reopen the Lisbon Treaty if it's rati-fied, wouldn't they? So how are you altering your position on Europe?
I don't take it as a fait accompli that it will be ratified and while it remains unratified I will continue to press for the referendum that we ought to have.

I've seen you at many, many events with Gordon Brown – both in public and in private. Some people find it rather amusing that you can share the same space in situations like this. How do you find those meetings? What goes through your mind?
When we meet at state occasions we get along perfectly well, you know we're both able to do that. We don't share a similar outlook about poli-tics or the future of the country and we do have some very major disagreements and we have them in public in the House of Commons.

No, but in private?
We get along. It should be perfectly easy to get on with your political opponents in a reasonable and polite way and I've always managed to do that. With Blair, with Clegg, with Ming Campbell, and with Brown.

William Hague is now your deputy in everything but name, and, rightly or wrongly, there is an assumption that Hague is now closer to you than George Osborne. Not only this, but Osborne was heavily criticized during the first months of the credit crisis for not appearing to have any plausible alternative solution. Would there ever come a point when you might have to sideline George, because it's something that people talk about a lot?

I don't accept that. I think that if you look at George's record through what has been incredibly testing economic times I think he basically got the big judgement right. The judgement to oppose the VAT cut, that was right; the judgement that we should back the government over rescuing the banks, I think that was right; the judgement that we should have a big national loan guarantee scheme rather than lots of fiddly small schemes that the government proposed – I think that judgement was right. To argue for the reduction of public spending has proved completely right as even Gordon Brown has had to abandon his entire lexicon of Tory cuts versus Labour investment. So I don't accept that. Of course I get people coming up to me all the time and reshuffling my Shadow Cabinet for me but I actually think that George has been very impressive as a Shadow Chancellor, and he's bested all the people he's been up against in the job. I think I have the right people in the right places – I think William does an excellent job as Shadow Foreign Secretary, where you really need knowledge and contacts and experience and he uses all of those to great effect. But I think George has done a very good job, and you can see from the polls that when they ask if they'd prefer us or the Labour Party to look after the economy and the public finances, we're now ahead of the government.

But what do you do about minimizing this gossip, because this is something that doesn't go away. Some people are desperate for his scalp.

I think it has rather gone away. Of course he took a knock over, how shall we say, the events of last summer, but that happens in politics. George took a knock, but there we are. It happens. He is tough and passionate about getting this right and I think he has rebuilt from that point in a very impressive way, I really do. And I stuck with him because I think he is the right person for the job and I think that was the right judgement.

I'd like to talk a little about Ivan, if I may. Can you take me through your last few days with him? Did you have any indication there might be anything happening with him that was out of the ordinary …
No, not really. What happened at the end was he had this very distended stomach and it got worse and worse that evening and that night. We were watching out all the time and seeing what we could do … we had so many dramas with Ivan in his life. And then we took him to the hospital. We thought, 'Well, this isn't right and it looks like it's getting worse.' So we took him to the hospital, and, and he died. I mean it was very, very quick. I think we had always worried about the severity of his epilepsy and that that might be what took him away from us but it wasn't, it was a breakdown of his digestion and his organs. It was totally unexpected and very sudden.

Is it possible for you to describe how his death has affected your other children?
They've been obviously grief-stricken. The sadness of the shock hits everybody and I think they knew that … they were old enough to understand, they were very sad, but the amazing thing about young children is that in situations like this they do handle their loss in a very positive way. They talk about it a lot, in a positive way, where as adults we moan. It's been extraordinary to see how positive they are about it.

Would you and Samantha *seriously* consider having another child?
We'd like to, but I don't know. We are very happy, we have a lovely family so fate will decide these things.

When you think of him now, what are your favourite memories, what are the images that spring to mind?
I think on the beach. We were lucky, we had some very good holidays where he wasn't ill, so I think of those. And bathtime, I think, is probably

the other because that was my … I was particularly good at handling him because he was getting bigger … But we have lots of good memories.

Finally on Ivan, did his passing have any effect on your attitude towards your work/life balance?
Yes, it does you know, your children only grow up once. So I do, I try. I took Elwen to school this morning on my bicycle; I tried to convince him that if we both clapped our hands at the same time we'd take off! You know it just brings home to you that you don't get a second chance with childhood so you must make the most of it, and it's for the best.

I want to talk about drugs again. In a year's time, any teenager caught smoking cannabis by their parents may well give the excuse in saying, 'Well, the Prime Minister did it!' Isn't it time you clarified the record about your alleged cannabis use in the past?
Ah, a genius way back into the question! No. I think the line that I drew between your private past and your public present is a fair one, and I don't intend to revisit this.

Yes, but in the past, you've spoken of how drugs have affected someone close to you. Given that you will shortly be in charge of drug policy, should you not tell people clearly how that experience informs or affects your judgement on drug policy - or does not?
I think I've said what I want to say about seeing at close hand the effect that drugs can have on life, I think I hope I've done it in a way that shows that I have some understanding of this issue but without jeopardizing someone's legitimate privacy.

Finally, the end of *Big Brother* – good thing or bad thing?
Good thing, I never really watched it, but what we need is the end of the Big Brother state!

Who would you rather be stuck in a lift with? Obama, Sarkozy, Berlusconi, Merkel, Putin or Carla Bruni?
I think Carla Bruni. But definitely not Carla Bruni with Berlusconi!

* * *

After arriving at Frome station Cameron was taken on a tour of Christ Church First School, and then on to a convivial meeting with Somerset county councillors. I'd heard many of Cameron's jokes before, but then being a successful politician is rather like being a successful stand-up comedian: you need to master the art of repetition to such an extent that it becomes second nature.

And then it was on to St John's Catholic Primary School in Bath, for the 49th Cameron Direct, public meetings to which anyone can come and throw a question at the Conservative leader. We were driven there in a large Mercedes, and on the way Cameron moaned light-heartedly about the Tory car-pool drivers trying to kill him – 'It's never a good idea to drive 100 yards the wrong way down a one-way street. At speed.' We were expecting some local protesters, who had campaigned for the scrapping of a park and ride scheme that involves building in an area of outstanding local beauty. But in the end they didn't come.

Tonight, in front of over 150 people Cameron answered questions on everything from tax to defence, from MPs' expenses to the economy. He said he wasn't going to stop university tuition fees, defended his relative inexperience, denied he is worth £30 million ('And if my wife is worth £30 mill then I haven't seen any of it'), discussed inequality ('The inequality we should chiefly be worried about is the gap between the poorest in our country and what I call the middle. I don't think we'd all be happier if suddenly David Beckham was earning a little bit less money'), said he couldn't wait to get rid of police paperwork, championed banning cheap booze, praised gay marriage, advocated empowering carers, tore into the state ('It should be our servant and not our master'), refused to rule out tax rises, said that public service cuts were unavoidable, repeated his position on Heathrow's third runway (doesn't want it), and was passionate in his espousal of the family ('I want us to be if we win the election the most pro family government this country's ever had'). He also discussed the following ...

Transparency: The MPs' expenses saga has been a national scandal, and we all owe you an individual and collective apology, but one good thing has come out of it. I'm now getting the Shadow Cabinet to publish their expenses online as they claim them. When that happens, some interesting things happen. People start behaving better and they start claiming less money. And if that's good enough for the MPs why don't we do that for the public sector? Make all the information about government spending available online so you can search it, like you search everything else online. I think that will get people more involved in politics and they could really see where the money is going.

Energy: Obviously this is a concern, because so much of it comes from the Middle East and from Russia. I hope we see some progress in the Middle East, and I think that Obama has an opportunity to make progress on the key issue of Israel and Palestine. I think when you have a Democrat President and a leader in Israel who won't be outflanked by the right, there is a potential of a deal, so let's hope that we get some stability. But too much of our energy comes from dangerous and unstable parts of the world, like Russia, like the Middle East. So what should we do? We should secure ourselves in the short term by making sure we have gas storage and making sure we have adequate generating capacity – particularly gas to start with, so that the lights don't go out and we have a secure supply. We also need to make sure we have a wide range of energy supply, including the renewable ... not just wind power but also wave and solar power and all the rest of it. And I think we need to also make a profound change in our thinking about energy. Up to now when it comes to electricity we've got the big national grid, great big power stations, mostly in the north and in the midlands, and we have a huge and inefficient energy loss as we plug in to the national grid and take our power off it ... We should encourage anyone who wants to generate some of their own electricity whether through solar or wind, or any business that wants to generate electricity alongside its business and sell it back to the grid. And if you have a decentralized energy system your source of energy becomes much more secure. You're much more likely to see yourself through difficult times.

MPs' expenses: I fill out my expenses on a monthly basis. I don't actually now claim the maximum amount, and the approach I always have taken to this issue is this – first of all I want to be a Member of Parliament whether the pay is twice as much or half as much, I want to be a Member of Parliament because I believe in this service, I love my constituency, I love the job I do, I think it's worthwhile. The second thing to say is the expenses are for maintaining two homes, because in my case my constituency home is not really commutable from London, not if you're sitting in the House of Commons until ten o'clock at night. So I have two homes, one in the constituency and one in London. And for my constituency home in West Oxfordshire, the one I claim for, I fill in a monthly form, and claim for the basics that go with running a second home. So I claim for the mortgage interest, I pay for things like gas, electricity and the phone bill, and I don't claim for 100 per cent of those either. I never claimed for food, cleaners or furniture because I thought you should claim for the basics of a second home. It's certainly right that I come from a prosperous background, but we don't means test our MPs, we have salaries and expenses and they are there to meet the needs of two homes. I would argue that I have taken a lead in this issue. I was the first party leader to whip my MPs through a vote saying 'no more claiming for furniture, no more claiming for the things that are not really justified apart from the second home'. I was the first one to say that even if you have obeyed the rules there is actually still a need to pay back money, you should recognize the public anger about this issue. And I was the first to say that if people claim badly they shouldn't stand again and a number of people on my side have done that. No party's record on this has been perfect, of course it hasn't, but in terms of leadership, I got there first.

Common agricultural policy: I had a wonderful letter from a constituent the other day, who wrote to me to say that a friend of his who is a farmer, was now being paid not to rear pigs. And my constituent said, I would like, Mr Cameron, to go into the business of not rearing pigs. He said, I'm not a very ambitious man, so I'd like to start by not rearing 100 pigs. Over time I'd like to get more ambitious and think I could get up to not rearing 1000 pigs. And as I won't be rearing pigs, but will actually be unemployed, will I still be eligible to get unemployment benefit? It was an absolutely brilliant letter and highlighted the absurdity of the situation we're in.

The odds on winning: I actually met someone once, in the 2005 election and they got me 33 to 1 to be leader of the Conservative Party and they put on around £500 and I think they went on a round-the-world cruise. So I've made one person happy.

* * *

Gordon Brown's conference speech on 29 September came grinding to a halt as soon as he promised to cure cancer during the 'next' Labour term. And then, just in case we thought we hadn't heard correctly, a few minutes later he said it again.

Optimism? Oh yes, this was optimism all right. It was a *coup de grâce* without grace notes, a preposterous and unhelpful promise with no basis in fact. First he gave us Tony Blair's greatest hits, then a litany of hastily-assembled policies (many of the social disorder policies looking like nothing but a knee-jerk reaction to the Fiona Pilkington story: she killed herself and her 18-year-old daughter, who had a mental age of four, having suffered more than ten years of abuse from a gang of feral teenagers living in their Leicestershire street), and finally, yes, the cancer thing.

From that moment on, he was doomed. Although you didn't know quite how doomed he was until you caught a glimpse of the expressions on the faces of Brown's Cabinet, looking on with horror as they sat in the cheap seats – the ones near the front – in the Brighton Centre. Harriet

Harman, David Miliband, Alan Johnson and Ed Balls all looked as though they were having their pay-cheques torn up in front of them, as though their careers were being shredded in full view of the whole country. Which they sort of were. This was the New Labour end-game, with Brown still being so convinced he had made the right call on the economy and growing increasingly petulant about our obvious misreading of his genius.

This was old-school Gordon, the one who used to walk in and out of Downing Street with gravitas – although I have the weight of the world on my shoulders, he seemed to imply, my shoulders are so broad and so sturdy that none of you have anything to worry about. Everything was fine, he appeared to say, everything was AOK (not that the Big Clunking Fist would ever say AOK). The smile he had been encouraged to employ having failed to convince the public that he hadn't lied about his reasons for not holding an election two years previously – well, it looked as though it had gone for good. He had reverted to the Stalinesque solemnity he does so well, espousing the qualities of his expensive safety net. Even though David Cameron has said that he believes all politicians should be allowed a private past before assuming public office – a neat way of refusing to talk about his drug past – it is still unnerving to read the advice in a student handbook edited by a 22-year-old Gordon Brown while he was still at Edinburgh University in the 1970s: 'If you're British and can give an address, free money is available from social security. Never be reticent about claiming benefits. For whatever reason the so-called welfare state was brought into being, and it can and must be used to its full extent.'

Brown's conference speech was less a call to arms, and more a plea. Even on the way down to Brighton one could tell the tempests of ill-feeling were starting to brew. The papers were filled with Peter Mandelson's performance the day before – the *Daily Mail* deriding his appeal for the party faithful to behave 'like insurgents, rather than incumbents', while the *Guardian* ran a series of images of the Business Secretary gesticulating wildly at the conference podium like Gaddafi at his most maniacal.

Mandelson made the best speech, however, and the way in which he demonized the Conservatives – continuing to paint them as a terminally divided, ideologically fractured party (even though the Tories had proved that Labour were going to cut public services by as much as 10 per cent) – was even more impressive if you closed your eyes. Listening to his rather sinister Scrooge-like scaremongering, you were reminded of Malcolm McLaren, or the Child Catcher from *Chitty Chitty Bang Bang*. Scary. Otherworldly. But then he went and ruined it later that night, calling up Rebekah Brooks and allegedly, ahem – calling her and the assembled News International big-wigs, 'c****' after he had been made aware that the *Sun* had officially dropped the Labour Party in the following day's paper (when quizzed later about this, he told TV crews, 'What c-word are you referring to? Cuts?' before agreeing he'd originally said 'chumps').

Dodging the pamphleting red-rinse brigade, the disgruntled union members and hung-over lobbyists, the atmosphere wasn't so much sombre and resigned – as had been reported earlier that week – but combative and frustrated. As the *Sun*'s promotional van reminded us – as we handed our laminated identity cards over to ensure smooth passage into Labour's safe and secure Green Zone – 'Don't You Know There's a Bloody War on?' Indeed, one man in particular was in for the fight of his political life.

Frankly, the town hadn't felt this electric since Fat Boy Slim held the last of his big, loud, hedonistic parties on the beach. We talked about pills, too, as we sat in the main conference hall, ignored Jack Straw on the big screen and debated whether or not it was right for Andrew Marr to ask the PM about his alleged use of antidepressants. The consensus was that Marr had been perfectly within his rights to ask such a question, and the fact that Brown had reacted so badly was merely another sign of his steadily fraying nerves. Of course, every Labour MP we approached stuck to the party line and insisted they'd be boycotting Marr's show from here on in, something which will do their campaigning the world of good in the run-up to the election.

Sarah Brown was the obligatory warm-up act, looking notably relaxed – she becomes more ambassadorial by the month – and introducing a video 'about' Gordon. Perhaps the PM had watched Glastonbury on tele-vision last year as the five-minute skit looked suspiciously like the video Jay Z played before he came on to headline the Pyramid Stage. You almost expected to hear Noel Gallagher's Mancunian timbre saying, 'David Cameron? F**king no chance!' Sadly all we got was a herogram from Bono, a rather limp montage from various world philanthropists, including about three snaps of Nelson Mandela (still the go-to guy for humility and image enhancement) and – bizarrely enough – TV presen-ter June Sarpong talking about how much poor Sarah has to put up with at home. Trust us, we believe you June.

Still, Mrs Brown was the only person on stage in Brighton to step down from it with any dignity.

How different Manchester was to Brighton.

'You could come here and say you're going to nationalize every bank in Britain and you'd get a standing ovation,' said one frontbencher at the Conservative Party conference the following week. 'So it should be no surprise that Boris went down so well. Here, we'd clap anything.'

Well, they certainly clapped BoJo. The Tory conference was initially derailed by its unwieldy, uncontainable celebrity mayor. On his way to the Manchester Central complex, Boris Johnson called for a referendum on the Lisbon Treaty after the Irish voted 'yes' the day before (having quite clearly said 'no' 18 months previously), and the media soaked up the mess with glee, loudly trumpeting disruption in the Tory ranks as Blondie stirred up a lot of unwanted EU trouble. The Tory leader managed to downplay Boris's very deliberate faux pas, asking his own party not to allow the issue to overshadow the conference: 'Let this not be the week when we talk to ourselves.'

But this treachery is unlikely to be forgotten, and it's difficult to overemphasize just how angry certain members of the party were about Boris's outburst. As soon as you got to Manchester you could tell that Boris had burned the most important bridge of his life, and, while his aides think he carried the day through sheer force of personality ('Boris is Boris, and there is nothing anyone can do about that, includ-ing David Cameron,' said one, as we milled about the Midland Hotel one night), there are others somewhat closer to the flame who think differently. 'The party will be vengeful,' said a close confidant of Cameron. 'You can't play to the Tory faithful and ignore the party line, as it always ends in tears.' Boris has always been good at playing the long game, but if he really wants to step into Dave's polished Oxfords in two terms' time, he needs to watch what he says a little more carefully.

Elsewhere, though, the Tories put flesh on policy bones under the scrutiny of a press who finally admitted they were watching a party preparing for power. Everyone had been told not to be triumphal, but of course they were – quietly, secretly, although actually rather obviously. Most of the MPs were walking around looking like people who have just been told they've been promoted, but who aren't allowed to tell anyone. They weren't smug, but they were certainly looking forward to being exactly that.

The British famously like their chancellors to be either bookies or undertakers, and this year George Osborne played the latter role with aplomb, wearing a Savile Row suit and a hair shirt. However his austerity measures played rather well (bar his refusal to bin Labour's 50p tax rate, which was only kept as a sop to those who want them to be tough on the rich), Shadow Justice Secretary Dominic Grieve and Shadow Home Secretary Chris Grayling promised to get tough – really tough – on crime, and Shadow Schools Secretary Michael Gove showed why he is often talked about as a future leader.

Osborne's speech certainly resonated with David Brooks of the *New York Times*. 'The Conservatives have treated British voters as adults for a year now,' he wrote on 16 October, 'with a string of serious economic positions. The Conservatives supported the Labour government bank bailout, even though it was against their political interest to do so. Last November, Osborne opposed a cut in the value-added taxes on the grounds that the cuts were unaffordable and would not produce growth. It is not easy for any Conservative party to oppose tax cuts, but this one did it … In the US, the economic crisis has caused many to question capitalism. But Britain has discredited the centre-left agenda with its unrelenting public spending, its public development agencies and disappointing public-private investment partnerships.'

But it was Cameron who stole the show, as he was always going to. On the eve of his forty-third birthday, Cameron made if not his most impassioned speech, then certainly his toughest and most funereal. He even co-opted Bono, who appeared on video before Dave took to the stage, praising the Conservatives for their pledge to preserve Britain's commitments on international aid. Oh, how Gordon Brown must have hated that bit (apparently Alastair Campbell was so incensed by Bono's betrayal he called up Bob Geldof – Bono's lobbying partner – to berate him). Cameron focused on welfare, the family, Afghanistan ('Our method should be clear – send more soldiers to train more Afghans to deliver the security we need. Then we can bring our troops home'), crime, 'society' ('We've got to stop treating adults like children and children like adults,' he said at one point), and – how could he not? – the debt mountain. He mentioned 'country', 'Britain' and 'the family' 30 times each, and only mentioned 'cuts' once. There were ethical tax cuts, piety, but none of the stage stalking he's done in the past, nor any of the obvious Blair mannerisms, like placing his open hand on his chest, to emphasize his points. This was wake-up call, hard-line message time. This was the speech where Cameron finally showed he wasn't quite as liberal as he may have enjoyed being painted in the past, while committing himself once more to trying to fix 'Britain's broken society'.

No, he didn't promise to cure cancer, but then you can't have everything. He'll probably save that one until he really needs it.

* * *

Cameron's character – and the collective doubts about it – is still a topic that divides people. Some like his openness, and apparent frankness. Others still think he's just a charlatan who decided on a whim in the Eton schoolyard that he wanted to lead the country one day. *The Spectator*'s Fraser Nelson once wrote in *GQ*, 'I've interviewed Cameron too many times to expect to get the better of him. He has this knack of sounding fluent, while keeping to a carefully vetted line of argument.'

It's very difficult to ruffle Cameron; you can mention his drug history, his rich background and aristocratic roots (the perils of privilege will always be his Achilles' heel, although one wonders when the commentariat will begin to start thinking that going to such a good school might actually have been a plus rather than minus), his inexperience, and he will bat you away as though none of this matters. Press him on the record, as I have, and he will simply get irritated. And like any politician, ask him the same question half a dozen times and he can get a little petulant. His opponents also accuse Cameron of being too smooth, smug and superficial. 'He may be likeable and sometimes hard to disagree with, but he is empty,' David Miliband has said.

Of course one of his biggest problems is his eagerness to please, to come across as a 'nice guy'. His innate confidence and breezy PR manner has made him an easy target, especially as he can turn the charm on like a tap. Yes, he can be dismissive and not listen and talk over you if he thinks what you're saying isn't particularly of any interest, but I've rarely seen him be downright rude. He appears to save that particular approach for his opposite number in the Commons. He would deny it, but there's always been a part of David Cameron that has believed he can do anything, and he has an arrogance that he learned at an early age, a divine superiority that his critics still find unpalatable. The birth of Ivan was probably the first thing that made him doubt his divine right. Ivan's birth taught him that the road ahead might not be as smooth as he was perhaps led to believe. Asked whether, on hearing about the extent of his son's disability, there might have been a moment when he thought he might not love him because of it, Cameron said, 'I never worried that I wouldn't because when your first child is born, that's an incredibly precious feeling that you have and you love him from the moment he pops out.' And while Ivan's death may have come as a blessed relief in some respects, his passing has no doubt compounded his father's doubts about his own destiny.

Cameron is certainly more of a progressive centrist leader than anyone left in Gordon Brown's Cabinet, but this won't define him. The big question about Cameron's tenure is whether or not he will turn out to be a Thatcher-style radical, or a more tempered Macmillan-style moderate. One feels that even Cameron doesn't know himself, and that it's only in the heat of the battle, or when he finally has his feet under the desk in Number 10, that we – and perhaps Cameron himself – will find out. He does have a radicalism about him, though, and this is certainly what could define him.

With the country still mired in a deep recession, Cameron will have to take the axe to public spending just like Margaret Thatcher did 30 years ago. As a result, the next election will be fought over an age-old battle-ground in British politics: the size of government. In this respect the party leaders have reverted to type, with, on the one hand, Cameron saying, 'The age of irresponsibility is giving way to the age of austerity ... Unless we deal with this debt crisis, we risk becoming once again the sick man of Europe' ... and Brown, on the other, proclaiming, 'The choice is clear: a Labour plan to grow Britain out of recession ... Or the Tory route: help the wealthiest few and cuts to public services for everyone at the worst possible time.' Bizarrely, the dog-end of New Labour will spend the next few years fighting the New Conservatives on very traditional party lines, and in this respect Cameron doesn't appear to be revolutionary at all. In fact so far he has been rather cautious. 'What you need is thoughtful radicalism,' he says, the 'long runway' approach to change, and only power will prove whether or not this radicalism will have any effect. I happen to think it will.

Cameron still has huge problems ahead, though. Even if voters trust him to lead them on that steep climb out of recession, many experts say that the suggested Tory cuts will amount to no more than a fifth of what is needed to balance the books (by October 2009 the budget deficit was £175 billion). The Tories have offered what William Hague calls 'a large dollop of honesty', although promising a decade of austerity has never been a traditional vote-winner. To win a majority the Tories need to hold every seat they won in 2005 and then capture a further 117. To do that Cameron would have to make history. The Tories have fewer MPs than Labour during the Michael Foot years, and they still need the biggest swing in modern times – a swing, as Broonites like to point out, even larger than the one achieved by Margaret Thatcher in 1979 with the assistance of the Winter of Discontent. The prospect of a hung parliament makes it crucial that the Tories entertain some sort of relationship with the Liberal Democrats (they might need their support to put through any major spending cuts). Plus there is the protest vote issue, with the distinct possibility that aggrieved voters will opt instead for the Lib-Dems, the Greens, UKIP or – God forbid – the BNP.

Then, of course, there is Europe. Even though Cameron has abandoned promise of a referendum on the Lisbon treaty, a successful Conservative government is pledged to attempt to return social and employment legislation to national control. If this is done by treaty change, it would require 26 other EU countries to agree to it. And why would they? As Sir Stephen Wall, a former adviser to Tony Blair, says, 'No concession would be made to Britain without us giving something in return. Would we, as other EU members might well demand, give up our budget rebate [£3 billion a year] in exchange?' And then there's defence, and General Sir Richard Dannatt, the former army chief, who was recruited to the Conservatives by Cameron to advise on, amongst other things, armed forces policy in Afghanistan. Cameron appears to have overlooked the fact that there is no love lost between Dannatt and the recently appointed army chief, General Sir David Richards. As both disagree over the future of the armed forces (Dannatt is a big fan of hardware and set-piece operations), all that Cameron has to look forward to here is a war of attrition.

Journalists often say that David Cameron has the sort of easy charm that can make you want to forget you're being charmed. But his problem is that there are still many people who have no interest at all in allowing him to charm them. He is, for them at least, a smarmy Tory with ulterior motives. He might always say that 'It's not where you're from, it's where you're going,' but this doesn't always wash. He has to accept that there will always be those who refuse to believe he has any understanding of ordinary people. Elsewhere there is a suspicion that Cameron will turn out to be considerably less reasonable and compassionate than he seems, although – ironically – there are those who warm to him because of this, those who understand the modernization process Cameron has initiated, but who also detect a traditional Tory heart beating beneath his cosy metrosexual exterior.

Perhaps David Cameron will turn out to be far more orthodox than originally advertised. He is certainly tougher, although, as the journalists Francis Elliott and James Hanning have pointed out, with toughness comes an exceptional capacity for putting people at their ease, and an attractive bigness of personality. And all that this involves. According to *Times* journalist Ginny Dougary, who researched a piece for her paper in May 2009, during the period Cameron worked at the Conservative Research Department, 'He was described to me as a "toadying suck-up" to those above him and a "petty tyrant" to those below.' Dougary said that there were numerous stories of him behaving like that at Carlton. I've seen him patronize people too, although I've always thought this is simply due to his indifference to those whose opinions he has no interest in. For a politician, he is hardly alone in this. I have watched enough people become famous to see how their confidence grows, and this is certainly the case with Cameron.

His ambition for Britain is simple. He wants to fix it. Not through revolution. But through stealth. Cameron's Conservatism isn't remotely Thatcherite, and doesn't revolve around personal prosperity, any kind of rapacious entrepreneurial spirit or the cult of the individual. The orthodox and instinctive Conservative element of his 'belief file' is a fundamental mistrust of the state and Britain's blind acceptance of and dependency on top-down government. However, while minimizing the state he wants to bring the people with him, rather than let them fend for themselves. What David Cameron proposes is something altogether different, focusing as much on social responsibility as individual responsibility. He wants us to assume a real sense of duty, a sense of collective paternalism, of genuine community spirit. And that involves everything from education to the voluntary sector. As Matthew d'Ancona so trenchantly put it in the *Sunday Telegraph*, just a few days after Cameron's 2009 conference speech, 'The radicalism of [his] approach has not been fully appreciated. This is neither the paternalism of the old Tory patricians, nor the rugged individualism of the Thatcher era. It is an audacious attempt to fashion a notion of social solidarity from the bricks of centre-Right ideas. For three decades, we have been told that solidarity of this sort is the hallmark of the Left, and that it is achieved through the agency of the state. Cameron disputes that orthodoxy completely. His mantra that "There is such a thing as society, it's just not the same thing as the state" is not just a nifty soundbite; it is also his most deeply rooted belief.'

Social responsibility – this was the phrase he used when we first met in the spring of 2006, all those years ago, a phrase that echoed through our conversations like a mantra. This is his radicalism, his revolution, his mission.

Cameron's future is equivocal. A lot has changed since December 2005, when Cameron became leader. Back then, back when 'Dave' was walking around with his big inclusive smile, his green agenda, the nod to the ethnic and gay communities and 'Hug a hoodie' soundbites, his mission was to project an image of moderation, to project an image of an inclusive party that had had its knuckles rapped by three general election defeats, a party ready to embrace anyone who wanted embracing, a party willing to reject seasoned ideological philosophy in favour of something altogether more pragmatic. But then the global economy crashed, the possibilities of growth evaporated over the space of a few months, and the last thing any future leader of the country needed was to look unsure of his principles.

Cameron has equipped himself well, and in the four years since becoming party leader has turned into an appreciably tougher politician, a politician who has not just found that he has had to adapt to the changing fortunes of the country he hopes to inherit, but also found that he can do this without abandoning the driving principles which encouraged him to attempt it in the first place.

INDEX OF QUESTION-AND-ANSWER TOPICS

DC denotes David Cameron
IDS denotes Iain Duncan
    Smith

Abbas, Mahmoud 257
AC/DC 237
Afghanistan 45, 174, 239,
    258–9, 345, 346, 347,
    380–2, 383
ageing population:
    exempting pensioners from
        tax 290
    pensions 288–9, 355, 368
    residential care 289, 356
    savings 289–90
AIDS 260, 266
Alan Partridge 237
alcohol:
    abuse 63, 167, 286
    binge drinking 139, 226
    family breakdown and 226
    poverty and 286
    underage drinking 140, 226
Allen, Lily 238
Andrew Marr Show, The 129
anti-Semitism 179
Archbishop of Canterbury
    137, 170, 172
ASBOs 146–7
Ashdown, Paddy 259
Asian community:
    Conservative Asian
        candidates for MP 28
    role models 138–9
Aston Villa 238

Australia:
    immigration points system
        175
    pension contributions, cuts
        taxes on 289
    welfare reform 134

Balkans 265
Balls, Ed 114
Bank of England 68, 344, 375
BBC 53
Berlusconi, Silvio 268, 389
Big Brother 237, 388
Big Issue 147
Bill of Rights, UK 177
Black Wednesday 70–1
Blair, Tony 43, 143, 169
    academies, involvement with
        188, 354
    crime and 14
    DC meets with on Middle
        East 257
    dictatorial style 114
    differences between Brown
        and 131, 306
    EU President, bid for role as
        385
    failures 43, 213–14, 310, 314
    foreign policy 43, 263, 264
    Granita deal with Brown 48
    influence upon DC 213–14
    liberal interventionism 43,
        263, 264
    London Mayoral race,
        involvement in 307

mandate, 1997 379
PMQs 253
religious beliefs 181
return of 351
self-deception 43
succeeds John Smith 66
welfare reform 134
William Hague and 75
Bloomberg, Mike 187
BNP (British National Party)
    296, 348, 371
Bradford 137–8
Brasenose College, Oxford 47,
    207
British Airways 234
Britishness 136
Broken Society 351, 365–6
Brown, Gordon 240, 311
    accession 30–1, 61–5
    ambition 43
    backbenchers, relationship
        with 294
    Blair, relationship with 48,
        214
    casinos, view on 140
    as Chancellor 49, 50
    character 31, 43, 64, 65
    Crewe and Nantwich By-
        election and 306
    DC, relationship with 63–4,
        131, 132, 385
    election that never was, 2007
        129–30, 131, 132
    honeymoon period 54, 59,
        60, 61, 62, 132, 133

incompetence 63
leadership style 31, 63, 64, 65, 132
lies 130
Northern Rock and 130
PMQs 63, 253
prisons policy 221
public spending 344, 363, 386
resignation, possible 283
steals Conservative policies 131, 293, 314
10p tax rate, abolishes 304, 306
unpopularity of 314
Browne, Des 114
Bruni, Carla 389
Bullingdon Club 213
Bush, George 188, 233, 260, 263
business:
  businessmen DC admires 291–2
  The City 290–2, 375
  criticising bad business practice 291
  link between Conservative Party and 290, 312
  privatisation 79
  protectionism 78
  role in tackling environmental and social problems 290–1, 292
  spirit of enterprise in UK 313
  see also economy
Butt, Ronald 42
By-elections:
  Ealing, 2007 28, 29, 58–61
  Crewe and Nantwich, 2008 304–6, 364, 379
  Norwich North 348, 368, 379

Callaghan, James 39
Cameron, Alex (brother) 36–7, 40
Cameron, Clare (sister) 206
Cameron, David:
  abuse from public 28–30
  art, favourite work of 237
  best moment in politics 212
  blasphemy laws, votes to abolish 108
  building, favourite 237

campaigning 28–9
celebrity 46
character
  aloof and cliquey 371–2
  ambitious 32–4, 42–3, 44–5, 109
  calculating 108
  cautious 108
  co-operative 108
  feline 108
  listener 104
  optimistic 108, 109, 363–4
  pragmatic 110
  professional politician 310
  rebel 37
  rural 31, 74
  ruthless 112
  salesman 310
  scepticism 43, 107
  self-confidence 45–8
  self-satisfied 108, 112
  sociability 46
  stubbornness 183
childhood 31, 36–40
conservatism 47–8
cooking 207
cycling 106, 213
dog lover 108
drugs and 210–12, 388
expenses 376–7, 391
family life 37, 38–40, 53, 188–9, 202–10, 349–50, 387–8
fear, greatest 108
films, favourite 236
football and 238
'heir to Blair' 213–14
holiday, 2009 349–50
hope, greatest 109
household, childhood 37, 38–40
hunting 213
ideology 105–8, 109–10
instincts 111
jobs outside politics 64, 71–4
jokes 239–40
Leader of the Opposition
  campaigning 28–9
  daily battle versus big picture 136, 310
  decides to run for 49, 82
  diary 81
  driver takes papers to Commons whilst DC cycles 106

first days as 85
  leadership contest 49, 82–5, 105, 141, 203, 311–12
  leaks from office 65
  devolving style 54, 108
  morning meeting 204
  role in UK constitutional set-up 267
  speeches 82–4, 105, 128–30, 212, 262
  stress of job 110–12
  success aids ability to get things done 86, 136
love life see Cameron, Samantha
manifesto 308–15
media, relationship with 46, 52
memory, bad 37
message, getting across 310–11
mistakes, biggest 106
motoring offences 212–13
MP 44
  ambition to become a 203, 210
  love of job 44, 79
  selected as candidate 74
  wins Witney seat 74
music, favourite 237, 238, 239
newspapers 39, 40, 41, 53, 54, 65
party politics, thoughts on 42–3
philosophy, political 104–5, 107, 308–13, 353, 355–6
piece of wisdom 105
PM, plans for role as 349
policy see under individual policy area
political development in youth 32, 37, 38–45
political development since becoming Leader of Opposition 109–10
private office 204
public relations, experience in 73
public meetings 348–9, 362
radio, favourite stations 207–8
reading 235–6
regrets, greatest 109

schooldays 40, 46
sibling rivalry 36–7
sleep 213
smoking 212
snooker 237
speeches 70, 82–4, 105,
    128–30, 212, 262
swimming 213
television, favourite shows
    207, 208, 236, 361
underwear 213
university 37, 42–3, 47, 254
weaknessses 364
wedding 205
work/life balance 388
worst moment in politics
    212
Cameron, Elwen (son) 388
Cameron, Ian (father) 38, 40,
    198–9, 292
Cameron, Ivan (son) 148,
    194–9, 209, 356, 387–8
Cameron, Mary (mother) 39,
    40
Cameron, Nancy (daughter)
    41, 111
Cameron, Samantha (wife)
    35, 54, 109–10
  as an asset to DC 204–5
  DC becoming Leader of the
    Opposition, reaction to
    85
  DC discusses policy with
    205, 206
  DC discusses running for
    leadership with 203–4
  DC does not discuss
    becoming PM with
    372–3
  DC falls for 206
  DC meets 50–1
  DC, life with 207
  effects of public life upon
    202–3
  green issues and 205
  Ivan and 194, 196, 197, 198
  Michelle Obama, meets 383
  mother 194, 196, 197, 198,
    204, 209
  prefers Clarke to IDS as
    leader 77
  rows with DC 206
  similarities with DC 206
  TV watching 207
  wedding 205

Campbell, Alastair 51–2, 68,
    180
Canada 260
car parking 148
Carlton Communications 64,
    71–4
Carter, Jimmy 54
casinos 62, 140
CBI 290
CCTV 144
Channel 4 41
Cheyne Centre, London 197
Churchill, Winston 260, 312
City, The 50, 290–2, 375
Clark, Alan 51
Clarke, Ken 71, 77, 349, 371,
    372
class system 34, 164–5, 238,
    239, 284–6, 306–7
Clegg, Nick 239, 284, 296, 297,
    378–9
Clinton, Hillary 53, 261, 383
CND 40
Coe, Seb 309
Cold War 32, 33–4, 258
Common Agricultural Policy
    392
Commonwealth 258, 380, 384
community 139–43, 285–6 see
    also society
Community Academy,
    Hackney 187
community service 141–3
Conservative Party:
  brand 292–3
  British Asian candidates 28
  by-elections, record at 29
  Central Office 130, 203, 293
  changing focus of 288,
    312–13, 355
  Compassionate
    Conservatism 287
  complacency, danger of
    364–5
  conference, 2002 78
  conference, 2003 78
  conference, 2005 82–4
  conference, 2007 127–30, 131
  core support, alienating 368
  corruption within 295–6
  DC's loyalty to 78, 79
  DC's successor as leader of
    50
  decline after 1997 election
    75–82

expenses scandal used to
    replace older, less
    compliant MP's 377
  funding 294, 295, 296
  gay rights and 28
  'hares' and tortoises 48n
  lurch to right in last three
    parliaments 61, 76, 80
  modernising the 292–5,
    312–13, 350, 351, 379
  one nation 136, 138
  open primaries 378
  party cohesion 65–6
  philosophy 308–10
  plans for power 349
  policy see under individual
    policy area
  policy direction, present 61,
    104–5, 107, 308–15
  policy makers, disagreement
    between 374–5
  popularity, effect of
    economic policy upon
    342–3
  poverty and 286, 287
  press office 293
  race and 28, 176–7
  sets of values 106–7, 133
  trades unions members vote
    for 36
  under Hague 75–6
  under Howard 79–82
  under IDS 77–8
  under Major 34, 44–5, 48,
    50, 169
  under Thatcher see
    Thatcher, Margaret
  women candidates 62, 293
  women MPs 351
Conservative Research
  Department (CRD) 42,
    48, 50, 69–70
Conway, Derek 295–6
corruption, political 295–6
Coulson, Andy 48n, 52, 112,
    374, 375
Crewe and Nantwich By-
    election 304–6, 364, 379
crime:
  ASBOs 146–7
  burglary 144, 225, 228
  CCTV and 144
  DC as victim of 144, 145
  domestic violence 147, 167
  DNA database 145

drugs, illegal 42, 63, 147, 148–9, 167, 226, 255, 286
gun and knife 225, 229
ID cards 62, 65, 144, 146
sentencing 226, 228–30
stop and search 135–6, 229
street 144–7
voluntary/charitable sector and 147–8
see also police and prisons
Criminal Justice System 225–8
crime see crime
police see police
prisons see prisons
sentencing 226, 228–30

Daily Express 39, 40
Daily Mail 36, 39
Daily Mirror 51
Daily Telegraph 53
Darfur 267
Darling, Alistair 111
Davis, David 84, 112, 114, 128, 204
Department of Health 201
Disraeli, Benjamin 107, 311, 312
DNA database 145
Dobson, Frank 307
drugs, illegal 42, 63, 147, 148–9, 167, 226, 255, 286, 388
Duke of Edinburgh's Awards 141, 142, 143

Ealing By-election 28, 29, 58–61
EastEnders 236
Economist, The 70
economy:
ageing population and 288–90
bank regulation 343, 375
Conservative Party focus on 63, 64, 65, 132, 288, 309, 312
consumer power 79
credit crunch 130, 283, 312, 343, 386
debt 286, 342, 344, 347, 362, 363, 364, 365, 370
free trade 78
FSA 343
inequality, income 285–6, 287
interest rates 363

Northern Rock 130, 283
pensions 288–9
philanthropy 285–6
poverty 62, 77, 285, 286, 287, 309
public spending 342–3, 344, 353, 355, 362, 363, 366, 369–70, 386
rate of growth 168
recession 343, 347
taxes see taxes
Thatcher's reform of 135, 288, 308, 313, 315
underclass and 286, 287
VAT cut 364, 386
wealth creation and GWB (General Well-Being) 285, 288, 312
wealth, too much 285
education 68
academies 188
allowing any group of teachers or parents to set up schools by themselves 185–6
American system 185
appeals panels, abolishing 314
as a priority 109
city technology colleges 188
curriculum 189
current state of 354
DC's children and 188
discipline, strong 187–8
11+ 183, 354
exam boards, independent 186
exclusions 354
faith schools 181, 182
for disabled children 196–7
good school places, lack of 184
grammar schools 181, 182–3, 212, 293
head teachers 187, 314
higher 189–90
history, teaching 189
independent sector 185–6
Labour's focus on admissions 184–5
leaving age 188
new schools 313
nursery 42
poor schools 286
private sector schools 188–9

school leaver programme 311
Schools Secretary 184
selection 182–5
smaller schools 187
special schools, stopping closure of 314
state school children going to Oxford, increasing number of 189–90
streaming 185
Swedish system 185
testing, importance of 186, 189
Elizabeth II, Queen 169
End of the Affair, The 236
energy:
decentralised energy 234–5
electricity bills 358, 372
energy security 265–6, 390
gas 265
nuclear 233–4
oil 265
renewables 390–1
Engleby (Faulks) 236
entrepreneurialism 147, 284
environment 62, 232–5
aviation and 232–3, 234
Bush and 233
business and 292
climate change bill 233
DC's awakening to problem of 205, 232
decentralised energy policy and 234–5
environmentally proofing your home 358, 372
John McCain and 232, 233
national parks and 358
nuclear power and 233–4
recycling 205
taxes 234
transport and 232–3, 234
Zac Goldsmith and Tory policy on 235
Eton 46, 48
European Convention on Human Rights 177
European Union 255–6, 257, 265, 268, 296, 385
expenses scandal, MPs' 347, 348, 376–7, 390, 391

Falklands War 40–1
Fall, Catherine 83

family:
  breakdown 63, 68, 143,
    164–9, 226, 286, 309, 314
  child benefit 167
  child care 167
  core values of 350
  importance of 106–7, 311
  parental responsibility
    209–10
  politicians and 167
  single parents 32, 165, 166,
    167, 187
  see also marriage
Fathers for Justice 168
Financial Services Authority
  (FSA) 343
Finkelstein, Danny 83
fixed terms for governments
  378
Fleming, Ian 235
floods, 2007 86
foreign policy:
  Afghanistan 45, 174, 239,
    258–9, 345, 346, 347,
    380–2, 383
  armed forces 266–7
  Blair's liberal
    interventionism 43, 263,
    264
  China 267, 384
  defence review 380
  democracy, exporting 258
  Eastern Europe 264–5
  energy security 265–6
  European Union see
    European Union
  Georgia 382
  in Afghanistan 258–9
  India 384
  international development
    86, 87
  Iran 259
  Iraq 41, 43, 62, 174, 256, 259,
    261, 346, 380
  Israel/Palestine 257
  Middle East 257–9
  policeman, Britain as a
    global 380
  population growth 266
  South Africa 260, 266
  Turkey and EU membership
    265
  US 260–3, 382–3
  Zimbabwe 258, 264, 267,
    384

  see also National Security
    and under individual
    head of state
Formula One 142, 143
Fox, Liam 114, 128
Friday Night With Jonathan
  Ross 237–8
Friends of the Earth 205
funding, party 59, 263, 294,
  295, 296

gay rights 28, 166, 169
Gaza Strip 257
Geldof, Bob 260
General Election:
  1979 38
  1992 50, 51
  1997 67, 75
  2001 76
  2005 44, 81–2, 203
  2010 347, 362, 364
  that never was, 2007 127–30,
    131, 132
Georgia 264, 382
Goldman Sachs 73
Goldsmith, Zac 235
Goodbye to All That (Graves)
  236
Gorbachev, Mikhail 33
Gove, Michael 112, 114, 374
Graves, Robert 236
Grayling, Chris 367
Great Western 287
Green, Michael 71–2
Greene, Graham 236
Greenham Common 39
Greenpeace 205
Guardian 39, 53
Guernica (Picasso) 237
Gurkhas 379
GWB (General Well-Being)
  138, 288, 312

Hackney 142
Haggard, Rider 236
Hague, William 75–6, 80, 112,
  114, 128, 131, 204, 349,
  371, 386
Hamas 257
Hastilow, Nigel 176
Healey, Denis 342, 362
Heath, Edward 39
Hilton, Steve 48n, 50, 83, 111
homelessness 147–8
Homelessness Foundation 311

Home Office 70, 147, 230
hospices 356
House of Commons, smaller
  342, 363, 370, 377–8
Howard, Michael 49, 71,
  79–82, 139
Howe, Geoffrey 372
Human Rights:
  Act 177–8
  European Convention on 177
  in China 267
Hume, David 353
hung parliament, possibility
  of a 296
Hurd, Douglas 254
Hussein, Saddam 256

ID cards 62, 65, 144, 146, 342,
  352, 363
I'm A Celebrity 237
immigration 133, 164, 172–7
India 384
Independent 374
individual, freedom and the
  32, 33, 34, 106, 128
inner cities 138
International Development
  366
internet 295
  Conservative Party use of
    295
  DC's use of 53–4
  fundraising on 295
  role in next UK election 53
  US Presidential race and
    53–4, 295
Iran 259, 268
Iraq 41, 43, 62, 174, 256, 259,
  261, 346, 380
Islam 179, 256, 265 see also
  Muslim community
Israel 257
ITN 72, 73
iTunes 54

Jack Tizard School,
  Hammersmith 196–7
Jerusalem 257
Johnson, Alan 351, 367
Johnson, Boris 29–30, 307,
  308, 313, 378
Johnson, Paul 42

Kant, Immanuel 353
Karzai, Hamid 259

Kelly, David 52
Khan, Amir 138
Kosovo 265

Labour Party:
  accession to power, 1997 67, 68
  Blair and 214, 351, 354
  change and 107
  Crewe and Nantwich By-election 304–6, 365
  economic incompetence 281, 342, 362
  legislative obsession 145, 225
  management consultant culture within 199–200
  short-term decision making 347
  spending cuts 344
  spin 68, 140
  state control, top-down, centralising philosophy 32, 65, 78, 132, 199–200, 214, 287, 309, 309–10, 311, 314
  steal Conservative policies 131, 293, 314
  Union with Scotland, approach to 268
  welfare reform 133
  see also Blair, Tony and Brown, Gordon
Lama, Dalai 293
Lamont, Norman 48, 70, 71, 203, 372
Lancashire County Council 368, 379
Lansley, Andrew 114
Lawrence of Arabia 236
Lawson, Nigel 372
Lebanon 257
Led Zeppelin 237
Lewis 207
Liberal Democrats:
  back bench rebellion on EU Treaty referendum 296, 297
  co-operation with Tories 378–9
  Ealing By-election 60
  hung parliament, hopes for a 296
  leader of 296, 297
  tax policy 284

Lilley, Peter 314
Lisbon Treaty 385
Lit, Tony 59, 60
litter, dropping xiii
Little Britain 237
Livingstone, Ken 209
Locke, John 353
London Mayoral election, 2008 29–30, 305, 307

Mackay, Andrew 377
Madonna 239
Magic FM 208
Major, John 34, 44–5, 48, 50, 169
Mandela, Nelson 239
Mandelson, Peter 365
Marks & Spencer 213, 291, 292
marriage 32, 164–9
  benefits system and 165, 167, 168
  civil partnerships 28, 166, 169
  divorce and 168
  forced 137, 147
  tax breaks for married people 167, 168
  value of 165–8
  see also family and family breakdown
Maude, Francis 374
Mayoral election, London, 2008 29–30, 305, 307
Mayors and First Ministers 29–30, 305, 307, 308
Mbeki, Thabo 264
McCain, John 232, 233, 261, 263
Merkel, Angela 268
Merrill Lynch 73
Middle East 257–9
Mill, John Stuart 353
Miners' strike, 1985–6 35, 36
minimum wage 355
ministers pay cut 363, 370, 377
Misuse of Drugs Act, 1971 149
Monarchy 169
Morse 207
MPs
  cutting number of 342
  expenses 347, 348, 376–7, 390, 391
  pensions 342

Mugabe, Robert 264, 384
multiculturalism 136, 137–9, 172–4, 256, 312
Murdoch, Rupert 73, 350
Muslim community 137, 138–9, 171–2, 174, 175, 178–9, 256 see also Islam and multiculturalism
MySpace 54

national citizen service 141–3, 312
national parks 358
National Service 141
National Security:
  preachers of hate and 174, 256
  Security Minister 231
  terrorism 62, 174, 177–8, 230–1
  see also foreign policy
National Union of Miners (NUM) 35
NATO 39–40, 105, 257, 264, 265, 268, 380, 382
Neighbours 236
Neville-Jones, Pauline 231
Newbury bypass 39
News of the World 375
9/11 174, 179, 346, 380, 382
NHS (National Health Service) 62, 64, 65, 68
  budget 344, 366–7
  change for change sake 199
  DC's experience of 199
  decentralisation 200–1
  drugs budget 366
  future of 201–2
  GPs 201, 202
  hospitals 62, 201, 293
  independence from government 201, 202
  lottery in care, postcode 357
  matrons 293
  mixed-sex wards 202
  opting out of with tax breaks 183
  polyclinics 199
  private medical care and 183
  Spanish system 202
  Swedish system 202
  target culture 200, 367
  top down centralisation 199–200
  waste 366–7

non-doms 131, 281
North Sea oil 265
Northern Alliance 259, 283
Northern Rock 130, 283
Norwich North by-election 348, 368, 379
nuclear power 233–4
nuclear weapons 380–1

Obama, Barack 261, 262, 295, 382–3
Obama, Michelle 383
OECD 362
Olmert, Ehud 257
Olympics, 2012 308
Osborne, George 48–50, 81, 82, 83, 112, 114, 128, 139, 280, 349, 386–7
Our Island Story (Marshall) 236
Our Man in Havana 236
Oxford Union 254
Oxford University 37, 47, 48, 254

Pakistan 382, 383
Palestine 257
Parkhurst Prison 229
Parris, Matthew 42, 83
Peel, Robert 311, 312
pensioners:
  exempting from tax 290
  pensions 288–9, 355, 368
  residential care 289, 356
  savings 289–90
Phillips, Trevor 133, 173
Pickles, Eric 137
police 225
  cuts in spending 367
  local control of 314
  1.9 per cent pay increase, 2008 227
  paperwork/form filling 226, 229
  past Conservative policy 293
  political correctness and 226
  stop and search 135–6, 229
  targets 145
  waste 367
  see also crime
political correctness 145, 175, 226
pornography 177–8
Porridge 236

'post-bureaucratic age' 287, 314
Pot Noodle 238
poverty 62, 77, 285, 286, 287, 309–10
Powell, Enoch 175–6
Price, Lance 67
primaries, open 378
Prime Minister:
  DC's ambitions to become 43, 44–5
  first goal of 103
  importance of character over policy 104
  messianic 104
  nature of job 53, 86, 111
  planning for role as 349
  principled 104–5
  teamwork and role of 349
Prime Minister's Questions (PMQs) 111
  Blair at 253
  Brown at 253
  DC's attacking/aggressive style at 63, 64, 253, 254
  DC's experience of 252–3
  DC's first 85
  DC's involvement in John Major's 44, 69
  importance of 77
Prince of Wales Trust 141
prisons:
  Afro-Caribbean population within 227–8
  conditions in 227
  conviction rates 223
  DC visits 221, 222, 224, 225
  drug problems within 220, 221–2
  illiteracy within 222, 227
  Labour policy 221, 224, 226–7, 228–30
  overcrowding/population 220–2, 226
  payments by results 222–3
  prisoner releases 64, 226–7
  private sector 223–4
  rehabilitation of prisoners 220, 221–2, 228
  re-offending rate 221, 222–3, 227
  selling old and building new 223
  training schemes 220
  volunteer groups and 227

young offender institutes and 226, 227
Private Eye 132
public meetings 348–9, 362
public services:
  pay 344, 366, 369
  pensions 368, 369
  unreliability of 287
  value for money of 288
  see also under individual service

Question Time 254–5

race 28, 172, 175–7, 348, 355–6, 370–1
racial tension, fears of 369–70
Radcliffe Camera, Oxford 237
Radio 1 207
Radio 4 207
Radio 5 207
Railways 287, 288
Rathbone, Tim 42
Ratner, Gerald 288
referendums 378
regional assemblies 342, 363
religion 170–2, 179–82
  Blair's beliefs 181
  DC's beliefs 179–81
  faith schools 181–2
  multicultralism and 170–2
  Sharia law 170
Rock, Patrick 66
Rolls-Royce 291
Rose, Sir John 291
Rose, Stuart 291–2
Russia 33–4, 265
Rwanda 62, 86, 87

Saatchi & Saatchi 50
Saga 289
Salisbury, Lord 312
Sanghera, Jasvinder 236
Sarkozy, Nicolas 54, 268, 269
schools see education
Scotland 164, 267–8, 307, 356–7
Security Minister 231
security services, funding of 346
Serbia 265
Shadow Cabinet:
  compared to Labour's Cabinet 111, 114

co-operation within 112
DC style within 108, 112
first 100 days, plans for
    government 374
reshuffles 112, 113
team, breadth of 371–2
unity of 374
Shame (Sanghera) 236
Shameless 207
Sharia law 137, 170
Sierra Leone 380
Simpsons, The 238
Sky News 73
Smith, Iain Duncan 61, 77, 79
Smith, Jacqui 114, 145
Smith, John 66
Smiths, The 239
Social Justice Policy Group 61
society xiii, 78
broken society, mending 63,
    77, 106, 138, 230, 308–9,
    311, 365–6
building one nation 136,
    138
building strong civic
    institutions for the
    benefit of 138
change and the role of 309
individual, freedom and 32,
    33, 34, 106, 128
responsible 32, 309–10
reviving 135
social justice 61
social mobility 189
social responsibility xiii,
    140–1
South Africa 260, 266
speed cameras 352
Spelman, Caroline 112, 114,
    128
spin 62, 140
Spin Doctor's Diary, The
    (Price) 67–8
St Mary's Hospital,
    Paddington 201
Sunrise Radio 59
surveillance state 352
Swampy 39

Tabernacle School, Notting
    Hill 185
Taliban 258–9, 381
tax 131
breaks for married couples
    165, 167–8, 312

breaks for private medical
    care 183
capital gains 284
council 288, 352–3, 378
credits 309
environmental 234
income 280–3, 284, 304, 306
inheritance 131, 281–2, 293
Liberal Democrat policy 284
middle classes and 284–5
non-doms 131, 281, 282
pensions and 355
raising 344, 352–3, 363
savings 355
sharing the proceeds of
    growth 282
stamp duty 283
tax cuts, Tory first term
    280–1, 282–3, 308
10p tax abolition 304, 306
top-rate, 50p tax, reducing
    344
see also economy
Technicolor 73
terrorism 62, 174, 177–8,
    230–1, 346, 352
Tesco 292
Thatcher, Denis 35
Thatcher, Margaret 34–5, 260,
    364, 368
Blair and 214
council house policy 106,
    209
DC's meetings with 35, 237
economic reform 135, 308,
    309, 313, 315
environment and 232
influence on DC 34, 35, 237,
    238
trade unions and 36, 183
Thorpe, Jeremy 38
Three Peaks Challenge 142,
    143
'Tickets for Troops' initiative
    346
Times, The 35, 39, 40, 42, 53,
    181
Today 207
Totnes primary 378
trade unions 35–6, 79, 134,
    183, 312
transport 148, 232–3, 234,
    287, 288
Treasury 48, 70–1, 75, 132,
    203, 266, 280

Trident 380–1
Turkey 265

UKIP 296
Ukraine 264
unemployment 63, 176, 313, 370
United Nations 256, 257
United States:
democracy, attempts to
    export 258
environmental policy 233
in Afghanistan 258–9, 382–3
in Iraq 261
Muslim integration within
    171–2
neo-cons 258
philanthropy within 285
Presidential race, 2008 53,
    260–2
torture and 261
UK and 260–3
welfare reform 134

Virgin Radio 208
voluntary sector 147–8
financial aid for projects
    based on ethnic
    background 171
national citizen service and
    141–3
prisoner literacy, help with
    227
welfare reform and 134
youth organisations and
    141–3, 147

Wales 307
Wandsworth Prison 220–1,
    224, 225, 227
Wapping dispute, 1986 35, 36
Warsi, Sayeeda 138–9, 170
WebCameron 53
welfare reform 133, 134–6,
    176, 286, 309, 313
White's Club, London 213
Wilson, Harold 39
Winehouse, Amy 238
Witney, Oxfordshire 74, 148
Woodward, Shaun 74, 79

Young, George 371–2
youth 139–43

Zimbabwe 258, 264, 267, 384
Tsvangirai, Morgan 384